SWIFT AND THE DIALECTICAL TRADITION

Swift and the Dialectical Tradition

James A. W. Rembert

Professor of English
The Citadel, Charleston, South Carolina

St. Martin's Press   New York

17202792
DLC

3-23-89

© James A. W. Rembert 1988

First published in the United States of America in 1988

Printed in Hong Kong

ISBN 0–312–01160–1

Library of Congress Cataloging-in-Publication Data
Rembert, James A. W. (James Aldrich Wyman), 1939–
    Swift and the dialectical tradition.

    Bibliography: p.
    Includes index.
    1. Swift, Jonathan, 1667–1745—Technique.
2. Swift, Jonathan, 1667–1745—Philosophy.
3. Dialectic—History.   4. Logic in literature.
4. Satire, English—History and criticism.
I. Title.
PR3728.T4R46   1988   828'.509   87–14077
ISBN 0–312–01160–1

To my sons André and Wyman

Contents

Preface   xi

Acknowledgements   xiii

Introduction   1

Part One: The Dialectical Tradition

1   Dialectic   11
    Dialectic and rhetoric   11
    Dialectic and logic   12
    Dialectic, sophistic, eristic   15

2   Dialectic: Antiquity to the Renaissance   19
    Dialectic in Ancient Greece   19
    Scholasticism   22
    The medieval universities   25
    The university disputation   31

3   Dialectic since the Sixteenth Century   37
    Scholasticism   37
    University logic studies   39
    The disputation   44
    The tripos or prevaricator speeches   54
    Criticism of logic and disputations   57

4   Dialectic at Trinity College, Dublin   63
    Swift at Trinity   63
    The founding and early development of TCD   63

Contents

Logic at TCD   64

Disputations at TCD   66

Part Two: Swift and Dialectic

5 First Principles and Contexts   75

   Substance versus style   75

   The peace of church and state   76

   The benefit of mankind   78

   The importance of opinion to the age   80

   Singularity of opinion   81

   Opinions of the wise and the majority   83

   Reason   85

   Pamphlet warfare   91

   University education   94

   Controversy   98

6 The Language of Logical Argument   101

   Dialectic   101

   The language of disputation   103

   'Topicks', syllogism, argue   105

   Prove, reason, deduce, conclude and consequence   107

   The language of the syllogism   109

7 Questioner against Answerer   114

   The questioner   114

   The opposition   118

   Refutation   119

   Extension of opponent's thesis   121

   Turning of opponent's argument   122

Argumenta ad . . .   124

Argument from contraries   128

The dialectical question: either/or   132

Offering two unacceptable extremes   133

The dilemma   134

8   Answerer against Questioner   144

The answerer   144

The opposition   147

Dialectical superiority   149

Refutation   152

Reductio ad impossibile   154

The dilemmatic response   159

The unacceptable extremes   160

Manipulating an opponent's argument   161

Drawing distinctions   163

Attacking definitions   164

Contempt for opponent's reasoning   167

Exposing fallacious reasoning   167

Citing opponent's dialectical tricks   169

Attacking metaphors   171

Exposing wit and sources   172

Criticising style   174

Personal attack   176

9   Dialectic and Satire   181

Satire   181

Irony   184

Wit and humour   186

    Paradox   190

Appendixes

1 Dialectic and Demonstration   194
2 University Logic Studies – an Epilogue   196
3 British Library MS Cotton Faustina D. II   198

Notes   202

Select Bibliography   243

Index   259

Preface

Dialectic is not as widely known as grammar and rhetoric, and one might conclude after glancing at the infrequent syllogisms and frequent references to Aristotle below that a knowledge of formal logic and philosophy is requisite to an understanding of this account of the dialectical tradition. Accordingly one might hesitate in making an investment of time in what might turn out to be too technical a subject for the student of literature. The reader may rest easy. The aim is to provide an elementary introduction to the subject readily within reach of anyone interested in Swift, literature or argument. Students of philosophy might bear in mind the propaedeutic function of the opening chapters.

Besides being an introduction to dialectic and its use by Swift and in literature in general, these chapters are inadvertently a kind of handbook on how to win an argument and how to preclude defeat by an opponent. Swift is staunch, vehement, clever and artistic in defending principles in which he believes and in attacking those he deplores, so that studying his art almost necessarily involves one in the spirit of attack and defence. Analysing the many stratagems Swift uses in perpetrating valid and fallacious arguments and in demolishing those of an opponent tends to make a reader want to practise the dialectical art. Plato warns against the destructive power of dialectic when practised by young men before the age of thirty-five, and Schopenhauer concludes one of the best expositions of the art of controversy with two reminders for those who learn the art of dialectic, Voltaire's suggestion that *la paix vaut encore mieux que la vérité* and an ancient Arabian proverb: on the tree of silence hangs a fruit which is peace.

NOTE ON REFERENCES

Quotations from Plato are from the translation of B. Jowett, 4 vols, Oxford (4th ed., 1953); those from Aristotle from the Oxford translation, ed. J. A. Smith and W. D. Ross, 12 vols (1908–53). In later chapters references to Swift's works often are cited parenthetically in the text, with the volume and page numbers (for example, III 82) of the Herbert Davis edition, *The Prose Writings of*

Jonathan Swift, 14 vols, Blackwell (1939–68), except for *Gulliver's Travels*, which is cited by voyage and chapter (for example, iv 5). Quotations from that work are from the Davis edition, vol. xi. *A Tale of a Tub, The Battle of the Books* and *The Mechanical Operation of the Spirit* are cited by page numbers of the Guthkelch–Smith edition of the *Tale* etc., 2nd ed., Oxford (1958). The *Drapier's Letters* are cited by page numbers of the Herbert Davis edition, Oxford (1935) and the *Contests and Dissentions Between the Nobles and Commons in Athens and Rome* is cited by page numbers of the F. H. Ellis edition, Oxford (1967). References to the poems are given by title, date and line numbers, so that they may be found either in the Oxford editions by Harold Williams, 3 vols (1st ed., 1937; 2nd ed., 1958) or in the Oxford Standard Authors edition, 1967, ed. Herbert Davis.

JAWR
Oakington, Cambridge

Acknowledgements

I should like to acknowledge with gratitude the generosity and kindnesses in Cambridge of Howard Erskine-Hill and Ian Jack of Pembroke College, Timothy Smiley of Clare College, whose ideas form most of Appendix 1, the late Garrett Sweeney, Nicholas Lash and Michael Parker, formerly of St Edmund's College, and the late Brian DuPré and Elizabeth DuPré, formerly of Landbeach, Cambridgeshire; at The Citadel in Charleston, James Duckett, Wallace Anderson, Roger Bender, the Citadel Development Foundation and the Pickett Fund; and in Charleston and Columbia, South Carolina, David H. Rembert, Mary Aldrich Rembert, Louisa T. Hagood and my sons André and Wyman, to whom this book is dedicated. Others to whom longstanding debts of gratitude are due are Robert Achurch, Milledge Seigler and Dougald MacMillan. Thanks are also due to the British Library for permission to quote extensively from MS Cotton Faustina D. II and to the Syndics of Cambridge University Library for permission to quote from MS D. d. 6. 30.

Introduction

Swift's satiric and ironic essays, chapters and passages, and his straightforward essays, are more dialectical in style than Swift studies heretofore have shown, dialectical analyses of literature not only having fallen behind rhetorical analyses but indeed being virtually nonexistent. Swift's style is due a dialectical analysis, and the importance of the dialectical tradition in literature calls for exposition. What here is provided for Swift can be done for any of a number of authors from the period when dialectic was the foundation of university studies and of philosophy and theology, from before the time of Chaucer to the time of Blake. An exploratory exposition would naturally settle on a competitive age of pamphlet warfare, a time when writers were conscious of what they considered the perfection of prose and verse styles in the land, and an age of satire. Dryden, Locke, Steele and others of their period could supply the examples, but Swift best shows the persistent use of dialectic and, as the best satirist, he shows one of the main contentions of this inquiry: that satire, rather than using logic or dialectic, is in fact an adjunct of dialectic, is the child of disputation.

An inquiry into the dialectical element in literature would not at first seem to break new ground in the light of all the attention paid to rhetorical analyses of literary works over the past three decades. Such analyses often draw inadvertently and unconsciously on dialectic to make their points, so that a dialectical analysis of literature may seem vaguely familiar. Nor can a single volume exhaust the subject of dialectic in the works of Jonathan Swift. Nothing, however, seems to have been done with the dialectical analysis of literature on a comparatively large scale, and so an introductory section on dialectic and its transmission from its origins through the universities to Swift may not only be useful but indeed indispensable.

Formal logic and dialectic today are so foreign to literature and to common knowledge that some readers who would normally disdain so elementary an explanation of a subject related to earlier literature might welcome a brief account of the history and methods of dialectic. A range of subjects related to university dialectic, especially the disputation, takes up the first three chapters. These subjects show the context of Swift's many references to dialectical disputation and the context of dialectical stratagems which he used in his many arguments, stratagems which are contributions to the distinctive style of one of the great stylists of the English language.

It is simple to propose that the writings of Swift and his contemporaries were strongly affected by academic dialectic, but the question arises, if so, was there not a comparable effect on Marlowe and his contemporaries, on Thomas More and his, and so forth? The answer lies in the realisation that however similar the dialectic Marlowe and Swift, for example, learned at Cambridge and Dublin, the social milieu in Marlowe's day did not allow an expression of that influence in popular dialectical combat to the extent that such expression was available to Swift. The unusual connection between university dialectic in the decline of scholasticism in the seventeenth and eighteenth centuries and the literature of the Augustan age has something about it that distinguishes it from the influence of university education on Marlowe, Spenser and Sidney. The scholastic synthesis of church and state,[1] with dialectic traditionally at its foundation, endured in the universities through the upheavals of civil war and commonwealth and provided a much-needed stability for conservative minds both during those upheavals and in the lingering political and religious unrest throughout the rest of the seventeenth century and into the first part of the eighteenth. But the scholastic dialectic of the universities was at the service of the new interests as well as the old, Whig as well as Tory, dissenters as well as the Church of England. With the progressive opening up of society after the civil war, the Revolution of 1688 and the establishment of the Bank of England – with the new moneyed interests challenging the old landed interests, the City challenging the country – public opinion grew enormously in its influence on public concerns, and the writers of the time took advantage of what was then a new relationship between writer and reader. Dryden, Swift, Addison, Steele, Defoe, Pope and others reflect the contemporary necessity of coming to terms with public opinion, with persuading an audience; and of these writers, Swift goes farthest beyond the often emotional persuasion of rhetoric to the more forceful persuasion of logic through dialectic, whose aim, like that of satire, is not only the establishing of an arguer's thesis or set of values but the demolishing of his opponent's as well.

II

In the British Library apparently only a single manuscript records examples of complete dialectical disputations such as were practised in European universities for almost seven hundred years, from the twelfth century to the middle third of the nineteenth. Few if any manuscripts or printed accounts elsewhere record so completely what were as central to academic exercises and testing for hundreds of years as are weekly quizzes or essays, hour tests and end of semester/term or end of year examinations today. This lack of historical, pedagogical data concerning testing in university life is not surprising, because even today, with the exception of none too numerous published examinations like the Cambridge Tripos, examinations – like the lecturer or professor who wrote them – usually slip away to retirement at the end of a teaching career. And the statutorily required disputations had the added disadvantage of being oral.

The concern with lack of knowledge about dialectical disputations and indeed about the actual academic life behind all the scholastic curriculum in the Renaissance (1350 to 1650) and beyond is not limited to readers of literature. As late as 1973 a historian of science said of the subject and the period in question, 'Much further work remains, before our picture will be anything but cloudy and vague. We still need to know much more about the universities of the period and how the basically Aristotelian curriculum – which was almost always set down clearly by statute – was actually applied in practice. To do this involves the laborious study of the lectures actually given at the universities, as well as student notes, correspondence and other primary materials, which at present are not only largely unstudied, but even uncatalogued.'[2] The next year a longer study repeated the observation: 'Despite the profusion of [seventeenth-century logic] books to which [Keckermann] refers, and despite the dominant position occupied by logic in the educational system of the fifteenth, sixteenth, and seventeenth centuries, very little work has been done on the logic of the post-medieval period. The only complete study is that of Risse.'[3] Nor is the subject satisfactorily explored today.

For all the attention given to humanistic studies, especially classical and Renaissance rhetoric and lately grammar under the name of semiotics, the wonder is that no readily available book exists explaining classical dialectic as it persisted in the educated mind since the founding of the universities in the twelfth century.[4] The closest attempt in English at explaining what actually went on in a dialectical disputation seems to be Charles Wesley's *Guide to Syllogism* (Cambridge, 1832) whose date is a commentary on the state of dialectical studies in the present time. For the reader who may wonder after the many pages of stage setting below, 'Will I ever be shown an example of a dialectical disputation? Will I ever have a chance to see just how one was conducted?' the answer is yes. But the background is necessary. It has never been given in such detail in one volume, and the reader's patience is sought, because a survey of various aspects of dialectic is needed before attention can be focused on the disputation itself and then on its application to Swift and literature.

The oral, dialectical examinations in the university called more immediately upon a student's wit and ingenuity than does today's usual examination, and the results have been noted as favourably by some as they have been noted unfavourably by Bacon, Milton, Sprat, Locke, Blake, Wordsworth and others. The dialectical disputation and its methods were in the consciousness and subconscious of both university men and non-university men more than the methods of the weekly or bi-weekly essay have been in the consciousness of college and university graduates in this century. The direct effects of disputations were limited to the relatively small number of university graduates in Europe and the New World, but they reached to non-university writers like Blake and Keats, who saw little use in analytical reasoning as practised in the university, and some of whose writings – Keats's letters, for example, and Blake's 'Marriage of Heaven and Hell' – show the influence of dialectic in their stated opposition to its study.

Accordingly, readers interested in the atmosphere, tone and intellectual milieu of a work of literature from the ages of the university disputation have been hard put to gain access to an influence, positive or negative, on the mind and art of almost any writer of note before the middle years of the nineteenth century. With little to build on in the way of critical studies, the following chapters go about supplying the elements of a study of dialectic and literature in the form of a compendium, with brief sections within chapters trying to cover the bases of a broad subject, so that a reader may take away fundamental rather than refined knowledge of dialectic and its use in literature. The publication of this study may stimulate others to write some more sophisticated accounts of the subject.

III

When D. W. Jefferson said three decades ago that it would be a formidable and lengthy task to analyse the dialectical basis of Swiftian satire in just one of the better-known pamphlets, he was pointing to an obvious vacuum. Such an investigation was even then long overdue, if only to serve as a foundation for the cliché that the bite of Swiftian satire often derives from unacceptable premises taken to logical extremes. Not long after Jefferson's remarks, R. S. Crane and Irvin Ehrenpreis commented on Swift's undergraduate training in logic and dialectic as a basis for his later writing, Crane with respect to a simple allusion, Ehrenpreis with respect to the irony.[5] Jefferson's essay had linked Swift's later dialectic with his undergraduate education and had raised provocative questions which the two later commentaries did not attempt to answer. The following chapters are a partial answer to these questions and an attempt to indicate the neglect of this rich field of the dialectical basis for literature, when lately so much attention has been given to the rhetorical and to the grammatical in the form of semiotics.

Those aware of the problem see analysers of Swift's satire rarely getting away from passing references to his use of logic. W. B. Carnochan, in a perceptive analysis of Swift's ironic satire and its use of negation,[6] tries near the end of his essay to come to terms with being and non-being. With a near-Hegelian quasi-synthetical *both/and* (rather than a true synthesis) deriving from *nothing* and *something* he admits a degree of puzzlement: 'The subject of negation, philosophically considered, is a very rough thicket of argument for the amateur'.[7] But he presses on with assistance from Eric Toms' *Negation and Logic* (Oxford, 1962), drawing on the language of logic to the extent of 'not-p implies p' and the like, and returns to Hegelian dialectic. He escapes a philosophical/logical paradox with an exit reference to literature, which is what literary critics sometimes do when bogged down in the morass of philosophical self-reference, the present writer included. Carnochan is close to discovering the importance of dialectic to an understanding of Swift's satire, but he chooses the path of Hegelian dialectic rather than Aristotelian dialectic and after an illuminating discussion concludes, as others investigating Swiftian satire have concluded, with a virtual admission that words fail.

Titles of other essays and studies suggest a look into the dialectic which influenced Swift's art, among them 'The Poetry of Swift: Dialectical Rhetoric and the Humanist Tradition', 'The Subversion of Logic in Some of Swift's Poems', 'Comedy, Satire, Dialectics' and 'Man and Yahoo: Dialectic and Symbolism in Gulliver's "Voyage to the Country of the Houyhnhnms"'.[8] But the analyses focus on rhetoric or humanism or Hegelian dialectic, not traditional dialectic and its influence on literature. Familiarity with Hegel, particularly, has blinded modern readers to a great part of the significant influence of Aristotle before the time of Hegel.

A look at Swift's dialectic would naturally attempt to reach some conclusions about his satire and about satire in general. Readers of Swift in this century have focused largely on his irony and satire, an understanding of which usually involves an awareness of the satiric norm, as it has been called, the position from which a satirist ridicules aberrations from what he regards as accepted ways of thinking, speaking and acting. Swift's irony and ironic satire are sometimes so refined, as his close readers know, that the position from which he writes is not always easily determinable, as in the 'Project' and the 'Digression on Madness'. The following chapters on Swift deal less with the ironic and satiric masterpieces than with his mind and the art of dialectic in his non-satiric works. Yet this look into his principles and the way he defends them and attacks opposing principles yields more insight into the satiric norm of Swift's ironic satire than one at first might suspect in a study of Swift and dialectic. A consideration of Swift's dialectical stance is necessarily a commentary on his satire long before the final chapter which focuses on the elemental relationship of dialectic and satire.

Satire and irony aside, a look into Swift's dialectic shows his mind at work in the defence of the Anglican Church and the Tory ministry, demonstrating the resources of his education and the natural bent of his mind in defending his views of common sense and reason and his convictions in religion and politics. Through his dialectic one also sees his mind and heart revealed in his attacking Tindal, Steele, Burnet and others for their lapses in thinking and writing and for assuming morally, spiritually or reasonably indefensible positions. This look at the other Swift, the writer beyond the satires and the poetry, reveals in some ways a new Swift, one which sheds some light on the old puzzling satirist.

It is possible for anyone to enjoy the combat of wits in comedies of manners of the seventeenth century, early and late, but more enjoyable to read them with some understanding of the dialectical disputation. It is possible to enjoy the pamphlet wars of the late sixteenth, seventeenth and early eighteenth centuries without an introduction to dialectic, but more enjoyable to see the workings of dialectic in them. And it is possible to enjoy satire without a foundation in dialectic, but it is more enjoyable to see the germ of satire grow from the dying body of dialectic, to see the humour and playfulness which in part destroyed the Aristotelian curriculum destroy the victim of satire.

The most useful books of literary criticism at present seem to be those dealing with theory. The present volume offers little theory except for the last chapter on dialectic and satire. But in the old, pedestrian sense of useful, the hope is that these chapters will provide a useful starting point for inquiry by others and for later theories on the relationship between dialectic and literature, especially dialectic and satire.

Part One
The Dialectical Tradition

1
Dialectic

Dialectic is the use of the question and answer method in the pursuit of truth, or logical argumentation aiming at victory in pursuit of truth rather than at testing of validity of inferences, which is the province of logic. Nor is dialectic rhetoric aimed at persuasion, without the give and take of intellectual combat of opponents. To be sure, Plato's dialectic is sometimes argument with minimal use of an opponent; however, the dialectic of the schools up to the time of Swift and beyond was not modelled on Plato's dialectic but on Aristotle's, which is nothing if not combative. Dialectic is neither logic nor rhetoric, although it uses the one and is used by the other, and its function and theirs are sometimes identical. This blurring of the distinctions of the three is only apparent; their differences are real and undeniable in spite of a tendency in literary criticism to overlook the differences. The widespread rhetorical analysis of literary works in the last three decades, for example, has often appropriated dialectic to serve its ends. Dryden's poems have been described in the name of classical rhetoric as verbal battles against opponents in which he 'answers objections, offers evidence, and appeals to the "old rule of logic"' and in which he offers 'a formal and logical argument, more like a public debate than a conversation'.[1] This concern with public argumentation is the province of dialectic far more than of rhetoric. Of late, rhetorical analyses of literature have rather unhistorically enlisted dialectic under the banner of rhetoric, although dialectic traditionally had a larger banner of its own.

To be fair, one should admit that modern rhetorical analyses using dialectic are in good company. Aristotle, Cicero and the English rhetorics of the sixteenth century acknowledge the place of logic or dialectic – the terms were often interchangeable from the Renaissance to the nineteenth century – in rhetoric, and Thomas Wilson's *Rule of Reason* (1551) and seventeenth-century guides to university studies give what had become the commonplace of Zeno that logic is to rhetoric as closed fist is to extended hand.[2]

Milton's *Logic* (1672–3), a rhetoric by Obadiah Walker in 1682 and another under Hobbes's name published a year before Walker's all describe the rhetorician as an orator who uses logic or dialectic. In the first chapter of the last-mentioned rhetoric the author gives the common explanation that rhetoric consists chiefly in proofs, which are inferences, which in turn are syllogisms, and a logician who uses enthymemes instead of syllogisms would make the best rhetorician. But when he says that 'the end of *Rhetoric* is victory, which consists of having gotten belief', he is attributing to the rhetorician not just the characteristics of the logician but of the dialectician. This tendency to dialectic is amplified in book II chapter 27 'Of the wayes to answer the Arguments of the Adversary'.[3] It has always been undeniable that rhetoric uses logic, specifically the enthymeme, but that use does not make rhetoric dialectic. When the rhetorician answers arguments of an adversary in debate, he has virtually entered the realm of dialectic unless the answers are long set speeches without the give and take of logical argument.

The rhetorical concern with proving a point against an adversary is properly the province of dialectic, as opposed to logic, which strictly speaking is as distinct from dialectic as is rhetoric. Schopenhauer's explanation of the provinces of the three disciplines is as simple as any and clearer than many. Logic, he says, is the technique of our own thinking, dialectic of disputing with others and rhetoric of speaking to many, which corresponds to the singular, dual and plural, and to the monologue, dialogue and panegyric.[4] For all its clarity, however, Schopenhauer's explanation is oversimplified, because the common borders of dialectic and rhetoric disappear for Hobbes (Fenner/Talaeus) and others, not to mention modern literary criticism. It would be an improvement to say that the aim of rhetoric is to move the audience and that of dialectic is to do so while defeating an opponent. The audience are the judges[5] and the dialectician's goal is to get them on his side, to have them, and ideally the opponent too, convinced that the opponent's reasoning has been refuted.

DIALECTIC AND LOGIC

Modern logic does not so much distinguish between logic and dialectic as ignore dialectic altogether. The techniques of logical inference which lead from premises to conclusions are valued in themselves as connections only. The premises and conclusions may concern themselves with any subject in ordinary language, but the modern logician to expedite his task transforms ordinary language into the technical ideography of modern logic. This symbolic logic has an application to science and everyday discourse in its justification and criticism of inference, in showing technically that a given statement does or does not 'follow logically' from another.[6] But it has very little to do with dialectic, of which logic (the logic of verbal argument rather than symbolic logic) was an integral part from Greek antiquity until a century and a half ago: what we now call 'logic' was in the first stages of philosophy technically described as 'dialectic'. Alexander of Aphrodisias, the third century AD commentator on Aristotle, first used the word 'logic' in its modern sense.

Stephen Toulmin's *Uses of Argument* (Cambridge, 1958) is an attempt to broaden the scope of modern logic beyond the elaborate mathematical systems of symbolic logic, but despite its title it is concerned far more with epistemology than with dialectic. To be fair to symbolic logic, and some critics are not, it is necessary to remember that Aristole, in creating formal logic in the *Prior* and *Posterior Analytics*, used no concrete terms in syllogisms in the former treatise and only infrequently used them in the latter; both are filled with alphabetical letters standing for premises and conclusions. But Aristotle, unlike most modern logicians, also wrote two treatises totally concerned with logical debate of topics in everyday life and largely concerned with getting the better of one's opponent in a dispute. One of the few exceptions to modern logic's aversion to dialectic is C. L. Hamblin's *Fallacies* (London, 1970), which gives a history, classification and criticism of logical fallacies and some space to logical argument.

Thus dialectic seems to have been absorbed by modern rhetorical studies and ignored by modern logic. Once dialectic has been distinguished from logic and rhetoric from the modern viewpoint, however, there remains the task of ascertaining the sphere of dialectic in the age of the author whose dialectical approach is under examination. The problem of discussing the dialectic of Swift's time is that the logic, or demonstration, of Aristotle's *Analytics* and the dialectic, sophistic and eristic of his *Topics* and *Sophistical Elenchi* were largely viewed as a single art or science from the Middle Ages to the nineteenth century.

In what manner, then, had logic and dialectic merged when Swift confronted 'logic' at Trinity College, Dublin, in the penultimate decade of the seventeenth century? The history for the most part is clear. Aristotle had distinguished between logical demonstration and dialectic in four separate logical treatises and in his *Metaphysics*[7] by defining demonstration as scientifically true conclusions reached by necessary inference from scientifically true premises and dialectic as probable truths reached by necessary inference from probable premises based on general opinion, that of the wise, the majority or everyone.[8] It is uncertain whether the supremacy of dialectic as a mode of thought, investigation, teaching and establishing truth in the Middle Ages was due more to imitation of Abelard or to the recovery of Aristotle's *Topics*, but the *ars disputandi* was practically unchallenged as the queen of philosophy by medieval theologians, and not without irony, because they used the dialectical art perfected by Aristotle, yet like Plato they held the art in greater esteem than did Aristotle.[9] That the seventeenth century in Britain regarded logic in much the same way as the Middle Ages had done is evident in logic manuals and student notebooks of the time, which were influenced by popular logics of the second half of the sixteenth century. Thomas Wilson's *Rule of Reason, Conteinying the Arte of Logique* (1553), laying down definitions in the first pages, describes logic in terms of the dialectic of the *Topics* rather than the demonstration of the *Analytics*: 'Logique is an Arte to reason probably, on bothe partes, of al matters that be putte foorth, so ferre as the nature of every thing can beare', and 'Logique, otherwise called Dialectic (for thei are bothe one) . . .'. This identity of logic and dialectic as the art of disputing well opens other logics in the sixteenth century, like Ramus's *Dialectique* (1555) and Thomas Blundeville's *Arte of Logike* (1599), and in the next century logic is still 'the Art of Reasoning, or Disputing', as in Thomas Blount's dictionary *Glossographia* (1656), or of argumentation, as in Thomas Good's *Brief English Tract of Logick* (1677). Other seventeenth-century logics maintain the identity of logic and dialectic, usually on the opening page of the text proper, with definitions like '*Logica, quae & Synedochicè Dialectica, est Ars Rationis*' and '*Logica (seu Dialectica) est ars instrumentalis . . .*'.[10] In student logic notebooks of the period the identity also occurs – logic is the science of examining 'probably' and closely[11] – but more significantly in these notebooks questions are raised about the province of dialectic, or logic, asking whether it is speculative or practical, reflecting the unresolved confusion of Aristotle.[12]

The dictionaries reflect the definitions of the logic manuals. The anonymous *Glossographia Anglicana Nova* (1707), Edward Phillips' *The New World of Words* (1706), Bailey, Johnson and others, whose definitions of 'dialectic(al)' refer to the art of logic, or reasoning, or arguing, show the synonymity of the term with logic. Johnson mentions 'logical dispute' and 'logical arguments' in examples under the word 'logical'. Phillips and Bailey in the entry 'Dialectical Arguments' stress the unconvincing or 'barely probable' quality of that procedure and thus make the major Aristotelian distinction between logic (or demonstration) and dialectic.[13]

Despite the substantial acceptance in logics and dictionaries of the identity of the aims of logic and dialectic, criticism of their indistinguishable character came from a quarter besides that of the school of Bacon and Sprat, which would reform logic altogether largely by ignoring the deductive mode in favour of the inductive. In this quarter the critics were purists, like the authors of two English translations from the French who accuse the schoolmen of having clogged and fettered logic with their wrangling disputes and instead of rectifying, perverting our understanding by teaching the art of disguising our thoughts.[14] Their advocacy, however, is not for the new philosophy but for a return to the method of the philosopher-logician[15] as opposed to that of the dialectician, whose methods are too susceptible to sophistry.

DIALECTIC, SOPHISTIC, ERISTIC

The accusation of sophistry is important in the history of dialectic, because it seems to have been levelled at the art practically from the beginning and was largely the cause of dialectic's going out of fashion and virtually out of existence in the first half of the nineteenth century. The art of proving and of concealing the direction of one's own logical argument while exposing the weak sides of that of an adversary, taught by Aristotle[16] and relished by many of the scholastics, was an integral part of university life until a combination of growing interest in mathematics, classical literature and written instead of oral-disputation examinations did what the New Scientists of the seventeenth century could not do: that is, do away with the scholastic disputation in its old form for good. At least, this was true for Protestant universities and colleges; James J. Walsh gives an informative account of the retention of the scholastic disputation in Roman Catholic education in 'Scholasticism in the Colonial Colleges' in the *New England Quarterly* for July 1932. Amazement that dialectic, especially in the form of the dialectical disputation, managed to last so long in the post-Renaissance world might be allayed by going to Aristotle to see what was so appealing in this instrument of thought.

Like Zeno, Socrates and Plato, Aristotle valued the questioner–answerer method of dialectic,[17] for which he was the first to lay down rules and formulate methods, not with an eye to the philosophic conception of Plato but with an eye to actual Greek practice. Although Aristotle is explicit in stating that the forms of demonstrative and dialectical proof are the same[18] in spite of the difference in certainty of their premises, he nowhere gives an example of a dialectical syllogism, and from what he explains of the practice of the questioner–answerer method of dialectic, especially in book VIII of the *Topics* and in the remarks on dialectic in the *Sophistical Elenchi*, one might with reason wonder whether in fact there is such a thing as a dialectical syllogism.[19] The question of the existence of the dialectical syllogism arises because the two treatises just named propound techniques of practical debate which seem more applicable to natural argument, however skilled and refined, than to formal syllogistic disputation.

The popularity of dialectic in ancient, medieval and Renaissance times was chiefly the result of the power it gave the disputer in gaining victory over his opponent, a fact often veiled, even in Aristotle, with observations about searching for the truth. A relatively recent discussion of Aristotle's advocacy of dialectic as opposed to eristic in the *Topics*, or truth-seeking as opposed to victory-seeking debate, concludes that the conflation of dialectic with eristic seems to do little justice either to Aristotle's theory or to his practice.[20] However, the argument of the discussion is so fair, and the evidence offered on both sides so elaborate, that the reader might well be left in doubt whether to accept the conclusion or that advanced more than a century earlier by Schopenhauer.

In 'The Art of Controversy', from *Parerga and Paralipomena* (1851), Schopenhauer takes a characteristically pessimistic view of human nature regarding disputation. The 'art' which he explains is justifiable by the *Topics* and *Sophistical Elenchi* if one disregards certain brief passages scattered in the two treatises, but, as Schopenhauer might have said, it seems necessary to do that no matter what consistent theory of dialectic one extracts from the treatises. When one begins a dispute, Schopenhauer maintains, one does not know whether one is in the right or the wrong, the truth not being determinable until the close. Dialectic then, as the art of disputation or of getting the best of it in a dispute, should consider the truth as much as a fencing master should consider who is in the right in a duel: thrust and parry are the sole concerns in real as well as in intellectual fencing. Only by viewing dialectic in this light can we consider it a branch of knowledge, because if we aim for objective truth rather than victory, we are reduced to mere logic, or demonstration. If we aim to maintain false propositions, it is mere sophistic, and both in sophistic and in logic it is assumed we know what is true and what is false beforehand, which is not the case with dialectic.

In Schopenhauer's sense of the word, dialectic has no other aim but to reduce to order the arts most men employ in a dispute when they observe that truth is not on their side but still attempt to gain the day. This science is mainly concerned with analysing and classifying dishonest stratagems so that in a real debate they can be recognised and defeated. Such knowledge put into practice is dialectic, the art of getting the best of it in a dispute, which art Schopenhauer is at some pains to distinguish more than Aristotle does from logic, and in which he includes what he believes Aristotle wrongly excluded as sophistic and eristic. This art of disputing in such a way as to hold one's own whether one is in the right or the wrong becomes for Schopenhauer controversial or eristical dialectic, the sole dialogic counterpart of the monologic logic, or analytic.[21]

Such a view of dialectic is in some measure what Aristotle actually propounds, in spite of his protestations to the contrary. But Schopenhauer's view of dialectic overlooks a major, integral part of the framework of the dialectical disputation explained by Aristotle and adopted in academic exercises from the foundation of the universities: that is, the answerer's defence of the right side of the question and the questioner's attack from what was agreed to be the wrong side. In university disputations the nomenclature was usually 'respondent' for answerer and 'opponent' for questioner. The answerer's and questioner's roles are explained in the *Topics*, book VIII, chapter 4; chapters 5 to 10 give the rules of how to answer in dialectic, and there is no comparable portion of the *Topics* given to the methods of the questioner. In the *Sophistical Elenchi*, chapters 3 to 15 explain the perpetration of fallacies, those which are advanced by the questioner under the guard of the answerer, if possible, to overthrow his thesis. Chapters 16 to 32 explain the solution of fallacious refutations, a guide to the answerer in meeting the sophistical attacks upon his thesis by the questioner. 'In a competition the business of the questioner is to appear by all means to produce an effect upon the other, while that of the answerer is to appear unaffected by him' (*Top.*, 159ª30–2). This is the sense in which Socrates is dialectical in the dialogues of Plato and Xenophon, in which as questioner he elicits a thesis from his answerer and at length reduces him to silence by showing the contradictions involved in his position. It is in this sense of dialectic that the methods used in the early eighteenth-century pamphlet wars and in other contexts are analysable in terms of the stratagems and counter-stratagems of dialectic. A survey of the historical background of dialectic from Greek antiquity to Swift's day and beyond will show the tradition upon which Swift was drawing when he used dialectic to refute books and pamphlets, to argue a thesis of his own and to introduce that satiric irony which he first refined and 'shew'd its Use'.

2

Dialectic: Antiquity to the Renaissance

DIALECTIC IN ANCIENT GREECE

Dialectic properly begins with Zeno, its founder or inventor, who used an indirect form of argument to defend his master Parmenides' paradoxical thesis of the immobility of the real against the Pythagoreans' pluralism. Zeno maintained the impossibility of *kinesis* not by arguing in favour of his theory but by showing its contraries, change and motion, to be absurd or illusory. Such *argumentum* (or *reductio*) *ad impossibile* or *ad absurdum* was later analysed and otherwise commented upon in various places by Aristotle.[1] Stated simply, as Aristotle did in the *Prior Analytics*, arguments *per impossibile* 'infer syllogistically what is false, and prove the original conclusion [one's own thesis] hypothetically when something impossible results from the assumption of its contradictory' (41ᵃ23–6); or, as a modern logician laconically explains, it is a last resort in argument, consisting 'in assuming the contradictory of what is to be proved and then looking for trouble'.[2] Zeno's method had an influence on Socrates in his deduction of contrary conclusions from the same hypothesis and in turn upon Plato, whose Parmenides (135d–136c) advises Socrates to practise this kind of argument. It influenced Gorgias's proofs of philosophical nihilism in both substance and form, Protagoras's view that contradictory conclusions could be constructed for every question, Euclid's question–answer method characteristic of his school of dialecticians at Megara, and the antinomian arguments of the *Dissoi Logoi*, a late fifth-century Sophistic manual of theses with particular arguments *pro* and *contra*, to which Aristotle was probably referring, along with others like it now lost, at the conclusion of the *Sophistical Elenchi*.

Of the state of dialectic before Socrates the conclusion of the *Sophistical Elenchi* is a valuable description. Here, in practically his only statement about himself, Aristotle explains that he developed the theory and technique of dialectic in the *Topics* with no precedent to build upon;[3] his reference to the 'paid professors of contentious arguments' is made with little respect, especially for their question and answer manuals with arguments on either side for memorisation, with which 'they used to suppose that they trained people by imparting to them not the art but its products' ($183^b37-184^a3$).

Although Zeno is represented as using the question and answer method of dialectic in his millet-seed puzzle, his contributions to dialectic do not lie mainly in that direction. The best *examples* of the art of disputation by question and answer are the dialogues of Plato, as the best *analyses* of the art to date are the logical treatises of Aristotle. Plato developed dialectic metaphysically in connection with analysing Ideas, especially the ultimate idea of the Good (*Republic*, 534b–c), and he developed it practically in the dramatised elenctic disputations of the early dialogues. The *Euthydemus*, probably the oldest treatise on logic, stands apart from the other dialogues as a satire on logical fallacies, some of which later appear in the *Sophistical Elenchi*. It is not surprising that Jowett finds a correspondence between Plato's ridicule of uncommonsensical philosophical disputes in the ancient world and Pope's and Swift's satire in the modern.[4]

Calculation, geometry and other elements of instruction are a preparation for dialectic, which for Plato is in one sense identical with philosophy and in another the end which philosophy achieves. This exalted praise of dialectic culminates in the statement that dialectic is 'the coping-stone of the sciences, and is set over them; no other study can rightly be built on and above this' (*Rep.*, 532a–34e). When Aristotle ranked dialectic among the philosophical sciences, he reversed the positions of mathematics (or demonstrative proof) and dialectic as Plato had ranked them, explaining that mathematics or the demonstrative sciences are based on true propositions and dialectic only on opinion (*Top.*, $100^a27-{^b}23$). Mathematics, Plato had said, lacks proper contact with Being because unlike dialectic it does not go directly to first principles (*Rep.*, 533b–c). This function of criticising first principles made dialectic in Aristotle's view a progymnastic or propaedeutic of philosophy but no more (*Top.*, 101^a28, $34-{^b}4$), and philosophy for Aristotle is synonymous with demonstration (*Top.*, 105^b30-1).[5]

If Zeno is the inventor of dialectic, Aristotle, the inventor of the syllogism, is the father of logic; and because of his *Topics* he, more appropriately than Zeno, can be called the father of dialectic also.

That treatise is one of six grouped together in what has come to be called the *Organon* (instrument, tool), the name apparently given by the Peripatetics, who maintained that logic was an instrument of philosophy, against the Stoics, who said it was a part of philosophy. (The Platonists said it was equally a part and an instrument.) The work itself shows but little unity, being variously grammatical, metaphysical and logical, and apparently Aristotle did not compose it as a unit. It is supposed to have been collected into one volume about the first century BC, was translated into Latin by Boethius and between the sixth and fifteenth centuries acquired the title *Organon*. Of all the ancient writings on logic this group of six is easily the most important and most influential. As usually arranged it begins with the *Categories*, a brief discussion of the ten classes of predicates (substance, quantity, relation, etc.); followed by *On Interpretation*, a briefer analysis mainly of propositions (affirmation, denial, possibility, necessity, etc.); the *Prior Analytics*, in which Aristotle formulated the theory of the syllogism, analysing the various figures and moods and the reduction of imperfect figures into the first and thus indebting all subsequent logic; the *Posterior Analytics*, a philosophical logic dealing with the demonstrative science and the most powerful instrument of thought known to the Middle Ages; the *Topics*, an investigation of probabilities, which comprise most human knowledge, in which premises and thus conclusions are based on the opinion of the wise or the majority or all; and last the *Sophistical Elenchi*, a treatise on fallacies, or more properly on tricks advanced in contentious argument by one person to another. These last two treatises are fundamental to a discussion of dialectic, and so they will prove to be throughout this brief history of dialectic and in the analysis of its use by Swift.

Post-Aristotelian logic in antiquity is mainly that of the schools of the Peripatetics, the Epicureans and the Stoics, all of which made some refinements on Aristotle's system, such as the Peripatetics' attention to hypothetical and disjunctive propositions and syllogisms. The Stoics, from a modern viewpoint, can be credited with having originated the study of propositional logic (the ancestor of the modern propositional calculus), which Aristotle markedly ignores. This distinctive contribution of Stoic logic, however, does not seem to have been properly recognised until modern times, so that in terms of their historical impact on logic the Stoics were not especially significant.[6]

SCHOLASTICISM

The most celebrated book of Porphyry (233–c. 305), his *Isagoge* or introduction to the *Categories* of Aristotle, was translated into Latin by Boethius, the translator of Aristotle's *Organon*, who also wrote two commentaries on Porphyry's work, one on Aristotle's *Categories* and two on *On Interpretation*. These two 'introductory' treatises of the *Organon* (the *Categories* and *On Interpretation*), Porphyry's *Isagoge*, Boethius's commentaries on these and on Cicero's *Topics*, together with some other logical works by Boethius such as his original treatises on categorical and hypothetical syllogisms, accounted for the whole knowledge of Aristotle available to medieval students from the sixth century to the twelfth. When in about 1128 James of Venice translated the *Prior* and *Posterior Analytics*, the *Topics* and the *Sophistical Elenchi* from Greek into Latin, the entire *Organon* thus became available in Europe. The newly-discovered books became known as the 'new logic' or *logica nova* as opposed to what was accessible from the time of Boethius, the 'old logic' or *logica vetus*.

The dark ages following the fall of Rome had however, long before the twelfth century, welcomed a glimmer of light when in 782 Alcuin of York took over the direction of the Palace School of Charlemagne and revived the old Roman curriculum of the seven liberal arts, the *trivium* and *quadrivium*. With the *trivium* (logic, rhetoric, grammar) dialectic was renewed; it remained the most durable element in European education and was synonymous, in fact, for centuries with philosophy itself.

The controversy between Anselm (1033–1109) and Roscelin (c. 1050–1120), over whether *genera* and *species* are subsistent entities or consist in concepts alone, in some respects determined the subsequent course of medieval philosophy, and dialectic with it. A brief and cautious statement on the nature of universals made by Porphyry in his *Isagoge* prepared the battleground for a persistent medieval controversy between the Nominalists and Realists. This question of universals, whether they are mere *flatus vocis* or *percussio aeris* (Nominalism) or whether they are the only reality (Realism), is in a way a controversy between the Aristotelians and the Platonists. The problem was alive enough in the eighteenth century to draw satire from the *Memoirs of Martinus Scriblerus* and to serve as a basis for the Idealist position, and it remains with us today.

Abelard (1079–1142), who was trained on the *logica vetus* and knew the *logica nova* only superficially, was enough ahead of his time to champion dialectic as the queen of sciences. More than that, he glorified dialectic, saying in his thirteenth epistle that logic is derived from *logos* and is thus connected with the *verbum Dei* and with Christ the Logos incarnate, who convinced the Jews often with dialectical disputations and who promised to the disciples logic as the ultimate wisdom. Dialectic remained for Abelard the *ars disputandi*, by which one detects fallacies and recognises good from bad arguments, and he admits his passion for it in his *Historia Calamitatum*: 'since I preferred the panoply of dialectical arguments to all the documents of philosophy, I exchanged other arms for these and esteemed the conflict of disputation more than the trophies of war'.[7] In spite of his advancing a Conceptualist position midway between Nominalism and Realism, Abelard's contribution to philosophy was limited by his engrossment in a dialectic that was seldom more than an ingenious art of words. His contemporary, Hugh of St Victor (1096–1141), whose influence was of a different kind but perhaps just as great as Abelard's, drew on Boethius to remind contemporary and later thinkers that logic does not deal with things and because of that is indispensable to those who would inquire into the nature of things. But also because it is the study of words and speech rather than of things it is distinct from metaphysics and the wider theory of knowledge. Such a setting of the boundaries of dialectic in some respects vindicates the limitations of Abelard and of subsequent medieval dialecticians, who drew as much fire in their own times as Bacon and Sprat were to level at them in the seventeenth century.

Another contributor to the study and practice of dialectic, Gilbert de la Porrée (1076–1154), wrote a logic textbook, *Liber de Sex Principiis*, which was more highly esteemed than any other composed in the Middle Ages. It is a commentary on Aristotle's ten categories which initiated a longstanding controversy over whether relation is real or merely a device of reason. Along with Abelard, Peter Lombard and Peter of Poitiers, Gilbert de la Porrée was considered one of the 'dialectical theologians' who were attacked by reactionary theologians but who eventually won the day. John of Salisbury (c. 1115–80) in his *Metalogicon*, a treatise on education based largely on Aristotle's *Organon*, remarked that the *Topics* is of more value than almost all the books of dialectic which his contemporaries use in the schools. Albert of Cologne (1206–80) and his pupil Thomas

Aquinas (1224/5–74) were the first to envisage a theological system based on a conscious differentiation of the roles of philosophy and theology, and to effect this system Aquinas, it has been suggested, had to make Aristotle say many things which he never said. For all his dialectical acumen Aquinas was more theologian and metaphysician than dialectician.

Duns Scotus (c. 1266–1308) founded a school strong enough for a time to divide the world with the Thomists in disputes over matter and form, universals and individuals. Scotus himself in a series of folios seemed to revel in dialectical disputation as much as Abelard had done, and he showed the joy in destruction against which Plato warned when young men are in the first fever of dialectic (*Rep.*, 539b). Although Swift anachronistically suggests that the theologians' deposition of Plato in favour of Aristotle occurred as late as the time of Duns Scotus, the spirit of his comment in the *Battle of the Books* rings true:

> *Books* of Controversy, being of all others, haunted by the most disorderly Spirits, have always been confined in a separate Lodge from the rest; and for fear of mutual violence against each other, it was thought Prudent by our Ancestors, to bind them to the Peace with strong Iron Chains. Of which Invention, the original Occasion was this: When the Works of *Scotus* first came out, they were carried to a certain great Library, and had Lodgings appointed them; But this Author was no sooner settled, than he went to visit his Master *Aristotle*, and there both concerted together to seize *Plato* by main Force, and turn him out from his antient Station among the *Divines*, where he had peaceably dwelt near Eight Hundred Years. The Attempt succeeded and the two Usurpers have reigned ever since in his stead: But to maintain Quiet for the future, it was decreed, that all *Polemicks* of the larger Size, should be held fast with a Chain.
>
> (*Tale*, p. 223)

Mention could be made of other thinkers and other schools of philosophy emphasising aspects of dialectic before and after 1300. But the second half of the thirteenth century can be regarded as the classical period in the development of medieval scholasticism, and after 1350, it has been suggested, one could be forgiven for thinking the plague had a predilection for logicians.

The last eminent representative of scholasticism is generally considered to be the Spanish Jesuit theologian Francisco Suarez (1548–1617), who took a middle position on the question of universals between the Realism of Duns Scotus and the Nominalism of William of Ockham (c. 1290–1349). His two-volume *Disputationes Metaphysicae* (1597), in which he mainly follows Aristotle and Aquinas, was used as a textbook in both Roman Catholic and Protestant universities until the first part of the eighteenth century, and when Leibniz speaks of Suarez's philosophy as the *philosophia recepta* it is chiefly the *Disputationes* to which he refers. In the Scriblerus memoirs (c. 1714) fourteen metaphysical and theological theses for disputation are listed for satiric purposes, and of the nine taken from particular authors, seven are from Aquinas and two are from Suarez.[8]

THE MEDIEVAL UNIVERSITIES

The seven liberal arts

The curriculum of the medieval universities had its origin in the imperial rhetoric schools of Rome, which by Roman tradition had always subordinated logical to rhetorical studies. The seven liberal arts studied in these schools were the familiar grammar, rhetoric, dialectic, geometry, arithmetic, astronomy and music, later divided by Boethius into two groups, the *trivium*, consisting of the first three, and the *quadrivium*, the last four. Grammar consisted of the Latin classics, rhetoric of the tropes and figures and dialectic of the logic of Porphyry. These seven arts were the basis of the educational reforms of Alcuin under Charlemagne, and, studied primarily in the compendiums of Boethius and Martianus Capella, they comprised the curriculum of monastic and cathedral schools – like Rheims, Laon, Chartres and Notre Dame in Paris – long before the foundation of the universities. A twelfth-century renaissance saw a brief period of humanism in Europe culminating in John of Salisbury, who with men like Peter of Blois was as devoted to Latin literary works as he was to dialectic, and who lamented the growing preoccupation with dialectic in the twelfth century. It was two centuries before something approaching a balance among the seven liberal arts was regained, after being smothered in what has been described as 'a dust-pall of dialectic'.[9]

Aristotle and the Arabs

Until the seventh century most of the works of Aristotle had remained in Greek in a Byzantine milieu, and there had grown up around them a body of professional comment making a system with a relatively consistent world view. This system – the original Aristotle (except for the *Politics*, whose practical rather than theoretical character little interested the Arabs), some pseudepigraphs and the commentary – was translated into Arabic between 750 and 1050 by the polyglot Syrian Christians, who were able to control the Greek original as well as the Arabic of their patrons in the court of Baghdad. Western scholars visiting Byzantium produced translations of the *Organon*,[10] and the union of Greek and Arabic at the court of Palermo brought together the intellectual cultures represented by those two languages, but the widest diffusion of Moslem knowledge into western Europe came by way of Toledo, where Archbishop Raymond had instituted a college of translators in the second quarter of the twelfth century. Translations made available to Europeans at the time of the founding of the universities a systematic interpretation of Aristotle, which served as content to be dealt with by the method of dialectic. The two most important of the Arabic philosopher-interpreters of Aristotle were Avicenna (980–1036), born near Bokhara in Persia, and Averroës (1126–98), born in Cordoba, who especially exalted Aristotle, declaring that philosophical truth is synonymous with the philosophy of Aristotle. Although much of the energy of Albert the Great and Aquinas was directed at refuting the Avicennian and Averroistic heresies, the scholastics in general, including Albert and Aquinas, were impressed with the conciseness and clarity of these two Arabic Aristotelians who had explained Islamic theology in the forms of the logic of Aristotle.[11]

The founding of the universities

The transformation of the oldest schools, at Bologna, Paris and Orleans, into universities in the twelfth century cannot be precisely dated. After 1200 founding dates are generally available because older schools were transformed officially into universities, or new universities were begun, like Padua (1222) and like Cambridge (1209), created by an influx of students from Oxford just as Oxford had begun, apparently, about forty years earlier from an influx of students from Paris. Others were created by kings or princes, or by the church: Salamanca (c. 1220), Naples (1224), Toulouse (1229), Lerida (1300), Prague (1347), Vienna (1365), Heidelberg (1386), Cologne (1388), Erfurt (1389) and in the fifteenth century Leipzig, Uppsala, St Andrews and others.

From the beginning the traditional subjects of the monastic and cathedral schools were retained in the university curricula, but both the content and framework of pursuit were transformed to meet a demand which was no longer abstract learning but training for a profession. The new vocational education offered by the universities qualified their members for service in the church, the law, medicine or teaching, and presented them with licences to practise. This independent professional nature of the universities is reflected in their organisation under a corporate form of control, like guilds, and in the novel idea of degrees in education. The relatively unimportant bachelor's degree was awarded in arts for four years' study of the *trivium* and the master's degree, an authorisation and obligation to teach, for four years' study of the *quadrivium*. In theology at Paris the master's or doctor's degree, at first synonymous, required twelve or thirteen years' study beyond the master of arts degree, and the candidate had to have reached his thirty-fifth year.

The Greco-Arabian body of knowledge and ideas gave the traditional arts course an Aristotelian character, so that all the arts were either subsumed by or in some way subservient to logic and philosophy. Dialectic, or 'dialogue-logic', was practically the sole method of discussion and with the read lecture the major method of teaching. Not only was the method of teaching mainly Aristotelian, but also its content, with the *Organon* overshadowing the whole of the *trivium* and Aristotle's scientific works monopolising the *quadrivium*.

The dependence on Aristotle created an antinomy, because the authority of his logic and natural philosophy was universal, yet some authorities believed his philosophy denied or threatened the principles of Christianity. In 1210 at Paris a provincial council prohibited the public or private study of his books of natural philosophy and their commentaries, and in 1215 the papal legate Robert de Courçon renewed the interdiction.[12] Various other prohibitions of Aristotle's philosophy followed past the middle of the thirteenth century, but his works continued to be studied at Paris, usually in quiet defiance of the extramural authorities.

Dialectical, literary and scientific studies

From the 1215 statutes of the university at Paris, the 1252 statutes of the English–German nation there and the 1255 syllabus of the arts faculty, one can see the evolution both of the total reliance of the arts course upon Aristotle and of the academic exercises based on dialectical disputations or determinations. The pre-eminence of dialectic in medieval studies can be accounted for by the prevailing attitude which for more than four hundred years echoed the sentiments of John of Salisbury in the *Metalogicon* (1159) II 13: 'while each study is fortified by its own particular principles, logic is their common servant, and supplies them all with its "methods" or principles of expeditious reasoning. Hence logic is most valuable, not merely to provide exercise [for our faculties], but also as a tool in argumentative reasoning and the various branches of learning that pertain to philosophy. One who has command of a method for doing so, can proceed with ease in argumentative reasoning'. In the universities of northern Europe generally, and at Paris particularly, theology was queen;[13] and because the method of theology was dialectical, with questions raised and solved by arguments *pro* and *contra* a thesis (compare Abelard's *Sic et Non*), dialectic was raised to eminence as a heavenly gift for determining the truth.

The overshadowing of literary and scientific subjects by dialectic began in the twelfth century, when for a time literary, scientific and dialectical studies were developing together. The success of Abelard's dialectical methods of teaching in Paris at Notre Dame and at the collegiate church of Ste Geneviève and other places contributed greatly to the popularity of dialectic and to the eclipsing of other humane and liberal sciences. John of Salisbury, in the *Metalogicon* III 1, has a notable description of Abelard as a teacher. The dialectical form of question and disputation, popularised by Abelard, became the standard form for studying both the mass of twelfth-century translations of Aristotle's works and Greek and Arabian science and thought, and for handling biblical exegesis in the cathedral schools of Italy. Twelfth-century humanism was dealt a particularly hard blow, resulting in the decline of the classics and of literary pursuits in general, because Aristotelianism found its staunchest supports in northern France where the humanist tendencies had been the strongest. 'Practical' dialectic drew students from the study of belles-lettres, stifling the literary tendencies of

Chartres and Orleans and providing instead what students now wanted: logic as a stepping stone to theology and law.

Grammar, virtually excluded from Paris and Oxford as an independent subject by the middle of the thirteenth century, was the chief casualty among the seven liberal arts. Rhetoric was adapted to the study of law, the *quadrivium* to medicine and metaphysics. The banning of Aristotle's natural philosophy at Paris accentuated the logical and philosophical character of the arts faculty there, while at Oxford the *quadrivium* remained more in balance with the *trivium* in the thirteenth century, thanks in part to the scientific bent of Robert Grosseteste (c. 1170–1253) and of Roger Bacon (c. 1212–after 1292) and to the vigour of the latter's insistence on experimental science. Logic was not however superseded by the sciences at Oxford, as one is reminded, among other places, in Chaucer's description of the Clerk from that university, whose major study was apparently 'logyk' and whose twenty books of philosophy at the head of his bed were all by Aristotle. Nor was logic, or dialectic, superseded at Cambridge; indeed, it was the predominant study, as the Elizabethan statutes of 1570 point out: *'Primus annu, rhetoricam docebit: secundus et tertius dialecticam. Quartus, adjungat philosophiam.'* Two of the four undergraduate years were thus given to dialectic.[14]

Medieval university textbooks

Most facets of university life and studies continued with little major change from earliest times to seventeenth-century Trinity College where Swift encountered them, and textbooks are not an exception. The first regulations for the arts faculty at Paris in 1215 required that the masters lecture on the Old and New logic of Aristotle ordinarily and not cursorily: *'Quod legant libros Aristotelis de dialectica tam de veteri quam de nova in scolis ordinarie et non ad cursum.'*[15] 'Ordinary' lectures were formal lectures given by a master who raised philosophical and theological questions while expounding the text. They were usually more speculative and analytical than 'cursory' lectures, which were seldom more than a running commentary on the text given by bachelors and were more rapid than ordinary lectures, as their name suggests. The same regulations at Paris required that masters lecture on the fourth book of the *Topics* of Boethius, and they mention other books on other disciplines,

Priscian's grammar and Aristotle's *Ethics* for example, but dialectic is predominant.

Among the books on which students had to hear lectures according to the 1252 statutes of the English nation at Paris were Aristotle's *Categories* and *On Interpretation*, the first three books of Boethius's *Topics* (the Old logic) and Aristotle's *Topics*, *Sophistical Elenchi* and *Prior* and *Posterior Analytics*. The statutes required that students completing the BA course should have heard these books once or twice in ordinary lectures and usually once in cursory lectures.[16] The 1255 statutes for the arts course at Paris are directed to the reading masters rather than to the listening students and include largely the same books mentioned in the 1252 statutes. Porphyry is mentioned by name in the Old logic. The 1366 statutes for all faculties at Paris required that students completing the BA course should have heard the same logic books mentioned in the 1215, 1252 and 1255 statutes, and at Bologna a 1405 statute concerning student fees paid to doctors lecturing in philosophy shows emphasis on physics and metaphysics and a prescription of the *Prior* and *Posterior Analytics* and the *Sophistical Elenchi*. Oxford statutes in 1408 required that candidate bachelors should have heard Porphyry's *Isagoge* and Aristotle's *Sophistical Elenchi*, and at the University of Erfurt, according to a statute of 1420, the undergraduate curriculum was almost entirely devoted to dialectic, including Porphyry's *Isagoge* and the whole of the *Organon* except the *Topics*. Oxford statutes of 1431 for licence and inception, that is for bachelors becoming masters of arts, prescribed Aristotle's *On Interpretation* or the first three books of Boethius's *Topics* or Aristotle's *Prior Analytics* or *Topics*. Among the objects found in the room of Master Thomas Cooper of Brasenose Hall, whose lodgings were entered on 31 July 1438 by order of the Chancellor of Oxford, were, besides a broken lute and other personal objects, a folio commentary by Boethius on Aristotle's *On Interpretation*.

A fifteenth-century Cambridge manual of logic, the *Logica Cantabrigiensis*, found in Gonville and Caius College, Cambridge, MS 182/215, is a copy of a tract that was important in the fifteenth-century logical curriculum in Europe and especially influential on logic teaching in Italy and Spain. It is not surprising that Cambridge logic greatly influenced that at Trinity College, Dublin, in the seventeenth century.[17]

THE UNIVERSITY DISPUTATION

The BA course

The Paris and Oxford statutes mentioned above contain references to 'determination' and 'inception', the final qualifying examinations for the BA and MA degrees respectively.[18] The determination required at the end of his course of study what the undergraduate had practised for two years, the dialectical disputation. Apparently from the beginning of the universities disputations were, with read lectures, the major forms of imparting and testing knowledge and understanding. The Cambridge statutes of c. 1250 mention days on which disputations could be held and those on which they could not. The statutes of Peterhouse, Cambridge, in 1338 required that scholars 'dispute together' two days a week, on Wednesdays in logic and physical sciences and on Fridays, when sufficient doctors and bachelors of divinity were present, in theology. In the original statutes of Corpus Christi College, Oxford, in 1517 (supplemented 1528), undergraduates were to hear logic lectures and practise 'arguments and the solution of sophisms', and after six to thirty months of such study of logic were to witness the public disputations in the schools. The Elizabethan statutes of 1558 for Cambridge limited responding (the Respondent or Answerer defended a thesis, which the Opponent or Questioner attacked) in public disputations to undergraduates who had passed beyond the second year. Such a student was to propose three questions, one in mathematics, another in logic and a third in natural or moral philosophy, which were to be affixed to the doors of his school three days before the disputation. (Luther's ninety-five theses – or questions – nailed to the church door of All Saints in Wittenberg in 1517 were proposals for a strictly academic proceeding. He was surprised at their reception because, he said, he had never meant to determine, in the academic sense, but to debate.) The other sophisters[19] were to maintain the contrary side of the question, and if the respondent hesitated, one of the moderators would solve the difficulty if he was able. These disputations took place on Mondays to Fridays, from one to three in the afternoon. The Cambridge statutes of 1570 left these regulations for the public disputations of the sophisters unchanged.

At Oxford at this time (1571–1622) the procedure at the formal disputations *In Parvisis* was similar. Three questions or subjects for disputation were affixed to the door of the schools at eight o'clock on the morning of the disputation, during which three students disputed at one time, one as respondent and two as opponents, a procedure used at Trinity College, Dublin, as late as the middle of the nineteenth century. Students completing these disputations *pro forma* were given a kind of quasi-degree in logic and grammar and received a copy of the *Logic* of Aristotle, after one of the moderators, a regent master presiding over disputations, had made a speech 'in praise of Aristotle and true logic'. These disputations, called 'responsions', survived until recently (1960) at Oxford in the form of the first examination for the BA degree, which could be taken in the first term of residence or even before matriculation.

By the turn of the seventeenth century attendance at Oxford responsions had fallen off so much that in 1607 *Novissima Decreta* required that each undergraduate proceeding to the BA take an oath that he has studied dialectic for six terms before disputing in responsions, that he has disputed in responsions in each of the four terms before he seeks the BA and that he has been 'sedulously present' at the disputations when others disputed. A form of this requirement survived until 1856.

According to the Paris faculty of arts statutes of 1275, responsions had to be completed by the Christmas before the Lent in which determination took place. Determination itself, which first emerged as a separate examination in the 1252 statutes of the English–German nation at Paris, took place throughout the whole season of Lent in the form of a series of disputations. There has long been a question over the precise status of an undergraduate determining in Lent, but one admitted to determine apparently became a bachelor in status, that is to say, after he had completed responsions and had satisfied the authorities that he had met certain requirements, such as four years' attendance at courses in the arts faculty during which time, he had to declare on oath, he had heard in lectures all the books of the Old and New logic.

The procedure during determination was formal, beginning at Oxford with an Ash Wednesday procession from St Mary's Church to the schools. The disputations began on the first Monday in Lent and continued to the Friday before Palm Sunday. On Mondays to Thursdays, with few exceptions, the disputations took place from one to five in the afternoon on questions taken from the logic of Aristotle. On Fridays and some special days they took place from nine to twelve in the morning on questions chiefly in grammar, but also in rhetoric, politics and ethics. The statutable length of each disputation was one and a half hours. Determining bachelors were the opponents and scholars who had studied four terms *in dialectica* were the respondents, whose official function was *respondere sub Baccalaureo in quadragesima* (Lent). Each determining bachelor had to dispute at least twice, defending Aristotle, or the disputation did not count.

The disputation was the most distinctive university exercise of scholasticism and one in which a young scholar might win a great reputation. Disputations were public in the schools, as in responsions and determination, and private in college, where they were usually provided for in college statutes and occurred as often as three times a week or more. Ideally the intention was, at Cambridge at least, also to have disputations in each faculty at least once a week. The procedure was very briefly as follows: after a college or faculty lecture a master or student might pose a problem (*questio*), to which other students replied with reasoned arguments in Latin syllogisms. The master's summing up or 'determination' gave its name to the public exercises in Lent. In those and other more formal public exercises respondent and opponent debated dialectically, using Latin syllogisms, on opposite sides of a question (or problem, thesis or proposition – depending on its expression as a question or a statement: see Aristotle, *Top.*, 101ᵇ28–37), after which there was a determination often indicating the victor.

Another method of university disputation, identical with that of Abelard in the *Sic et Non*, was an individual's presentation of two sides of a question in alternately reasoned arguments. No matter how effectively presented, this method would obviously lack the dramatic effect of the better dialogic disputations in which respondent met opponent in oral syllogistic combat. In the 'monologic' disputation the result of the argument was a foregone conclusion, with a false impression of objectivity created by arguing both sides of a question and eventually showing the weight of evidence on one side or the other. Another reason it was objective in appearance only is that the discredited side was presented as the only possible alternative to the side the arguer eventually championed. Such a stratagem, however, is basic in dialectical argument of whatever variety and is not the point of distinction between the monologic and dialogic. The single-reasoner method of argument has its relevance to literature, in which a writer maintains a thesis and examines and refutes opposing theses, somewhat in the manner of *Religio Laici*, although the foregone conclusion there is perhaps too obvious. Dialectic in its more common literary form is closer to *The Hind and the Panther*, where the poet refutes not only opposing ideas and opinions, but also those who argue those ideas and opinions. When Dryden says 'God Save King Buzzard' (III 1140), referring in the allegory to Gilbert Burnet, Bishop of Salisbury, one sees that, while satire was not particularly his aim in the poem, there is an affinity between satire and dialectic. It is through satire as much as through normal polemical writing that dialectic finds its way into literature.

The MA course

The MA degree, towards which Swift was studying when the disturbed state of Ireland caused his departure for England early in 1689, had essentially the same requirements as the BA: residence for a stated period (three years in the English universities by the sixteenth century), attendance at lectures and disputations, two distinct sets of disputation exercises and final disputations called 'inception', corresponding to 'determination' for the BA. The BA course, however, was *in dialectica*, or grammar, rhetoric and logic from a dialectical viewpoint, and the MA course was *in utraque philosophia*, or moral and natural philosophy. The candidate for MA must have taken a BA and must give certain lectures to show his capacity for lecturing when he became an MA. The statutes of Paris, Oxford and Cambridge show that dialectic was not neglected but that MA studies comprised a broader range than those for the BA, including for example Aristotle's *Rhetoric* and Boethius's *Consolation of Philosophy*. Traditionally, and very broadly speaking, candidates for the MA pursued the *quadrivium* of music, arithmetic, geometry and astronomy.

A BA at Oxford seeking an MA had to dispute *pro forma* in two exercises, the Austin disputations (derived from the custom of scholars disputing with the Augustinian monks) and the quodlibet disputations. The former exercises took place from one to three p.m. on Saturdays during full term, and every BA had to dispute in them once a year, responding or opposing. These disputations at Cambridge, not called Austins there, sometimes took place from nine to eleven o'clock on Friday mornings (1570 statutes). In the Oxford quodlibet disputations the bachelors of arts responded to the regent masters on three questions and to any other (*quodlibet*) disputant on any question whatsoever.

At Paris, Oxford and Cambridge admission to the MA was called inception, after which the new MA had to dispute for forty consecutive disputable days or for six weeks. The procedure at inception at Oxford, which was not much different from the other two universities, consisted in a formal disputation called 'Vespers', which usually took place the evening before the degree ceremony. The next day, or two days later, the new master delivered an inaugural lecture followed by another disputation (or set of disputations, since several or many candidates incepted at a time) called the *Comitia* or 'the Act'. The tedium of the *Comitia* was relieved by a farcical element whose buffoonery would produce laughter in the audience, as some of the questions and theses debated show: 1600, 'What is the right way to tame a shrew? Ought Aristotle to have included a wife among the goods of a philosopher?' 1610 (for inceptors in law and medicine), 'Lovers require the same remedy used for curing madmen'. The comic element in the undergraduate disputations was provided by the Tripos or Prevaricator or Terrae-Filius, discussed in Chapter 3.[20]

Medieval and Renaissance disputations

During the long history of scholasticism, the last vestiges of which vanished from Protestant universities only in the nineteenth century, many attacks were levelled against it, especially against its most characteristic feature, the dialectical disputation. The condemnations by Bacon, Milton, Hobbes, Sprat, Locke and Pope should not blind one to the fact that disputations provided a way to fame and fortune, were important to the stability of church and state and were popular. In his defence of the doctrine of the Immaculate Conception at Paris, Duns Scotus showed such dialectical ingenuity that he was given the title *Doctor Subtilis* and caused the university's formal condemnation of the Thomist doctrine in 1387. In 1445 a young man of twenty, Fernando of Cordova, who had five degrees in arts, medicine, law and theology, came to the college of Navarre and in front of an audience of more than three thousand, including fifty masters, argued four doctors of divinity out of countenance. At Navarre and at Paris, where he travelled the same year, he was both hailed as something of a universal genius and suspected of being a magician or the Antichrist. Johnson's *Adventurer* no. 81 contains an account of the Admirable Crichton, the sixteenth-century Scotsman who studied at St Andrews University and was renowned for his learning and athletic skills. He won a great reputation for prowess in formal, public disputation in Paris, Rome and Padua.

An Oxford statute of 1408 recognised that the logical acumen displayed at disputations had largely contributed to the fame of the university, and St Andrews similarly recognised the importance of disputations. More importantly, disputations affected the course of history, as did Luther's which led first to his excommunication and then to the open division of Christendom. Following a public disputation on the question 'Whether the Roman Pontiff has, granted him by God in the holy scriptures, a greater authority and power in this kingdom of England than any other foreign bishop', the Cambridge House of Regents on 2 May 1534 drew up 'An Instrument Presented to Henry the Eighth by the University of Cambridge, Renouncing the Pope's Supremacy'. Henry II had considered submitting his dispute with Becket to the judgment of the masters at Paris, and Cranmer, when a theological master at Cambridge, suggested that Henry VIII refer the question of divorce to the universities for disputation.

Dialectic was popular not only among the major scholastic philosophers. Wolfgang Meurer (1513–85), a bachelor of arts at the University of Leipzig about 1533, held private disputations in his home with his friends on Saturday nights after supper, partly to search out the truth and partly to prepare themselves for future battle. The numbers attending these private disputations grew so large that they had to move to a public hall. At Cambridge Simonds D'Ewes (St John's College, 1618–20) found disputations not a grievance as Milton did, but an amusement. He prepared for them diligently and was crestfallen when he did not acquit himself well. This same spirit of optimistic pugnacity is reflected in the eighteenth century by Richard Cumberland, who regarded highly not only the disputations but the entire scholastic system: 'the extreme usefulness' of these academical exercises in training men in principles of right reasoning demonstrates that this is 'the best system, which this country offers, for the education of its youth'.[21]

3

Dialectic since the Sixteenth Century

SCHOLASTICISM

At Paris in the middle years of the thirteenth century the tendency towards harmonising philosophy and theology reached its perfection, one could say, in the scholasticism of Aquinas which implied the harmony of faith and reason. The beginning of the decline of scholasticism has been attributed to the doctrines of Duns Scotus (d. 1308) and William of Ockham (d. 1349), both of whom reintroduce the dualism between faith and reason which for centuries scholasticism had tried to overcome. After the fifteenth century, it is sometimes said, scholasticism ceased in effect to exist, except perhaps in its lone, late champion, Suarez.

Such was not the case in British universities, however. Milton at Cambridge in 1625, Locke at Oxford in 1652 and Bentley at Cambridge in 1676, for example, encountered an undergraduate curriculum that was still considered by some to be medieval. Outside the universities, too, scholasticism was still a force in 1667 when Sprat wrote the *History of the Royal Society*: the scholastics 'are still esteem'd by some men, the onely Masters of Reason'. Notebooks of English and Scottish undergraduates in the seventeenth century show that the curricula, in spite of the challenges of humanism, Ramism, the new science and the puritan rebellion, remained scholastic and Aristotelian throughout the century. Dr Fell at Christ Church, Oxford, later in the century was as partial to the old philosophy as was Neville at Trinity College, Cambridge, at the beginning of the century. Suarez's *Disputationes Metaphysicae*, Magirus's *Physics*, Scheibler's *Metaphysics* and other works of scholastic theology continued to be bought by college libraries or to be presented to them by fellows.

Puritan Cambridge was academically as conservative as Royalist Oxford, and at both universities the student notebooks of the 1650s

are indistinguishable from those of the 1640s. The Scottish
universities were if anything more conservative. There is no hint of
Baconian ideas at Glasgow, St Andrews or Aberdeen in the 1650s,
and at Oxford at this time science generally was no further advanced:
at Exeter and Corpus Christi students were learning Aristotelian
physics and astronomy and discussing the motion of the sun in pre-
Copernican terms. The curriculum for medical degrees at seventeenth-
century Oxford consisted of Aristotle, Galen, Hippocrates, Avicenna
and some botany and herbals. The collection book of Christ Church,
which gives the required reading for undergraduates during vacations,
shows that Burgersdicius's *Metaphysics* was not taken out of the
reading lists until 1744, the year in which Locke's *Essay concerning
Human Understanding* was finally recommended.

> Prompt at the call, around the Goddess [of Dulness] roll
> Broad hats, and hoods, and caps, a sable shoal:
> Thick and more thick the black blockade extends,
> A hundred head of Aristotle's friends.
> Nor wert thou, Isis [Oxford]! wanting to the day,
> (Tho' Christ-church long kept prudishly away.)
> Each staunch Polemic, stubborn as a rock,
> Each fierce Logician, still expelling Locke,
> Came whip and spur, and dash'd thro' thin and thick
> On German Crouzaz, and Dutch Burgersdyck.
> As many quit the streams that murm'ring fall
> To lull the sons of Marg'ret and Clare-Hall [Cambridge].

> Pope, *Dunciad*, iv

It would be interesting to know whether the *Dunciad*'s attack on the
Oxford curriculum in 1742/3 had a part in the curriculum change of
1744.

The major reason scholasticism was so difficult to unseat is that it
was the court philosophy, defending the status quo by emphasising
religious and social authority, a point not lost on Pope (*Dunciad*,
iv):

> May you, may Cam, and Isis preach it long!
> 'The Right Divine of Kings to govern wrong'.

The scholastics had brought the rationally ordered world of

Aristotle's politics, ethics, nature and metaphysics into conjunction with Christian doctrine, and this comfortable and articulate synthesis appealed to the conservative mind threatened by Anabaptism. In one sense the division in British society in the seventeenth century was not along religious or political lines but along the social. The civil war was fought between two sections of the gentry, but they grew more and more to fear social radicalism as the war continued. In science too the division in society was reflected: both the Wadham Group and its successor the Royal Society were intellectual clubs for the social élite. At bottom it was the universities with their requirements of Latin and Greek for admission, with their emphasis on the classics and their distrust of the 'mechanick arts', that maintained the social division. The decline of the universities in importance and in numbers of undergraduates from the Restoration to the second half of the eighteenth century was the result of many factors, including the exclusion of dissenters from the universities as a result of the Clarendon Code, the decline of the clergy and gentry in both numbers and importance, and reaction against the new England which was advancing with the Whigs and the City of London. The relevance of university conservatism to Swift is not only through a curriculum which stressed Aristotle and dialectic but also through the broader social issues which pitted the universities (including Trinity College, Dublin, a replica of Cambridge and Oxford) and what they stood for against the spirit of the post-Restoration world which saw the establishment of the Bank of England, the national debt and the City as powerful influences in English life. With the growth of merchant wealth and tolerance of dissent, the universities lost their central position within the state, and Swift, who moved up socially as much through the university and the church as through unassisted genius, reflects the opposition of the new and old élite in the premises from which he argues throughout his career.[1]

UNIVERSITY LOGIC STUDIES

Bartholomaeus Keckermann, whose logic was popular in seventeenth-century British universities, said at the beginning of the century, 'never from the beginning of the world was there a period so keen on logic, or in which more books on logic were produced and studies of logic flourished more abundantly than the period in which we live'.[2] It was taken for granted that logic was the basis of university education, but some logic had crept into the public schools, much to the dismay of Locke and Fuller, who said of 'The Good Schoolmaster': 'He spoils not a good school to make thereof a bad college, therein to teach his scholars logic'. Some like Milton thought that difficult logic and metaphysics were introduced too early even at the university. Magdalene College, Cambridge, MS F. 4. 21, an anonymous mid-seventeenth-century commonplace book, comments on the 'Custome ancient & generall, yet notwithstanding held erroneous; wch is, that Schollers in vniuersities come too soone, & for vnripe to Logique & Rhetoricke' (p. 97). At St Paul's School in the early seventeenth century, for example, students bound for university were taught, besides writing, declaiming and orating, the elementary principles of logic and disputation. Once at university the boys, often as young as fourteen, encountered a course of study only slightly revised since medieval times by Elizabethan statutes (1570) at Cambridge and Laudian statutes (1636) at Oxford, both of which remained in effect until the nineteenth century. In *Of Education* (1644) Milton says early on, 'I deem it to be an old errour of universities, not yet well recover'd from the Scholastick grosnesse of barbarous ages . . .', a remark that can be read in conjunction with his Prolusion III, '*Contra Philosophiam Scholasticam*'. The main undergraduate studies in the seventeenth century were still logic and philosophy, and it was largely for these that Latin and Greek were studied. Hobbes's Latin verses on his studies at Oxford, where he was sent at fourteen, show the emphasis on logic.[3]

The 1628 statutes for the University of Edinburgh show that the undergraduate was taught Aristotle's *Organon* and Porphyry's *Isagoge* and examined regularly in them for the last three of his four years. Although the least given to thoroughgoing Aristotelianism of the Scottish universities, Edinburgh was still soundly Aristotelian in spite of the passing challenge of Ramism, as student notebooks show: like John Robertson's '*Prolegomena in Duos Libros Posteriorum Analyticorum*' (1628), a volume of notes from lectures delivered by John Brown, a regent in the university.[4] A bound volume of manuscripts in the Edinburgh University Library relates to the meetings of the principals of the four Scottish universities in the last decade of the seventeenth century to discuss curricula and textbooks. A carefully recorded meeting took place on 15 September 1693, and by 1697 a draft manuscript of a logic textbook prepared by St Andrews University, the most Aristotelian of the four, had been criticised in detail by the universities of Glasgow, Aberdeen and Edinburgh. Two results of the discussions were *An Introduction to Logicks* and *An Introduction to Metaphysicks*, both printed in London in 1701. The logic is predictably Aristotelian and traditional. Logic notebooks at the English universities show the same Aristotelian method: for example, the '*Systema Logicae*' (1677) of Humphry Hody of Wadham College,[5] the notebook (1681) of John Smith of Gonville and Caius College,[6] the anonymous late seventeenth-century 'Discursus upon Logic'[7] and an anonymous '*Institutio Dialectica sive Epitome totius Artis Logicae*' (1703).[8] Others treat subjects like Aristotle's *Of Generation and Corruption* in a traditional dialectical method.[9] Henry Docker of St John's College, Cambridge, in his notebook dated 1686, has several pages of written-out arguments, for example, '*Argumenta ad probandum Deum esse unum*' (p. 51), consisting of three brief arguments.[10]

The abundance of undergraduate logic notebooks in the seventeenth century is a reminder that printed books at that time were relatively rare and expensive and that students depended on lectures for basic information. Daily logic lectures (except feast days) like those provided for in the original statutes (1505) of Christ's College, Cambridge, were also common in other colleges, and new lectureships were instituted in the seventeenth century. In 1611 the will of John Cowell, Master of Trinity Hall, Cambridge, provided maintenance towards a college lecture in logic from six to eight a.m. four days a week in term, and King James provided for a university lectureship in logic at Cambridge in 1620. This resurgent interest in lectures is balanced by the fact that by the mid-seventeenth century sparsely-attended lectures had come to be called wall lectures.

The lecture technique, which generally consisted of a methodical reading of the same texts to which medieval undergraduates had listened, was no more out of date, judged from a twentieth-century vantage point, than the textbooks used. Descartes, Bacon, Harvey and Copernicus were for the most part slighted in curricula still adhering to the teachings of Aristotle, Galen and Ptolemy. The popular logics of Robert Sanderson[11] at the beginning of the century and Henry Aldrich[12] at the end were Aristotelian, as were those of Smiglecius and Samuel Smith, and other logics Locke assigned to his students in the 1660s. An end-of-the-century study guide at Oxford, 'Some Short Hints at a Method of Study in the University for the first eight years',[13] recommends Descartes, Bacon and other moderns, although less frequently than Aristotle and his commentators. It is likely, however, that this and other similar 'advanced' directions for study were more exercises in wishful thinking than seriously-followed proposals. More in line with what actually seems to have been studied is 'A Library for Younger Schollers', by Thomas Barlow, Provost of Queen's College, Oxford, from 1657, who ignores the practical views of 'modern' educators like Samuel Hartlib and lists in logic de Trieu, Smiglecius, Scheibler, Massius and other Aristotelians.[14]

At Cambridge Simonds D'Ewes under his tutor at St John's College, Richard Holdsworth, was taught in 1618 the Aristotelian logics of Seton, Keckermann and Molineus, and 'Holdsworth's' 'Directions for a Student in the Universitie' (1651/2)[15] recommends Burgersdicius, Crackanthorp, Keckermann, Molineus, Sanderson, Smiglecius, Massius and Ramus, all traditionally Aristotelian except Ramus; the same recommendations are found in the reduction of the 'Directions'[16] about 1696 by Joshua Barnes, Professor of Greek at Cambridge from 1695. At Harvard Burgersdicius and Keckermann seem to have been the most popular.

The belles-lettres of the seventeenth century, descendants of the humanism of the Renaissance, give few hints of the pervasiveness of Aristotle and dialectic in the universities. At Cambridge the statutes of Clare Hall, Trinity and St John's Colleges and at Oxford the Laudian statutes insist on the authority of Aristotle in interpretation of philosophy and in dialectic. 'In your answering reject not lightly the authority of Aristotle' was the advice to disputants given by James Duport, the teacher of Newton's teacher Isaac Barrow and fellow of Trinity and master of Magdalene College, Cambridge, from 1688. His 'Rules to be Observed by Young Pupils and Schollers in the University' (1650–60)[17] in addition to disputations gives advice in logic: 'Follow not Ramus in Logick nor Lipsius in Latine, but Aristotle in one and Tully in the other'.[18]

At the beginning of the eighteenth century Aristotelian logic seems to have been entrenched in university life as much as ever. William Reneu, an undergraduate at Jesus College, Cambridge, in 1705, wrote to a friend that his tutor read lectures to him daily from Burgersdicius's logic and the New Testament. Daniel Waterland, when he was dean and tutor at Magdalene College, drew up about 1706 'Advice to a Young Student, With a Method of Study for the Four First Years',[19] which like 'Holdsworth's' 'Directions' divides the studies into the four undergraduate years and recommends books to be read during certain months. Burgersdicius's logic is recommended in June of the first year in the 1730 edition; a later edition substitutes Wallis's logic. In 1755 at Trinity College there were daily lectures in hall from Duncan's logic[20] and weekly *viva voce* examinations in logic conducted in Latin. Jesus College in 1772 held lectures in Duncan's logic and in algebra. At Oxford in 1721 there was a call for a reformation of learning because of the 'philosophical popery' of Aristotle prevailing in the universities.[21] An undergraduate at Brasenose College wrote in 1742, 'We are here quite taken up with logic, which is indeed a very dry study'.[22] The state of logic on the continent at this time seems to have been at least as conservative as that in Britain, judging from the lectures on logic (1755) of F. J. Philipart of Louvain University, which are reminiscent of seventeenth-century English logics and notebooks: '*Quid est Dialectica? est ars disserendi. . . . quid e[st] finis Dialecticae? est acquirere habitum recte intende lumine rationis, de qualibet re cognitando, judicando, ratiocinando.*'[23]

University conservatism of a kind which forbade circulation of Locke's *Essay concerning Human Understanding* at Oxford upheld scholasticism into the eighteenth century, supported by the declining gentry and clergy. In 1714, approximately when the *Memoirs of Martinus Scriblerus* were written, scholasticism was still reckoned a suitable object for parody, as Chapter 7 on logic and metaphysics amply shows.[24] As late as 1780 in a brief article in the *Gentleman's Magazine*,[25] 'Observations on the University of Oxford', a writer commends the present age for passing beyond an interest in scholastic metaphysics but censures the universities for still adhering to the ancient method of education which is preparatory to the useless and perplexing studies of the scholastics. In spite of its tenacity, however, scholasticism throughout the eighteenth century was giving way to classical studies at Oxford and, as an equally socially acceptable form of intellectual activity, to pure mathematics at Cambridge.[26] Daniel Waterland's 'Advice to a Young Student' (c. 1706) says that mathematics is more useful than logic towards 'the conduct of the understanding',[27] and Richard Cumberland, Richard Bentley's grandson the dramatist, wrote a panegyric to 'the demonstration and discovery of positive and mathematical truth' in which he excelled as an undergraduate at Trinity in 1751.[28]

THE DISPUTATION

For all the centuries of formal disputing at the universities, surprisingly few disputations have survived. Cambridge has relatively few extant medieval records,[29] and although ample material relating to the university has been available since the Renaissance, only one complete disputation seems to have survived, a late sixteenth-century defence of two theses, one about crime deterrence and one about possession of private goods,[30] which show more of the dialogic drama of the academic disputations than do the plodding examples of disputations in Magdalen College, Oxford, MS 38,[31] and in Lambeth Palace Library MS 221.[32]

Examples of disputation in literature abound, such as the debate with Despair in the *Faerie Queene* (i 9), and are often in parody of serious dialectic, like Feste's dialectical catechising of Olivia proving that she is a fool (*Twelfth Night*, I v), the gravediggers' debate at the opening of Act v of *Hamlet*, the dialectical foolery of Petulant and Witwoud in *The Way of the World* (III xiii 15–31) and the debate between the executioner, the king and the queen about decapitating the Cheshire Cat in *Alice in Wonderland*. On a serious note, the laconic descriptions of Jesus's confrontations of the Pharisees, Herodians and Sadducees in Matthew 22 and the silencing of his hierarchical opponents with a dilemma at the opening of Luke 20 have long been familiar examples, but they lack the length and complexity required to show the many surprising turns a disputation can take. Examples of serious disputations, then, are relatively rare – that is, disputations inside or outside a university context in which a consciousness of the techniques of argument is maintained.

The earliest and one of the best of these selfconscious disputations is Plato's *Euthydemus*, in which the skill of Euthydemus and Dionysodorus in the war of words is such 'that they can refute any proposition whether true or false' (272a–b). In spite of its comedy and irony and the obviousness of its logical fallacies to post-Aristotelian minds, the *Euthydemus* is a valuable example of disputation because of its emphasis on the dialectical question and answer method: Euthydemus and his brother are willing to teach the young Cleinias philosophy and virtue at Socrates's request, 'if the young man is only willing to answer questions'; to which Socrates replies, 'He is quite accustomed to do so . . . , for his friends often come and ask him questions and argue with him; and therefore he is quite at home in answering' (275b–c). Aristotle's *Sophistical Elenchi* and the eighth book of the *Topics*, unsurpassed as guides in how to argue, contain enough examples to bring the concept of disputation to life; however, since these treatises will be drawn upon extensively in later chapters on Swift's use of dialectic, they will be passed over here. Cicero's *Tusculan Disputations* are characterised far more by continuous exposition than by the dramatic question and answer method, and the opponent is far too easily defeated (I 17, 76, 112; II 14–15) to show the conflict which must have been characteristic of those disputations on which Aristotle drew in writing his dialectical treatises, and of many of those from the Middle Ages to the seventeenth century in universities.

Something of the spirit of dialectical refutation can be seen in a controversy in 1436 over the draining of the Cambridge fens. Fuller in his history of Cambridge lists in parallel columns the contemporary arguments against and for the undertaking: 'Argument I. Some objected, that God saith to the water, "Hitherto shalt thou come, and no further", Job. xxxviii. 11. It is therefore a trespass on the Divine prerogative for man to presume to give other bounds to the water, than what God had appointed . . .'. In a parallel column: 'Answer I. The argument holdeth in application to the ocean, which is a wild horse, only to be broken, backed, and bridled by Him who is the Maker thereof. But it is a false and lazy principle, if applied to fresh waters; from which human industry may [rescue] and hath rescued many considerable parcels of ground'. Fuller lists nine more arguments and answers, some of which are adroitly clinched (Answer III) and some whose reasoning is as questionable as parts of the *Euthydemus*. Because of their elenctic answers, these arguments which Fuller lists are more dialectical than the method of arguments in favour of each of two contradictory assertions characteristic of the ancient *Dissoi Logoi* and of Abelard's *Sic et Non*. The fen drainage arguments resemble part of the first chapter of the logic of John Case (1598), containing a brief, stylised disputation between opponent and respondent on the necessity of dialectic, in which the respondent, as usual, has the last word. A like method is used in theological disputations in the Samuel Ward notebooks (early 1590s) at Sidney Sussex College, Cambridge, (Ward, BA Christ's 1593, was master of Sidney Sussex 1610–43) and in the notebook of Jonathan Mitchell (BA Harvard 1647), which gives outlines of several Harvard disputations, one of which Morison prints in his history of the college: 'The Cause as Cause passes into the Effect', 3 April 1646. The latter is in such abbreviated form that it has little value as an example of disputation other than as a reminder that Harvard education was practically indistinguishable in the seventeenth century from that at British universities.

All of these disputations, however, lack a feature of the formal scholastic exercises practised in the universities: the denying of an opponent's major or minor proposition or the nexus of his argument. University disputations were largely and consciously syllogistic, with propositions maintained and overthrown with the help of syllogisms. Case's and Mitchell's examples are syllogistic, but not dialectical enough to show denials of antecedents, for example, or demands for proofs of propositions. Robert Sanderson's *Logicae Artis Compendium* (1680) discusses these elements of formal disputation which occur in the next century in Amhurst's *Terrae-Filius* and in the *Gentleman's Magazine*. After complaining of Aristotle's domination of university studies and quoting part of the Oxford statute requiring disputants to maintain and defend all Peripatetic doctrines, Amhurst fills the rest of his essay with a partly humorous example of a disputation held at Oxford three years earlier (1718). The more serious part of it here shows the form of the argument, although from what one can know of academic disputations through another transcribed example (the Cotton Faustina MS) and from many accounts of the excitement they raised, this sample is pale indeed:

> *Opponens*. Propono tibi, domine, hanc questionem, (viz.) – An datur actio in distans?[33]
> *Respondens*. Non datur actio in distans.
> *Oppon*. Datur actio in distans; ergo falleris.
> *Resp*. Negatur antecedens.
> *Oppon*. Probo antecedentem;
>> Si datur fluxus virium *Agentis*, cum distat *Agens*, tum datur actio in distans.
>> Sed datur fluxus virium agentis, cum distat agens.
>> Ergo datur actio in distans.
> *Resp*. Negatur minor.
> *Oppon*. Probo minorem;
>> *Vice-Cancellarius*[34] est agens;
>> Sed datur fluxus virium *Vice-Cancellarii*; cum distat *Vice-Cancellarius*.
>> Ergo, datur fluxus virium agentis, cum distat agens.
> *Resp*. Negatur minor.

Oppon. Probo minorem;
   Si disputans parviis . . .[35]

(*Opponent.* I propose to you, sir, this question – Whether
   action occurs at a distance?
Respondent. Action does not occur at a distance.
Op. Action does occur at a distance; therefore you are mistaken.
Resp. The antecedent is denied.
Op. I prove the antecedent;
   If power flows from an agent when the agent is at a distance,
      then action occurs at a distance.
   But power does flow from an agent when the agent is at a
      distance.
   Therefore action occurs at a distance.
Resp. The minor premise is denied.
Op. I prove the minor premise;
   The Vice-Chancellor is an agent [or powerful person – a play
      on the word];
   But power flows from the Vice-Chancellor when the Vice-
      Chancellor is at a distance.
   Therefore power flows from an agent when the agent is at a
      distance.
Resp. The minor premise is denied.
Op. I prove the minor premise;
   If disputants in a formal disputation . . .)

The opponent supplies proofs to support two more minor premises,
proving other ways,[36] until the moderator steps in and draws two
distinctions which are humorous, quibbling defences of the
respondent's position. Even before the moderator brings it to a
close the disputation has degenerated from what had seemed to be a
serious argument over the possibility of action occurring at a distance
into a mock-logical joke over the vice-chancellor's power to cause
fear in undergraduates.

A disputation example in the *Gentleman's Magazine* (1780) also
follows a complaint that scholastic exercises at Oxford are woefully
out of date and are but farces enacted for sake of tradition. This
example, which the author gives in translation from the Latin, is not
a ridiculous example, he insists, but a fair representation of those
held in the schools. The respondent has affirmed that universal ideas
are formed by abstraction.

Opponent. Universal ideas are not formed by abstraction; therefore you are deceived.

Resp. I deny the antecedent.

Opp. I prove the antecedent – Whatever is formed by sensation alone is not formed by abstraction: but universal ideas are formed by sensation alone; therefore universal ideas are not formed by abstraction.

Resp. I deny the minor.

Opp. I prove the minor. The idea of solidity is an universal idea: but the idea of solidity is formed by sensation alone: therefore universal ideas are formed by sensation alone.

Resp. I deny the major.

Opp. I prove the major . . .[37]

The opponent soon abandons his proofs through sensation for proofs through relation, and the disputation ends with the respondent's conceding the opponent's last proof but drawing a distinction and so maintaining his own original thesis. The respondent (answerer) seems to be thoroughly Platonic and the opponent Aristotelian, a role reversal of what should be followed by statute and tradition. Here the opponent (questioner) follows the concepts laid down in the *Posterior Analytics* ii 19, and in so doing he should be the respondent who takes the school position and not the opponent. But the writer of the article has the sides assigned, and no matter who defends and who attacks, one can see the drift of the argument and the style in which it is done.

Although these examples are authentic in form, they cannot be expected to be complimentary to academic disputation, their intention being to show the foolishness of such exercises as they had degenerated in the eighteenth century. That is not the case, however, with the Elizabethan disputation at Cambridge, British Library MS Cotton Faustina D. II, probably the best and most complete example of a disputation in a long line of examples, usually of an abbreviated or fragmentary nature. Part of the manuscript account of this disputation is given a spirited exposition by Costello, who points out the formal contexts of the disputants' thrusts and parries and the vigour with which they are pressed home.[38] The disputation, which probably took place between 1594 and 1600, consists of two questions, on each of which a Mr Boyes, possibly of Clare Hall, meets two opponents. Costello passes over Boyes's first opponent and discusses the second opposition to the first question: Knowledge of the existence of prisons is sufficient crime deterrent (rendering the gallows unnecessary). The debate with the first opponent on this question is not as dramatic as that with the second, but it has more concrete terms and has parts which show the occasional lightness in these formal exercises, which were often either too arid or too virulent for contemporary tastes. To prove an antecedent Boyes has denied, the opponent argues that if the possibility of imprisonment deters wrongdoing, the possibility of being hanged deters wrongdoing the more; therefore the possibility of being hanged is the ultimate deterrent in human things. Boyes replies, 'I concede everything. Honestly, your syllogism has four terms' (*Concedo omnia. Habet enim iste syllogismus quatuor terminos*).[39]

In the second question, whether the possession of private property violates the law of nature, Boyes drives his first opponent to distinguishing between primary and secondary nature and then to calling upon the authority of Aristotle. This brief excerpt will give an idea of the style of argument.

Op. Rerum priuatarum possessio non est secundum naturam.
  Ergo naturae refragatur.
[*B*.][40] Nego antecedens.
Op. Quod naturae decretum violat non est secundum naturam;
  Priuatarum rerum possessio naturae decretum violat;
  Non est igitur secundum naturam.
B. Proba assumptionem.
Op. Tollit aequalitatem inter omnes;
  Ergo violat decretum naturae.
B. Nego argumentum.
[*Op*.][41] Natura aequalitatem imperat;
  Ergo hanc abrogando naturae aequalitatem violat.
[*B*.] Vt huic argumento satisfiat necessario est distinguendum.
  Natura enim duplex est, Primaria et secundaria. Naturae
    primariae non nego hanc placere aequalitatem sed imperfecta
    est et illis etiam, animantibus communis quae ratione carent.
  Natura autem secondaria quae ex rationis fonte manat hanc
    abrogauit penitus.
Op. Probabo ex secundariae naturae consideratione non abrogari
    aequalitatem.
  Quod dissentiones ciuium animos ad concordiam reducit a natura
    secundaria non abrogatur;

Sed bonorum aequalitas dissentientes ciuium animas ad concordiam reducit;

Non abrogatur igitur a natura secundaria.

B. Nego minorem.

Op. Probo primum ex Philosopho Polit. 5. Docet enim exulceratos ciuium animos aequali bonorum diuisione facillime placari et quamuis illud non affirmavit infinitis tamen Atheniensium et Romanorum exemplis possit confirmari . . .

(*Op*. The possession of private property is not according to nature.

Therefore it is against nature.

[*B*.] I deny the antecedent.

Op. Whatever violates a decree of nature is not according to nature;

The possession of private property violates a decree of nature;

Therefore it is not according to nature.

B. Prove the minor premise.

Op. Private property removes equality between people;

Therefore it violates a decree of nature.

B. I deny the proof.

[*Op*.] Nature demands equality.

Therefore private property violates this natural equality by doing away with it.

[*B*.] For that argument to stand up, a distinction is necessary. There are two kinds of nature, primary and secondary. I do not deny that primary nature rejoices in equality, but this primary nature is incomplete – and is held in common with non-rational living creatures. Secondary nature, however, which springs from reason, completely does away with equality.

Op. I shall prove from a consideration of secondary nature that it does not do away with equality.

Whatever restores the discordant minds of fellow citizens to concord is not done away with at the level of secondary nature;

But equality of goods restores the discordant minds of fellow citizens to concord;

Therefore it is not done away with at the level of secondary nature;

B. I deny the minor premise.

Op. I prove it first from the Philosopher [Aristotle], in *Politics* v. He teaches that the aggravated minds of fellow citizens are most easily quietened by an equal distribution of goods, and although he did not say so, this could easily be proved by countless Athenian and Roman examples . . .)

BA and MA requirements of prolonged and intensive study and practice of dialectic and disputations like these of Boyes had an effect on the literary world just as the conservatism of the curriculum had an effect on the political and social worlds.[42] Swift's use of the language and methods of dialectic is part of the evidence of the permeation of this effect. The dialectic of writers who had no formal connection with a university, like Shakespeare, is better evidence of the degree to which the dialectic emphasised in the academic world penetrated the literary world in the seventeenth and eighteenth centuries. The Third Earl of Shaftesbury, who attended Winchester but no university, did not need Locke, the director of his education, to advise him on an old trick in disputation: '*Grimace* and *Tone* are mighty Helps to Imposture. And many a formal Piece of Sophistry holds proof under a severe Brow, which wou'd not pass under an easy one'. In many seventeenth- and eighteenth-century comments on wit and raillery reference is made to informal disputation, but information about manners, strategems and procedures in formal disputation naturally comes from academic sources. John Sanderson's *Institutionum Dialecticarum* (Oxford, 1602), for example, has a brief concluding section, 'Rules to observe in disputing', which begins with advice against useless altercations that waste words and fail to search out truth.

As good a source as printed logics for guides to formal disputation are lectures on logic, in which Scottish lecturers seem to have been the most conscientious, lecturing slowly so that undergraduates could transcribe carefully and neatly. (Scottish undergraduate notebooks are usually neater than their English counterparts.) One such unsigned student notebook,[43] a typical example, has as a final chapter 'Concerning the Rules of Disputation' a list of seven sensible guides governing formal academic debate. Under Rule 6 concerning the conduct of the respondent, the fourth principle, for example, is that 'if the [opponent's] thesis should contradict [one's own] and the form be good, the false proposition should be denied or the ambiguous one distinguished', a principle given also in Rule 10 of Colin Vilant's 'Course of Logicks', lecture notes given when he was Professor of Philosophy in St Salvator's College, St Andrews, in 1724.[44] Also in both of these '*Leges disputandi*' is the reminder that

'No one should be keen to win empty glory, but each should search for truth with the sincerity becoming a noble mind'.[45] Other rules for disputing in these notebooks are similar to Duport's 'Rules' (1650–60), which, however, are unlike many other lists because they are in English and are unusually concrete and informal in style: 'Use often to dispute & argue in Logick, and Phylosophy with your Chamberfellow, and acquaintance when you are together' (*Cap.4, De exercitiis Scholasticis*).

Such rules provide at best a random and general view of academic disputations. For what actually occurred in the contests the manuscript account of Boyes's Act gives an example but no commentary, and the commentaries on the public disputations, or 'Acts and Opponencies' as they were called, are sometimes cryptic, sometimes contradictory and generally unsatisfactory in their attempts to explain the procedures of disputation in the schools. Christopher Wordsworth gives a superficial view of disputations at Oxford from the seventeenth to the nineteenth centuries[46] and Peacock does little better with those at Cambridge.[47] From these and other sources one gets an idea of their importance, of the ritual, of the questions debated and of the undergraduates' opinions of them. It seems to be only in the nineteenth century, when arguments to abolish academic disputations were receiving more and more attention, that one finds a serious attempt to explain just how the disputing was done. Charles Wesley's *Guide to Syllogism* (1832) has an appendix 'On Academical Disputation' which explains precisely the roles of the respondent and opponent in disputation, including accepted strategems each uses in trying to overthrow the other's position. This explanation is followed by examples of forms (with letters replacing substantive reasonings) of four arguments which, after more explanation, are followed by five substantive arguments in a divinity act held at Cambridge in the early nineteenth century and by comments on acts in civil law.[48] Although Wesley's *Guide* is valuable as an explanation of the workings of a disputation, it is so technical that we are left with little sense of the combativeness inherent in a good disputation. The best accounts of the dialectical spirit of the disputation, in the sense of Aristotle's *Topics* and *Sophistical Elenchi*, are Schopenhauer's 'Art of Controversy',[49] Costello's section on 'The Disputation'[50] and Paul Moraux's 'La joute dialectique d'après le huitième livre des *Topiques*',[51] which should be considered along with university statutes and contemporary descriptions of procedures for a relatively thorough view.[52]

Another view of the disputation which helps to convey its liveliness is the contemporary account, which deserves a chapter to itself but of which only bare mention can be made here. Bishop Usher's disputation at age nineteen with a Jesuit is described as comparable with David challenging Goliath;[53] at a Cambridge disputation in 1614 King James stood up and entered the Act;[54] on another occasion in the presence of James I, Dr William Chappel of Christ's, 'known as a fierce and subtle arguer', opposed a Dr Roberts of Trinity so closely and subtly that the latter fainted away and the king completed the disputation in his place;[55] the Bishop of Exeter wrote to a friend in 1647 concerning a commencement disputation at Cambridge on the punishment of heretics and referred to the current upheavals: 'That bloody syllogisme wch y^u mention, ye maior whereof was framed by their old masters, & ye minor added by ye present disciples . . .';[56] Locke in his valedictory speech to the bachelors of arts, delivered in Christ Church hall in 1664 upon stepping down from his office of Praelector Rhetoricus, emphasises in a good-natured way the combativeness of the BAs' disputations;[57] 'Holdsworth's' 'Directions' urge the study of Latin and oratory: 'without those you will be bafld in your disputes, disgraced & vilified in Publick examinations';[58] Richard Cumberland of Trinity, Cambridge, in a 1751 Act opposed 'a North-country black-bearded philosopher' from St John's and when he had caught the fallacy in his opponent's syllogism 'pursued it with advantage, keeping the clue firm in hand till I completely traced him through all the windings of his labyrinth';[59] other eighteenth-century disputants 'kept a very capital Act' (1790), 'came off very gloriously' (1711), 'came down without much disgrace' (1708) and one, on a mathematical question from Newton's *Principia*, had an opponent who 'brought an argument against me fraught with fluxions' (1752);[60] another resorted to verse, begging off describing his Act (1790):

> of important days,
> Examinations, when the man was weighed
> As in a balance! of excessive hopes,
> Tremblings withal and commendable fears,
> Small jealousies, and triumphs good or bad –
> Let others that know more speak as they know.
> Such glory was but little sought by me,
> And little won.

So said Wordsworth in *The Prelude* (iii 68–75), describing his disputations at St John's College, Cambridge.

THE TRIPOS OR PREVARICATOR SPEECHES

A statutorily sanctioned comic disputant to provide light entertainment at public exercises was called at Oxford the *terrae-filius*, at Cambridge the varier, prevaricator or tripos and at Trinity College, Dublin, the tripos. The tradition of the comic interlude seems to have started in the late fifteenth or early sixteenth century, and by the seventeenth various statutes provide for it. It may be noted that a decree of the University of Heidelberg in 1518 prohibited under severe penalty the practice of former years of masters, bachelors and other alumni proposing *facetiae* at quodlibetical disputations, where 'shameful, lascivious and impudent' displays of wit might provoke youth innocent in sexual matters to unseemly or illicit lust.[61] At Oxford the *terrae-filius* at the commencement disputations underwent successive metamorphoses from a grave participant in the exercises, to a humorous attacker of thesis questions, to a ridiculer of the university and its members and, after he became scurrilous, to a tradition cut short because of its abuse.[62] At Cambridge the metamorphoses were from a wooden tripod, to a comic disputer (the tripos), to a tripos speech, to printed tripos verses, to a sheet of foolscap paper on which examination results were printed, to a system of examination[63] still called the tripos today.

Because instances when the prevaricator fell foul of the university are recorded more faithfully than occasions when he was simply witty and diverting, the evidence shows a turbulent career for him in the seventeenth century. A grace of the Cambridge Senate in 1608 exiled beyond the purlieus of the university all buffoon-like raillery, unsuitable, indecent, unmannerly wit, brawling, invective and derisive laughter: '*Scurrilis omnis dicacitas, ineptae, impurae, inurbanae facetiae, rixae, convitia, theatralem cachinnum moventia, ab oribus orisque academicorum longe exulent*', but approved charming, pleasant and learned witticisms in the prevaricator. In 1626 a decree of the heads of the Cambridge houses stated that 'buffooneries and scurrilous jests are not to be any longer permitted at the public disputations', which, like the grace of 1608, is more vivid in Latin than in English: *'Interpretatio seu decretum de auferendis moronium ineptiis et scurrilibus jocis in publicis disputationibus'*.[64]

Undaunted prevaricators, however, occasionally abused their privileges. Seth Ward, later bishop of Exeter, as prevaricator when he took his MA in 1640 so angered the vice-chancellor that he was suspended his degree, but was granted it the next day.[65] Marsden summarises a prevaricator's speech of 1660, showing the gibes at the dons, Oxford men present, beadles and the vice-chancellor, in which there is an audacity that exceeds the senior proctor's exhortation 'to be witty, but modest withall'.[66] A decree of 1667 required that the prevaricator show his speech to the vice-chancellor before the disputation exercises, and if he subsequently added to it without official approval he was to be expelled.[67] Oxford was if anything harder on its *terrae-filii*, who were expelled following their speeches at public Acts in 1592, 1632 and 1658. Troops were called in to quieten a disturbance at the Act of 1651; and a speech was burned by the Common Beadle in the theatre yard in 1713.[68] When a *terrae-filius* of Merton repeated a local scandal, the son of one of the parties involved, 'who was there, cudgelled him afterwards in the Row-Buck yard'.[69]

The Act in July 1669 must have been especially outrageous. John Evelyn described it as 'ribaldry' and 'a tedious abusive, sarcastical rhapsody', in which 'the old facetious way of rallying upon questions was left off, falling wholly upon persons, so that it was rather licentious lying and railing than genuine and noble wit. In my life, I was never witness of so shameful entertainment'. After the ceremonies he complained to the vice-chancellor and to the heads of several colleges, who resolved to take action against such speeches. On 19 July 1669 John Wallis wrote to the Hon. Robert Boyle concerning the recent Saturday and Monday Acts, which included the object of Evelyn's indignation and at which the *terrae-filii* were 'abominably scurrilous', representing the heads of houses and other eminent persons in the university and their relations 'as a company of whore-masters, whores, and dunces . . . Since the act (to satisfy the common clamour) the vice-chancellor hath imprisoned both of them; and it is said, he means to expel them'.[70] In 1680 Cambridge University received both a sharp reprimand and threatened interference from parliament because of a prevaricator's ridicule of the Titus Oates plot,[71] and in 1684 both the Saturday and Monday *terrae-filii* were expelled on Wednesday following the Acts.[72] The decline of the prevaricator at both universities dates from about this time, although at Cambridge the tradition survived probably until the middle of the eighteenth century, and at Oxford apparently the last *terrae-filius* speech, an innocuous one, was delivered in 1763.

Besides the slander and coarse language of the prevaricator's speeches, it was chiefly their lewdness which called down the wrath of the authorities. Commentators on these speeches, like Costello and Burton, generally confine themselves to polite and ingenious wit and humour, having little occasion to point out examples of the risqué. Burton, for example, prints an English translation of an early seventeenth-century Latin disputation (St John's College MS S. 34) in which Alexander Bolde frivolously attacks the proposition 'Matter does not stir unless it is moved' (*Nullum corpus agit, nisi moveatur*) by playing on the idiomatic meanings of the verb *agere*. It shows wit of the kind authorised by statute in a prevaricator's speech.[73] But at least some mild examples bordering on the indecent appear to be called for in viewing the prevaricator tradition as part of the background of a writer who was accused, with less than complete exaggeration, of never missing an opportunity 'of talking obscenely' and of writing 'in the Language of the Stews'.[74] A modest example occurs in the Oxford Musick Speech[75] of a Mr Thurman,[76] who addresses the ladies in the audience with mock concern that 'if any should have bene bigge bellyed wee should not putt you to the labour of a paire of staires . . . , and wee scholars being not to marry in the university judged it not fitting to heare [you] crye out in our mayden university, which if you had Ile assure you I had bene the man midwife. But wee have saved you y^t labour'.[77]

In another Oxford Musick Speech the address to the ladies begins with the question of saluting them, not with 'a civility which is as common as your lippes, but I mean I am at a losse with what titles to acouch you'. Some, he says, call you deities because you have so little humanity; angels, but evil, fallen ones; paradise because of the old serpent in you.

Another calls his mistresse the paragon of nature, a title invented by a taylour who being about to court his love, having fingered away half his buttons, and not knowing how to expresse himself cast his eyes upon hir petticoate and from thence took up this course [*sic*] complement. And indeed you are beholding to this man of measure for an other very pregnant title who will be sure to call you his bellypiece but I will not descend further to seeke after any thing else.[78]

It is doubtful whether this was acceptable to ladies and gentlemen alike in the audience at a degree ceremony, and later in the speech one would certainly guess that the wag offended the modesty of some. He is concluding a comment on the ladies, head to foot:

A great Master of love compares his mistresses legges to the colosse of Rhodes, tis a very broad expression and for owne to speake it in the Cambridge dialect tis to call the privy chamber of love a common road: some compare their Laydes to the world I shall not neede to tell you where the Low countrys lye; which the gulphe where Lapland is, or question whither there be any terra incognita here, but only admonish those y^t designe to compasse this globe, y^t they take heede y^t they hover not to long under the line least they gett a Calenture.

His most successful and most risqué metaphor, as witty as some of Swift's dialectical jabs in simile, follows a reference to the scented ointments pomatum and 'jessimy butter': 'and now I mention butter tis the fittest embleme in the world of y^r sexe, for you are just like butter in its extreames, either you melt in ones mouth at the first kisse and salute, or els you are so stiffe and frozen y^t tis impossible to make you spredde'.[79]

CRITICISM OF LOGIC AND DISPUTATIONS

Attacks on the pre-eminence of Aristotle and dialectic in the intellectual and academic worlds began long before Francis Bacon's call to arms. John of Salisbury in book II of the *Metalogicon* (1159), Peter of Blois in a letter (c. 1160) to the Archbishop of Nantes[80] and 'The Battle of the Seven Arts', a poem written about 1240, all level against scholastic dialectic what was to become the criticism by the New Scientists in the seventeenth century. With probably a deeper understanding of what he was about, Roger Bacon in the thirteenth century was to some degree turning his back on scholastic learning in strongly advocating the same inductive approach to

science that Francis Bacon was to champion in the seventeenth.
John Colet complained that dialecticians carped, quibbled and
analysed 'everything so minutely'; Juan Luis Vives suggested that
they claimed to have conquered their adversaries when they had
only confused them; Lorenzo Valla wanted to do away with the
entire structure of traditional logic and construct a new one closer to
oratory; and Erasmus's Folly says that after lawyers, sophists and
dialecticians are the most self-satisfied class of people. Thomas
More in his letters and in *Utopia* criticises the nonsensical scholastic
perversions of 'the sort of dialectics that Aristotle teaches', and says
ironically that the philosophers of Utopia are no match for 'our
modern logicians' who teach children from 'Small Logicals', almost
certainly a reference to the *Logica Parva* of Paul of Venice (1369–
1429), found in more than seventy-five manuscripts and published in
more than twenty-five editions from 1472 to 1563. Rabelais in
Gargantua and Pantagruel specifically satirises scholastic dialectic
with a mock-syllogistic argument in Latin, or 'donkey-Latin', about
recovering the bells of Paris: 'Every bellable bell to be belled in the
belfry', and so on.[81] But it is generally the seventeenth-century
critics of scholasticism who are remembered today: Raleigh ('But
for myself, I shall never be persuaded that God hath shut up all the
light of learning within the lantern of Aristotle's brains'), Dryden,
Butler, Locke, Hobbes, Milton and of course Sprat, who contrasted
the learned scholastics and the experimental scientists somewhat in
the fashion in which Swift was later to contrast the Spider and the
Bee: 'the one in his *Library, arguing, objecting, defending,
concluding,* with himself: the other in his Work-hous, with Tools
and Materials'.[82]

But however important the ramifications of the conflict between
the Old and New Philosophies to the history of science, at bottom
the controversy had little foundation, because Aristotle had conceded
what was to be the experimental scientists' argument in the *Posterior
Analytics* II 19: Primary premises or basic truths 'are neither innate
in a determinate form, nor developed from other higher states of
knowledge, but from sense-perception. . . . we must get to know the
primary premises by induction; for the method by which even sense-
perception implants the universal is inductive' ($100^a9–11$, $^b4–5$; one
should see all of the brief chapter 19). Aristotle's position is not
without its seventeenth-century explicators. Narcissus Marsh, Provost
of Trinity College, Dublin, when Swift was an undergraduate there,
says in his *Institutiones Logicae, In Usum Juventutis Academicae*

Dubliniensis (Dublin, 1681), 'Inductionis *praecipuus usus est ad probandum* prima & Universalissima Scientiarum Principia, *quorum non dantur Causae seu priora & notiora, per quae possint demonstrari*', and so on (p. 202). A 1680 manuscript in the Bodleian advises, 'You may remb^r in Logick, ye Rule of settling probable opinions is by Sense, observation, Experience & Induction'.[83] And to be accurate concerning what may be a small point, seventeenth-century logicians like twentieth-century logicians in the face of scientists could proffer a deduction entitled to claim necessity, and no conclusion of an inductive argument could then or can now do that.[84] Logic and disputations were denounced as dry and dull, but they were, or could be, exact, and thus they were not open to the same kind of ridicule as that directed towards the experiments of the New Philosophers.

Most criticism of university disputations and logic in the seventeenth century is less good natured than Chaucer's Reeve's glancing remark about the two Cambridge scholars' powers of logical argument. It ranges from language approaching diatribe in Milton's *Prolusion* III ('these joyous wranglings of crabbed old men') and John Webster's *Academiarum Examen* of 1654 ('it is meerly *bellum intestinum Logicum*, a civil war of words, a verbal contest, a combat of cunning')[85] to the reasoned complaints of Sprat and Locke: 'disputing is a very good instrument, to sharpen men's wits, and to make them verstil, and wary defenders of the Principles, which they already know:[86] but it can never much augment the *solid substance* of Science itself'; 'be sure not to let your Son be bred up in the Art and Formality of Disputing, . . . an insignificant Wrangler, Opinionater in Discourse, . . . thinking there is no such thing as truth to be sought, but only Victory in Disputing'.[87] Some were remarkably succinct: 'Logic is a very dull science, especially that which relates to disputation.'[88]

In the eighteenth century the criticism of logic and disputations is usually no less severe than that in the seventeenth, but it is often more metaphorical. To Bishop Hoadly (1715), 'the Art of *Wrangling*' is 'a Game at *Learned Racket*. The *Question* is the *Ball* of *Contention*: and *He* wins, who shews himself able to keep up the *Ball* longest'. Chapter 7 of the *Scriblerus Memoirs* (c. 1714), a series of metaphors, is probably the best satire ever written on the logical and metaphysical disputations of the schoolmen. To Nicholas Amhurst it was 'this syllogistical hocus-pocus', to Pope,

> Snip-snap short, and Interruption smart.
> And Demonstration thin, and Theses thick,
> Major, Minor, and Conclusion quick,

and to Cowper it was a

> solemn farce, where Ignorance in stilts
> His cap well lin'd with logic not his own,
> With parrot tongue perform'd the scholar's part
> Proceeding soon a graduated dunce.

Vicesimus Knox (1782) said of these public disputations in the schools, 'The first step in this mighty work is to procure arguments. These are always handed down, from generation to generation, on long slips of paper, and consist of foolish syllogisms on foolish subjects, of the formation or the signification of which, the respondent and opponent seldom know more than an infant in swaddling cloaths'. Amhurst (vol. 1 p. 108) explains the phenomenon more concretely: A student's disputation *pro forma* for his degree 'is no more than a *formal* repetition of a set of syllogisms upon some ridiculous question in *logick*, which they get by *rote*, or, perhaps, only read out of their *caps*, which lie before them with their Notes in 'em'.[89]

Poets generally had the strongest comments against dialectic and disputations: Blake in 'The Voice of the Ancient Bard' in *Songs of Innocence*, in 'The Marriage of Heaven and Hell' and in 'Jerusalem', Wordsworth in 'Composed on the Banks of a Rocky Stream', Keats in *Lamia* and in letters to B. Bailey on 22 November 1817[90] and on 13 March 1818: 'I shall never be a Reasoner because I care not to be in the right, when retired from bickering and in a proper philosophical temper', and Thomas Moore in 'The Devil among the Scholars, A Fragment', speaking of a son of Lucifer who

> fought the combat syllogistic
> With so much skill and art eristic,
> That though you were the learn'd Stagirite,
> At once upon the hip he had you right.

Philosophers like Kant were quieter in their denunciations: 'In former times the dialectic was studied with great diligence. By this art false principles were propounded under the appearance of truth, and it was endeavoured, comformably to them, to maintain things in appearance . . . In logic, it was for a time propounded under the name of the art of disputation . . .'.[91]

Much of the criticism of disputations reflects the tradition of the farce Act, which throughout the seventeenth and eighteenth centuries rivalled the efforts of serious and sometimes enthusiastic disputers like Richard Cumberland and Simonds D'Ewes. Evidence in the nineteenth century shows that by then the mock disputations had practically won the day, a natural prelude to the abolishing of the medieval-style Acts altogether. But the problem of the degeneration of disputations is as old as the Middle Ages: a lawsuit in 1426 at Paris concerned the right of a student to his licence no matter how poorly he had acquitted himself in the public exercises. Anthony Wood wrote on 17 February 1683, 'Lent disputations decay'. The most obvious manifestation of the problem during and after the seventeenth century was the practice of 'huddling', or putting facetious questions on any subject and so hurrying through the exercises.[92] In 1717 Serjeant Miller, one of Bentley's many opponents, complained that 'huddling' was the practice of the day, because there were too many scholars and too little time for performance of the traditional exercises. Christopher Wordsworth recounts an incident of six Acts completed in less than two minutes.[93] A candidate bachelor at Oxford in 1770 was examined in Hebrew and history, replying to two questions which made up the entire examination: what is the Hebrew for the place of the skull, and who founded University College? With the answers (one correct and one not) Golgotha and King Alfred he was bachelor of arts. Often the answers were drolly flippant, as in 1811 when an undergraduate was asked, '*Quid est* aes?' (then pronounced 'ease') and he replied, '*Nescio, nisi finis examinationis*'.[94] Usually, however, it seems that some form of the disputation was retained, whether it was as bare as the opponent's reply of '*Recte non statuit Newtonus*' to the respondent's assertion of '*Recte statuit Newtonus*' (repeated to serve as a disputation as often as the statutes required) or whether it was a witty mock disputation playing on ambiguity.[95] These mock disputations of the nineteenth century are part of the tradition of the parody of logic evident in the sample disputation from Amhurst's *Terrae-Filius* essay (1721) and in the prevaricator of the seventeenth century. In Swift the tradition of mock logic finds expression as obvious as the reversal of values in the clothes philosophy of section 2 of *A Tale of a Tub* and the 'Words are but Wind' syllogism in section 8, or as subtle as the example of the legal dispute over the stolen cow in chapter 5 of the 'Voyage to the Houyhnhnms', to be examined in dialectical detail in Chapter 7 below, at the end of the section on 'The dilemma'.[96]

4

Dialectic at Trinity College, Dublin

SWIFT AT TRINITY

This roughly chronological survey of the dialectical tradition has proceeded from the general (dialectic) to this chapter on the particular (dialectic at a certain college), which begins with a few facts regarding Swift at Trinity College, Dublin. From 1674 to 1682, aged six to fourteen, Swift was sent by his uncle, Godwin Swift, to Kilkenny Grammar School midway between Dublin and Cork, described as the best school in Ireland, one of the best in the British Isles, the Eton of Ireland. The connections between Kilkenny and Trinity were close, with the Duke of Ormond patron of the one and chancellor of the other, and the Provost of Trinity always one of the three visitors of Kilkenny. Swift entered Trinity on 24 April 1682 at the age of 14 and remained there seven years, taking his BA degree in February 1686 and staying on for three years' study towards the MA, until the enforcing of James II's Catholic programme in Ireland caused such fears that by early 1689 Swift sailed for England, about the time that the college plate and manuscripts were sent over.

THE FOUNDING AND EARLY DEVELOPMENT OF TCD

Trinity College, Dublin, was founded in 1591 under the auspices of Queen Elizabeth and established in 1593, with Adam Loftus, Archbishop of Dublin, as its first provost. Like Harvard, founded 45 years later, TCD had close connections with Emmanuel College, Cambridge, and through that university and Oxford and Paris[1] it inherited the predominantly dialectical curriculum and examination traditions of European universities. From the beginning the influence was particularly that of Cambridge: the first five provosts, Loftus, Travers, Alvey, Temple and Bedell, were educated at Trinity (two),

St John's, King's and Emmanuel; and Burghley, the first Chancellor of TCD, was also Chancellor of the University of Cambridge. In fact one of the original statutes said that 'no member of any foreign College shall be admitted to the same Degree in our College, that he possesses in his own; except he has first taken the same Degree in the University of *Cambridge*, where the same Statutes, and the same Time for taking Degrees, are observed as with us'.

With Cambridge, TCD in the first part of the seventeenth century was largely Puritan in religion and Ramistic in dialectic. Sir William Temple, provost from 1609 to 1627, published in 1584 an annotated edition of Ramus's *Dialecticae Institutiones* (1st ed., Paris, 1543), which may have been an early textbook at TCD. But the Laudian statutes of 1637 restricted religious freedom and undermined the dominant Ramism in favour of a purer Aristotelianism; Aristotle's *Organon* was now to be studied without commentary. With the appointment of Narcissus Marsh, Fellow of Exeter, as provost in 1678, a conservative brand of Oxford scholasticism came to TCD to uphold the post-Restoration status quo, primarily by educating those who were to become Anglo-Irish gentlemen and Church of Ireland ministers, and to ensure that the Anglican ascendancy was retained in the face of the Roman Catholic and Presbyterian threats. The influence of such a collegiate atmosphere on Swift is obvious in the political and religious principles he defended and asserted throughout his career and in his intellectual preference for the Ancients.

LOGIC AT TCD

In the first years after the establishment of the college in 1593 the tutors read the Greek text of Aristotle to their undergraduates, but the Laudian statutes do not specify the Greek original, so presumably they allowed Latin translations from 1637 until the nineteenth century brought about major changes in the curriculum. The Laudian statutes in fact are so concise that they mention few texts (and no textbooks) at all: only Porphyry's *Isagoge*, which was to be read through at least twice a year to Junior Freshmen,[2] Aristotle's *Organon*, explained in parts only and without scholastic commentary to the Senior Freshmen, his *Physics* explained as above to the Junior Sophisters and his *Metaphysics* explained to Senior Sophisters, except in Lent, when they heard all or part of the *Nicomachean Ethics*. The college retained this curriculum for a hundred years, after which a revised curriculum brought into the course a number of Greek and Latin poets and historians.

The emphasis on logic, both in lectures and in thrice-weekly disputations, is normal when viewed against the inherited medieval university tradition. That logic was 'the most engrossing subject' or 'the chief mental pabulum'[3] is reflected in statutes not connected with the curriculum. Various residential and financial restrictions govern the candidates for election as scholars in the college, but the only academic one is that those elected must be 'fit to learn Logic in the Hall'. Each fellow has the statutory right to admit one 'poor Scholar or Sizer' into college, '(provided he be fit to learn Logic)'. During the summer vacation (9 July to 1 October) Junior and Senior Freshmen 'shall frequently dispute, whereby they may be the better prepared for the Study of Logic'.[4]

Besides the statutes of 1637, the other most important determinant of the dialectic Swift learned and practised was the 'Provost's Logic', Narcissus Marsh's *Institutiones Logicae in Usum Juventutis Academicae Dubliniensis* (1681), a reissue of his *Institutio Logicae* (Dublin, 1679), which in turn is largely a revision of Philippe Du Trieu's *Manuductio ad Logicam* (Douai, 1615), subsequently published at Oxford in 1662 and reprinted in 1678.[5] Marsh's 1681 textbook remained on the course until 1783, when it was replaced by the logic of Richard Murray, afterwards provost: *Artis Logicae Compendium* (London, 1773). Other seventeenth-century logics used at Cambridge and Oxford were also used at TCD in the seventeenth and eighteenth centuries – Keckermann, Smiglecius and Burgersdicius – and they, unlike Marsh's more readable logic, seem to have drawn the usual amount of undergraduate criticism about the arid study of logic, especially Burgersdicius, who was for a while burned ceremoniously every year. According to the *Dublin Evening Post*, 6 November 1733, 'Last Tuesday Franco Burgersdicius was burnt according to annual custom at Molesworth's Fields near the Gallows, by the class of candidate Bachelors of our University, and was carried in a wheel-barrow to the place of execution, attended by two or three hundred scholars and six mourners'. After a funeral oration and an elegy, 'the scholars contributed their books with great alacrity, so that 'tis hop'd that this unintelligible author will soon be out of print'. It is not surprising to find it said two years later in the anonymous *Difficulties and Discouragements which Attend the Study for a Fellowship in the College of Dublin* (Dublin, 1735), 'At present, Logic is in no Esteem' and 'the Logic in the

Schools . . . is a disagreeable, dry Study' (pp. 4–5). These attitudes
toward logic extend at least from Swift's student days at TCD to
Burke's: Act II of the Tripos at commencement in 1688 mentions 'a
piece of an Old Smiglesius' procured 'for a natural use'; a versifier
writes of the 'painful task' of scouring 'the knotty Page/Of
BURGERSDICIUS' in the anonymous *College Examination: A
Poem* (Dublin, 1731); Goldsmith speaks of the 'cold logic of
Burgersdicius' and 'the dreary subtleties of Smiglecius', and Burke
in an undergraduate letter from college refers to Burgersdicius's
logic as 'hideous'. In 1794 a criticism of the college was that 'They
sup on syllogisms, are enamoured of their cobwebs' and 'spend four
years in pouring over majors and minors'.[6]

In short, dialectic or logic at TCD was virtually indistinguishable
from that at other British universities in the seventeenth century; in
fact the college embraced two traditions, the Ramism of Cambridge
in the first part of the century and the Aristotelianism of Oxford in
the latter part. Seventeenth-century lecture notes, guides to study
and commonplace books are not as plentiful for TCD as for English
and Scottish universities, but the latter two give a fairly accurate
picture of the logic studied at the English college in Dublin. Before
Swift arrived at college he had to prove he was fit to learn logic;
once there he listened to more logic lectures than he desired; and he
put that logic to use in thrice-weekly dialectical disputations. The
memory of the exercise of dialectic was with him more than a
decade after leaving TCD, so much so that he seems to have
required of himself a kind of purgation of its effects in *A Tale of a
Tub*, which is rife with the terms of dialectic and exercises on the
wrong sides of questions. After the *Tale* he seems to have been able
to put much of the foolery of dialectic in the Tripos tradition behind
him, to get on with serious disputation with his religious and political
enemies and to develop a kind of unanswerable satire both in its
comic exuberance and in its tragic vision.

DISPUTATIONS AT TCD

Directions concerning disputations in the college statutes of TCD
are at least as explicit as those of the colleges and universities of
Cambridge and Oxford, and from their careful explanation it seems
that at Trinity more emphasis was placed on them than on lectures
and declamations. All undergraduates of the first two classes, Junior

and Senior Freshmen, were to dispute three times each week on a question taken from logic, the third and fourth classes as often on one taken from natural philosophy or metaphysics. Each undergraduate was to take his turn as respondent and opponent, beginning with the junior in each class. 'Our [Charles I's] will is', the statutes continue, 'that what relates to Logic shall be handled Logically, that is, Syllogistically, not with the flourishes of Rhetoric'.[7] Without introductory positions explained, the disputants were to enter into the dispute immediately. 'The Opponents, (who shall always be four at least,) shall reduce their Arguments to a Syllogistic Form, concerning which the Respondent and the Moderator are to take Care that this Disputation be ended within an Hour. The Days appointed for Disputation shall be Mondays, Wednesdays, and Fridays, from Two of the Clock in the Afternoon to Four'. The statutes mention the punishments for failing to respond and oppose in disputations and for failing to attend regularly the disputations of others. They vary from a penny fine to expulsion, depending on the number of violations. The tradition Swift inherited in dialectic and disputation and which he was required to practise becomes unmistakable. The influence on his thinking and on others of his generation in Dublin must have been enormous, and yet this influence has only been hinted at in more than two hundred years of Swift studies.

Bachelors of arts were to dispute every Tuesday in term at two p.m. on questions in mathematics, physics or metaphysics, and masters of arts, including BDs and DDs, were to dispute each in his turn on two questions in divinity every Thursday at two p.m., except on festival days. The divinity disputations were to involve points of disagreement between Protestants and Papists (germ of *A Tale of a Tub*?) and if possible the respondent and opponent were to change sides and finish the disputation the following week. Fines for BAs and MAs who failed to dispute in turn were considerably heavier than for undergraduates; after four lapses they were expelled from the college. There was also a provision against a bachelor's or master's performing in a disputation or other exercise 'negligently, or ludicrously, or in any way unbecoming his Degree'. The same regulations regarding divinity disputations governed the disputations of masters of arts in civil law and medicine.

Compared with the regular disputations every week in term, the public commencement disputations were more exciting because of the large audiences and the importance of the occasion. Together, the two kinds of disputations, the one by their regularity and the other by their importance, inculcated in the scholars the dialectical habit, at least until the statutory exercises degenerated into academic farces, and the evidence suggests that they did not do that in large measure until after the seventeenth century. Public commencement took place each year on the Tuesday following 8 July, when each candidate for BA, besides making a Greek and a Latin declamation and performing other exercises, was twice respondent and four times opponent. Candidates for MA were to be once respondent and once opponent, besides performing other exercises, and within the next year they were to dispute publicly on a question in philosophy.

Thus far the BA and most of the MA requirements would have applied to Swift. The following statutory requirements show further how deeply the college was committed to dialectical disputations. A graduate was admitted to the degree of bachelor of divinity only after seven years as MA, and at public commencement he was to be once respondent, twice opponent, and was to preach twice, once in Latin to the clergy and once in English to the people. After five years as BD a candidate could proceed to the degree of doctor of divinity by performing certain exercises, including one respondency to a doctor or public professor and one opponency, and within a year of taking his degree he was to determine a question in a public disputation, that is, act as moderator. Candidates for bachelor and doctor of laws were to be once respondent and one opponent in commencement law disputations, and candidates for bachelor and doctor of medicine ('Physic') also were to perform one respondency and one opponency, on two questions in medicine.

The evidence of the conduct of Cambridge and Oxford disputations, more plentiful than similar evidence of disputations at TCD, shows that while 'huddling' and other abuses existed, some disputations were carried on in the spirit of the statutory requirements, and that some undergraduates approached them with enthusiasm, fear or both. For a picture of what Trinity College disputations in Swift's day might have resembled, it seems appropriate to go back about eighty-five years to the serious, lively, competitive dialectical arguments of Mr Boyes and his opponents in the British Library manuscript (Chapter 3 above) or to return sixty or seventy years to the accounts of the intense Cambridge disputations in which King James entered the fray (Chapter 3 also). The most complete modern biography of Swift, however, offers a picture of the disputations Swift practised by drawing on a description of Trinity

College disputations as conducted more than one hundred and sixty years after Swift left the college, when it is acknowledged on all hands that disputations had degenerated into arid ceremonies or solemn farces. It is no wonder that Ehrenpreis regards the commencement disputation as a 'final and perfunctory ritual' (pp. 62, 200), because he bases his view of the commencement exercises and the college disputations in general on an account of 'that part of the procedure which survived into the nineteenth century' (p. 63), which is understandable when little in this century has been written about dialectical disputations in the universities. The account to which he refers and from which he quotes is one entitled 'Swift: Dryden: Herrick', in *Notes and Queries*, 21 August 1875, whose author (his initials B. E. N. are given) draws on a previously unpublished document to show the state of Trinity College, Dublin, disputations in 1851. This document, which both B. E. N. and Ehrenpreis quote, says that 'each candidate is required to write *twenty-four* syllogisms on the *wrong* side, and *twelve* upon the right' side of the disputation questions. Written-out syllogisms, like the inherited strings of syllogisms Amhurst and Knox mention (last section, Chapter 3), are a foundation for farcical exercises which are a far cry from various accounts of spirited debates in the seventeenth century or from the aggressive engagement of Richard Cumberland and the 'North-country black-bearded philosopher' in 1751, sixty-five years after Swift's commencement and a century before the account by B. E. N. in *Notes and Queries*.[8]

At Trinity College, Dublin, a tripos, like the Cambridge prevaricator or tripos and the Oxford *terrae-filius*, flourished in the seventeenth century and seems to have been totally suppressed early in the eighteenth century. He was as disrespectful of authority and ribald as his counterparts at the other universities, and he sometimes received punishments as stern. Swift's classmate John Jones (later DD) for his performance of the tripos at the 1688 commencement exercises was first deprived of his degree but later only suspended from several college privileges. As a commencing BA in 1685 and an '"old" Bachelor' in 1688, Swift was in a position to write parts of the triposes of these two years, the only two complete triposes which have survived from Swift's time at TCD, perhaps because of a contemporary belief that Swift had a hand in them.[9]

The tripos of 1688 has some of the elements of the seventeenth-century prevaricator, *terrae-filius* and Musick speeches, like parody of disputation jargon – '*Probo antecedens*', '*Probo minorem instantiam*' – near the end of Act I (p. xxx of Scott's reproduction), farcical syllogisms for absurd proofs, occasional references to 'Respondent' and 'Opponent' and scurrility, like the reference in the will of Mary Hewetson, sister to the Rev. Michael Hewetson, at whom fun is poked at the opening of the tripos. She leaves her breasts to one lady, her paint to another, and although she leaves her nose to one gentleman, 'out of her great charity' she gives permission to another 'to furnish himself after the Hudibrasian manner with a supplemental snout out of her posteriors' (Act II). Both this tripos and the one of 1685, however, differ from the examples of Oxford Musick speeches quoted in the last chapter in that they are in the form of three-act plays with stage directions rather than simply speeches or mock debates. The value of the two triposes as repositories of insights into the style of Swift is far less than the value of the tripos or prevaricator tradition at British universities in general, and that in turn is of less value than the dialectical tradition in general, as the succeeding chapters will attempt to show.

The statutes of Swift's college show what was required of him dialectically during his years at Trinity, but some account must be taken of the following remark in his unfinished autobiographical essay which he entitled 'Family of Swift', written when he was past seventy: 'he too much neglected his Academical Studyes, for some parts of which he had no great relish by Nature, and turned himself to reading History and Poetry'. This remark is often enough quoted in biographical accounts of Swift's undergraduate career, and this or the confession of 'Dullness and Insufficiency' following it often enough attributed to exaggeration,[10] that questions on either side could be raised as to the extent of Swift's participation in the scholastic exercises called for in the statutes. Two decades before Swift came up to Dublin John Potenger (1647–1733) entered Corpus Christi College, Oxford, from Winchester: 'I did not immediately enter upon logick and philosophy, but was kept for a full year to the reading of classical authors, and making of theams in prose and verse'.[11] If Potenger had been kept for a year from the study of dialectic laid down in the college statutes,[12] doubtless Swift could equally have arranged some time off from dialectic, or he could have 'neglected' it to some degree for several years together, but since he admits in the sentence following the one quoted above that 'he lived with great Regularity and due Observance of the Statutes', it is hard to imagine his avoiding a stiff measure of the study of logic and the practice of dialectical disputations during his seven years in college. It is hard to imagine that even if he were exaggerating his regularity and due observance of the statues.

The most intriguing remark about Swift's study of logic is made by Thomas Sheridan (the son of Swift's close friend) who was a student in Dublin shortly before Swift's mind decayed:

> He told me that he had made many efforts, upon his entering the College, to read some of the old treatises on logic writ by Smeglesius, Keckermannus, Burgersdicius, &c., and that he never had patience to go through three pages of any of them, he was so disgusted at the stupidity of the work. When he was urged by his tutor to make himself master of this branch, then in high estimation, and held essentially necessary to the taking of a degree; Swift asked him what it was he was to learn from those books? His tutor told him, the art of reasoning. Swift said that he found no want of any such art; that he could reason very well without it. . . . In going through the usual forms of disputation for his degree, he told me he was utterly unacquainted even with the logical terms, and answered the arguments of his opponents in his own manner, which the Proctor put into proper form. There was one circumstance in the account which he gave of this, that surprised me with regard to his memory; for he told me the several questions on which he disputed, and repeated all the arguments used by his opponents in syllogistick form, together with his answers.[13]

Forster places little value on Sheridan's biography largely because he was only sixteen at most when he could have talked with Swift before his mind was gone,[14] and Leslie Stephen says that in this account of Swift and logic at Trinity 'there is probably a substratum of truth'.[15] It is perhaps best to suspect in the account a 'colouring from the ironical tone' which Forster suggests.[16]

Thus much for the dialectical tradition as it comes to bear on the college life of Jonathan Swift. Had elucidators of Swift's style, analysers of his and others' satire, even chroniclers and interpreters of his life shown sufficient evidence of the dialectical background which significantly influenced the minds and art of Swift and others of his generation, the survey of the dialectical tradition in these pages would have been briefer or perhaps unnecessary. But the neglected state of matters dialectical is such in the current world of literary studies that an introduction to dialectic is requisite to an analysis of Swift's employment of the dialectical tradition in his satire and in his attacks on Steele, Burnet, Tindal and others, which are more extensive than his purely satirical writings. With the second part of this inquiry into Swift and the dialectical tradition, the tradition is put to use; and evidence shows that the tradition was not neglected, nor was Swift dull and insufficient in dialectic. Rarely has a writer in any language put dialectic to such extensive use in straightforward argument and in satire. Before the close of Part II satire and argument will be seen to grow not one from the other or both from rhetoric as is often assumed, but both from dialectic.

Part Two
Swift and Dialectic

5

First Principles and Contexts

SUBSTANCE VERSUS STYLE

The premises of a dialectician regarded *qua* dialectition are generally not as important as the nexus of his arguments and the speed and acumen with which he overthrows the arguments of his opponent. If the dialectician is regarded *qua* both arguer and author, however, some account must be taken of the principles from which he argues, if for no other reason than that an author is usually a *committed* person and we need to know what principles in his commitment he defends and what contrary principles he attacks. In literature, if not in logic, substance cannot be separated from style. The simplicity and obviousness of Swift's principles have dismayed some commentators, who point out the poverty of his commitment, his unphilosophic mind, even his lack of intelligence.[1] In this instance, however, what is loss for the philosopher is gain for the dialectician,[2] if the criticisers of Swift's intelligence[3] are correct, because a proper dialectician can argue either side of a question with success, his strength lying in wit and style and not necessarily in insight and commitment. That is one view of dialectic. But nowhere is it mandated that the truth must be dull and unconvincing. There is little one can say in reply to a charge that Swift is not a great or profound thinker but only a brilliant stylist with intense feelings; one may hold up the 'Voyage to the Houyhnhnms' and the 'Digression on Madness' and suggest that they are piercing, philosophic commentaries on human nature, society and the mind, but as yet there is no consensus on that view.

For all the disagreement over Swift's meaning in places like Gulliver's Fourth Voyage, the 'Digression on Madnesss' and the 'Project for the Advancement of Religion and the Reformation of Manners', and the resultant questions about the depth or lack of it of his world view, this much not only can be said with certainty but has been said convincingly since the publication of the *Tale*: Swift is an exceptionally good stylist, satirist and ironist, who can express intense feelings with clarity, simplicity and force. Side by side with what some call a narrow political and religious conservatism, he appears to maintain a liberal view of common people in the social structure in his fight for human liberty: '*Strenuum pro virili/Libertatis Vindicatorem*'. This accepted, one can with singularity but not narrowness of purpose take account of some of the principles from which he argues in the role of dialectician, which role, it will become clear, is central to his acclaim as a stylist.

THE PEACE OF CHURCH AND STATE

One of the closest principles to Swift's heart, the belief that mankind is not 'any where directed in the Canons, or Articles, to attempt explaining the Mysteries of the Christian Religion' (IX 77), is a view common enough in the seventeenth century: 'Disputations in Religion are sometimes necessarie, but alwaies dangerous; drawing ye best spirits into ye head from ye heart, & leaving it either empty of all; or too full of fleshly zeale & passion, if extraordinary care be not taken still to supply & fill it anew wth pious affections towards God, & loving towards men'.[4] If, as Kathleen Williams says, for Swift 'the world can only be properly interpreted in a context of moral truth enforced by divine authority',[5] also intricately bound up in his religion is a somewhat Erastian view of the place of the Anglican Church in the state. His aggressive and defensive championing of Anglicanism against the threat of the dissenting sects, one of the consistent positions from which he argues, has at its foundation a political view of the relationship of religious sects to the state, as two of the sermons show: 'On Brotherly Love' (IX 171–9) and 'A Sermon upon the Martyrdom of K. Charles I' (IX 219–31).[6] Both his dislike of the questioning of the first principles of Christianity and his legalistic insistence upon the privileged status of the Anglican Church are reflections of the scholastic synthesis of government, religion, philosophy and science, which was the substance of his years of academic training as well as of much of his reading in Temple's library. Swift demonstrates the scholastic concern with preservation of the status quo in church and state by his insistence on unity and simplicity, and the inversion of this position is often the basis of his irony: 'I affirm, that if Ten thousand Free Thinkers thought differently from the received Doctrine, and from each other, they would be all in Duty bound to publish their Thoughts

. . . though it broke the Peace of the Church and State, Ten thousand times' (IV 36). His real position seems to be reflected in certain aspects of the Houyhnhnms, who 'have no Letters, and consequently, their Knowledge is all Traditional' (iv 9), whose 'Subjects are generally on Friendship and Benevolence; or Order and Oeconomy; sometimes upon the visible Operations of Nature, or ancient Traditions; upon the Bounds and Limits of Virtue; upon the unerring Rules of Reason' (iv 10), and who could civilise Europe 'by teaching us the first Principles of Honour, Justice, Truth, Temperance, publick Spirit, Fortitude, Chastity, Friendship, Benevolence, and Fidelity. The *Names* of all which Virtues are still retained among us in most Languages, and are to be met with in modern as well as ancient Authors' (iv 12).

Freethinkers like Collins were as much a threat to the state church, in Swift's view, as were dissenters. Freethinkers, another name for deists,[7] 'endeavour to overthrow those Tenets in Religion, which have been held inviolable almost in all Ages by every Sect that pretends to be Christian' (II 60), by writing books 'against those Doctrines in Religion, wherein all Christians have agreed', in which they seek to 'undermine the Foundations of all Piety and Virtue' (II 10–11). With a simple ironic inversion this position becomes one from which ironic satire strikes: 'If Christianity were once abolished, how would the Free-Thinkers, the strong Reasoners, and the Men of profound Learning be able to find another Subject so calculated in all Points whereupon to display their Abilities' (II 36).

His principles were not always perceived as conservatively as he held them, particularly when he resorted to irony and satire, as early on he did in the *Tale*. Rather than criticise the harmless *Tale of a Tub*, Swift says in the Apology, the indignant Anglican clergy should condemn books by those 'illiterate Scriblers' who endeavour to pull up 'those very Foundations, wherein all Christians have agreed'. Wotton's charge in the *Observations on The Tale of a Tub* is that the author 'shews at bottom his contemptible Opinion of every Thing which is called Christianity' in writing 'so crude a Banter upon all that is esteemed Sacred among all Sects and Religions among Men'. He suggests that the *Tale* and the *Mechanical Operation of the Spirit* have 'undermined Christianity'. Belated Apology or no, this apparent breach in his conservative defence of Anglican principles (it was only apparent) hurt him considerably in the eyes of many, not the least in those of the queen.

Considering his defensively Anglican principles, it is natural for

Swift to lash out at Whigs in practically the same language he uses against dissenters. In *Examiner* no. 39 he says, 'I look upon the Whigs and Dissenters to be exactly of the same political Faith' (III 145), because the principles of Whigs, Irish Whigs in particular, consist 'in nothing else but damning the Church, reviling the Clergy, abetting Dissenters, and speaking contemptibly of revealed Religion' (IX 30). His satiric attack on Collins's *Discourse of Free-Thinking* uses the ploy of assuming the identity of his opponent, a freethinker who is a Whig, and he shows their interests to be identical. Swift never questioned the Whig principles of the Revolution of 1688 and the Protestant succession after Queen Anne, but the Whig tenderness towards dissenters and freethinkers made it easy for him to change political allegiance in 1710: 'as to religion, I confessed myself to be an High-churchman, and that I did not conceive how any one, who wore the habit of a clergyman, could be otherwise' (VIII 120).[8]

THE BENEFIT OF MANKIND

The committed clergyman who saw himself in the phrase '*Strenuum pro virili/Libertatis Vindicatorem*' is sometimes forgotten among readers who usually see the politically-minded high-churchman, the man of disappointed ambitions, the wit and the negatively-oriented satirist. When he shows Gulliver explaining that at Glubbdubdrib 'I chiefly fed mine Eyes with beholding the Destroyers of Tyrants and Usurpers, and the Restorers of Liberty to oppressed and injured Nations' (iii 7), he is expressing a quarter of a century's concern with liberty and tyranny, from the *Contests and Dissentions* (1701) to the *Drapier's Letters* (1724) and the *Travels*. The succeeding sentence in the Third Voyage, which concludes chapter 7, is a confession that words fail him on a subject so close to his heart, a phenomenon so rare in Swift that we are not surprised to find this subject in two of his most heartfelt writings after *Gulliver's Travels*: 'A Modest Proposal'[9] and his epitaph. He wanted to be remembered for his struggle against tyranny: another epitaph of sorts in his verses on his death announces, 'Fair LIBERTY was all his Cry;/For her he stood prepar'd to die'.

Underlying the love of liberty is the broader concern with public benefit which is the ironic foundation of the three best known of his works: the *Tale* is 'Written for the Universal Improvement of Mankind'; Gulliver 'wrote for their Amendment, and not their

Approbation',[10] and 'the Benefit of Publick as well as private Life'
was his 'sole Design in presenting this and other Accounts of his
Travels to the World' (ii 1); and because of his beneficial scheme the
Modest Proposer 'would deserve so well of the Publick, as to have
his Statue set up for a Preserver of the Nation'. At the conclusion of
the pamphlet the Proposer says that he has 'no other Motive than
the *public Good of my Country, by advancing our Trade, providing
for Infants, relieving the Poor, and giving Pleasure to the Rich*'. But
the familiarity of these ironic protestations should not mask for the
reader their underlying sincerity or overshadow the many expressions
of serious concern with benefiting the public. He wrote the *Examiner*
papers 'with no other Intention but that of doing good', having
'never received injury from the late Ministry; nor Advantage from
the present, farther than in common with every good Subject' (iii 9).
He wrote his 'Proposal for Correcting . . . the English Tongue'
because 'nothing would be of greater Use' (iv 5) and his 'Hints
towards an Essay on Conversation' because it is 'so useful and
innocent a Pleasure' (iv 88). In 'Doing Good: A Sermon' he
observes 'That there are few people so weak or mean, who have it
not sometimes in their power to be useful to the public' (ix 234); in
'On Brotherly Love', in a statement resembling the 'two Blades of
Grass' remark in *Gulliver's Travels* (ii 7), he says that there is no
Christian duty of mankind greater than brotherly love, 'which
whoever could restore, in any Degree, among Men, would be an
Instrument of more Good to human Society, than ever was, or will
be done, by all the Statesmen and Politicians in the World' (ix 171).
Perhaps his most reasoned observation on the subject is in the
sermon 'On Mutual Subjection': 'he who doth not perform that Part
assigned him towards advancing the Benefit of the Whole, in
proportion to his Opportunities and Abilities, is not only a useless,
but a very mischeivous Member of the Publick: Because he taketh
his Share of the Profit, and yet leaveth his Share of the Burden to be
borne by others, which is the true principal Cause of most Miseries
and Misfortunes in Life' (ix 142). These remarks, together with
those complaining of a heedless public ignoring his warning and
advice in the *Drapier's Letters* and other places,[11] suggest that in
spite of his ambition, wit and negativeness, and perhaps partly
because of these, he 'served human liberty' as Yeats phrased Swift's
view of himself, and that this is one of the major positions from
which he argues.[12]

THE IMPORTANCE OF OPINION TO THE AGE

Although he said that he expected and desired no other reward for
ridiculing the world's corruptions and follies than the pleasure of
laughing with a few friends in a corner (xii 34), Swift was in fact
much concerned with the opinions of the majority of men. A
dialectician bases his premises on the opinions of the wise (the
philosophers), or of the majority, or of everyone,[13] and Swift shows
a constant awareness of opinion in the most basic premises from
which he argues. The *Tale*, he protests in the Apology, 'advances no
Opinion' the Anglican clergy reject, 'nor condemns any they receive'
(p. 5). 'Dangerous Opinions', he says, 'fill the Readers Mind with ill
Idea's' (p. 18); they are able 'to inflame the Nation' (iii 4), 'to
poison the people' (ix 227). In defence of the church he writes to
expose 'wicked opinions' (ix 227) and 'horrid Opinions' (iv 4), and
when the state is attacked by Whigs denigrating the present ministry
chosen by the queen, he writes against 'so vile an Opinion as this'
(iii 33) and declares that because of such party violence 'the People
throughout this Kingdom should, if possible, be set right in their
Opinions by some impartial Hand' (iii 13).

'Opinion' in the *Battle of the Books* is 'light of Foot, hoodwinkt,
and headstrong, yet giddy and perpetually turning', the daughter of
Ignorance and Pride and the sister of Criticism, and a false leader of
men in the 'Ode to Dr. William Sancroft':

> But foolish Man still judges what is best
> In his own balance, false and light,
> Foll'wing Opinion, dark, and blind,
> That vagrant leader of the mind,
> Till Honesty and Conscience are clear out of sight.

The same Opinion can also lead to battle between men, as Gulliver's
Houyhnhnm Master learns when he asks the causes of European
wars. Besides ambition of princes and corruption of ministers,
'Difference in Opinions hath cost many Millions of Lives: For
Instance, whether *Flesh* be *Bread*, or *Bread* be *Flesh* . . . Neither
are any Wars so furious and bloody, or of so long Continuance, as
those occasioned by Difference in Opinion, especially if it be in
things indifferent' (iv 5).

Most of Swift's attention is absorbed, however, in exposing or
influencing opinion before it leads to armed conflict. One of the

reasons he took over the *Examiner* 'was to undeceive those well-meaning People, who have been drawn unaware into a wrong Sense of Things', partly by 'foul Misrepresentations' (III 31). By implication these are what Swift would call persons of quality, but they are no more important in his eyes than the common sort where opinion is concerned. The Whig view of the Pretender, for example, 'is very unseasonably advanced, considering the Weight such an Opinion must have with the Vulgar, if they once thoroughly believe it' (III 146–7). And more than a decade later he says, 'If this Copper should begin to make it's Way among the common, ignorant People, we are inevitably undone; it is they who give us the greatest Apprehension, being easily frighted, and greedy to swallow Misinformations'.[14] What persons of quality must beware is betraying 'very dangerous opinions in government' (IX 31), and thus passing for disaffected persons,[15] by holding opinions opposed to those of the present ministry, which should reflect the opinion of the majority. To argue in support of a party that it should retain or regain the power of government, as Swift did throughout his career, one must always keep an eye to opinion:[16] 'every Body knows, that *Authority* is very much founded on *Opinion*' (III 150); 'It is said the World is governed by *Opinion*, and Politicians assure us, that all Power is founded thereupon' (XII 289).

SINGULARITY OF OPINION

A complement of acknowledging the power of general opinion is denouncing the presumption of singularity of opinion. Socrates ironically praises Euthydemus and Dionysodorus:

> There is much, indeed, to admire in your words, . . . but there is nothing more magnificent than your total disregard of any opinion – whether of the many, or of the grave and reverend signiors – you regard only those who are like yourselves. And I do verily believe that there are exceedingly few who are like you, and who approve of such arguments; the majority of mankind are so ignorant of their value, that they would certainly be more ashamed to use them in the refutation of others than to be refuted by them.[17]

Swift also ironically plays on this theme: ''tis certain that all Men of

Sense depart from the Opinions commonly received; and are consequently more or less Men of Sense, according as they depart from the Opinions commonly received' (IV 47), and 'It is the indispensable Duty of a *Free Thinker*, to endeavour forcing all the World to think as he does, and by that means to make them *Free Thinkers* too' (IV 36). With more polished irony in the 'Letter Concerning the Sacramental Test' he suggests that the English House of Commons has the interests of Ireland at heart, but 'I have the Misfortune to be something singular in this Belief, and therefore I never attempted to justify it, but content my self to possess my own Opinion in private' (II 113). In a middle ground between irony and literal statement at the opening of the 'Argument against Abolishing Christianity' he plays with this same dialectical view of opinion: 'I am very sensible what a Weakness and Presumption it is, to reason against the general Humour and Disposition of the World' (II 26). His most common method, however, is simply to inveigh against 'Affectation to Singularity' (XII 37), 'such a Piece of Singularity' (IV 57) and men who are 'obstinate in maintaining their own Opinions, and worrying all who differ from them' (XII 246), like Tindal, 'who had published as singular and absurd Notions as possible, yet hath a mighty Zeal to bring us over to them' (II 103).

He has provisions for breaking the bounds of received opinion, but only on special conditions: 'I do not mean by a true Genius, any bold Writer, who breaks through the Rules of Decency to distinguish himself by the Singularity of Opinions; but one, who upon a deserving Subject, is able to open new Scenes, and discover a Vein of true and noble Thinking, which never entered into any Imagination before: Every Stroke of whose Pen is worth all the Paper blotted by Hundreds of others in the Compass of their Lives' (IV 19). But his predominant attitude is that behind the irony in the 'Digression on Madness': The more a man 'shapes his Understanding by the Pattern of Human Learning, the less he is inclined to form Parties after his particular Notions; because that instructs him in his private Infirmities, as well as in the stubborn Ignorance of the People'. Swift's position on opinion is no different from the standard university treatment of the subject as reflected, for example, in Joshua Barnes's 'Directions and Advice to Students' (c. 1696): 'If in yo[ur] Authors you meet wth Diversity of Opinions, follow [that which] is most consonant to Reason, & most generally received in the Schools'.[18]

OPINIONS OF THE WISE AND THE MAJORITY

A way to defeat an opponent in argument is to lead him into paradox, which Aristotle advocates doing in two ways, by making the opponent oppose professed opinions and secret wishes and by making him oppose nature and law. By means of a related tactic, and one more fundamental in dialectic, the arguer can lead his opponent into opposing the views of the majority and the wise, which would almost certainly lead to defeat, or more subtly he may lead him into a position in which he finds himself opposing the majority *or* the wise. Chapter 7 below discusses these dialectical strategies in the sections '*Argumenta ad . . .*' and 'The dilemma'. As the opening of Aristotle's *Topics* asserts, dialectical arguments are won by an arguer's keeping an eye to the opinions of the wise, the majority, or all. Swift's written debates and attacks are filled with the consciousness of this basic concern of the dialectician.

In Swift's view the majority opinion usually not only rules, but has about it something of a heavenly mandate. He says to the Irish Parliament, 'whenever You shall please to impose *Silence* upon me, I will submit; because, I look upon your *unanimous Voice* to be the Voice of the Nation; and this I have been taught, and do believe to be, in some Manner, the *Voice* of *God*'.[19] His humility is only apparent, however, because he knows the people and the Parliament support him in these letters from the drapier, and that explains the unanimity insisted upon here, which is unusual; a majority was almost always sufficient. '*We* are the Majority, and *We* are in Possession' (II 124), he says of the Anglicans as opposed to the Presbyterians, and when he is writing in defence of the Harley ministry he also reminds the opposition of the majority's support of the Tories: a wise prince, an able ministry and a freely-chosen parliament form a power not easily challenged by faction (that is, the Whigs) – 'To this we may add one additional Strength, which in the Opinion of our Adversaries, is the greatest and justest of any; I mean the *Vox Populi*, so indisputably declarative on the same Side' (III 168). He speaks elsewhere ironically of the danger of 'a Design to oppose the Current of the People; which besides the Folly of it, is a manifest Breach of the Fundamental Law, that makes this Majority of Opinion the Voice of God' (II 26). The Whigs, he says, appeal to the *vox populi* 'only when they have been so wise as to poison their Understandings beforehand' (III 105), a distinction similar to that in the *Contests and Dissentions*, where he says, 'I should think that the

saying, *Vox Populi, Vox Dei*, ought to be understood of the
Universal Bent and Current of a People, not of the *bare Majority* of
a few Representatives, which is often procured by *little Arts*, and
great Industry and Application, wherein those who engage in the
Pursuits of Malice and Revenge, are much more Sedulous than such
as would prevent them.'[20]

One must of course consider whose side Swift defended at a given
time and whether that side was in or out of power, realities which
governed his dialectical strategies as they would those of any adept
arguer. Because it suits his purpose in defending the four former
Whig ministers impeached by the Tories in 1701, Swift speaks in the
Contests and Dissentions of a '*Dominatio plebis*, or *Tyranny of the
People*' (p. 97), and of giving way to 'Popular Encroachments' and
'Popular Clamours' (p. 115). 'I think it is an universal Truth', he
says, 'that the People are much more dexterous at pulling down and
setting up, than at preserving what is fixt; And they are not fonder
of seizing more than their own, than they are of delivering it up
again to the *worst Bidder*, with their own into the bargain' (p. 108).
When the Tories were in power a decade later and he was their
spokesman, his views of the intelligence of the mass of people
changed.

Swift's position on the opinion of the majority often depends on
what he sees as common sense. Accordingly, despite distinctions
over the size, delusion or danger of the majority, it often suits his
purpose to place 'much weight in the opinions of the people',[21] like
those who checked the project of the Academy of Lagado to replace
words with things carried on one's back, which would have taken
place 'if the Women in Conjunction with the Vulgar and Illiterate
had not threatened to raise a Rebellion, unless they might be
allowed the Liberty to speak with their Tongues, after the Manner
of their Forefathers: Such constant irreconcileable Enemies to
Science are the common People. However, many of the more
Learned and Wise adhere to the new Scheme of expressing
themselves by *Things*' (iii 5). Yet there are always instances to the
contrary, depending on the circumstances of Swift's allegiance. The
'*Clamour* of Enemies to the Church' is not 'the *Voice* of the Nation'
(ix 57) when he is defending his established church, and 'It is the
Folly of too many, to mistake the Eccho of a *London* Coffee-house
for the Voice of the Kingdom' (vi 53), but the '*clamour of a few
disaffected incendiaries*', in the Whigs' phrase, is actually 'the true

voice of the people' (v 114) when he is speaking of the popular discontent over the corruptions of Walpole's administration.[22]

A good dialectician knows when to argue from the opinions of the majority and when from those of the wise. Swift calls to the support of his theses the clergy,[23] the learned,[24] the wise[25] and various kinds of experts.[26] In the apology to the *Tale*, he tacitly acknowledges the weight of the arguments of critics charging him with satire of religion by calling almost frantically to his aid 'a great Majority among the Men of Tast', 'all Church of *England* Men', 'the Men of Tast', 'a fair Majority', 'All the Men of Wit and Politeness', 'any Reader of Tast and Candor', 'the judicious Reader', 'the Men of Wit and Tast' and 'the Publick'. Tindal, at whom Swift directs some of his strongest *ad personam* language, sits on the wrong side of the opinion of what is phrased to sound like both the wise and the majority: 'Here is the whole lower House of Convocation, which represents the Body of the Clergy and both Universities, treated with Rudeness by an obscure, corrupt Member, while he is eating their Bread' (II 103). In many of these examples, especially in the apology to the *Tale*, there is an implied opposition between the majority and the wise, which is a normal dialectical stratagem.[27] In some places the opposition is explicit, as in his sarcastic reference to 'that *happy Majority*, which I am confident is always in the Right' (XII 162), in his observation that the opinion of 'a man of common prudence' is often more in the right than that of the majority of an assembly (v 79) and in his remark that 'the unbiassed Thoughts of an honest and wise Man' are more acceptable 'than the Results of a Multitude, where Faction and Interest too often prevail. As a single Guide may direct the Way, better than five Hundred who *have contrary Views*, or *look asquint*, or *shut their Eyes*' (II 61). The most extreme statement of the opposition of the wise and the many is found in Gulliver's 'Letter to His Cousin Sympson', in which he says, 'The united Praise of the whole Race would be of less Consequence to me, than the neighing of those two degenerate *Houyhnhnms* I keep in my Stable' (XI 8).

REASON

To Swift reason was most important as it pertained to religion and politics, especially the latter. The 'meanest person' (IX 227) of 'plain honest sense' (IX 28) knows whether he is well or ill governed, because politics, as the king of Brobdingnag observes, is first of all 'common Sense and Reason' (ii 7); and the bulk of mankind would be easily governed by reason if it were left to their choice (VIII 77), that is, without faction clouding political issues.[28] Apart from religion and politics, reason considered *per se* is as clear cut and simple a matter as government: 'when Reason plainly appears before me, I cannot turn away my Head from it',[29] and 'no Person can disobey Reason, without giving up his Claim to be a rational Creature'.[30] Such bare assertions are deceptive, however, because reason cannot cure wrong opinions (IX 78), it sometimes pries too deeply or where it should not[31] and in man it is generally untrustworthy: '*Reason* itself is true and just, but the *Reason* of every particular Man is weak and wavering, perpetually swayed and turned by his Interests, his Passions, and his Vices' (IX 166). Further, as Gulliver points out, reason is a negative force which in humans improves and multiplies the vices of the Yahoos (iv 10), transforming natural appetites into unnatural ones (iv 7).

The contradictory nature of Swift's conception of reason is nowhere more obvious than in the description of the Houyhnhnms, who are said to be wholly governed by it. In an account reminiscent of the perplexing attitude towards reason in the 'Digression on Madness', Gulliver explains that the Houyhnhnms could not perform a simple deduction concerning his wearing shoes; yet the contemporary dictionaries and logic manuals show that reason was for the most part synonymous with deduction or logic.[32] The dapple grey and the brown bay, when they discover Gulliver his first morning on the island, are under 'great Perplexity' about his shoes and stockings, which they examine closely, behaving like two philosophers attempting 'to solve some new and difficult Phaenomenon' (iv 1). Later that morning the grey, who has become Gulliver's master, examines him again and wonders about his clothes; and on a third examination at noon his master is perplexed at the gloves Gulliver is wearing, which he had not had on earlier and which he sheds upon request. At this point the horses are satisfied regarding the gloves, but they remain perplexed about his other coverings, his clothes and shoes.

The Houyhnhnm Master continues to think about Gulliver's clothes after the physical examination on the day they meet. For weeks after Gulliver came to live with the Houyhnhnm family, the master horse 'was most perplexed about my Cloaths, reasoning sometimes with himself, whether they were a Part of my Body; for I never pulled them off till the Family were asleep, and got them on before they waked in the Morning' (iv 3). One morning, four and a half months after Gulliver's arrival, the master's servant nag discovers Gulliver asleep, half naked, and Gulliver consequently confesses his use of clothes to his master, who finds the explanation 'all very strange' (iv 3). His reasonable master, who had examined him as a philosopher would have done and had subsequently compared him side by side with a Yahoo (iv 2), noting similarities, cannot reason A is to B as C is to D, or hand is to glove as C is to shoe, where Gulliver is thought to be basically a Yahoo and Yahoos have feet, just as they have hands similar to Gulliver's. With all of these knowns, neither the master nor his family, servants or friends can, in spite of four and a half months' intimate acquaintance with Gulliver, proceed to the simple unknown: what Gulliver has at the end of his legs must be coverings just as the gloves are, and underneath must be feet like those of Yahoos, just as his hands resemble theirs. For a considerable time Gulliver takes advantage of this deception (or dullness) of the Houyhnhnms regarding the true nature of his Yahoo-like body in order to insinuate himself into their confidence and company, to partake of the reason he so often praises, which is, one sees, not worthy of quite so high a praise as he offers it. After explaining the wearing of clothes to his master, Gulliver offers to 'give him immediate Conviction, if he pleased to command me' (iv 3). It is possible to convince the Houyhnhnm immediately by showing to his senses the disrobing which, had he deduced it from prior evidence, would have been called reason.

That certainty of which the Houyhnhnms are capable in their thought processes and for which Gulliver praises them they reach not by deductive inference, nor by inductive inference, but by analogical inference, which unlike the other two is not properly reasoning at all. Both induction and deduction are characterised by universal inference, the former adding a universal premise to a particular premise to draw a universal conclusion, the latter adding a particular premise to a universal premise to draw a particular conclusion. Universal inference is reasoning and the Houyhnhnms, who add a particular premise (Gulliver is an animal similar to a Yahoo) to a particular premise (a Yahoo is a depraved brute)[33] to draw a particular conclusion (Gulliver is a depraved brute), cannot be said to use reasoning, but only analogical inference. Had they inferred inductively that if the Yahoo is a depraved brute and all animals who resemble Yahoos are like them in nature,[34] then all animals who resemble Yahoos are depraved brutes, the Houyhnhnms could have proceeded to the deductive inference that if all animals who resemble Yahoos are depraved brutes[35] and Gulliver is one of those animals who resemble Yahoos, then Gulliver is a depraved brute – not sophisticated reasoning to some twentieth-century minds, but logical nonetheless.

Because the logics of Marsh and Burgersdicius used during Swift's years at Trinity College dealt with different kinds of inference and with logical propositions about reason and unreason in men and animals, Swift was familiar with both subjects.[36] In a brief discussion of induction, Marsh touches upon a topic which especially concerns the question of the Houyhnhnms' ability to reason.[37] In a syllogistic example showing species inferring genus, Marsh has as the major term a reference to the senses in both men and beasts:

Nec homo nec brutum est sensus expers.
Sed animal est homo et brutum. Ergo,
Nullum animal est sensus expers.[38]

(Neither man nor brute is without sensation.
But a man or a brute is an animal.
Therefore no animal is without sensation.)

Through sense perception, common to both men and beasts, impressions are made in the mind and it is this process that Gulliver celebrates as the reason of the Houyhnhnms. Whether Swift, as opposed to Gulliver, meant by 'reason' the obtaining of knowledge through sense perception, or the drawing of conclusions by universal reference, is a difficult question and one for which it is helpful to turn to Aristotle for an answer.

In the *Posterior Analytics* Aristotle explains that primary immediate premises (basic truths from which the most elementary demonstration proceeds) are not innate in us, nor are they reached through demonstration (scientific deduction). These primary or first premises are states of knowledge developed from sense perception and apprehended by intuition. Sense perception gathers many particulars which in turn form the basis of a lesser number of universals.[39] What is suggested by the 'reason' of the Houyhnhnms, which 'strikes you with immediate Conviction' (iv 8), and by a statement of Swift's written after *Gulliver's Travels* that 'a man may be persuaded into a wrong opinion wherein he hath small concern: but no oratory can have the power over a sober man against the conviction of his own senses' (v 112) seems to be the same as the apprehension of basic truths as described in the *Posterior Analytics*. A biographer suggests that 'reason' to Swift and Gilbert Burnet 'meant not formal logic but "the clear conviction of our senses" ', a phrase of Burnet's which, it is said, describes their views of reason throughout their lives.[40] Such a suggestion seems to be at variance with Swift's lines from the 'Ode to the Athenian Society', which argue the necessity of deduction to complete the initial step of sense perception:

> *The Wits*, I mean the Atheists of the Age . . . ,
> Wondrous *Refiners* of Philosophy. . . .
> By the new *Modish System* of reducing all to sense,
> Against all Logick and concluding Laws,
> Do own th'Effects of Providence,
> And yet deny the Cause.[41]

The intuitive–inductive apprehension of universals against which Swift argues in the poem is of extremely limited value without a complementary ability at deduction, as the *Organon* shows and as the Houyhnhnm Master shows negatively by knowing it is 'impossible that there could be a Country beyond the Sea, or that a Parcel of Brutes could move a wooden Vessel whither they pleased upon the Water' (iv 3): that is, his intuitive knowledge in this instance is blind to an advance of knowledge resulting from deductions Gulliver could provide for him.[42]

Despite the Houyhnhnms' reluctance to accept Gulliver's account of sea travel,[43] they accept other testimony of his in order to reason dialectically to 'approve' and 'affirm' the tradition of the two original Yahoos' being driven to Houyhnhnmland by their companions (iv 9). The Argument of chapter 9 indicates the dialectical character of this discussion: 'A grand Debate at the General Assembly of the *Houyhnhnms*; and how it was determined'. Despite, also, Gulliver's high praise of the Houyhnhnms' limiting themselves to certain truths which give immediate conviction (iv 8), he commends their dialectical reasoning when he says of his master 'That his Honour, to my great Admiration, appeared to understand the Nature of Yahoos much better than my self. He went through all our Vices and Follies, and discovered many which I had never mentioned to him, by only supposing what Qualities a *Yahoo* of their Country, with a small

Proportion of Reason, might be capable of exerting. And concluded, with too much Probability, how vile as well as miserable such a Creature must be' (iv 10). Here Gulliver's master shows an ability to reason probably and to advance his knowledge deductively, although he was unable to do so with respect to Gulliver's wearing of clothes.

So it seems that in spite of Gulliver's attempt in the Fourth Voyage to advocate conviction through sense perception to the exclusion of deduction, Swift himself was not of the same mind, certainly not in his other writings and not even, in fact, in the Fourth Voyage, as evidence of the Houyhnhnm Master's deduction shows. Swift would not want to eradicate the scholastic tradition of deductive inference from his view of truth even if he could, because that kind of inference had long shaped the character of his mind and was an important part of his writing style. The value of deduction to Swift lay in the quality of the conclusions it draws. As the *Posterior Analytics* suggests,[44] induction, which results from a comparison of the particulars of sense perception, does not, even when the enumeration of the particulars is complete, reach a probative force. Induction remains a syllogism of fact, not of reason; it makes it *clear*, but it does not *prove*. Induction does not offer incontestable conclusions until the inquiry, of which induction forms the first part, reverses its process and shows that from an inductively-reached principle a certain conclusion necessarily follows. As Wesley's guide to university disputation explains, 'The term "Induction" is sometimes employed to designate the process of investigating and collecting facts; which is not a process of argument, but a *preparation for it*.'[45] It is the quality of necessity[46] in deductive conclusions which seems to have impressed Swift, and as a result one encounters time and time again references to proof, argument, deduction, consequence, reasoning, determining and conclusion, all of which refer to syllogistic reasoning.

Speaking very simply, induction encompasses two drawbacks which disqualify it as superior to deduction in what Russell calls 'the search for certainty'.[47] First are the basic problems of appearance and reality, the existence of matter and the extent to which we can trust our senses.[48] Second is the problem of enumeration of instances: there is always the possibility of finding one to the contrary. 'Do *any* number of cases of a law [like the law of gravitation or of motion] being fulfilled in the past afford evidence that it will be fulfilled in the future? . . . The man who has fed the chicken every day throughout its life at last wrings its neck instead, showing that more refined views as to the uniformity of nature would have been useful to the chicken.' Will the sun rise tomorrow? 'Have we any reason, assuming that they [natural laws] have always held in the past, to suppose that they will hold in the future?' Russell concludes that however close we may approach to certainty using the inductive principle, 'probability is all we ought to seek' (ch. 6). Swift seems to prefer the force of the necessary (deductive) inference to the comparative mildness of the probable (inductive) inference.[49] 'A Modest Proposal' with its careful computation and air of exigency has about it a kind of necessity. The 'Project for the Advancement of Religion and the Reformation of Manners' is based explicitly on the 'necessary Consequence' (II 54) of improved faith and morals which 'must needs' (II 61) follow the rewarding of virtue and piety in high places.

On a smaller scale, too, Swift's style in sentences and paragraphs reflects his regard for the cogency of deduction, whose combination of premises compels a conclusion which follows the premises of necessity. Induction allows doubt as to the universality of its conclusions, and analogical inference requires less evidence than does induction. It is through necessary or deductive reasoning, Swift believes, that 'Truth always forceth its Way into rational Minds'. Gulliver makes this statement with reference to the reception of his account of his sojourn in Brobdingnag by the sea captain who rescued him (ii 8). The captain's belief is gained by conclusions reached deductively, given the premises of Gulliver's account. Yet Gulliver, 'further to confirm' what he has recounted, shows the captain 'the small Collection of Rarities' he brought from Brobdingnag. Swift also believes that it is through deduction that 'the Force of Reason' can overcome irrational influences (II 144) and that when fancy and imagination attempt to gain control of the mind, reason and the senses are on the same side opposing them.[50] One has simply to look at Swift's use of the language of deductive logic, the subject of parts of the next chapter, to see that he valued deduction highly, with some reservations, and employed it often.

PAMPHLET WARFARE

Swift had an edge over many of his opponents in various pamphlet combats because he possessed, in addition to a forceful style and dialectical acumen, a knowledge of history and a facility for drawing

upon it which proved formidable in disputation.[51] Referring to his
History of the Four Last Years of the Queen he mentions his moral
purpose in writing history (VIII 141–2), which seems to be a concern
of his no greater than simply recording accounts of men and events
for posterity,[52] a task for which he felt he was suited.[53] His several
historical writings have their value, but from an artistic point of view
the value which his historical knowledge gave his dialectic and satire
is greater.[54]

Most of Swift's references to and engagements in pamphlet
warfare are confined to religion, learning and politics. In religion he
was no stranger to the history of 'that Spirit of Opposition, that
lived long before Christianity, and can easily subsist without it'
(II 34), having familiarised himself with the petulant and scurrilous
Puritan pamphlets of the sixteenth century, especially those of
Martin Marprelate, and having found, 'by often rumaging for old
Books in *Little Britain* and *Duck-lane*, a great Number of Pamphlets
printed from the Year 1630 to 1640, full of as bold and impious
railing Expressions against the lawful Power of the Crown, and the
Order of Bishops, as ever were uttered during the Rebellion, or the
whole subsequent Tyranny of the Fanatick Anarchy' (XII 264). The
best Anglican pamphlets against Popery, he judged, were written
during the reign of James II, but the Presbyterians at that time were
either strangely silent or such poor writers that their tracts no longer
survive (XII 270). In the eighteenth century, however, they were
anything but silent, especially concerning abolishing the Sacramental
Test, over which Swift suffered their stock arguments in a hundred
conversations and twenty pamphlets (XII 259).

The pamphlet – and book – warfare in the realm of learning is
described in Swift's unsurpassed account of the subject, *The Battle
of the Books*, where he explains that '*Ink* is the great missive
Weapon, in all Battels of the *Learned*', which is 'convey'd thro' a
sort of Engine, call'd a *Quill*'. The *Battle* concludes in the ultimate
martial metaphor of dialectical controversy in literary criticism:
Boyle's skewering Wotton and Bentley. Swift's concern with such
controversy is apparent as late as *Gulliver's Travels*, in which
Gulliver protests that he wrote only for the truth as far as he could
perceive it, in a plain style, without prejudice or ill will against any
man: 'I hope, I may with Justice pronounce myself an Author
perfectly blameless, against whom the Tribes of Answerers,
Considerers, Observers, Reflecters, Detecters, Remarkers, will
never be able to find Matter for exercising their Talents' (IV 12). The

list is reminiscent of that in *The Battle of the Books* where the battles of the learned 'are known to the World under several Names: As, *Disputes, Arguments, Rejoynders, Brief Considerations, Answers, Replies, Remarks, Reflexions, Objections, Confutations*' (p. 222).

The satire of pamphleteers had begun in the *Tale*, where he said, 'Fourscore and eleven Pamphlets have I written under three Reigns, and for the Service of six and thirty Factions' (p. 70). In the *Battle*, after describing the Moderns' horse, light horse, bowmen, foot and so forth and the 'confused Multitude' led by Aquinas, Scotus and Bellarmine, he describes in the last place the 'Swarms of *Calones*', or soldiers' servants, signifying political pamphlets (p. 238 and nn.). After having so ridiculed mercenary writers for political parties, he was obliged when he began writing in support of the Harley ministry in 1710 to declare more than once 'that I do not write for a Party' in answer to the many accusations that he was a tool of the Tories. In this same *Examiner* no. 39 he continues, 'Neither do I, upon any Occasion, pretend to speak their Sentiments, but my own'. Later in the paper he says, 'as an Answer once and for all, to the tedious Scurrilities of those idle People, who affirm, I am hired and directed what to write: I must here inform them, that their *Censure* is an Effect of their *Principles*: The present Ministry are under no Necessity of employing prostitute Pens; they have no dark Designs to promote, by advancing *Heterodox Opinions*'. He had said as much in *Examiner* no. 29: 'I never received Injury from the late Ministry; nor Advantage from the present, farther than in common with every good Subject', and later in no. 41 he was still asserting, 'I never let slip an Opportunity of endeavouring to convince the World, that I am not Partial; and to confound the idle Reproach of my being hired or directed what to write in Defence of the present Ministry, or for detecting the Practices of the former'.

Needless to say he was not entirely convincing to his opponents. In 1721 he still complained: 'it is with great injustice I have these many years been pelted by your Pamphleteers, merely upon account of some regard which the Queen's last Ministers were pleased to have for me' (ix 30). The Whigs during and after that ministry, he believed, wrote no pamphlets of value because they had no just cause to defend. Writing as the Examiner facing his Whig opponents, he suggests that if both sides wrote with fairness, sense and manners, it would be both entertaining and a means to reconciliation. 'But I am apt to think, that Men of great Genius are hardly brought to prostitute their Pens in a very odious *Cause*; which, besides, is more properly undertaken by Noise and Impudence, by gross Railing and Scurrility, by Calumny and Lying, and by little trifling Cavils and Carpings in the wrong Place, which those *Whifflers* use for Arguments and Answers' (III 35–6). In 1730, with the tables turned, Swift makes the same charge, this time against Walpole's hired pamphleteers defending the Whig ministry: 'Should we allow them to be masters of wit, raillery, or learning, yet the subject would not admit them to exercise their talents; and, consequently, they can have no recourse but to impudence, lying, and scurrility' (v 113).

After successfully soliciting the restoration of First Fruits and Twentieth Parts for the Irish Church in 1710, Swift was told by Harley, who had helped with the restoration, that several in the ministry were aware of the useful things he had 'written against the principles of the late discarded faction; and, that . . . the Queen was resolved to employ none but those who were friends to the constitution of church and state: That their great difficulty lay in the want of some good pen, to keep up the spirit raised in the people, to assert the principles, and justify the proceedings of the new ministers' (VIII 123). Swift the Tory pamphleteer is one part rhetorician (keeping up the spirit of the people) and two parts dialectician: as asserter of principles and justifier of acts he takes the part of the 'respondent' in a disputation, just as he takes that of the 'opponent' when he attacks theses maintained by others. In many of his pamphlets the style of his argument is partly determined by his position as one or the other of the disputants, the one who answers or the one who opposes, the latter of which he had done when writing 'against the principles of the late discarded faction'.

UNIVERSITY EDUCATION

In the digressions of *A Tale of a Tub* Swift satirises learning, but there is no satire directed at the universities themselves, nor is there in *Gulliver's Travels*, where the satire of learning is aimed at experimental scientists, unless the intermittent foolishness of Gulliver is attributable to his education at Emmanuel, one of the most Puritan of Cambridge colleges in the seventeenth century. The Tory satirists' occasional bias for Oxford and against Cambridge might have been instrumental in determining Gulliver's university. In the Ancients–Moderns controversy Swift took the side of the Christ Church wits (Henry Aldrich, dean of the college, Charles Boyle,

Francis Atterbury and others) of Oxford against Bentley and Wotton, both products of St John's College, Cambridge. An inherent contradiction in the Tory bias, however, is that Temple, whom Swift was primarily defending in *The Battle of the Books*, was educated at Emmanuel College, Cambridge. There seems to be no educational pattern in the targets of Swift's satire or abuse: Tindal studied at Oxford, Collins at Cambridge, Toland at Glasgow and Leyden, Asgill at the Middle Temple and Partridge at Leyden. There are no comparable Oxford references to match Gulliver's alma mater; or the first line of 'Cassinus and Peter': 'Two College Sophs of *Cambridge* Growth'; or 'A Modest Defence of Punning', which is dated 'Cambridge, Nov. 8th, 1716' (IV 205), and the etymology of *pun*, traceable to Cambridge, 'where this Art is in highest Perfection' (IV 206) – except perhaps the career of Corusodes at Oxford, in *Intelligencer* nos 5 and 7 (XII 41–4).[55]

Swift staunchly defends university education in *Intelligencer* no. 9 (XII 48–9, 51–2), 'A Letter to a Young Gentleman' (IX 78) and ironically in 'A Vindication of Lord Carteret' (XII 160). In the *Dunciad* Pope ridiculed the universities' maintaining of the status quo in church and state – 'The Right Divine of Kings to govern wrong' (iv 188) – but to Swift these 'Prejudices of Education' merited defence, which he gave them.[56] One of the reasons the Whig pamphleteers defending Walpole's administration were such poor writers is that they had 'enjoyed the happiness of a very bad education' (v 96), which meant that they lacked clarity of style and did not know how to argue as did, for example, Bacon, Milton and Dryden,[57] all Cambridge men incidentally.

Swift's view of the Aristotelianism on which university education was based contains a distinction between Aristotle and his commentators, the scholastics. Although in his 'Sermon upon the Excellency of Christianity' he criticises the philosophies of Plato and Aristotle as not conducive to virtue and happiness (IX 244–5)[58] and through Peter disparages '*Aristotelis Dialectica*, and especially that wonderful Piece *de Interpretatione*',[59] he generally regards Aristotle rather highly: 'He writ upon *logick*, or the art of reasoning; upon *moral* and *natural philosophy*; upon *oratory, poetry*, &c. and seems to be a person of the most comprehensive genius that ever lived.'[60] At Glubbdubdrib, when Gulliver wants to see those ancients 'most renowned for Wit and Learning', he calls up Homer and Aristotle and finds the latter ('this great Philosopher') especially to be 'out of all Patience' with his commentators (iii 8). In *The Battle of the*

Books Aristotle, who with Plato is one of the two greatest ancient
philosophers (p. 238), dispatches Descartes with an arrow (p. 244).
And castigating Tindal, who in his *Rights of the Christian Church*
(1706) had referred to 'this miserable Gibberish of the Schools',
Swift makes his most telling remark concerning the basis of the
dialectic he had learned at Trinity College, Dublin: '*Aristotle* . . . is
doubtless the greatest Master of Arguing in the World: But it hath
been a Fashion of late Years to explode *Aristotle*, and therefore this
Man hath fallen into it like others, for that Reason, without
understanding him. *Aristotle's* Poetry, Rhetoric, and Politicks are
admirable, and therefore it is likely, so are his Logicks' (II 97).

Rarely, however, did Swift have a good word for scholasticism.
He speaks of the 'Lumber' and the 'Stale Memorandums of the
Schools',[61] and of being 'long inur'd to musty Rules/And idle Morals
in the Schools'.[62] The *Tale* describes Dryden's 'Hind and the
Panther' as an abstract of 'sixteen thousand Schoolmen from *Scotus*
to *Bellarmin*' (p. 69), and in *The Battle of the Books* those two
schoolmen with Aquinas lead 'a confused Multitude, . . . without
either Arms, Courage, or Discipline', who follow the Moderns'
horse, bowmen, foot and so forth (pp. 237–8). The cause of the
battle, in fact, was affirmed by some to be Bentley's habit of eating
worms picked out of scholastic volumes, which perturbed both his
spleen and his brain (p. 226). The 'Followers of *Aristotle*', who by
'the old Evasion of *occult Causes* . . . endeavour in vain to disguise
their Ignorance',[63] in Swift's view belong in the jakes with commentators and German divines, where they may at least be of
practical use (IX 283). Turning an argument of the freethinkers back
upon themselves, he uses the scholastics to disparage Tindal: 'The
Free-thinkers may talk what they please of Pedantry, and Cant, and
Jargon of Schoolmen, and insignificant Terms in the Writings of the
Clergy, if ever the most perplexed and perplexing follower of
Aristotle from Scotus to Suarez could be a Match for this Author'
(II 81), and similarly he criticises an oath-filled 'Volley of Military
Terms, less significant, sounding worse, and harder to be understood
than any that were ever coined by the Commentators on *Aristotle*'
(XII 49).

In the *Tale* he satirises scholasticism through parody of its
terminology, as Peter 'the Scholastick Brother' (p. 89) adds clauses
for the public good 'though not deductible, *totidem verbis*, from the
Letter of the Will' (p. 90) and draws distinctions increasingly minute,
totidem verbis, *totidem syllabis*, and *tertio modo* or *totidem litteras*,

trying to justify the use of shoulder knots (p. 83).[64] Such 'Scholastick Midwifry' (p. 186), which delivers authors of their meanings by drawing distinctions, seems to be the object of parody in *The Mechanical Operation of the Spirit*, where in one passage in particular the conciseness and distinguishing have a strong Peripatetic flavour: 'Upon these Examples, and others easy to produce, I desire the curious Reader to distinguish, First between an Effect grown from *Art* into *Nature*, and one that is natural from its Beginning; Secondly, between an Effect wholly natural, and one which has only a natural Foundation, but where the Superstructure is entirely Artificial. For the first and the last of these, I understand to come within the Districts of my Subject' (p. 269). One might compare, for example, the style of Aristotle's observation:

> Can the cause of an identical effect be not identical in every instance of the effect but different? Or is that impossible? Perhaps it is impossible if the effect is demonstrated as essential and not as inhering in virtue of a symptom or an accident . . . though possible if the demonstration is not essential. Now it is possible to consider the effect and its subject as an accidental conjunction, though such conjunctions would not be regarded as connexions demanding scientific proof.[65]

The satire of scholasticism often focuses on the disputation, as one might expect, having considered the relationship of university disputations to scholasticism in Part I above. Although Swift can without satire speak of having heard a particular question 'disputed in publick Schools . . . , which was held in the Negative',[66] he usually speaks of a disputation as something 'dark', 'a weak argument by force maintained,/In dagger-contests, and th'artillery of words'.[67] In an explicit reference to university exercises, the goddess Criticism boasts that through her, 'Sophisters debate, and conclude upon the Depths of Knowledge'.[68] When the Bee accepts the Spider's challenge to dispute, 'the *Spider* having swelled himself into the Size and Posture of a Disputant, began his Argument in the true Spirit of Controversy, with a Resolution to be heartily scurrilous and angry, to urge *on* his own Reasons, without the least Regard to the Answers or Objections of his Opposite; and fully predetermined in his Mind against all Conviction' (p. 230). In the debate the tones of their language show that the Spider is vehement and the Bee calm, a reflection of the recklessness with which Jack in the *Tale* stripped his coat of ornaments and the moderation with which Martin stripped his: 'as in Scholastick Disputes, nothing serves to rouze the Spleen of him that *Opposes*, so much as a kind of Pedantick affected Calmness in the *Respondent*; Disputants being for the most part like unequal Scales, where the *Gravity* of one Side advances the *Lightness* of the Other . . . ; So it happened here, that the *Weight* of *Martin*'s Arguments exalted *Jack's Levity*, and made him fly out and spurn against his Brother's Moderation. In short, *Martin*'s *Patience* put *Jack* in a *Rage*' (p. 140). In the *Battle* the Bee at length grows bored and flies off to a bed of roses, leaving the Spider inflated with polemic (pp. 232–3). Aesop, noting that the disputants have 'exhausted the Substance of every Argument *pro* and *con*', acts as moderator and determines the debate in favour of the Bee (pp. 233–4).

Shaftesbury, in a remark on scholastic debates in his 'Essay on the Freedom of Wit and Humour', supplies reasoning behind the object of Swift's extended analogy:

> If a Philosopher speaks, Men hear him willingly, while he keeps to his Philosophy. So is a Christian heard, while he keeps to his profess'd Charity and Meekness. In a Gentleman we allow of Pleasantry and Raillery, as being manag'd always with good Breeding, and never gross or clownish. But if a mere Scholastick, intrenching upon all these Characters, and writing as it were by Starts and Rebounds from one of these to another, appears upon the whole as little able to keep the Temper of Christianity, as to use the Reason of a Philosopher, or the Raillery of a Man of Breeding; what wonder is it, if the monstrous Product of such a jumbled Brain be ridiculous to the World?[69]

CONTROVERSY

For all Swift's references to the techniques of disputation and his use of them in his writings, he voiced in several places an antipathy to controversy both in writing and in conversation. He says of Stella, 'She was never positive in arguing, and she usually treated those who were so, in a manner which well enough gratified that unhappy disposition. . . . when she saw any of the company very warm in a wrong opinion, she was more inclined to confirm them in it, than oppose them. The excuse she commonly gave when her friends asked the reason was, That it prevented noise, and saved time.'[70] Of 'Daphne' he says,

> To dispute, her chief delight,
> With not one opinion right:
> Thick her arguments she lays on,
> And with cavils combats reason:
> Answers in decisive way,
> Never hears what you can say.

(1730) ll. 9–14

In his introduction to 'Polite Conversation' he observes, 'When this happy Art of polite conversing, shall be thoroughly improved; good Company will be no longer pestered with dull dry tedious Story-tellers, or brangling Disputers' (IV 117) and in 'Hints on Good Manners', 'Argument, as usually managed, is the worst sort of conversation; as it is generally in books the worst sort of reading' (IV 222).

Regarding books and pamphlets one sees the same attitude: 'I know very well how soon the World grows weary of Controversy', he says of the attacks of the Whig paper, the *Medley*, on the *Examiner* (III 154). 'Books of Controversy', he says in the *Battle of the Books* (p. 223), 'being of all others, haunted by the most disorderly Spirits', are always kept separate from the rest and bound with strong chains. In the *Battle* and in 'A Sermon upon the Excellency of Christianity' he attributes these disorderly spirits to the 'Peripatetic forms' which, he erroneously suggests, 'were introduced by Scotus, as best fitted for controversy. And, however this may have become necessary, it was surely the author of a litigious vein, which hath since occasioned very pernicious consequences' (IX 250).[71]

Bentley is the object of satire because of his polemical vein, particularly because of his 'low and mean' style in disputation. The generals of the Moderns' army make use of him because of his 'Talent of Railing',[72] which he turns against them when the Moderns are losing the battle: 'He humbly gave the *Modern Generals* to understand, that he conceived, with great Submission, they were all a Pack of *Rogues*, and *Fools*, and *Sons of Whores*, and *d—mn'd Cowards*, and *confounded Loggerheads*, and *illiterate Whelps*, and *nonsensical Scoundrels*.'[73] Scaliger, taking the generals' side, scolds

Bentley in turn: '*Miscreant* Prater, said he, . . . *Thou railest without Wit, or Truth, or Discretion, the Malignity of thy Temper perverteth Nature, thy* Learning *makes thee more* Barbarous, *thy Study of* Humanity, *more* Inhuman.'[74] Like the children of 'a malignant Deity, call'd *Criticism* – *Positiveness, Pedantry*, and *Ill-Manners*' – whom the goddess leads into battle on the side of the Moderns (p. 240), like the 'heartily scurrilous and angry' Spider who urges his arguments 'without the least Regard to the Answers or Objections of his Opposite, and fully predetermine[s] his Mind against all Conviction' (p. 230) and like Peter in the *Tale*, who was 'extream wilful and positive, and would at any time rather argue to the Death, than allow himself to be once in an Error' (p. 120), Bentley characterises what Swift most objects to in argument, for which 'railing' is as good a name as any. In some of his *ad personam* replies to Tindal, Steele and Burnet, Swift makes admirable use of the art of insult, but he rarely lowers his style to railing.

When controversy grows too rancorous, 'when Parties in a State are violent', a solution comes by way of a doctor in the school of political projectors in the Academy of Lagado. His proposal, a kind of internal dialectic, is that surgeons remove the occiputs of a hundred leaders from each party, exchange half of the brain of each leader with that of his counterpart in the other party, and 'the two half Brains being left to debate the Matter between themselves within the Space of one Scull, would soon come to a good Understanding, and produce that Moderation as well as Regularity of Thinking, so much to be wished for in the Heads of those, who imagine they came into the World only to watch and govern its Motion' (iii 6). Gulliver valued the conversations of the Houyhnhnms, in which 'there was no interruption, Tediousness, or Heat' (iv 10). But the horses had no 'Difference of Sentiments', which is the stuff of dialectic.

6
The Language of Logical Argument

DIALECTIC

Swift's use of the language of logic has often been noticed and sometimes stressed, but rarely from a dialectical perspective. It is a commonplace to see his usual satirical method as 'that of a devastating logic' but one more in appearance than reality, a 'logic on the basis of a preposterous major premise'.[1] His 'mocking echoes of . . . logic' are sometimes a 'unique Swiftian amalgam of wild fancy and perverse logic', a 'perverse consistency of . . . preposterous logic', 'a kind of "internal logic of error" '.[2] A brief discussion of 'The Sentiments of a Church-of-England Man' contains (unflattering) references to the essay's logical framework, logical outline, logical surface and logical skeleton.[3] Largely overlooking the *dialectical* basis of Swift's language,[4] as opposed to the *logical*, and the dialectical foundation of much of his satire, is perhaps less of a disservice to the dialectical perspective than is confusing it with *rhetorical* analysis of his style, by including, for example, rhetorical devices like 'aposiopesis' and 'epiphonemas' in a passage explicitly concerned with Swift's use of the terminology of the logic taught in the schools[5] or by unnecessarily substituting for 'dialectic' a phrase like 'polemic rhetoric'.[6] Ehrenpreis goes a small way towards righting the imbalance of concern with Swift's rhetoric and monologic logic to the exclusion of dialectic by pointing out that by statute the candidate for the BA at Trinity College, Dublin, was required to argue twelve times on the right side of the disputation questions and twenty-four on the wrong side, a procedure likely to engender an ironic viewpoint in a fertile mind.[7] The most explicit statement of the importance of dialectic to Swift's style is no more than several brief passages in an essay, but they are significant, as this one shows:

The witty use of these techniques in literature belongs historically

to the age when dialectic was still important in education, when
the ability to dispute on either side of a question was an accepted
accomplishment in schools and universities. The English masters
of ratiocinative wit, of the art of developing a plausibly outrageous
argument, are Donne, Dryden and Swift, of whom the latter is,
surely, the most astonishing. But dialectical dexterity declined in
importance, the new philosophers and scientists of the seventeenth
century having no use for traditional logic, and English writers
after this period show much less skill in these arts.[8]

The value of Ehrenpreis's and Jefferson's remarks is real but limited,
because they refer almost exclusively to the dialectical basis of
Swift's often witty use of irony and satire, but not to the
straightforward dialectic which is often the basis of his clarity and
force, stylistic characteristics as remarkable as his satire and irony.

Swift succeeds as a dialectician partly because he neither is nor
considers himself an expert,[9] but rather an examiner of first
principles, which are usually based on general opinion.[10] In *Examiner*
no. 20 he proposes to discuss the military, which he confesses is 'a
Matter wholly out of my Trade' and one that 'hath suffered great
Changes, almost in every Age and Country of the World; however,
there are some Maxims relating to it, that will be eternal Truths,
and which every reasonable Man must allow' (III 40).[11] In dialectical
examinations like this *Examiner* paper, the *Contests and Dissentions*,
the 'Argument against Abolishing Christianity' and 'A Letter to a
Young Gentleman', he argues from the first principles of dialectic,
that is, from premises based on general opinion rather than scientific
truth (*Topics*, 100ª27–31): *''Tis agreed'*, the *Contests and Dissentions*
begins; the 'Argument' opens with ironic references to reasoning
'against the general Humour and Disposition of the World' and to
'the Fundamental Law, that makes this Majority of Opinion the
Voice of God'; and the 'Letter' opens by acknowledging 'the present
Dispositions of Mankind towards the *Church*' and a reference to 'the
general Practice and Opinion'.

In his 'Letter to a Whig Lord' and the third Drapier's letter,
addressed 'To the Nobility and Gentry' of Ireland as opposed to the
tradesmen and common people to whom the first two letters are
addressed, the forceful reasoning could be said to derive in part
from the presence of a relatively learned audience. But generally the
most dialectical of Swift's pamphlets are not appeals to an audience
but answers to writings he wishes to refute, this being nothing more

than the difference between rhetoric and dialectic. The third Drapier's letter, for example, is such a reply: 'Some Observations upon a Paper, Call'd, The Report of the Committee of the Most Honourable the Privy-Council in England, Relating to Wood's Half-Pence'. The language and methods of dialectic, the attention to definition, to distinguishing terms and to style, flourish especially where there is an opponent to be dealt with, such as Steele in 'The Publick Spirit of the Whigs' and 'The Importance of the *Guardian* Considered', Tindal in the 'Remarks' against his book and Burnet in 'A Preface to the Bishop of Sarum's Introduction'. By contrast, 'Memoirs Relating to That Change which happened in the Queen's Ministry' is barren of dialectical ploys and of references to language and logical processes; nor can 'An Enquiry into the Behaviour of the Queen's Last Ministry' match Swift's dialectical writings for force and wit. The reason for this lifelessness is the absence of a dialectical opponent. Swift agreed with the principles of the queen's ministry.

THE LANGUAGE OF DISPUTATION

His denunciation of controversy aside, Swift believed more in dialectic, the reasoning between two people leading, it is hoped, to agreement, than he did in solitary reasoning. The former must anchor itself to the *consensus gentium* or to the conclusions of the wise, whereas the latter can go too wildly astray, leading to singularity of opinion and nonsensical speculation. Those with minds turned inwards require gentle strikes with air-filled bladders to prevent bouncing their heads on every post, or sometimes they require an encounter with a lamp post to draw their attention to the practical world.[12] The internal dialectic produced by an occipital exchange among contending party leaders[13] is an extreme and undesirable measure; conciliation is possible if the opposing causes are just and the arguers adept. Only rarely, however, does Swift concede opponents' justness or adeptness, as the succeeding chapters will show. He generally seeks victory, not conciliation, but in order to conceal the conclusion he is trying to secure,[14] he can be deceptively compliant: 'I am ready to grant two Points to the Author of the *Crisis*';[15] but later in the *Crisis* when Steele argues from a conditional premise – '*There can be no Crime in affirming, (if it be a Truth) that* . . .' – Swift is not so generous in granting premises: 'I will for once allow his Proposition. But if it be false, then I affirm, that whoever advanceth so seditious a Falsehood, deserveth to be hanged' (VIII 58).[16] So much for the stakes of dialectical disputation with Swift.

Swift himself when reasoning towards a conclusion is careful to begin with acceptable dialectical premises: 'I suppose, nothing will be readier granted, than . . .' (XII 246); 'I believe you will please allow me two Propositions'.[17] Such mildness in securing propositions[18] contrasts with Burnet's 'taking it for a *Postulatum*', which Swift criticises (IV 62). But mild openings are sometimes rebuffed. When an Ancient 'offered fairly to dispute the Case, and to prove by manifest Reasons' that the Ancients should have priority of place over the Moderns, the latter 'denied the Premises'[19] as simply as Swift denied one of Clarendon's conclusions in a marginal note to *The History of the Rebellion*: '*Nego*' (V 296).

Besides the granting and denying of premises and conclusions, the language of disputation encompasses the posing of dialectical questions. The Author of the *Tale* suggests an inquiry 'whether' the religion of the Aeolists was wholly compiled by Jack or had a Delphic origin (p. 161).[20] 'Whether the Banishing all Notions of Religion whatsoever, would be convenient for the Vulgar', Swift suggests, 'may perhaps admit a Controversy' (II 34). A proper dialectical question is phrased to allow the opponent only the choice of one of two contradictories, often stated to require a simple Yes or No answer. A dialectician would not ask, 'How many meanings has "the good"?' but rather, 'Good means this, or this, does it not?'[21] In this way the dialectician can more easily control the direction the argument will take, often having beforehand, like a chess player, reasoned through two or more series of moves depending on the response of his opponent. The King of Brobdingnag seems to have been a proficient dialectician. After taking notes during five audiences with Gulliver, in the sixth, 'consulting his Notes, [he] proposed many Doubts, Queries and Objections, upon every Article', and on English parliamentary elections he 'multiplied his Questions, and sifted me thoroughly upon every Part of this Head; proposing numberless Enquiries and Objections' (ii 6) and thus pursued with dialectical advantage the fallacies and weaknesses in Gulliver's account of English life. At the end of the examination, acting as moderator in the discussion, the king makes his famous determination about 'the most pernicious Race of little odious

Vermin that Nature ever suffered to crawl upon the Surface of the Earth'.

References to the determination at the conclusion of disputations are also a part of Swift's diction. Whether Jack or the Greeks originated the Aeolist religion, says the Author of the *Tale*, 'I shall not absolutely determine' (p. 161). On whether the Hanoverian successor to Queen Anne should reside in London before her death, the leaders of both parties 'when they were in Power did positively determine the Question in the Negative' (VIII 179). Concerning the confinement of the enormous plants and animals to the continent of the Brobdingnags, Gulliver decides he will 'leave the Reasons to be determined by Philosophers' (ii 4). Swift speaks of points 'already determined, whether wisely or not' (VIII 171) and of desiring 'to open this Matter, and leave the *Whigs* themselves to determine upon it' (III 154). In explicit references to academic disputations he speaks in passing of 'Moderators in an Assembly of Divines' (III 43) and entitles a poem '*Probatur Aliter*', a moderator's direction in disputations, requiring that a certain conclusion be proved from other premises.[22]

'TOPICKS', SYLLOGISM, ARGUE

The word 'topics' used by Aristotle and Cicero meant *loci communes*, general arguments, which do not grow out of the particular facts of a case but are applicable to any class of cases; topics are the grounds of proof, the points on which proofs are founded or from which they are deduced. In this sense Swift speaks of advancing topics (V 115), of 'the only Topicks of Quarrel' (VI 127), of 'many Arguments drawn from the Topicks of Policy as well as Justice' and says that 'To prove this he made use of the most plausible Topicks'.[23] References like 'the *Postulatum* already laid down' (XII 46) imply a succeeding deductive inference or syllogism; he also explicitly refers to 'the first proposition of an hypothetical syllogism' (XII 123) and to the 'sort of Sophistry that the Logicians call *two Mediums*, which are never allowed in the same Syllogism' (VIII 43).[24] 'As to that Argument used for repealing the *Test*', he asks in logical terminology, 'I wonder by what Figure[25] those Gentlemen speak, who are pleased to advance it' (II 120–1).

The words 'argue' and 'argument' in Swift's writings usually refer to self-consciously formal reasoning, as in 'Reasoners may argue' (III 18). The parody of logical argument in many parts of the *Tale* results in an exaggerated show of certainty, when, for example, the Author speaks of 'an undisputed Argument for what I affirm' (p. 34), 'an uncontestable Argument' (p. 147) and 'an unanswerable Argument' (p. 181).[26] In one passage concerning argument the diction is unmistakably characterised by the terminology of dialectical disputation, the establishing and overthrowing of propositions: 'But if no other Argument could occur to exclude the *Bench* and the *Bar* from the List of Oratorical Machines, it were sufficient, that the Admission of them would overthrow a Number which I was resolved to establish, whatever Argument it might cost me', even if it should include forcing 'common Reason' (p. 57). To Swift, whose strength of style requires more than just the persuasion of rhetoric, the *necessary* inference of logic[27] is indispensable: 'our Reason can find no way to avoid the Force of such an Argument' (IX 155), 'my Arguments offered to prove the foregoing Head' (IX 192) and 'producing many Arguments to prove that Opinion' (XII 276). To him arguing was the proper means to a reasonable goal, like purging the language of abbreviations, cant and harsh-sounding words, which should be corrected 'First, by Arguments and fair Means' (II 176), but if those fail, then by a censor. Although when he confronts a personal opponent he often resorts to contentious argument, when he challenges an opposing idea he often uses 'fair Means', as in his responses to arguments against the Sacramental Test (II 122–3, 133–4).

Swift seems to have shared Aristotle's view that induction should be used to convince the mass of men (the province of rhetoric) but deduction, which Aristotle calls 'reasoning', being more forcible, is more effective against contradictious people – that is, against dialectical opponents.[28] The contrast is between arguing from individuals to universals and the converse. Swift speaks favourably of those 'who might argue very well . . . from general Topicks and Reason, though they might be ignorant of several Facts' (VI 53) and of 'men who argued only from the Principles of generall Reason' (VIII 84). Conversely he says, 'I am sensible, it is ill arguing from Particulars to Generals' (III 107) and 'I made bold to tell him, That I thought we could not well judge from Particulars to Generals' (III 218). He also criticises 'very frivolous Arguments' (XII 173) and says on occasion that 'it is very false Reasoning . . . to argue that . . .' (III 141).

When each side has had its say, when the concluding and objecting are finished, it is time for the determination, as Swift suggests with respect to the question of Wood's halfpence: 'But it is needless to argue any longer. The Matter is come to an Issue.'[29]

PROVE, REASON, DEDUCE, CONCLUDE AND CONSEQUENCE

The concern with proving points, whether ironically in the *Tale*[30] or seriously in his political pamphlets,[31] reflects Swift's interest in the cogency of his language. In *Examiner* no. 44 he remarks that the Whig faction 'made use of those very Opinions themselves had broached, for Arguments to prove, that the Change of Ministers was dangerous and unseasonable' (III 168), thus exposing his opponents' violation of a principle of proof, in this case the fallacy of *petitio principii*, or begging the question. 'There is not one Argument used to prove the Riches of *Ireland*', he says, 'which is not a logical Demonstration of its Poverty' (XII 11). Of the various kinds of proof, demonstration is one of the most conclusive:[32] 'the contrary may almost be proved by uncontroulable Demonstration' (*Tale*, p. 34). And of the various kinds of demonstrative proof, the mathematical, praised highly by Richard Cumberland in his memoirs,[33] is one of the most certain: the *Tale*'s Author says that all the subjects to be written upon have been exhausted – he has been 'given a full Demonstration of it from Rules of *Arithmetick*' (p. 146). Gulliver speaks of a tutor's difficulty in teaching a Laputan lord 'to demonstrate the most easy Proposition in the Mathematicks' (iii 4).

Reason personified negatively in the *Tale* as an officious cutter, opener, mangler and piercer, 'offering to demonstrate, that [objects or bodies] are not of the same consistence quite thro'' (p. 173), is an accurate picture of the reason to which Swift refers in many of his other writings. True, he admires Bolingbroke's 'invincible Reason' (VIII 151), warns young clergymen against 'letting the pathetick Part swallow up the rational' in their sermons and urges instead using 'a plain convincing Reason' (IX 70), but generally his use of a more active form of the word 'reason' (reasoner, reasoning), while it implies the dialectical force suggested in the references to Bolingbroke and sermons, also suggests mangling, piercing or other destructive actions against the status quo of church and state. Of 'Enthusiastick Preachers', he says, 'I laugh aloud, to see these

Reasoners . . . engaged in wise Dispute, . . . seriously debating';[34]
he calls freethinkers 'the strong Reasoners' (II 36); the inhabitants of
Laputa 'are very bad Reasoners, and vehemently given to Opposition,
unless when they happen to be of the right Opinion, which is seldom
their Case' (iii 2). The wits of the present age, he says in the *Tale*,
might 'pick Holes in the weak sides of Religion and Government' by
'reasoning upon such delicate Points' (p. 39); predestination is
satirised by the force of Jack's 'Reasoning upon such abstruse
Matters' (p. 194); the Jesuits, Toland and Tindal are ironically
praised: 'the Reasoning they proceed by, is right' (II 37); and the
Examiner, who is defending the recent change of ministries, says,
'Among those who are pleased to write or talk against this Paper, I
have observed a strange Manner of Reasoning' (III 32). The static
quality of the noun 'reason' seems to imply to Swift an eternal first
principle and the active forms of 'reasoner' and 'reasoning' a
debased human reflection of the ideal form.

Swift uses 'deduce' and 'deduction' more often in the sense of
tracing a history to the present[35] than in the logical sense. He
'concludes' more often in a context of monologic logic than of
dialectic,[36] and at least twice comments on the relation of premises
to conclusion, once criticising the resolving 'upon a Conclusion
before it is possible to be apprised of the Premises',[37] and again
reflecting on the nature of current politics, 'I thought myself twenty
times in the right, by drawing conclusions very regularly from
premises which have proved wholly wrong. I think this, however, to
be a plain proof that we act altogether by chance; and that the
game, such as it is, plays itself'.[38]

The language of 'consequence' sometimes simply implies an
inference: 'These *Postulata* being admitted, it will follow in due
Course of Reasoning, that those Beings which the World calls
improperly *Suits of Cloaths*, are in Reality the most refined Species
of Animals' (*Tale*, p. 78). But often Swift more explicitly uses
phrases like 'the Consequences I shall deduce from it' (III 61) and
'deduce wrong Consequences by reasoning upon the Causes and
Motives' (VIII 79), or in response to a piece of shoddy reasoning by
an opponent, 'I do not well see the Consequences of this' (III 195).
References to consequences following of necessity reflect the
definition of a syllogism, whose conclusion follows necessarily from
its premises.[39] In the *Tale* the thinker 'consequently, must needs
conclude' (p. 103); in the 'Project for the Advancement of Religion
and the Reformation of Manners' he is shown a result which would

be 'the necessary Consequence of such a Reformation' (II 54); and in the 'Argument against Abolishing Christianity' he is advised to abolish not only Christianity but all religion, considering 'all the necessary Consequences, which curious and inquisitive Men will be apt to draw from such Premises', if religion is allowed to remain (II 37).

A passage in the 'Project' based on consequence shows Swift's particular knowledge of Aristotelian logic. He says:

> The Clergy are the only Set of Men among us who constantly wear a distinct Habit from others: The Consequence of which (not in Reason, but in Fact) is this, that as long as any scandalous Persons appear in that Dress, it will continue, in some Degree, a general Mark of Contempt. Whoever happens to see a *Scoundrel in a Gown*, reeling home at Midnight, (a Sight neither *frequent* nor *miraculous*) is apt to entertain an ill Idea of the whole Order; and, at the same Time, to be extreamly comforted in his own Vices.   (II 54)

The distinction between the inferential consequence of logic and the consequence of 'fact' is a reference to a logical rule in the *Prior Analytics* (53^b5–9): 'From true premisses it is not possible to draw a false conclusion, but a true conclusion may be drawn from false premisses, true however only in respect to the fact, not to the reason'.[40] The converse of this rule is that when the conclusion is false, one or both of the premises must be false (57^a36–7), and it is from this latter rule that Swift argues, indicating not that the public's conclusion is true in *fact* as opposed to *reason* (in spite of the misleading reference to the earlier rule by Aristotle), but that the public's conclusion is false because the minor premise (every clergyman is like a single reeling clergyman at midnight) is false. The ability to expose fallacies and cleverly to perpetuate them stands any debater in good stead, as the next chapter will show.

THE LANGUAGE OF THE SYLLOGISM

Formal syllogistic reasoning is appropriate to academic disputations in which opponents face each other, advancing, analysing and demolishing syllogisms, but a steady flow of such reasoning would not do in a polemical pamphlet. The sixteenth-century Boyes disputation, in fact, shows that a *steady flow* of such reasoning was not the rule in the more lively academic disputations, in which the excitement of argument often overcame the aridity of the syllogistic form.[41] It would be unusual, however, if a writer educated in university disputations did not from time to time reveal a formal syllogistic structure in his arguments. Concerning the Pretender's chances in 1714 Swift says in defence of the Tories, 'The Logick of the highest Tories is now, that this was the Establishment they found, as soon as they arrived to a Capacity of Judging; and that they had no hand in turning out the late King, and therefore have no Crime to answer for, if it were any' (VIII 92). The syllogism is not very deeply buried in this reasoning:

If turning out James II is what was possibly a crime,

and the Tories had no hand in turning out James II,

then the Tories had no hand in what was possibly a crime.[42]

In the 'Project' for advancing religion and reforming manners Swift reasons 'backwards', as most people do, giving his conclusion first and premises last. Speaking of his scheme for reformation he says, 'Besides; all Parties would be obliged to close with so good a Work as this, for their own Reputation: Neither is any Expedient more likely to unite them. For, the most violent Party-men I have ever observed, are such as in the Conduct of their Lives have discovered least Sense of Religion, or Morality; and when all such are laid aside, at least those among them who shall be found incorrigible, it will be a Matter, perhaps of no great Difficulty to reconcile the rest' (II 58). Again the skeleton of the argument is not difficult to find:

If the most violent party men are those with the least religion or morality,

and those with the least religion or morality are excluded from preferment,

then the most violent party men are excluded from preferment.

From that conclusion it is but a short logical distance to the conclusion that with the violent party men out of the way the reconciliation of the others will be a simpler matter than before.

He argues that the time is right for such a reformation as he proposes. 'Neither is this a Matter to be deferred till a more convenient Time of Peace and Leisure: A Reformation in Mens Faith and Morals, is the best natural, as well as religious Means to bring the War to a good Conclusion. Because, if Men in Trust performed their Duty for Conscience Sake, Affairs would not suffer through Fraud, Falshood, and Neglect, as they now perpetually do: And if they believed a God and his Providence, and acted accordingly, they might reasonably hope for his Divine Assistance in so just a Cause as ours' (II 57). Although the reasoning here could be reduced to simple hypothetical syllogisms denying consequents to show that the immorality and impiety of men in high places cause delay in winning the war, the thrust of Swift's reasoning can probably best be shown in a complex hypothetical syllogism, a kind not usually found in logic manuals:

If A is B, E is F; and if C is D, G is H;
A is B, and C is D;
therefore E is F, and G is H.[43]

If men in high places are immoral, the successful prosecution of the war suffers delay through fraud, etc.;

if men in high places are impious, the successful prosecution of the war suffers delay through the withholding of Divine Assistance;

men in high places are both immoral and impious;

therefore the successful prosecution of the war suffers delay from both natural and supernatural causes.

In other places the reasoning is signalled by diction which suggests a simple categorical syllogism. The following instance draws on the fact that a syllogism is much like the geometrical axiom that two things equal to a third are equal to each other: 'I believe it may pass for a Maxim in a State, that *the Administration cannot be placed in too* few *Hands*, nor the *Legislature in too* many. Now in this material Point, the Constitution of the *English* Government far exceeds all others at this Time on the Earth; to which the present Establishment of the *Church* doth so happily agree, that I think, whoever is an Enemy to *either*, must of necessity be so to *both*' (II 18). Again, after turning an argument from one between Whigs and Tories to one between men who are 'inclined to *Peace* or *War*, to the *Last*, or the *Present Ministry*', he signals syllogistic reasoning – in this instance an enthymeme – with a reference to logical consequence: 'I am apt to think your Lordship would readily allow this, if you were not aware of the Consequence I intend to draw: For it is plain that the making of Peace and War, as well as the Choice of Ministers, is wholly in the Crown; and therefore the Dispute at present lies altogether between those who would support, and those who would

violate the Royal prerogative. This Decision may seem perhaps too
sudden and severe, but I do not see how it can be contested'
(VI 123).

The part of the reasoning omitted might be supplied thus:

If the making of peace and war and the choosing of ministers are
royal prerogatives,
and the making of peace and war and the choosing of ministers
are subjects disputed by some men,
then the royal prerogatives are subjects disputed by some men.

The bare logic in this and other passages in Swift's writings can be
discovered and analysed, but it bears about the same relation to
dialectic as words in a dictionary do to poetry. In other words, the
logic in the passage above is part of a plan, one that is well executed
to drive an opponent in a corner where he *has* to agree with Swift's
conclusion. (See the selection on 'The dilemma' in Chapter 7
below.) The testing of the validity of arguments is usually a matter
of constructing syllogisms, the science of logic, but in the *finding and
applying* of arguments lies the art of dialectic, and in an inspection
of Swift's syllogistic reasoning the two, logic and dialectic, should
not be confused. Appendix 1 below analyses the difference.

The following argument, for example, whose diction contains
signposts showing the steps in the reasoning, can readily be analysed
logically. But to stop with a logical analysis without recognising the
art of arranging the logic as manoeuvres against an opponent is to
miss the spirit of Swift's style:

My second Proposition was, that we of *Ireland* are a free People:
This I suppose, you will allow; at least, with certain Limitations
remaining in your own Breast. However, I am sure it is not
criminal to affirm; because the Words *Liberty* and *Property*, as
applied to the Subject, are often mentioned in both Houses of
Parliament, as well as in yours, and in other Courts below; from
whence it must follow, that the People of *Ireland* do, or *ought* to
enjoy all the Benefits of the common and Statute Law; such as to
be tried by Juries, to pay no Money without their own Consent,
as represented in Parliament; and the like. If this be so, and if it
be universally agreed, that a free People cannot, by Law, be
compelled to take any Money in Payment, except Gold and
Silver; I do not see why any Man should be hindered from
cautioning his Countrymen against this Coin of *William Wood*;
who is endeavouring by Fraud to rob us of that property, which

the Laws have secured. If I am mistaken, and that this Copper can be obtruded upon us; I would put the *Drapier*'s Case in another Light, by supposing, that a Person going into his Shop, should agree for Thirty Shillings Worth of Goods, and force the Seller to take his Payment in a Parcel of Copper-Pieces, intrinsically not worth above a Crown: I desire to know, whether the *Drapier* would not be actually robbed of Five and Twenty Shillings, and how far he could be said to be Master of his Property? The same Question may be applied to Rents and Debts, on Bond or Mortgage, and to all Kind of Commerce whatsoever.[44]

Here the language of logic is a part of the syllogistic structure of his dialectical argument. Like a university disputant (a questioner) he argues a second proof of the conclusion he is trying to secure. In scholastic terminology he could have said '*Probo aliter*'.[45]

7

Questioner against Answerer

THE QUESTIONER

In dialectical argument the questioner's role, generally speaking, is that of an attacker of the thesis maintained by the answerer. In the dialectical debates of Aristotle's time, for which the *Topics* and the *Sophistical Elenchi* are analyses and guides, and in the academic disputations in the schools from the Middle Ages until the nineteenth century, the questioner (opponent) had the responsibility of securing propositions, some of which were accepted as obviously true by the answerer (respondent, who defended the received opinion) and for others of which the answerer demanded syllogistic proof. The questioner accordingly framed a syllogism whose conclusion was the proposition he was trying to secure. If the syllogism seemed free of fallacy, and if the conclusion did not lie too near the contradictory of the thesis the answerer was defending, the answerer would concede the proposition which was the conclusion of the questioner's syllogism. In order to triumph in the dialectical contest, the questioner had to secure two propositions which he then used as premises in another syllogism whose (necessary) conclusion the answerer and audience agreed followed without fallacy and which was in turn irrefutable by the answerer.[1] The triumph lay in the questioner's conclusion contradicting the thesis defended by the answerer.

The excitement of the disputation often lay in the answerer's quickness of mind in perceiving the direction of the questioner's argument, so that he would know which propositions (conclusions) to concede and which to overthrow. In order to secure propositions necessary to his final argument, the questioner often had to propose fallacious syllogisms, whose fallacies it was the responsibility of the answerer to expose. The most common fallacy, that of ambiguity, called for the answerer's quickness in distinguishing the meanings of

114

the subjects and predicates of the questioner's premises, which, the answerer then showed, did not lead with validity to the conclusion the questioner originally deduced. Among many other defences against the questioner's onslaught, the answerer could simply deny a premise, which the questioner was then required to prove, or he could use the questioner's conclusion as the premise of a syllogism of his own to prove the thesis he was maintaining. Appendix 3 shows some of these stratagems in action.

The questioner's and answerer's roles are explained in the *Topics* VIII 4, with chapters 5 to 10 giving the rules of how to answer in dialectic and no comparable portion of the *Topics* giving the methods of the questioner. Chapters 3 to 15 of the *Sophistical Elenchi* explain the perpetration of fallacies, those which the questioner advances under the guard of the answerer, if possible, to overthrow his thesis. Chapters 16 to 32 explain the solution of fallacious refutations, a guide to the answerer in meeting sophistical attacks upon his thesis by the questioner.[2]

According to the last book of the *Topics*, which contains the most practical advice in Aristotle on how to argue in dialectical disputations, the exercise consists almost completely in the answerer's defence of his thesis with yes and no answers (*Top.*, 158^{a}14–22, 160^{a}33–4), a procedure which hardly contributes to a real confrontation of arguments or an exchange of ideas.[3] Socrates generally assumes the position of questioner in the dialogues of Plato and Xenophon and is dialectical in the Aristotelian sense to the extent that he reduces his answerer to silence by showing the contradictions involved in his thesis. But while Socrates is engaged for the most part in a search for truth, dialectic according to Aristotle and Aristotelian dialectic as practised in the schools from the time of the Middle Ages has about it a largely competitive cast, which means that the opponents are more often out for victory than for the truth. The *Topics* VIII, the *Prior Analytics* II 19 and the *Sophistical Elenchi* so clearly advocate the concealing of arguments in order to deceive an opponent that they have drawn many objections from those who believe that dialectic should be a tool in the search for philosophical truth.[4] Cornelius Scriblerus, the father of Martin, calls scholastic logic and metaphysics polemical arts and compares them with fencing and cudgel-playing.[5] Schopenhauer finds that he cannot use the word 'dialectic', because that term would denote logical discussion between two rational beings, who because they are rational should think in common. Since man is naturally obstinate, however, he finds more accuracy in the expression 'Controversial Dialectic' ('Eristic is only a harsher name for the same thing'), which he defines as 'the art of disputing . . . in such a way as to hold one's own, whether one is in the right or the wrong', or 'the art of getting the best of it in a dispute'.[6]

Dialectical debate cannot easily be confined to the rigid system which Aristotle in places in the *Topics* attempted[7] to formulate, as one sees from other places in the *Topics*[8] and in the *Sophistical Elenchi*.[9] In both books he distinguishes between dialectic and contentious reasoning; however, since virtually the entire *Sophistical Elenchi* is a handbook for the perpetration and solution of fallacies in dialectical argument, it seems to be an acknowledgement that a competitive rather than a philosophical spirit is often the basis of Aristotelian dialectic and that such argument cannot easily be constrained within the framework of the answerer's yes/no responses to his opponent's questions. The Socratic dialogues, upon which Aristotle partly drew for his dialectical system, and Cicero's *Tusculan Disputations* and the scholastic disputations, which drew upon Aristotle's system, show that dialectical debate could not be expected to stay within a strict system of rules governing the responses of each opponent. When competitiveness is a basic element in debate, the rules of reason and fair play are a standard of judgment only where the disputant's (and the audience's) reasoning is quick enough to catch sophistical stratagems employed by his opponent in the heat of combat. With this in mind one can return to Swift, expecting to see him employing the techniques sometimes of questioner and sometimes of answerer, usually not in the strict sense of an Aristotelian or a scholastic disputation, but obviously drawing upon elements of the dialectical debate to defeat his opponent or an opposing thesis in the pamphlet wars of his time.

Concerning those who write against – or answer – the Examiner he says, almost as if describing the role of the questioner in a disputation, 'When I have produced my Facts, and offered my Arguments, I have nothing farther to advance; it is their Office to deny and disprove; and then let the World decide' (III 76).[10] He has produced 'a hundred Instances' of the Tory objections against the long-standing practices of the Whigs, but 'no Answer hath yet been attempted' in rebuttal of the Examiner (III 115): when the papers of the opposing party answer other objections of the Examiner, they resort to distorting quotations to make their points, and Swift finds he must warn the reader against this stratagem, directing him back to the original, confident in the validity of his arguments (III 121). In the dialectical question of the existence of Partridge, which Partridge maintains and Bickerstaff challenges, the language is that of a formal disputation, complete with audience and appeal to the learned (the wise). Partridge 'is pleased to contradict absolutely' his death in response to Bickerstaff's assertion (proposition): 'This is the Subject of the present Controversy between us: . . . In this Dispute, I am sensible, the Eyes not only of *England*, but of all *Europe*, will be upon us: And the *Learned* in every Country will, I doubt not, take Part on that Side where they find most Appearance of Reason and Truth' (II 161–2).

Wotton in his *Observations upon The Tale of a Tub*, a detailed refutation of the *Tale* and of Swift, takes the part of answerer to Swift's arguments in the *Tale*, the *Battle* and the *Mechanical Operation of the Spirit*. Swift acknowledges Wotton's role by referring to him several times as 'this Answerer' and reminding him 'that to answer a Book effectually, requires more Pains and Skill, more Wit, Learning, and Judgment than were employ'd in the Writing it'.[11] The Apology to the *Tale* is in effect a *probo aliter* argument to justify the original questioner's argument, the *Tale* volume, brought against the objects of Swift's satire. The answerers in the dispute, whether vocal like Wotton or silent, are put in the position of having to maintain a thesis which, like Partridge's, is in some measure that of their own existence, or at least their conduct, which Swift feels cannot be justified by reason. The usual answerer's response is to attempt to refute the questioner's attack by exposing the fallacies, inconsistences and weak points in his argument, which Wotton does.[12]

Like much about *A Tale of a Tub*, Swift's dialectical stance can be argued from opposed positions. A reader can view him, as above, as a questioner attacking received, erroneous opinions of those who abuse learning and religion. Or one can view him as an answerer upholding received opinions of church and state, a stalwart conservative defending what is best in the heart and mind against those questioners who would overthrow tradition in the interest of modern religious dissent, subversive Roman Catholicism and contemporary trends in learning and scholarship. But Swift calls Wotton an answerer in his Apology to the *Tale* and the matter is perhaps best settled there. In fact viewing Swift in the *Tale* dialectically as a questioner, a position he implies by calling Wotton an answerer, goes some way towards justifying those who saw the book as an injudicious attack on the church. Questioners traditionally in academic disputations attacked the received opinions of church and state which answerers defended. An analysis of the *Tale* from that perspective might yield interesting conclusions about the mind and art of the early Swift, who claimed he was attacking only abuses in religion and learning.

THE OPPOSITION

Like Wotton, many other opponents had valid objections against propositions Swift tried to secure. Since in this and succeeding chapters the focus is almost entirely on argument from Swift's viewpoint, it will be useful to show at the outset that his opponents were often formidable and clever and not easily put down by Swift's stylistic and dialectical impetus. Only rarely does he follow Aristotle's advice about bringing an objection against his position.[13] Although he is 'sensible that it is not reckoned prudent in a Dispute, to make any concessions without the last Necessity' (III 145),[14] he concedes that some Tories have stressed too much the principle of passive obedience. He draws a distinction concerning the object of passive disobedience, however, and thus takes some of the force out of occasions 'when the *Whigs* quote Authors to prove it upon us'. Only after the death of Gilbert Burnet, whom Swift vigorously refuted in his 'Preface to the Bishop of Sarum's Introduction', does Swift concede that 'After all, he was a man of generosity and good-nature,[15] and very communicative; but, in his last ten years, was absolutely party-mad, and fancied he saw Popery under every bush' (v 184). Here, as with passive obedience, the concession is not unqualified. He is too quick a dialectician to shrink from defending in debate principles or premises he believes are right; it is difficult to imagine him resorting to a device Junius was later to use: 'My premises, I know, will be denied in argument, but every man's conscience tells him they are true'.[16] When Swift disputes, any ground he gives the opponent is usually ironically offered. Speaking as an Irish MP to an English MP he comments on England's 'being so very industrious to teach us to see our Interests, in a Point where we are so unable to see it our selves. This hath given us some Suspicion; and although, in my own Particular, I am hugely bent to believe, that whenever you concern your selves in our Affairs, it is certainly *for our Good*; yet I have the Misfortune to be something singular in this Belief' (II 113).[17]

The pose of dialectical superiority, however, is not always justified. 'The Conduct of the Allies', for example, received many answers from the opposition,[18] the most successful of which – the most damaging to Swift – is that by Francis Hare, Marlborough's chaplain and the leading apologist of the war party. His lengthy book, *The Allies and the Late Ministry Defended against France and the Present Friends of France* (1712), reduces to absurdity some of Swift's arguments concerning the national debt and the landed against the moneyed interests, and criticises with justice Swift's refusal to acknowledge points proven against him.[19] John Oldmixon successfully applies *argumentum ad hominem* to the 'Proposal for Correcting the English Tongue' by pointing out that in the same pamphlet in which Swift disparages panegyric he offers a panegyric to Harley (IV xv).[20]

REFUTATION

Although a questioner will more often than not resort to stratagems of dubious or unacceptable logical validity in the attempt to overthrow the answerer's thesis, he sometimes brings valid refutations to demolish proofs brought by the answerer in defence of his thesis. In the Apology to the *Tale* Swift 'will not be at the trouble of defending' about a dozen passages Wotton ('This Answerer') attacks, but he assures the reader that for the greater part 'the Reflector is entirely mistaken' (p. 12). The simple denial of his opponent's argument here contrasts with the scornful denial of the Presbyterians' right to claim merit for their services towards the restoration of Charles II and in the revolution under Prince William: 'Which Pleas I take to be the most singular, in their Kind, that ever were offered in the Face of the Sun, against the most glaring Light of Truth, and against a Continuation of Publick Facts, known to all *Europe* for twenty Years together' (XII 263). Both these denials are assertions to the contrary of his opponent's conclusions without an element of proof, and a refutation is a *proof*, or reasoning or syllogism, of the contradictory of the opponent's conclusion or thesis.[21] Closer to a proper refutation is his argument that 'when the Clause enacting a *Sacramental Test* was put in Execution, it was given out in England, that half the Justices of Peace through this Kingdom [Ireland] had laid down their Commissions; whereas, upon Examination, the whole Number was found to amount only to a Dozen or Thirteen, and those generally of the lowest Rate in Fortune and Understanding, and some of them superannuated' (II 111).

Where Swift chooses to meet Wotton's attacks on the *Tale*, he counters with three refutations, only one of which is a refutation according to the rules of logic; but the other two are hardly less effective. Wotton provides evidence to show that in three instances Swift's 'wit' (invention) is not his own. To the first instance, Wotton's accusation that Swift borrowed the names Peter, Martin and Jack from a letter by Buckingham, Swift denies ever having heard of the letter until Wotton mentioned it, says that the names are obvious choices for the sects they represent and attacks the major term of Wotton's reasoning,[22] which can be said to follow these lines:

> If the conjunction of the names Peter, Martin and Jack in the *Tale* is an idea borrowed from another source,
> and an idea borrowed from another source is not an author's own wit,
> then the conjunction of the names Peter, Martin and Jack in the *Tale* is not the author's own wit.

Swift ignores the accusation of borrowing (the middle term), which is the substance of Wotton's criticism, and directs this part of his answer to the wit (invention) inherent in the three names: 'Whatever Wit is contained in those three Names, the Author is content to give it up, and desires his Readers will substract as much as they placed upon that Account' (p. 13). This reply is a playful equivocation on the names considered as a borrowed series and as three individual names, which of course contain no inherent wit. He treats Wotton's properly-reasoned[23] argument as merely an apparent argument by drawing a distinction between the lack of wit in the *borrowing* of the three names and the lack of wit in the names *themselves*.[24] It is Swift's argument, however, which is only apparent, because his reasoning is irrelevant to the point Wotton is arguing, a dialectical stratagem deserving of adverse criticism (*Top.*, 161ᵇ25–7).

While such a dialectical analysis of Swift's reply may be true and relevant, it overlooks the humour involved in Swift's statement. He deflates Wotton's charge by his willingness to treat insignificantly what he claims as his own invention. This humorous diminution is phrased in a commercial metaphor, that of deducting from the invention-assets in Swift's account a liability he concedes while not actually conceding a debt to Buckingham. It is only to silence Wotton that he concedes what he thinks is insignificant, and in conceding wit in the sense of invention he displays it in the sense of humour.

In the second instance of Wotton's accusation that Swift's wit is not his own, Swift once again responds with a simple denial, saying he saw the 'source' Wotton cites, Buckingham's pamphlet, about ten years after the *Tale* was written and a year or two after it was published. The second part of this answer, however, is a proper refutation, which summons evidence to overthrow Wotton's conclusion: 'Nay, the Answerer overthrows this himself; for he allows the Tale was writ in 1697; and I think that Pamphlet was not printed in many Years after'.[25] Wotton's third charge of plagiarism, that Swift took the *Battle of the Books* from a French book with a comparable French title, receives a simple denial as did the first two charges. But also, as in the first two answers, Swift adds an effective retort. He quotes Wotton's brief accusation, seizes upon Wotton's hedging in the statement of it and in effect countercharges Wotton with *ignoratio elenchi* – not knowing what a refutation is:[26] 'In which Passage there are two Clauses observable: *I have been assured*; and *If I misremember not*. I desire to know, whether if that Conjecture proves an utter falsehood, those two Clauses will be a sufficient Excuse for this worthy Critick. The Matter is a Trifle; but, would he venture to pronounce at this Rate upon one of greater Moment?' (p. 14). Summarising the three charges, Swift pronounces 'two of them meer Trifles, and all three manifestly false' and objects to such treatment by critics, 'where we have not Leisure to defeat them' (p. 15), a complaint he makes as answerer in *Examiner* nos 26 and 41 (III 75, 156).

EXTENSION OF OPPONENT'S THESIS

A dialectical manoeuvre disparaged by Aristotle (161^{b}20–4, 28–9) and advocated by Schopenhauer (Stratagem 1) is the making of certain additions to the premises to bring about the desired conclusion. In 'A Letter to a Member of Parliament in Ireland', which concerns fear of the Whigs' repealing the Test, Swift extends his specific objection to cover a larger objection which is more easily attacked: 'And I believe there are too many who would talk at the same Rate if the Question were, not onely about abolishing the

Sacramental Test, but the Sacrament itself' (ɪɪ 132). Such a
manoeuvre viewed as an extension of the grounds of the argument is
condemned by Aristotle as a vitiation of argument. But viewed as a
drawing of an opponent into the kind of statement against which
one is well supplied with lines of argument, it is just another
sophistical turn of argument a questioner might hope to use under
the guard of the answerer.[27] Another instance of Swift's resorting to
the extension stratagem is at the end of the first Drapier's letter, 'To
the Shopkeepers', where he exaggerates the debased value of the
coins Wood made and sent over in 1723–4, saying that they were
anything from one-ninth to one-twelfth of the nominal value, when
no one ever seriously suggested that they were more than about a
third less in value than English copper coins from the Mint.[28]

The opposition too was capable of extending the debate. As soon
as Carteret, the new Lord-Lieutenant, reached Ireland in 1724 he
told the Privy Council that he believed the agitation against Wood's
patent was a traitorous attempt to turn the people against the
monarchy and their dependence upon England. On the strength of
this reasoning he proposed prosecuting the printer of the Drapier's
fourth letter and offering a reward for the discovery of its author.[29]

Naturally the extension of an opponent's thesis is useful in ironic
argument. If, notwithstanding all Swift has said, a bill for repealing
Christianity is to be introduced, 'I would humbly offer an
Amendment, that instead of the Word *Christianity*, may be put
Religion in general; which I conceive, will much better answer all
the good Ends proposed by the Projectors of it' (ɪɪ 37). Humorous
exaggeration is also effective. After arguing against the repealing of
the Test, showing the unreason which underlies arguments for its
repeal, he shows how the Anglicans themselves will be grouped with
the Roman Catholics after the Presbyterians gain ascendancy on the
repeal of the Test. Even now, he says, they are writing pamphlets
disclaiming toleration, so that after the abolition of the Test an
Anglican bishop may be taken for a Jesuit in the dark and will have
to disguise his chaplain as his butler (ɪɪ 121).

TURNING OF OPPONENT'S ARGUMENT

Similar to extending an opponent's argument is turning it either in a
new direction where it can more easily be demolished or back upon
the opponent.[30] The *retorsio argumenti* consists in taking the stated

premise of an opponent's enthymeme, supplying a second premise different from the understood premise left unstated by the opponent and thus reaching a different conclusion, overthrowing the opponent's reasoning.[31] Swift employs this technique when Wood shows the necessity of a greater supply of copper money in Ireland by revealing 'that several Gentlemen have been forced to Tally with their Workmen and give them Bits of Cards Sealed and Subscribed with their Names'. The Drapier cites Wood's argument and replies, 'What then? If a Physician prescribes to a Patient a *Dram* of Physick, shall a Rascal Apothecary Cram him with a *Pound*, and mix it with *Poyson*? And is not a Landlord's Hand and Seal to his own Labourers a better Security for Five or Ten Shillings, than *Wood*'s Brass Seven Times below the Real Value, can be to the Kingdom, for an Hundred and Eight thousand Pounds?'[32] Swift shifts the argument from the shortage of coinage to the value of Wood's coinage compared to the value of the landlord's credit notes which Wood had used as evidence in his own argument. Wood's position had been from the beginning to fill the need caused by a coin shortage. Swift from the beginning had turned the argument to the value of Wood's debased coins. The exchange cited here is a particularly dialectical example of Swift's major position in the debate.

Swift's turning of the argument is in some measure a *retorsio argumenti* upon Wood, but it is not as cogent as another of his turns. High churchmen, he says, are distinguished by their opinion that 'the Clergy can never be too *low*'. The Church of England man 'thinks the Maxim these Gentlemen are so fond of; that they are for an *humble* Clergy, is a very good one: And so is He; and for an humble Laity too; since Humility is a Virtue that perhaps equally befits and adorns every Station of Life' (II 8). He takes the enthymeme of the High Church laity – Humility is a Christian virtue, therefore the clergy should be humble – and turns the tables upon the High Church laity, pointing to the disparity between their *High* Church principles and the *lowness* of humility they should embrace as Christians.

The controversial passage in the 'Project' in which Swift defends hypocrisy is similarly a *retorsio argumenti*. He concedes a predicted argument (objection) and provides reasons to show that it supports his own argument:

Neither am I aware of any Objections to be raised against what I

have advanced; unless it should be thought, that the making
Religion a necessary Step to Interest and Favour, might encrease
Hypocrisy among us: And I readily believe it would. But if one in
Twenty should be brought over to true Piety by this, or the like
Methods, and the other Nineteen be only Hypocrites, the
Advantage would still be great. Besides, Hypocrisy is much more
eligible than open Infidelity and Vice: It wears the Livery of
Religion, it acknowledgeth her Authority, and is cautious of
giving Scandal.   (II 56–7)[33]

He has taken a major objection an opponent might make against his
proposal[34] and has not only prepared a defence[35] but has also taken
the objection (or conclusion) as a premise in his argument justifying
the presence of hypocrisy in national life. First the objection stated
in syllogistic form:
> If making religion a necessary step to interest and favour is a plan
> which might encourage feigned religion for worldly gain,
> and a plan which might encourage feigned religion for worldly
> gain is one which might increase hypocrisy among us,
> then making religion a necessary step to interest and favour is a
> plan which might increase hypocrisy among us.

This and other syllogisms show the elementary nature of the
reasoning buried in discursive argument. The elemental arrangement
of the reasoning reveals the positioning of the major and minor
terms and the buried spine of the argument.
   Now Swift's response using the opposing conclusion as his first
premise:
> If making religion a necessary step to interest and favour is a plan
> which will[36] increase hypocrisy among us,
> and such a plan is one which will also decrease open vice,
> then making religion a necessary step to interest and favour will
> decrease open vice.

And to boot, one twentieth of the converted hypocrites might be
converted further to true piety.

ARGUMENTA AD . . .

In 'The Answer' (1728) Swift undertakes to prove a point

> By topicks, which tho' I abomine 'em
> May serve, as arguments *ad hominem*.
> Yet I disdain to offer those,
> Made use of by detracting foes.

(ll. 47–50)

Swift as questioner has far fewer occasions to advance arguments *ad hominem* and the like than he does as answerer, as the next chapter shows. When advancing an argument for an answerer's inspection it is less appropriate to attack him with *argumenta ad hominem* or *ad personam* than to bolster one's own reasoning with *argumenta ad verecundiam* (an argument which rests on respect for authority), *ad metam* (fear), *ad misericordiam* (pity) and so forth.[37] One that Swift relies on several times as questioner is that *ad verecundiam*, either jokingly as in the *Tale* – 'To confirm this Opinion, hear the Words of the famous *Troglodyte* Philosopher' (p. 183) – or seriously, as in the first Drapier's Letter, where he speaks in an especially simple manner to the working people: 'Having said thus much, I will now go on to tell you the Judgments of some great *Lawyers* in this Matter, whom I fee'd on purpose for your Sakes, and got their *Opinions* under their *Hands*, that I might be sure I went upon good Grounds'.[38] Later in the letter, referring to the question of the people's obligation to receive mixed money instead of gold or silver, he says that 'this Proceeding is rejected by all the best Lawyers as contrary to Law'.[39]

Although the genre of *argumenta ad* originated with Locke and most of the Latin names are from the nineteenth and twentieth centuries, many of these arguments are found scattered through Aristotle, such as that *ad verecundiam*[40] and the one which Schopenhauer calls *ab utili*. Aristotle explains this second kind of argument in a thoroughly dialectical manner, showing the questioner that he can argue from either of two positions depending on the line of argument the answerer takes up. 'Argue from men's wishes and their professed opinions', he says. 'For people do not wish the same thing as they say they wish; they say what will look best, whereas they wish what appears to be to their interest: e.g. they say that a man ought to die nobly rather than to live in pleasure, and to live in honest poverty rather than in dishonourable riches; but they wish the opposite' (*Soph. El.*, 172^{b}36–173^{a}2). Accordingly an opponent who argues from people's professed opinions must be led into admitting or stating their secret wishes, and *vice versa*. Either way the opponent is led into a paradox, speaking contrary to men's professed or hidden opinions, and an adept questioner will not be slow to exploit his opponent's dilemma.

Schopenhauer, naturally, would settle upon this kind of argument because of its pessimistic view of man's better nature and its reliance upon will, which Schopenhauer exploits. He gives it as Stratagem 35 in his 'Art of Controversy':

There is another trick which, as soon as it is practicable, makes all others unnecessary. Instead of working on your opponent's intellect by argument, work on his will by motive; and he, and also the audience if they have similar interests, will at once be won over to your opinion, even though you got it out of a lunatic asylum; for, as a general rule, half an ounce of will is more effective than a hundredweight of insight and intelligence. . . . If you succeed in making your opponent feel that his opinion, should it prove true, will be distinctly prejudicial to his interest, he will let it drop like a hot potato, and feel that it was very imprudent to take it up.

His second example illustrating this stratagem is that of a landed proprietor who argues in favour of the widespread use of farm machinery over manual labour because of the former's efficiency. 'You give him to understand that it will not be very long before carriages are also worked by steam, and that the value of his large stud will be greatly depreciated; and you will see what he will say.'

Loosely speaking, a person is said to be caught in a dilemma if he is forced to choose between two unpleasant or, to him, unacceptable alternatives. A formal dilemma is a carefully constructed argument advanced to place an opponent in such a position; the difference between a dilemma in practical life and one in dialectic is that in the former one has to choose between two courses of action, or not acting, and in the latter one must choose between two admissions.[41]

Swift's references to and employment of the *argumentum ab utili* range from the serio-comic to the thoroughly serious. In the fifth Drapier's Letter he confesses his resolve never to dispute with three sorts of persons, obviously because the argument *ab utili* is too much in the opponent's favour: 'A *High-way-man* with a Pistol at my Breast, a *Troop of Dragoons* who came to plunder my House, and a *Man of the Law* who can make a Merit of accusing Me. In each of these Cases, *which are almost the same*, the best Method is to *keep out of the Way*, and the next Best is to *deliver your Money, surrender your House*, and *confess nothing*'.[42] Swift's frequent satire of lawyers rarely if ever surpasses this passage, where the witty and powerful argument addressed to the will is reinforced by the argument *ad metum* (fear) and, one might say, that *ab pecunia*. In a discussion of the controversy generated by the question of repealing the Sacramental Test, he observes that 'in Religious Quarrels, it is of little Moment how few or small the Differences are; especially when the Dispute is only about Power' (XII 247). This dispute, he implies, will be virulent because its basis is personal interest, or will. In another place he observes with some cynicism that in the Irish Parliament a minority with an ill cause has an advantage in carrying a point against a majority with a good cause. The reason is that when favour and interest are on the side of the former, they are assiduous in their attendance and zealous in gaining over proselytes. A majority with a good cause cannot compete against favour and preferment. 'In short, they want a common Principle to cement, and Motive to spirit them. For the bare acting upon a Principle from the Dictates of a good Conscience, or the Prospect of Serving the Publick, will not go very far under the present Dispositions of Mankind' (II 129). United here are three consistent elements in Swift which underlie many of the first principles from which he argues: private morality, public service and the current malfeasance of humanity. In this pamphlet[43] he regards the argument *ab utili* as an evil device geared to men's selfish interests as opposed to the public good. In the 'Project' for advancing religion and reforming manners he cleverly entwines selfish interest with public benefit so that one necessitates the other. The exposition of this somewhat cynical morality, like Mandeville's in *The Fable of the Bees*, is the moralist's perfection of the *argumentum ab utili*. 'If Virtue and Religion were established as necessary Titles to Reputation and Preferment' (II 59), new laws for the regulation of taverns, censorship of the press and the building of more churches would be seen to be but 'airy Imaginations' (II 61), because they are addressed more to the intellect by argument than to the will by motive.

ARGUMENT FROM CONTRARIES

This subject of contraries[44] and the three sections which follow are concerned with one of the most basic elements in dialectic, its binary aspect, by which a disputer can take either side of an argument brought to him and drive it to a conclusion in favour of his position, or by which he can so address an argument to an opponent that, regardless of the line of reasoning the latter chooses to take, the former can refute him, show that he is committing a fallacy, lead him into paradox or reduce him to solecism or to babbling (*Soph. El.*, 165^{b}12–22). In order to improve one's ability at arguing either side of a question, Aristotle suggests bringing objections against the thesis one is trying to maintain (*Top.*, 160^{b}14–16) and making it a practice to find arguments *pro* and *con* the same thesis.[45] Swift was naturally aware of such advice: 'It is usual for Masters to make their Boys declaim on both Sides of an Argument; and as some kinds of Assemblies are called the *Schools of Politicks*, I confess nothing can better improve political Schoolboys, than the art of making plausible or implausible harangues; against the very Opinion for which they resolve to Determine. So Cardinal *Perron*, after having spoke for an Hour to the Admiration of all his Hearers, to prove the Existence of God; told some of his Intimates, that he could have spoken another Hour, and much better, to prove the contrary' (xii 159).[46]

His use of the argument from contraries is evident in various writings, often merely in a passing remark. In the sermon 'On False Witness' he says that 'a faithful Witness, like every Thing else, is known by his contrary' (ix 188)[47] and in 'A Letter to a Young Lady' he advises the recipient to notice the foppery, affectation, vanity, folly and vice of other females in Dublin and to behave 'directly contrary to whatever they shall say or do' (ix 88). Similarly William Pulteney is shown to value the libels and scurrilities conferred on him by the worst of men because they gain for him esteem and friendship from the best (v 119). Here a connection between the contraries, one generating the other, adds a dimension to the remark beyond that of a simple contrast, of false and faithful witnesses, for example, or affected and sincere ladies.

Another self-generating contrary is the well-known passage in *Intelligencer* no. 3, where Swift asks whether he has not as much right to laugh as men have to be ridiculous, and to expose vice as another has to be vicious. 'If those who take Offence, think me in the Wrong, I am ready to change the Scene with them, whenever they please' – that is, those in a court, ministry or senate who are amply paid by pensions, titles and power. Swift as exposer expects and desires 'no other Reward, than that of laughing with a few Friends in a Corner' (xɪɪ 34). His offer to exchange places, suggestive of arguing either side of the question, has about it a whiff of dilemma, the most powerful weapon available to the dialectical disputer. The opponents in this case wish neither to be ridiculed nor to relinquish their pensions, titles and power, and therefore Swift seems to have left them no recourse but to suffer under his laughter. His manoeuvre is not tightly enough constructed to be a dilemma, however; there are too many variables. Only those who take offence are caught in the trap, and an exchange of places is not really in question. The dilemma here is more rhetorical than logical, yet no less effective in achieving the goal it attempts.

Another mild dilemma arrived at through argument from contraries is indirectly related to Swift, occurring as it does in the final resolution of the Wood's Halfpence affair. Wood surrendered his patent to supply coinage in August 1725 and the Irish House of Commons drew up and unanimously accepted an address of thanks to the king in September. The not-so-submissive Lords, however, debated two or three days over the exact form the address of thanks should take, finally expressing their gratitude for the king's 'great Wisdom' in having the patent surrendered. The Archbishop of Dublin, who proposed the inclusion of those two words in the compliment, could not help pointing out its humorous irony once the wording was accepted. Dr Coghill in a letter to Edward Southwell, 9 October 1725, describes the scene: as soon as the vote on the archbishop's amendment ('great Wisdom') was passed,

he said to the Primate, who sat next him, that he had clinched the matter, for if it was Wisdom to gett the Patent surrendered, it must have been the contrary to have granted it, this gave the alarm, and upon the debate of the Adresse, after it was brought into the house, it was urged that this word was moved as an affront either to his Majesty or his ministers, and therefore would be improper and indecent to use it in an adresse of thanks for the greatest act of favour that cou'd be done us, on the other side it was urged that no body could deny his Majesties wisdom in all his actions, that the word was inserted by order of the House and could not be struck out, and that nothing could be a greater affront than putting a negative on that word, after three days debate, the word was left out 12 affirmative, 21 negative.[48]

The suggestion that 'political Schoolboys' should argue 'against the very Opinion for which they resolve to Determine' (XII 159) had been advised earlier by an ingenious doctor in the school of political projectors at the Academy of Lagado, although his was a reverse procedure. His recommendation was 'that every Senator in the great Council of a Nation, after he had delivered his Opinion, and argued in the Defence of it, should be obliged to give his Vote directly contrary; because if that were done, the Result would infallibly terminate in the Good of the Publick' (iii 6). The buried premise concerning man's selfishness shows that this is an argument *ab utili* as well as an ironic argument from contraries. Gulliver hears a more subtle argument *ab utili* from contraries in the same political school at Lagado, concerning the most effective means of raising money without grieving the subject. The first professor had suggested a universal tax upon vices and folly, the levy on each man to be determined by a jury of his neighbours. 'The second was of an Opinion directly contrary; to tax those Qualities of Body and Mind for which Men chiefly value themselves; the Rate to be more or less according to the Degrees of excelling; the decision whereof should be left entirely to their own Breast' (iii 6). The implication is that vanity in this instance would be as strong as is self-interest in the 'Project' for advancing religion and reforming manners; in each instance a would-be dilemma is evaded through pride, which produces better results, whether revenues or virtue and piety, and obviates the trouble and expense of juries of neighbours, new laws for regulating taverns, censoring the press and building churches.

Another example of argument from contraries shows the value of an ability to argue from the contrary not of an opponent's thesis but of one's own. A complaint was made to the king and council in Sweden that the large number of Scots pedlars in the kingdom might prove dangerous by joining with any discontented party. The prime minister, bribed by the Scots to defend their interests,

> told the Councill, he was assured they were but a few inconsiderable People, that lived honestly and poorly, and were not of any Consequence. Their Enemyes offered to prove the contrary. Whereupon an Order was made to take their Numbers, which was found to amount, as I remember, to about thirty

thousand. The Affair was again brought before the Council, and great Reproaches made the first Minister, for his ill Computation; who presently took the other handle, said he had reason to believe the number yet greater than what was returned; and then gravely offered to the King's Consideration, whether it were safe to render desperate so great a Body of able Men, who had little to lose, and whom any hard Treatment would onely serve to unite into a Power capable of disturbing, if not destroying the Peace of the Kingdom. And so they were suffered to continue.   (II 134–5)

An instance of Swift's offering to argue either 'handle' occurs in 'A Letter Concerning the Sacramental Test', where, describing the immigration of the Scots into northern Ireland and exaggerating the Scottish threat to the national religion and to the House of Lords if the Test is repealed, he says that the Scots, or dissenters, 'care not three Pence whether there be any Church or no; yet, because they pretend to argue from Conscience as well as Policy and Interest, I thought it proper to understand and answer them accordingly' (II 118). The distinction between arguing from conscience on the one hand and from policy and interest on the other is the same as a dialectical stratagem described by Aristotle as the one most widely applicable for leading men into paradoxical statements. It consists in opposing the standards of nature and law, meeting the man who argues from the standard of one with an argument from the standard of the other and thus either refuting him or leading him into paradox. The opposition comes about because the standard of nature can be seen as the truth and that of law is the opinion of the majority, and the two often disagree (*Soph. El.*, 173ª7–30). Socrates is said by Callicles to use this method of argument:

For the truth is, Socrates, that you, who pretend to be engaged in the pursuit of truth, are appealing now to the popular and vulgar notions of right, which are admirable by convention, not by nature. Convention and nature are generally at variance with one another: and hence, if a person is too modest and timid to say what he thinks, he is compelled to contradict himself. Perceiving this subtlety, you play fast and loose in your arguing; when a speaker is stating his case on the basis of convention, you insinuate a question based on the rule of nature; and if he is talking the rule of nature, you slip away to convention.

(*Gorgias*, 482e–83a)

In the *Drapier's Letters* Swift argues from law (convention)[49] and elsewhere shifts to nature (reason) for a better ground for argument: 'Therefore to lay aside the Point of Law, I would only put the Question, whether in *Reason* and *Justice*[50] it would not have been proper, in an Affair upon which the *Welfare of a Kingdom depends*, that the said Kingdom should have received timely Notice, and the Matter not be carried on between the Patentee and the *Officers of the* CROWN, who were to be the *only* Gainers by it' (p. 47).

THE DIALECTICAL QUESTION: EITHER/OR

A dialectician should pursue his argument by the question and answer method, avoiding questions like 'What is it?' which are not dialectical. The question should instead be one offering two alternatives, so that the division exhausts the genus which is the subject of the question; the answerer then will be faced with choosing one of two contradictories: for example, 'Should a man obey his parents in everything, or disobey them in everything?'[51] In this way the questioner can often predict the two possible answers his opponent will make, and in practice he can often determine the exact response the answerer will make by posing his question in such a way that one of the alternatives is immediately seen to oppose the views of the majority and the wise, as in the question whether to obey one's parents in everything or nothing.[52] In the *Tale* Swift plays with the concept of the dialectical question, based on an excluded middle, when he asks 'Whether a Tincture of Malice in our Natures, makes us fond of furnishing every bright Idea with its Reverse; Or, whether Reason reflecting upon the Sum of Things, can, like the Sun, serve only to enlighten one half of the Globe, leaving the other half, by Necessity, under Shade and Darkness' (p. 158). Later, in a passage of ironic philosophising, his dialectical question does not exclude a middle: 'the Question is only this; Whether Things that have Place in the *Imagination*, may not as properly be said to *Exist*, as those that are seated in the *Memory*; which may justly be held in the Affirmative, and very much to the Advantage of the former, since This is acknowledged to be the *Womb* of Things, and the other allowed to be no more than the *Grave*' (p. 172). In the *Battle of the Books* Aesop's clarification of the either/or nature of the dispute leads to combat (p. 235).[53]

In other places Swift seriously poses dialectical questions in which the either/or aspect is obvious. In his sermon 'On the Trinity' the contrast is glaring in order that he can easily make his point: 'Thus, we see, the Matter is brought to this Issue; we must either believe what God directly commandeth us in Holy Scripture, or we must wholly reject that Scripture and the Christian Religion which we pretend to profess: But this, I hope, is too desperate a Step for any of us to make' (IX 165). In another sermon, 'On the Poor Man's Contentment', he poses a dialectical question and answers it:

> The great Question, long debated in the World is, whether the Rich or the Poor are the least miserable of the two? It is certain, that no rich Man ever desired to be poor, and that most, if not all, poor Men desire to be rich; from whence it may be argued, that, in all Appearance, the Advantage lieth on the Side of the Wealth, because both Parties agree in preferring it before Poverty. But this Reasoning will be found to be false: For, I lay it down as a certain Truth, that God Almighty hath placed all Men upon an equal Foot, with respect to their Happiness in this World, and the Capacity of attaining their Salvation in the next; or, at least, if there be any Difference, it is not the Advantage of the Rich and Mighty. (IX 190)[54]

The question posed is suitable for Swift's purposes and his answer is rhetorically and theologically effective. But from a logical point of view a middle is not excluded, because generally speaking – and that is the basis of dialectic – men agree that while wealth may not bring happiness, at least some relief from the hardships of poverty tends to make one less miserable. His mentioning men's hopes for salvation in the next world is a diversion.

OFFERING TWO UNACCEPTABLE EXTREMES

As a kind of prologue to Swift's use of the dilemma, one might look at his tendency to place his opponents in a quasi-dilemmatic predicament. The manoeuvre is more rhetorical than dialectical because it asserts, or attempts to impose upon an opponent, two choices which are unacceptable to Swift[55] but not necessarily unacceptable to the opponent. In the *Tale*, for example, the refined and sublime agent of happiness, 'the possession of being well deceived', is also called 'The Serene Peaceful State of being a Fool

among Knaves' (p. 174). Although the opposition of fool and knaves
has been seen as two unacceptable extremes with a *via media*
implied,[56] one might with reason question whether a happily
deceived person, before he is undeceived, considers himself a fool.
After he is undeceived – which might follow the pointing out to him
of the cause of his happiness – it is likely that he would no longer be
happy, according to the given cause of happiness (perpetual
deception). Swift's happy fool is foolish to Swift, but not to the
happy person himself. Similarly Jack and Peter, or Calvinists and
Roman Catholics, are unacceptable religious extremes to Swift, but
Calvinism is acceptable to most Calvinists and Roman Catholicism
to most Roman Catholics. Swift's pointing out Jack's 'huge Personal
Resemblance to his Brother *Peter*' (p. 199) in disposition, shape,
size and mien has the appearance of a dilemma in offering two
extreme positions with the middle way of Martin, or the Church of
England, implied. Neither Jack nor Peter, however, is caught in a
dilemma: that is, neither is offered alternative positions, one of
which he must choose, with the result that no matter which he
chooses he will be committed to a conclusion that is unacceptable to
him.[57]

THE DILEMMA

The dilemma[58] was not analysed as a distinct kind of argument until
the third century BC,[59] so that when one encounters elements of the
dilemma in Aristotle prior to that time they are called paradox,
usually in the context of leading one's opponent into paradox.
Preceding pages have shown Aristotle's advocacy of two ways to
lead an answerer into paradox and Swift's employment of them: the
opposition of professed opinions and secret wishes, and the
opposition of nature and law. Another way similar to leading an
answerer into opposing the views of the majority *and* the wise (for
example, whether to obey one's parents in everything or nothing) is
to lead him into a position in which he must oppose the majority *or*
the wise. If he speaks according to the views of the philosophers,
lead him into opposing the views of the majority, and if he speaks
according to the views of the majority, lead him into opposing those
of the philosophers. For example: 'Ought one to obey the wise or
one's father? Ought one to do what is expedient or what is just? Is it

preferable to suffer injustice or to do an injury?' (*Soph. El.*, 173ª19–
30).

To Aristotle, these questions are a questioner's basis for 'an
Argument equally conclusive by contrary suppositions'[60] or
'an Argumentation of two Members, both which have some
Inconvenience belonging to them'[61] or, as Aristotle expresses it, a
basis for drawing an opponent's argument into paradox (*Soph. El.*,
172ᵇ11). Post-Aristotelian logicians in antiquity seem to have been
intrigued by the dilemma, if one can judge from the best examples
of various kinds of dilemmas in modern logics which were passed
down from the ancients. Logics of the sixteenth and seventeenth
centuries often devote only small space to the dilemma, generally a
definition ('*cornutus syllogismus*', or horned syllogism) followed by
a classical example, often the dilemma of marriage, where the
choice is shown to be between a fair and common wife and a
deformed and faithful one.[62] Whately points out that the accounts
usually given of the dilemma in logic manuals are 'singularly
perplexed and unscientific',[63] primarily because they discuss subject
matter to the exclusion of form.

Dilemmas can be said to take four forms, the simple and complex
constructive and the simple and complex destructive, some of which
Swift employs.[64] They can be evaded or defeated in three ways: by
going between the 'horns', by grasping the horns or by rebutting
with a counter-dilemma. One of the most popular examples of the
rebuttal or *retorsio* is that mentioned by Gellius (*Noctes Atticae*,
v 10), in which the dilemma advanced by Protagoras to his pupil
Euathlus is turned by the latter back upon the teacher.[65] This and
another classical dilemma are shown below in connection with
Swift's dilemmas.

A logical description of a dilemma is a syllogism or argument
whose major premise is a compound hypothetical proposition and
whose minor premise is a disjunctive proposition, which either
affirms alternatively the antecedents of the major premise or denies
alternatively its consequents. Definitions of a dilemma in seventeenth-
century logics are usually not as full as the considerably abbreviated
definition just given. They do, however, often mention its hypothetical
and disjunctive qualities: '*Hypotheticus Redundans* dicitur Dilemma.
Est autem *Dilemma* Argumentatio, quae facta disjunctione
membrorum. . .'.[66] If the disjunctive proposition excludes a middle
(exhausts the possibilities on either side) it often places the answerer

against whom it is advanced in a position of having to accept the consequences of the compound hypothetical proposition.

An example will show the technique, one from a seventeenth-century author educated at Gonville and Caius College, Cambridge, and later fellow of All Souls College, Oxford, Jeremy Taylor, whose *Rule and Exercises of Holy Living* (1650) contains several dilemmas. If sense, experience, grace and reason cannot convince a man that he should bear his troubles patiently, time will provide a cure. But Taylor does not want his reader to endure long suffering under misfortune, so he returns to the question of reasoning oneself out of the suffering: 'then consider, do you mean to mourn always, or but for a time? If always, you are miserable and foolish. If for a time, then why will you not apply those reasons to your grief at first with which you will cure it at last?' (ch. II sec. 6).[67] Put into syllogistic form, the reasoning would be:

If you mean to mourn under misfortune always, you are foolish because such a course is unnecessary and [Taylor implies] impossible;

if you mean to mourn under misfortune but for a time, you are foolish not to advance the ultimate reason for ceasing to mourn to the present;

either you mean to mourn always or for a time;

therefore you are foolish for mourning unnecessarily.[68]

The argument takes the form of a simple constructive dilemma:

If A is B, E is F; and if C is D, E is F;

either A is B, or C is D;

therefore E is F.

In another place in the same section Taylor advances a complex constructive dilemma when speaking of 'Means and Habits for procuring Contentedness':

When a sadness lies heavy upon thee, remember that thou art a Christian designed to the inheritance of Jesus; and what dost thou think concerning thy great fortune, thy lot and portion of eternity? Dost thou think thou shalt be saved or damned? Indeed if thou thinkest thou shalt perish, I cannot blame thee to be sad, till thy heartstrings crack; but then why art thou troubled at the loss of thy money? What should a damned man do with money, which in so great a sadness it is impossible for him to enjoy? Did ever any man upon the rack afflict himself because he had received a cross answer from his mistress? or call for the particulars of a purchase upon the gallows? If thou dost really believe thou shalt be saved, consider how great is that joy, how infinite is that change, how unspeakable is the glory, how excellent is the recompense, for all the sufferings in the world, if they were all laden upon the spirit? So that, let thy condition be what it will, if thou considerest thy own present condition, and comparest it to thy future possibility, thou canst not feel the present smart of a cross fortune to any great degree, either because thou hast a far bigger sorrow, or a far bigger joy.[69]

The dilemma takes this form:
  If A is B, E is F; and if C is D, G is H;
  either A is B, or C is D;
  therefore either E is F or G is H.
Stripped of Taylor's style the argument goes like this:
  If you believe you are to be damned, you should be too miserable to fret over worldly cares;
  if you believe you are to be saved, you should be too joyous to fret over wordly cares;
  either you believe you are to be damned or saved;
  therefore you should be either too miserable or too joyous to fret over worldly cares.
Swift has few references to dilemma in practical life[70] and he only infrequently uses them in argument, but those he does use have more bite to them than those we have seen in Taylor, as might be expected from a dialectical satirist compared with a rhetorical moralist. Two dilemmas in 'The Conduct of the Allies', for example, are complex destructive, intended more to disparage opponents than to persuade readers into a particular course of action. Swift shows how expensive the ten years' war has been, with the nation going three to four million pounds more into debt every year, and he asserts that the debt will double and treble if the war continues, so that it will be impossible to repay. 'This Computation, so easy and trivial as it is almost a shame to mention, Posterity will think that those who first advised the War, had either not the Sense or the Honesty to consider' (vi 19). Whately points out the conciseness of some arguments, a premise sometimes being suggested by a single word in an exhortation serving as a conclusion.[71] So it is with Swift's remark, where the two unpleasant choices in the conclusion – lack of intelligence or lack of honesty – are parts of the disjunctive conclusion of a complex destructive dilemma. In the complex

destructive dilemma, the minor premise alternatively denies the consequents in the major premise:

If A is B, E is F; and if C is D, G is H;
either E is not F, or G is not H;
therefore either A is not B, or C is not D.

In hypothetical-disjunctive syllogistic form Swift's reasoning would look like this:

If the Queen's Whig advisers were honest, they would not have given obviously bad advice designedly;
if they were competent, they would not have done so undesignedly;
they gave obviously bad advice either designedly or undesignedly;
therefore they were either dishonest or incompetent.

In proper dilemma technique he has left his opponents only alternatives which are distasteful to them.

Later in the pamphlet Swift comments on the first article of the Offensive Alliance with Portugal, which he shows is not at all in Britain's interest: 'They who were guilty of so much Folly and Contradiction, know best whether it proceeded from Corruption or Stupidity' (VI 25). Again he has offered only choices between dishonesty and lack of intelligence,[72] a dialectical manoeuvre which again could be put into syllogistic form. So too could another remark. In 'The Conduct of the Allies' he commented on the possibility of a future altering of the succession because of tyranny or some other dire necessity in a passage which provoked much debate and several answers, including a judgment of treason by the Lord Chief Justice. Swift defends the passage in 'Some Remarks on the Barrier Treaty': 'I am humbly of Opinion, that there are two Qualities necessary to a Reader, before his Judgment should be allowed: these are, common *Honesty*, and *common Sense*; and that no Man could have misrepresented that Paragraph in my Discourse, unless he were utterly destitute of one or both' (VI 93). While this remark might have the appearance of a dilemma because of the disjunction in the last clause, it imputes both lack of honesty and lack of intelligence to the opponents and therefore does not place them in the position of having to choose one or the other: they can choose one or the other or both. Because of the remark's loosening of the strictly formal dilemmatic form, what it gains in the way of abuse it loses in the way of logical force.

The denying of both parts of a conclusion, which thus would have to be conjunctive rather than disjunctive, can be effective in argument, but it is not the technique of the dilemma. Sprat has a remark, for example, in which he speaks of Christian doctrine: 'This is the place in which the Peripatetic *Philosophy* has long triumph'd: But I cannot imagine on what right. The spiritual and supernatural part of *Christianity* no *Philosophy* can reach: And in the plain things there is no need of any at all: So it is excluded on both accounts'.[73] By excluding both alternatives he has not forced his opponents (the Peripatetics) to make a choice of two unpleasant alternatives, but has dismissed them from the ground of the argument altogether. In a passage related to the same subject Swift advises against trying to explain the mysteries of the Christian religion: 'to me there seems to be a manifest Dilemma in the Case: If you explain them, they are Mysteries no longer; if you fail, you have laboured to no Purpose' (IX 77). Rather than a conclusion he has given the major premise of a dilemma, a compound hypothetical proposition. One can easily supply the rest:

either you will explain them or you will fail;
therefore you will have no Christian mysteries or you will have
   laboured to no purpose.

The import of the first conditional proposition in the major premise seems to suggest an obscurantist position but the dilemma, such as it is, is a valid complex constructive dilemma, like the second one of Taylor given above.

As with Swift's arguments secular and theological, so with parts of the New Testament: the well-known force and appeal of the style is sometimes the result of dialectical stratagems long unfamiliar to modern readers. Swift's dilemma about the Christian mysteries, for example, is reminiscent of one in Acts (5:34–40) where a Pharisee lawyer offers advice to the Jewish council concerning the treatment of the apostles in the form of the major premise of a dilemma: if their work and teaching is of men, it will come to nothing; if of God, you cannot overthrow it. The distinction between the work of men and the work of God bears a resemblance to that between the opposition of law and nature in the *Sophistical Elenchi*, 173^{a}7–18. A more pointed dilemma, and one which better shows the opposition of God and men, occurs in Luke (20:1–8) where Jesus asks the chief priests, scribes and elders whether the baptism of John was from heaven or from men. 'And they reasoned with themselves, saying, If we shall say, From heaven; he will say, Why then believed you him not? But and if we say, Of men; all the people will stone us: for they be persuaded that John was a prophet. And they answered, that they could not tell whence it was.'

A classical example of a dilemma will serve to point out an aspect of the preceding dilemma of Swift's and the one to follow: this example, like both Swift's, concerns the opposition of the wise and the majority (*Soph. El.*, 173ᵃ7–30), which in turn is reflected in the opposition of the gods and men. The traditional example is that of an Athenian mother who tried to persuade her son not to enter public life:

If you say what is just, men will hate you;
if you say what is unjust, the gods will hate you;
but you must say either the one or the other;
therefore you will be hated.

This example is invariably followed by the son's rebuttal:

If I say what is just, the gods will love me;
if I say what is unjust, men will love me;
but I must say either the one or the other;
therefore I shall be loved.

The rebuttal is one of three ways of evading or destroying the force of a dilemma, and Swift gives one of the three in response to the following dilemma in *Gulliver's Travels*. Explaining English law to his Houyhnhnm Master, Gulliver gives an example of a neighbour who might hire a lawyer

to prove that he ought to have my Cow from me. I must then hire another to defend my Right; it being against all Rules of *Law* that any Man should be allowed to speak for himself. Now in this Case, I who am the true Owner lie under two great Disadvantages. First, my Lawyer being practiced almost from his Cradle in defending Falshood; is quite out of his Element when he would be an Advocate for Justice, which as an Office unnatural, he always attempts with great Awkwardness, if not Ill-will. The second Disadvantage is, that my Lawyer must proceed with great Caution: Or else he will be reprimanded by the Judges, and abhorred by his Brethren, as one who would lessen the Practice of the Law. And therefore I have but two Methods to preserve my *Cow*. The first is, to gain over my Adversary's Lawyer with a double Fee; who will then betray his Client, by insinuating that he hath Justice on his Side. The second Way is for my Lawyer to make my Cause appear as unjust as he can; by allowing the *Cow* to belong to my Adversary; and this if it be skilfully done, will certainly bespeak the Favour of the Bench.   (iv 5)

The 'two great Disadvantages' under which Gulliver lies can be put syllogistically as a formal dilemma,[74] one which is complex constructive:

> If A is B, E is F; and if C is D, G is H;
> either A is B, or C is D;
> therefore either E is F, or G is H.

Or,

> If the lawyer pleads for justice poorly, which is to be expected from corrupt lawyers, he may lose the case through a poor performance;
> if he pleads for justice well, he may lose the case by prejudicing the corrupt judge against him;
> either he must plead poorly or well;
> therefore he is in danger of losing the case either because of his own corruption or because of that of the judge.

The form of the dilemma is valid, and it can be rebutted by one equally valid which, on first consideration, might seem to be the horns of Gulliver's two methods of preserving his cow. The counter-dilemma would take this form:

> If the lawyer pleads for justice poorly, he may win the case by prejudicing the corrupt judge in his favour;
> if he pleads for justice well, he may win the case through a superior performance;
> either he must plead poorly or well;
> therefore either he may win through the judge's prejudice or through a superior performance.

The conclusion of a counter-dilemma, one can see, contradicts or overthrows the conclusion of the original dilemma. Swift's complex constructive dilemma can be met, as shown above, by transposing the major premise's consequents and changing their quality from affirmative to negative. Schematically the counter-dilemma looks like this:

> If A is B, G is not H; and if C is D, E is not F;
> but either A is B, or C is D;
> therefore either G is not H, or E is not F.

Because this rebuttal, like the original it answers, concerns pleading a court case, Swift perhaps considered using such a rebuttal, reminiscent as it is of the classical courtroom dilemma and rebuttal of Protagoras and Euathlus mentioned in Marsh and given in Burgersdicius, both of whose logics Swift would have studied at

Trinity College. Protagoras, the fifth-century Sophist, specialised in the art of pleading before juries, and he agreed to train Euathlus as a lawyer although the latter could not immediately pay the required tuition. The arrangement was that Euathlus would pay after winning his first case, which he so long delayed undertaking that Protagoras brought suit against his former pupil for the tuition money, presenting his case in court with a seemingly unanswerable dilemma:

> If Euathlus loses this case, he must pay me (by the judgment of the court);
>
> if he wins this case, he must pay me (according to our agreement);
>
> he must either lose or win this case;
>
> therefore Euathlus must pay me.

Euathlus, who had profited by his instruction under the Sophist, offered the court this counter-dilemma in rebuttal:

> If I lose this, my first case, I shall not have to pay Protagoras (according to our agreement);
>
> if I win this case, I shall not have to pay (by the judgment of the court);
>
> I must either win or lose this case;
>
> therefore I do not have to pay Protagoras.

This rebuttal, like the one given above which Swift might have used, is logically valid because its conclusion actually contradicts the conclusion of the original dilemma. In the case of the Athenian mother and her politically-minded son, the conclusion of the counter-dilemma only apparently rebuts the original dilemma. The two conclusions are in fact compatible, because the second does not *contradict* the first. The contradictory of the first would be: 'Men will love me and the gods will love me'.

The idea of using such a counter-dilemma as the one above almost certainly would have presented itself to Swift, because the familiar Protagoras–Euathlus example is remarkably close to his subject and to the form his subject takes in the cow-ownership litigation in *Gulliver's Travels*. But his stratagem is not a *taking* of the dilemma *by the horns*, which would be showing that one or both of the consequents in the major premise do not follow from the antecedents. Rather than rebut, Swift chooses to evade the dilemma by escaping between the horns, that is, by showing that the minor premise, the disjunction, is incomplete and that another alternative remains. He adds his own kind of minor (disjunctive) premise:

> either the adversary's lawyer is bribed to plead for justice and thus *he* will be inept and unwilling and may lose the case, or the

defendant's lawyer pleads the opposite of the truth and thus may win the favour of the judge.

By supplying this alternative instead of a formal rebuttal, Swift evades the positive-sounding consequence of the second conditional proposition in the major premise of the counter-dilemma: that is, that he may win the case through a superior performance. Such a possibility would undermine the almost absolute system of corruption Swift has described. The closest he comes to an admission of an uncorrupt alternative in the case is the consequent of the first hypothetical proposition in the original dilemma: that he may lose the case through a poor performance. The implication is damaging to the system of corruption he is giving, but the statement, being negatively expressed, suppresses the just alternative. To admit in a formal counter-dilemma that the laywer may win the case through a superior performance would be far more damaging to the satire of corruption. Swift seems to have rejected such a counter-dilemma. A rebutting counter-dilemma in this case would in fact have to be advanced by Swift's opponent, someone defending the legal system, not by the adversary's lawyer, and therefore Swift himself would seem to be defeated. By offering an escape between the horns of the dilemma, he remains in control of the satire, underscoring the corruption in the practice of law.

8

Answerer against Questioner

THE ANSWERER

The beginning of the preceding chapter explained briefly the roles of answerer and questioner in dialectical debates in Ancient Greece and in university disputations. Two additional remarks in the eighth book of Aristotle's *Topics* help to explain Swift's attitude as answerer in his writings. One is advice on the four ways an answerer prevents a questioner from working his argument to a conclusion:

(1) he can demolish the point which produces the falsehood in the questioner's argument;

(2) he can ignore the questioner's argument and without demolishing it attack the questioner himself;

(3) he can object to the manner in which the questions are asked (or in which the argument is advanced), if the questioner is pursuing badly the conclusion he is trying to secure; and

(4) he can make an objection which would take the questioner more time to respond to than time is allowed for the discussion.

Of these four only the first is a solution to the false reasoning of the questioner: the other three are just hindrances and stumbling-blocks to prevent him from reaching the conclusion he desires (161^{a}1–15). Swift employs the first three regularly, and the fourth can be seen at the end of the section on 'Refutation' in the preceding chapter and to some degree later in this section. The other remark of Aristotle, that 'in a competition the business of the questioner is to appear by all means to produce an effect upon the other, while that of the answerer is to appear unaffected by him' (159^{a}30–2), seems to suggest a passive defence by the answerer, but to appear unaffected an answerer might need a Swiftian sense of dialectical superiority. Like Cicero he shows his dialectical if not his satirical skill better in the defence, as answerer, than in the attack, as questioner; but this does not mean that he cannot be aggressive and devastating when he champions principles he believes need his support in the face of the challenges of Whigs, deists, dissenters, freethinkers, the moneyed as opposed to the landed interests, and Moderns, both literary and scientific, who would overthrow the supremacy of the Ancients.

Swift took over the writing of the *Examiner* with issue no. 13 (2 November 1710) and continued the weekly essays, published on Thursdays, until no. 45 (14 June 1711). In these papers, especially, he argues as answerer to questioners attacking the establishment, the Tory party and the Church of England.[1] 'I must remember my Character', he says, 'that I am an *Examiner* only, and not a *Reformer*' (III 82), that is, that he is an answerer, examining the fallacious arguments of the Whig opposition: 'When this Paper was first undertaken, one Design, among others, was to *examine* some of those Writings so frequently published with an evil Tendency, either to Religion or Government.' Should one question the identification of examiner and answerer, Swift makes the matter clear on the same page: 'I know not whether I shall have any Appetite to continue this Work much longer; if I do, perhaps some Time may be spent in exposing and overturning the false Reasonings of those who engage their Pens on the other Side' (III 156). Swift's treatment of the opposition is in line with the plan of the *Sophistical Elenchi*, thirty-one of whose thirty-four chapters are given to explaining the perpetation of fallacies by the questioner and their solution by the answerer.[2] The answerer's role as solver of fallacies probably accounts for the relative scarcity of irony and satire in Swift as an answerer. Most of his ironic satire is generated when he tries to secure propositions as questioner, as the Author in the *Tale*, the *Battle* and the *Mechanical Operation of the Spirit* and as Gulliver advancing accounts and ideas to the King of Brobdingnag and the Master Houyhnhnm, who expose the fallacies in what Gulliver says. The answerer is not excluded from advancing fallacies, however. Sometimes a false proposition advanced by a questioner must be demolished by means of false propositions, because some men believe what is not the fact more firmly than the truth.[3] But as the many examples in this chapter will show, Swift as answerer is usually seriously trying to overthrow an opponent's sound reasoning or to expose his fallacious reasoning, or he is trying to win over the minority to the right path. His is the majority's opinion, he assumes.

In the *Examiner* he draws the line of the dispute clearly between his side, the Harley ministry, and the late Whig ministry. 'If you write in Defence of a fallen Party, . . . you have little more to do than carp and cavil at those who hold the Pen on the other Side. . . . You may affirm and deny what you please, without Truth or Probability, since it is but Loss of Time to contradict you' (III 75). He emphasises his role as answerer, defending the right side: 'It is notorious enough that the Writers on the other Side were the first Agressors' (III 68). It is they who are responsible for the invectives daily published against the Harley ministry (III 100) and against the Examiner himself, but, he says with the assurance of one on the side in power, he will not lose time 'in vindicating my self against their Scurrilities, much less in retorting them' (III 156). One reason he will not respond to railings against himself, such as those of the *Medley*, the best Whig paper next to the *Observator* (III 154), is that such a course would have diverted his design, which is to be of public use (III 153). Although such a remark is natural coming from Swift, it is less convincing as a reason for his aloofness than simply being on the side of the majority, so great an advantage for a dialectician that one who finds himself in that position hardly needs to argue: 'alas, I lye under another Discouragement of much more Weight: I was very unfortunate in the choice of my Party when I set up to be a Writer: Where is the Merit, or what Opportunity to discover our Wit, our Courage, or our Learning, in drawing our Pens for the Defence of a Cause, which the Queen and both Houses of Parliament, and nine Parts in ten of the Kingdom, have so unanimously embraced?' (III 30). The irony is so broad and lame that it passes for literal truth.

In other pamphlets besides the *Examiner* papers, written about the same time, he maintains his stance as answerer for the Tory ministry, as in his reference to overthrowing an 'idle affected Opinion'[4] of the opposition and in his complaint of the labour involved in an answerer's task, which requires refutations, arguments and disproof: 'This is the old foolish Slander so frequently flung upon the Peace, and as frequently refuted. These factious Undertakers of the Press write with great Advantage; they strenuously affirm a thousand Falsehoods, without Fear, Wit, Conscience, or Knowledge; and we, who answer them, must be at the Expence of an Argument for each: After which, in the very next Pamphlet, we see the same Assertions produced again, without the least notice of what hath been said to disprove them.'[5] Of Steele he says, 'he allows us to be his *Criticks*, but not his *Answerers*; and he is altogether in the right, for there is in his Letter much to be *Criticised*, and little to be *Answered*.'[6] The turning of Steele's assertion back on him is a practically unanswerable dialectical refutation, the *retorsio argumenti*. In the most dialectical of the Drapier's Letters, the third, which answers a pamphlet of the opposition, he points out his role as an answerer exposing fallacious arguments: 'I think I may affirm that I have fully answered every Paragraph in the *Report*, which although it be not unartfully drawn, and is perfectly in the Spirit of a Pleader who can find the most plausible Topicks in behalf of his Client, yet there was no great Skill required to detect the many Mistakes contained in it.'[7]

THE OPPOSITION

Swift's opponents were not always as poor in argument as he tried to make them appear: an example is Matthew Tindal in *The Rights of the Christian Church*, published in two editions in 1706 and a third in 1707, which Swift partly answered in his 'Remarks' the next year – but he never published his reply. His 'Remarks' on Tindal's book, which is a disguised attack upon the idea of a national, state-supported church, are often refutations of valid arguments or solutions of fallacious ones, but in places Tindal remains unscathed by Swift's attempts to answer him. Swift quotes from Tindal, for example: 'I cannot see but it is contrary to the Rules of Charity to exclude Men from the Church, &c.', and replies, 'All this turns upon the falsest Reasoning in the World. So if a Man be imprisoned for stealing a Horse, he is hindered from other Duties: And, you might argue, that a Man who doth ill, ought to be more diligent in minding other Duties and not be debarred from them. It is for Contumacy and Rebellion against that Power in the Church, which the Law hath confirmed. So a Man is outlawed for a Trifle, upon Contumacy' (II 92). What Tindal says on pages 88–90, however, shows that he has the better argument. For example: 'What can be more unaccountable, than to hinder a Man from performing one part of his Duty (especially so great a one as the Publick Worship of God) because he has fail'd in another? or if he has offended God publickly, what can be more absurd than to debar him from as publickly desiring his Pardon'. This convincing argument is reinforced by a further conclusion: 'But if the not doing of one Duty can make amends for the breach of another, he who neglects the Divine

Service, ought to be debar'd from doing his Duty to his Neighbour, as so *vice versa*'.[8]

Tindal's *reductio ad impossibile* is based on his taking the opposing thesis on the level of genus and showing it to be absurd on the level of species. From the specific question of church worship he has proceeded to the generic one of duty, altering in the process the word on which the argument is based: 'worship' becomes 'duty'. This response involves the dialectical stratagem of changing the terminology when opinion is divided: the division of opinion will conceal the appearance of trickery, and after the change the arguer's position will be irrefutable (*Soph. El.*, 176^{b}21–6). The *Topics* is more direct: to establish or overthrow a view, the disputant should alter a term to suit himself (*Top.*, 111^{a}8–13). He advances the generic antecedent 'if the not doing of one Duty can make amends for the breach of another' and examines a specific consequence,[9] which happens to consist of the two New Testament commandments on which depend all the law and the prophets: duty to (love of) God and neighbour. This placing of his opponents, Anglican clergymen, in a paradoxical position is the effect of Tindal's *reductio ad impossibile*. He assumes his own conclusion's contradictory, which happens to be the conclusion (or thesis) of the Church of England, and by arguing from that and reaching an impossible or absurd conclusion he proves his original conclusion hypothetically.[10] Swift's answer, an argument from analogy, does not successfully solve or refute Tindal's reasoning.

From another of Tindal's arguments Swift quotes a line, '"Tis plain, all the Power the Bishops have, is derived from the People, &c.', and gives a full counter-argument, beginning by making a distinction: the method used in solving merely apparent arguments as opposed to those properly reasoned, which are solved by demolishing them (*Soph. El.*, 176^{b}35–6). 'In general the Distinction lies here', he says, as if Tindal had no argument at all. 'The permissive Power of exercising Jurisdiction, lies in the People, or Legislature, or Administrator of a Kingdom, but not of making him a Bishop; as a Physician that commenceth Abroad, may be suffered to practice in *London*, or be hindered; but they have not the Power of creating him a Doctor, which is peculiar to a University' (II 104). Tindal's words in context mean something different from what Swift assumes when he leads the argument away from Tindal's line of reasoning in order to seem to refute him. Tindal says on page 333, 'But if every Nation can appoint the Number of its own Districts,

and diminish and enlarge 'em as they please, 'tis plain all the Power
the Bishops have is deriv'd from the People, since they cannot only
appoint what Number they think fit, and enlarge or diminish a
Bishop's Power with his District, but by consolidating or turning two
Districts into one they wholly deprive one Bishop of his Power, and
bestow it on another.'

Swift's argument is that the civil government can no more create a
bishop than it can a physician; its only power with respect to bishops
lies in determining a bishop's jurisdiction. This exactly is Tindal's
argument. His phrase 'all the Power' is an overstatement, but the
essence of his reasoning is virtually what Swift has conceded.
Although Swift affects a refutation by talking about a legislature's
inability to create a physician or a bishop, his answer, an apparent
refutation only, is sophistical (*Top.*, 162ª12–15). In a published
answer to Tindal he might have answered differently; yet his answer
as it stands is complete,[11] and to exonerate him from the charge of
sophistry would be difficult.

DIALECTICAL SUPERIORITY

Swift's infrequent failure to have the upper hand in argument is not
because of lack of spirit. He often exhibits an attitude that in a
lesser dialectician would be bluff and bravado. His speaking of those
'who pretend to answer the *Examiner*' (III 73) and of an opponent
'labouring to prove the contrary' (VIII 52) suggests an aloofness from
inferior opponents which in other places he states explicitly. 'Can
you think I will descend to vindicate myself against an aspersion so
absurd' (v 115), he asks in one place and refuses to descend so low
as to justify his computations to a caviller in another (XII 101). Such
instances of the dialectician's pride are similar to Gulliver's remark
to his Cousin Sympson about the Europeans who have hinted that
the Houyhnhnms and Yahoos might not actually exist: 'Do these
miserable Animals presume to think that I am so far degenerated as
to defend my Veracity?'

His assumption of dialectical superiority arises not from his
confidence in arguing either side of a question, like an actor who can
assume any character and play it with conviction, but from his self-
assurance that he is in the right: 'I am of a Temper to think no Man
great enough to set me on Work' (III 194). His confidence rests
partly on his belief that his knowledge is wide – 'whatever Charges I

bring, either general or particular, shall be religiously true, either upon avowed Facts which none can deny, or such as I can prove from my own Knowledge' (III 68)[12] – and that his opponents' knowledge is narrow, like Tindal's: 'it requireth more Knowledge, than his, to form general Rules, which People strain (when ignorant) to false Deductions to make them out' (II 98). His confidence rests partly on a kind of intuitive certainty: 'I am not in jest; and, if the fact will not be allowed me, I shall not argue it' (XII 124); 'I insist on my Opinion' (II 44); 'I am therefore as confident as a Man can be of any Truth which will not admit a Demonstration, that upon the Queen's Death, if we except Papists and Nonjurers, there could not be five hundred Persons in England of all Ranks who had any Thoughts of the Pretender, and among these, not six of any Quality or Consequence' (VIII 165).

But his confidence also rests in his certainty that his processes of reasoning (showing how 'the Effects and Consequences of Things follow') are superior to his opponent's; for example, the gentleman who wrote against 'The Conduct of the Allies': 'Hitherto therefore, the Matter is pretty equal, and the World may believe Him or Me, as they please. But, I think, the great Point of Controversie between us, is, whether the Effects and Consequences of Things follow better from His Premisses or mine: And there I will not be satisfied, unless he will allow the whole Advantage to be on my side' (VI 96).

Such confidence finds expression in the belittling of his opponents' dialectical skill, as in his references to 'those *Things*, which the Owners of them, usually call *Answers*' (III 14), 'those little barking Pens which have so constantly pursued me' (III 171), towards whom he will be wiser than Virgil and Horace had been and wiser than Pope was to be in the *Dunciad*, because he will 'disappoint that tribe of writers whose chief end next to that of getting bread, was an ambition of having their names upon record by answring or retorting their Scurrilityes; and would slily have made use of my resentment to let the future world know that there were such Persons now in being' (V 201). One of the most condescending of his remarks is directed to a gentleman, unknown to Swift, 'who has done me the Honour to write Three Discourses against that Treatise of the *Conduct of the Allies*, &c. and promises, for my Comfort, to conclude all in a Fourth':

I pity Answerers with all my Heart, for the many Disadvantages they lie under. My Book did a World of Mischief (as he calls it) before his First Part could possibly come out; and so went on through the Kingdom, while his limped slowly after, and if it arrived at all, it was too late; for Peoples Opinions were already fixed. His manner of answering me is thus: Of those Facts which he pretends to examine, some he resolutely denies, others he endeavours to extenuate, and the rest he distorts with such unnatural Turns, that I would engage, by the same Method, to disprove any History, either Ancient or Modern. Then the whole is interlarded with a thousand injurious Epithets and Appelations, which heavy Writers are forced to make use of, as a supply for that want of Spirit and Genius they are not born to.   (vi 95)

If he cannot find Whig opponents with spirit and genius enough to attack him, he threatens to supply the want and wittily denies rumours explaining the ineptness of the arguments on the other side: 'I declare once for all, that if these People will not be quiet, I shall take their Bread out of their Mouths, and answer the *Examiner* my self, which I protest I have never yet done, although I have been often charged with it; neither have those Answers been written or published with my Privity, as malicious People are pleased to give out; nor do I believe the common *Whiggish* Report, That the Authors are hired by the Ministry to give my Paper a Value' (iii 6). What he asks from his opponents is *proof* of the contradictory of the theses he maintains, not merely scurrilous attacks. 'I am tempted to draw some Conclusions, which a certain Party would be more ready to call False and Malicious, than to prove them so' (vi 95); 'What Proofs they bring for our endeavouring to introduce *Popery, Arbitrary Power*, and the *Pretender*, I cannot readily tell, and would be glad to hear' (iii 143); and when Burnet suggests that Tory clergymen who preach 'Obedience to the highest Powers' are practically the same as papists, Swift replies:

My Lord, I have a *little* Seriousness upon this *Point*, where your Lordship *affects* to shew so *much*. When you can prove, that one single Word hath ever dropt from any Minister of State, in *publick* or *private*, in Favour of the *Pretender*, or his Cause; when you can make it appear, that in the Course of this Administration, since the Queen thought fit to change her Servants, there hath one Step been made towards weakening the *Hanover* Title, or giving the least Countenance to any other whatsoever; then, and not until then, go dry your *Chaff* and *Stubble*, give Fire to the

Zeal of your Faction, and reproach them with Luke-warmness. (IV 75)

With the words 'when you can make it appear' Swift says he will even welcome apparent proof, that is, sophistry, which would at least show dialectical spirit and would be more to contend with than simple malicious assertions and suggestions.

REFUTATION

Swift's dialectic in the role of answerer consists largely in drawing distinctions, attacking definitions, offering witty, metaphorical retorts and attacking the opponent himself rather than his argument. In these and similar manoeuvres his dialectic, often with the help of irony, sometimes approaches and sometimes becomes satire. In his proper refutations, on the other hand, it is understandable that the levity often characteristic of his solution of fallacies and of his personal attack is missing. A proper refutation occurs when the conclusion of one's own argument is contrary to an opponent's conclusion,[13] a process requiring reasoning rather than the wordplay Swift often uses in the solution of fallacies. Yet he manages to achieve a refutation of a sort in the *Tale* and the wit rides heavily upon it: 'To affirm that our Age is altogether Unlearned, and devoid of Writers in any kind, seems to be an Assertion so bold and so false, that I have been sometime thinking, the contrary may almost be proved by uncontroulable Demonstration' (p. 34). The succeeding 'proof' is more loosely constructed, less forceful and less witty than most of his responses to the fallacious arguments of opponents. A better refutation in the *Tale* is the Author's 'proof' of the contrary of the first of several detractions aimed at true critics, which is that little expense is required for setting up as a true critic: 'on the contrary, nothing is more certain, than that it requires greater Layings out, to be free of the *Critick*'s Company, than of any other you can name. For, as to be a *true Beggar*, it will cost the richest Candidate every Groat he is worth; so, before one can commence a *True Critick*, it will cost a man all the good Qualities of his Mind' (p. 102).

One of Swift's few straightforward refutations, not involving analogy or *reductio ad impossibile*, is a reply to Burnet's 'Introduction' to the third volume of his *History of the Reformation of the Church of England.*[14] Swift's refutation is, as a proper refutation should be, reasoning involving the contradiction of Burnet's conclusion,[15] but it has throughout as well a colouring of scorn, or *argumentum ad personam*. In the first two volumes of his history, Swift says, Burnet was 'frightened with *the Danger of a Popish Successor in View, and the dreadful Apprehensions of the Power of* France. England *hath forgot these Dangers*, and yet is *nearer to them than ever*,[16] and therefore he is resolved to *awaken them* with this third Volume; but in the mean Time, sends this Introduction to let them know they are asleep . . . as if the *Pope*, the *Devil*, the *Pretender*, and *France*, were just at our Doors'. With the outline of Burnet's argument thus presented, Swift sets about demolishing the assertion.

> When the Bishop published his History, there was a *Popish* Plot on Foot: The Duke of *York*, a known *Papist*, was presumptive Heir to the Crown; the House of Commons would not hear of any Expedients for securing their Religion under a *Popish* Prince, nor would the King or Lords consent to a Bill of Exclusion: The *French* King was in the Height of his Grandeur, and the Vigour of his Age. At this Day [1713] the Presumptive Heir, with that whole illustrious Family, are *Protestants*; the *Popish Pretender* excluded for ever by several Acts of Parliament; and every Person in the smallest Employment, as well as Members in both Houses, obliged to *abjure* him. The *French* King is at the lowest Ebb of his Life; his Armies have been conquered, and his Towns won from him for ten Years together; and his Kingdom is in Danger of being torn by Divisions during a long Minority. Are these Cases Parallel? Or are we now in more Danger of *France* and *Popery* than we were thirty Years ago? What can be the Motive for advancing such false, such detestable Assertions? What Conclusions would his Lordship draw from such Premises as these? If injurious Appellations were of any Advantage to a Cause, (as the Stile of our Adversaries would make us believe) what Appellations would those deserve, who thus endeavour to sow the Seeds of Sedition, and are impatient to see the Fruits?   (IV 61–2)

Swift also refutes as answerer by means of the *argumentum ad verecundiam* or argument resting on respect for authority, a valid dialectical manoeuvre. He quotes Steele, who 'affirms, That *Men's Beings are degraded when their Passions are no longer governed by the Dictates of their own Mind*', and answers, 'directly contrary to the Lessons of all Moralists and Legislators; who agree unanimously, that the Passions of Men must be under the Government of Reason and Law; neither are the Laws of any other Use than to correct the Irregularity of our Affections' (VIII 46–7).

REDUCTIO AD IMPOSSIBILE

When Aristotle attributed the invention of dialectic to Zeno of Elea he was probably referring to Zeno's method of deducing the consequences of his opponents' hypotheses in order to show that they led to impossibilities. The *reductio ad impossibile* is treated at length in the *Prior Analytics* of Aristotle (I 29, 44; II 11–14) and is explained also in the *Posterior Analytics* (I 26). It is a kind of hypothetical negative demonstration which can be shown by the scheme: If P then Q; but not-Q; therefore not-P. This is a destructive hypothetical syllogism, or *modus tollens*, in which the consequent is denied and therefore the antecedent is denied.[17] Aristotle contrasts the process with the direct negative demonstration, which is the supposition that if A is not B, and B is C, then A is not C. In the *reductio ad impossibile*, on the other hand, if we are to prove that A is not B we would assume its contradictory: that is, that A is B. The second premise would be B is C (the truth of which is not questioned) and the resulting inference, A is C, we would know to be an admitted impossibility, according to the method of this kind of argument. Therefore A is not C: such a conclusion is impossible (*Post. An.*, 87ª1–11). Its impossibility means that one of the preceding premises is not true and we know that the minor premise, B is C, is true. Therefore the major premise must by necessity be false.

Swift's tendency to concreteness in diction finds an open field for play in the *reductio ad impossibile*, in which he indulges his love of analogy, applying his opponents' reasoning to cases in which the contradictory nature of the consequences is easily exposed. Tindal tries to show the absurdity of the great power enjoyed by clergymen, the prime ministers of God's authority, many of whom lately rose from poor servants to such great heights merely by the laying on of a hand. They cannot help being vain, giddy and insolent (Tindal, pp. 79–80). Swift replies, 'The Argument lieth stronger against the Apostles, poor Fishermen, and St. Paul, a Tent-maker' (II 92). Analysing Swift's reply as a *reductio ad impossibile* according to the scheme in the preceding paragraph requires awkward phrasing, which will perhaps be pardoned in the name of clarity, because (paradoxically) the phrasing broken into major and minor terms permits the reader to follow the scheme easily: Swift proposes to prove that A is not B: vain, giddy and insolent are not the preachers of the Christian faith, which is the contradictory of Tindal's conclusion and which, if proved, will overthrow Tindal's conclusion. He assumes the contradictory,[18] that A is B – vain, etc., are the preachers of the Christian faith – and adds an unquestionably true second premise, B is C, which is that preachers of the Christian faith were the Apostles. The resulting inference, or conclusion, that A is C – vain, giddy and insolent were the Apostles – is if not impossible at least unacceptable, and thus he has successfully effected the *reductio ad impossibile*.

The *reductio ad absurdum* results when the consequence drawn from an hypothesis is not self-contradictory but simply false. The *reductio ad impossibile* results when the consequence is incompatible with or contradicts the hypothesis from which it was derived. Both arguments lead to negative results and both may be viewed together as arguments reaching unacceptable consequences, thus causing the rejection of the hypotheses from which they were derived.[19]

One sees a similar technique when Tindal says, 'How easily could the *Roman* Emperors have destroyed the Church', and Swift answers, 'Just as if he had said; how easily could *Herod* kill *Christ* when a Child, &c.' (II 93). Swift's argument is that the destruction of the church by the Roman emperors would not only be man's overthrowing of the will of an almighty God, but in one respect the destroying of God himself, because the Holy Spirit of the Trinity, the foundation of the church, is the same as God. Swift emphasises the absurdity of man's destroying God in his impossible analogous conclusion that Herod easily could have killed Christ as a child.

Again by analogy, answering Tindal's disparagement of the clergy, Swift says, 'In the Judgment of all People, our Divines have carried practical Preaching and Writing to the greatest Perfection it ever arrived to; which shews, that we may affirm in general our Clergy is excellent, although this or that Man be faulty. As if an Army be constantly victorious, regular, &c. we may say, it is an excellent, victorious Army: But *Tindall*, to disparage it, would say, such a Serjeant ran away, such an Ensign hid himself in a Ditch; nay, one Colonel turned his Back, therefore it is a corrupt, cowardly Army, &c.' (II 97). The *reductio ad impossibile* in this passage can be

analysed, but again is somewhat awkwardly phrased in places. Swift
wishes to prove that the clergy in general do not deserve
disparagement, that is, that A is not B. He assumes the contradictory
of his conclusion (which is Tindal's conclusion): A is B, which in his
analogy is that a certain army is corrupt and cowardly. The second
premise, B is C, is that cowardly and corrupt are three who showed
fear. The impossible conclusion is that an army consists of three who
showed fear (A is C) or, by analogy, that the clergy of the Church of
England are discredited because a few of their members are at fault.

When Tindal says, 'The meanest Layman [is] as good a Judge as
the greatest Priest', Swift replies, 'As if one should say, the meanest
sick Man hath as much Interest in Health as a Physician, and
therefore is as good a Judge of Physick as a Physician, &c.' (II 96).
This *reductio ad impossibile* uses the physician analogy which like
the soldier analogy is one of Swift's stock answers.[20] Tindal argues in
another place that the laity can reject those preachers they judge
false and accept those they judge honest and sincere, the former act
being the same as unmaking or depriving some clergymen and the
latter the same as making or ordaining others, and 'no more Power
is requir'd for the one than the other' (p. 236). Swift replies again
with the physician analogy: 'That is, I dislike my Physician, and can
turn him off, and therefore I can make any Man a Physician, &c.',
and for good measure he adds a soldier analogy: 'So because it is the
Soldier's Business to knock men on the Head, it is their's likewise to
raise them to Life, &c.' (II 98–9).

Tindal, questioning the authority of two independent powers (civil
and ecclesiastical) governing, asks, 'if there may be two such in
every Society on Earth, why may there not be more than one in
Heaven?' Swift's simple reply suggests that he is prepared to take
the conclusion implied by Tindal's question and deduce it to an
impossibility. He answers only, 'A delicate Consequence' (II 90).
When Tindal cites Philippians for the authority of the people
preceding bishops and deacons, Swift turns the argument back on
him, citing 1 Samuel: 'I hope, he would argue from another Place,
that the People precede the King, because of these Words: *Ye shall
be destroyed, both you and your King*' (II 94–5). The reply is loosely
a *reductio ad absurdum* and also a *retorsio argumenti*, turning
Tindal's source, broadly speaking, back upon him. Tindal asks,
'Does not justice demand, that they who alike contribute to the
Burden, should alike receive the Advantage?' And Swift responds,
'Here is another of his Maxims loosely put without considering what

Exceptions may be made. The Papists have contributed doubly (being so taxed) therefore by this Rule they ought to have double Advantage' (II 101–2). He adds to Tindal's conclusion (maxim), which is the contradictory of his own thesis, a second undoubted premise, but one which concerns not the dissenters, as Tindal had intended, but the Roman Catholics. The deduced conclusion shows the absurdity of the first premise, at least to the satisfaction of one of Swift's persuasion.

Tindal does not have a monopoly on suffering Swift's rebuttals *ad impossibile*. In 'Some Arguments against Enlarging the Power of Bishops, in Letting of Leases', Swift answers a pamphlet called 'The Case of the Laity'. 'The Clergy, I conceive, will hardly allow that *the People maintain them*, any more than in the Sense, that all Landlords whatsoever are maintained by the People. Such Assertions as these, and the Insinuations they carry along with them, proceed from Principles which cannot be avowed by those who are for preserving the happy *Constitution* in *Church* and *State*' (IX 57). Later in the pamphlet, in response to the late Lord Molesworth's address to the Irish House of Commons on the encouragement of agriculture, Swift suggests that if the clergy should abate a portion of tithes to encourage agricultural improvements, why should not farmers abate a portion of the rents due them, for the same purpose? He asks, 'Would not a Man just dropt from the Clouds, upon a full Hearing, judge the Demand to be, at least, as reasonable?' (IX 59). In each instance he is overthrowing the opponent's premise by showing the absurdity to which it leads.

Such an invitation to examine the reasonableness, or absurdity by implication, of an opponent's argument is twice extended in 'The Sentiments of a Church-of-England Man'. Explaining the 'Absurdity of that Distinction' between a king *de facto* and a king *de jure* with respect to English government, Swift points out that every limited monarch is a king *de jure*. Jacobites unhappy with the Revolution of 1688, he says, 'insist much upon one Argument, that seems to carry but little Weight'. He states the argument and proceeds to demolish it with examples showing its absurdity. The advocates for succession argue that the crown is the prince's birthright and should be secured to his posterity as is the property of a private citizen. 'Now, the Consequence of this Doctrine must be' that the prince like the citizen can 'waste, mispend, or abuse his Patrimony' and will be held no more accountable to his subjects for misapplying revenues or alienating the crown than the citizen is answerable to the laws for squandering his property. The prince, they argue, is answerable only to God. 'Now, the Folly of this Reasoning will best appear, by applying it in a parallel Case.' According to the Jacobites' reasoning, he says, a physician prescribing poison and a divine preaching against religion are answerable only to God. 'In either of these two Cases, every Body would find out the Sophistry.' Their crimes 'are not purely personal to the Physician, or the Divine, but destructive to the Publick' (II 19–20). And much more so with respect to a prince, but not with respect to a private person who ill-manages his property.

This argument is the same kind of *reductio ad impossibile* that he uses often against Tindal. In those arguments Swift is usually brief, not bothering to comment on the method his refutation takes. In some places, however, he does signal his techniques: for example, when he says, 'At his Rate of arguing (I think I do not misrepresent him, and I believe he will not deny the Consequence) a Man may' etc. (II 88) and when he says, 'This is a Maxim deduced from a Graduation of false Suppositions. If a Man should turn the Tables,[21] and argue that' etc. (II 101). He also indicates his method of reduction when he observes that the 'Scheme of encouraging *Clergymen* to build Houses by dividing a Living of 500 *l.* a Year into ten Parts, is a Contrivance, the Meaning whereof hath got on the wrong Side of my Comprehension; unless it may be argued, that *Bishops* build no Houses, because they are so rich; and therefore, the inferior *Clergy* will certainly build, if you reduce them to Beggary' (XII 198).

In 'The Sentiments of a Church-of-England Man' he presents an argument which announces his technique as *reductio ad impossibile* (or *ad absurdum*) and 'proves' it both by hypothetical example and historical examples. Speaking of the objections of a 'very pious, learned, and worthy Gentleman' to the Revolution of 1688, Swift says, 'The Force of his Argument turned upon this'. He explains concisely the legal points involved in the gentleman's objection and divides the objection into two questions, the first of which is, According to the constitution under James I, could a King of England be deposed? Swift says he will not presume to determine this point – that is, he will not prove it by direct argument reaching a negative conclusion – but to all who hold the negative (that the king could not under the constitution be deposed) he will take the liberty of putting his case 'as strongly as I please'. He then proceeds by *reductio ad impossibile*. If the king cannot be deposed except by a unanimous vote of the three branches of the supreme power in England – King, Lords and Commons (each having a negative vote, no two able to repeal or enact a law without consent of the third) – then a king under English law can conduct himself like a Nero or a Caligula. He can 'murder his Mother and his Wife, . . . commit Incest, . . . ravish Matrons, . . . blow up the Senate, and burn his Metropolis; openly . . . renounce God and Christ, and worship the Devil'. These and more a king can do under the worthy gentleman's interpretation of the constitution, because in these acts the king does not need the advice of a ministry or the assistance of an army. Therefore, if such a king cannot be deposed except by his own consent in parliament, there would seem to be no protection of the people against him, no meaning in the term *limited* monarch and no validity in the idea of the people's consent in making and repealing laws, because the king, as the worthy gentleman understands the constitution, administers with no tie but conscience and is answerable only to God. Swift responds, 'I desire no stronger Proof that an Opinion must be false, than to find very great Absurdities annexed to it; and there cannot be greater than in the present Case: For it is not a bare Speculation, that Kings may run into such Enormities as are above-mentioned; the Practice may be proved by Examples'. He mentions the first Caesars and later emperors, modern European princes like Pedro (the Cruel) of Castile, Philip II of Spain, Ivan Basilovitz, first Czar of Russia, and in England, King John, Richard III and Henry VIII. To answer a possible counter-argument, Swift adds, 'But there cannot be equal Absurdities supposed in maintaining the contrary Opinion', because princes can keep a majority on their side 'by any tolerable Administration' which is free from continual oppressions (II 21–2).

THE DILEMMATIC RESPONSE

Swift's dilemmatic retorts are rarely if ever as dramatic as that of Jesus, who replied dialectically when the chief priests, scribes and elders asked him by what authority he did these things (he had purged the temple the day before), asking them whether the baptism of John was from heaven or of men. Not knowing how to negotiate the horns, they admitted they could not answer (Luke 20: 1–8; see Chapter 7 above, in the section 'The dilemma'). Swift's responses are usually consciously dialectical, like a remark Lord North was to

make in a speech concerning Junius: 'The public will see and feel
that he has either advanced false facts, or reasoned falsely from true
principles.'[22] When an opponent criticises the Tory ministry for
serving the queen with obsequiousness, humility and resignation,
Swift observes that the reverse[23] of these is rudeness, insolence and
opposition, which some Whigs have lately shown towards the queen
(III 201). The reply would not be dilemmatic directed to one of the
many Tories who accepted the doctrine of passive obedience, but it
would be so if directed, as it is, to a loyal Whig. His remark
concerning Steele's pamphlet the *Crisis* is a distillation of a proper
dilemma:[24] 'What shall I say to a Pamphlet, where the Malice and
Falshood of every Line would require an Answer, and where the
Dulness and Absurdities will not deserve one?' (VIII 36). He
discovers something of a dilemma in the *Crisis* – 'So, *whether*
France *conquer* Germany, *or be in Peace and good Understanding
with it*: either Event *will put us and* Holland *at the Mercy of*
France' – and belittles this 'Logick' with mild humour (VIII 64).
Referring to a letter Steele quotes, Swift reflects, 'how blind the
Malice of that Man must be, who invents a groundless Lye in order
to defame his Superiors, which would be no Disgrace, if it had been
a Truth' (VIII 67): in effect rebutting his opponent before and
behind.

THE UNACCEPTABLE EXTREMES

Swift as answerer will not usually let himself be impaled on the
horns of a dilemma brought against him by a questioner, nor will he
allow a single unpleasant *lemma* (λημμα, an assumption) to stand
directed against himself without an attempt to deflate or demolish it.
For example, he will not accept the view 'of those that call
themselves Protestants, who look upon our Worship to be idolatrous
as well as that of the *Papists*, and with great Charity put *Prelacy* and
Popery together, as Terms convertible' (II 121). 'Cannot I see things
in another Light than this Author and his Party do', he asks,
'without being *blind*? Is my *Understanding lost* when it differs from
theirs? Am I *cheated, bewitched* and *out of my Senses*, because I
think these to have been Betrayers of our Country, whom they call
Patriots?' (III 204). Hyperbolic and rhetorical arguments of both
sides in pamphlet warfare, he observes, if taken seriously would lead
to massacres and widespread hangings (II 13). In the thoroughly

political sermon on the martyrdom of Charles I he offers a remedy to those faced with such arguments: 'One great design of my discourse was to give you warning against running into either extreme of two bad opinions' (IX 230). Two such bad extremes are those of the dissenters and the Roman Catholics: 'here are on one Side two stupid illiterate Scribblers, both of them *Fanaticks* by Profession; I mean the *Review* and *Observator*. On the other Side we have an open *Nonjuror*', whose 'Rehearsal' is 'yet more pernicious than those of the former two' (III 13–14). In a stratagem reminiscent of his ridiculing his opponents in the *Tale* by showing how closely the mutually antipathetic extremes, Peter and Jack, resemble each other, Swift twice points out that Tindal's arguments against the Church of England are old arguments in favour of Roman Catholicism given a slight turn (II 93, 94).

In these several places Swift is aware of the danger of the dialectical question, both to himself when used against him and to opponents when he uses it. Properly phrased the dialectical question excludes a middle, forcing the opponent to choose between two extremes.[25] It is suggestive of the formal dilemma because it can almost by necessity put an opponent in a bad light, and because of this quality Swift was quick both to defend himself against the technique and to employ it.

MANIPULATING AN OPPONENT'S ARGUMENT

At about this point in the analysis of Swift's use of dialectic one passes from his refutation of valid arguments to his solution, or other treatment, of fallacious arguments. There are so many means of solving fallacious arguments – and Swift employs many of those means – that it is not practicable to give all the examples of even the best responses. A sampling, however, will easily show his various techniques.

In several places Swift turns his opponent's argument with a reply that from the opponent's point of view might seem unanswerable. Speaking as the Examiner about those papers that come out weekly against him, he says,

The Authors are perpetually telling me of my Ingratitude to my Masters; that I *blunder*, and betray the Cause; and write with more Bitterness against those who hire me, than against the

Whigs. Now, I took all this at first only for so many Strains of
Wit, and pretty Paradoxes to divert the Reader; but upon further
thinking I find they are Serious. I imagined I had complimented
the present Ministry for their dutiful Behaviour to the Queen; for
their Love of the old Constitution in Church and State; for their
Generosity and Justice, and for their Desire of a speedy,
honourable Peace: But it seems I am mistaken, and they reckon
all this for Satyr, because it is directly contrary to the Practice of
all those whom they set up to defend, and utterly against all their
Notions of a good Ministry. Therefore I cannot but think they
have Reason on their side:[26] For, suppose I should write the
Character of an Honest, a Religious, and a learned Man, and
send the first to *Newgate*, the second to the *Grecian Coffee-
House*, and the last to *White*'s; would they not all pass for *Satyrs*,
and justly enough, among the Companies to whom they were
sent? (III 118–19)

When Burnet makes light of the Church of Rome's view of
sacrilege, Swift turns the argument back on him (IV 65–6) with
admirable conciseness and force, which is surpassed, however, when
Bishop Burnet vilifies the lower clergy and Swift turns the argument
lightly and adroitly and refutes him on a side issue (IV 78). In a third
place in his answer to Burnet[27] he remarks, 'I could turn the
Argument against his Lordship with very great Advantage, . . . and
then conclude . . .' (IV 84), but the outline of the reply he gives
suggests that it would not be as effective as the former two turnings
of the argument. In all these examples a touch of *reductio ad
impossibile* persists, but they contain a grace (if that is not too gentle
a word here) beyond the reach of logic in the art of dialectic.
    Another of Swift's methods is showing that his opponent is
arguing beside the point.[28] He says that what has concerned Tindal
so much that he wrote a 'large swelling Volume' has been of almost
no concern to the majority of Christians or among disputing divines.
By showing amazement that Tindal 'raiseth such a Dust' over 'this
Opinion of the Independent Power of the Church' (II 76), Swift
brings to bear on him if not the antipathy at least the indifference of
the majority and the wise: Tindal's book 'is wholly turned upon
battering down a Sort of independent Power in the Clergy; which
few or none of them ever claimed or defended' (II 79). He similarly
deflates one of Burnet's laboured proofs (IV 67–8), and to one of
Wood's concessions on the coining of copper Swift replies that it is

beside the point: 'The King has given him a Patent to Coyn Half-pence, but hath not obliged us to take them'.[29] More damaging to an opponent than showing him to be arguing beside the point is showing him to be arguing one's own thesis, although Swift is less effective stylistically in the latter manoeuvre. He remarks that Tindal strongly argues the objections his adversaries would argue, including Swift himself (II 91), and he comments, again concerning Tindal: 'It is hard to think sometimes whether this Man is hired to write for or against Dissenters and the Sects' (II 102).

DRAWING DISTINCTIONS

An answerer solves arguments that are properly reasoned by demolishing them, but he solves those that are only apparent arguments by drawing distinctions (*Soph. El.*, 176b35–6), a technique especially useful when an answerer is about to be confuted (174b24–5). Sidney in his defence of poetry was thankful that he was 'a peece of a *Logician*' and was thus able to distinguish the fallacies in an enthusiastic argument.[30] In the *Drapier's Letters* (p. 106) Swift draws a surprising distinction which he calls 'an invincible Argument' because it shows that his opponent is arguing beside the point. Many distinctions are drawn in that most dialectical of his writings, his 'Remarks' to Tindal. 'His great Error all along is, that he doth not distinguish between a Power, and a Liberty of exercising that Power' (II 95). He says in another place, 'And here lies the Mistake of this superficial Man, who is not able to distinguish between what the Civil Power can hinder, and what it can do' (II 75). Sounding like a logic master, he says, 'Bad Parallels; bad Politicks; Want of due Distinction between Teaching and Government. The People may know when they are governed well, but not be wiser than their Instructors. Shew the Difference' (II 98). 'There is a Difference' (II 104), he says, and points out a distinction Tindal failed to make about apostolic succession. 'State the Difference here', he says, 'between our Separation from *Rome*, and the Dissenters from us, and shew the Falseness of what he sayeth' (II 104). 'Have they not trusted this Power with our Princes?' Tindal asks, and Swift distinguishes: 'Why ay. But that argueth not Right, but Power' (II 86). Tindal tries to show that ecclesiastical power cannot be totally separated from civil: they must clash. For example, he says, if a magistrate cannot deprive a clergyman of all offices and employments, he cannot put a clergyman to death. Consequently, he says, 'Without having the less, he could not have the greater, in which that is contained' (p. 37). Swift replies simply, 'Sophistical; Instance wherein' (II 90). Here, and in a distinction he draws between Ireland on the one hand and England and Holland on the other (VII 79), his aim is to expose the fallacy of combination,[31] which is solved, as Swift does in the second instance, by applying division to it (*Soph. El.*, 179ᵃ12–13).

Burgersdicius gives an example (taken *mutatis mutandis* from *Soph. El.*, 166ᵃ33): Two and three are even and odd; five is two and three; therefore five is even and odd. This fallacy occurs because things are spoken of in conjunction which should be divided.

ATTACKING DEFINITIONS

The starting point for dealing with people who advance eristical arguments is definition (*Metaphysics*, 1012ᵃ17–28), because defective definition is the most common fallacy in argument (*Soph. El.*, 168ᵇ19–21) and attacks are always more easily made on the definitions than on the reasonings in arguments (*Top.*, 111ᵇ12–16). The obviousness of such advice led some seventeenth-century authors of logics to acknowledge on their first pages that formal logic is no more than a categorising of the natural logic uninformed men use unconsciously.[32] Swift shows a regard for definition in marginal notes to books he read (V 248) and in his defence of his church and party. He criticises 'the Scribblers on the other Side' for 'affecting to confound the Terms of *Clergy* and *High-Church*' (II 8) and observes, 'A *Whig* asks, whether you hold *Passive Obedience*? You affirm it: He then immediately cries out, you are a *Jacobite*, a *Friend* of *France* and the *Pretender*; because he makes you answerable for the Definition he hath forced of that Term, however different it be from what you understand' (III 111–12). He will not consent to an opponent's conclusion 'untill he and I have settled the meaning of the word *Mischief*' (III 196) and he 'cannot by any Means allow' another argument to stand, because a distinction between *tool* and *instrument* will demolish it: 'I desire once for all to set them right. A *Tool* and an *Instrument*, in the metaphorical Sense, differ thus: the Former, is an Engine in the Hands of *Knaves*, the latter in those of wise and honest Men' (III 200). To establish or overthrow a view one should bring forward the meanings of a term appropriate to one's case and leave the rest aside (*Top.*, 110ᵇ28–32). In the preceding example Swift establishes his own view and overthrows his opponent's in the same sentence. He attacks the Privy Council's reliance on the word *obligatory*, which if allowed to stand would undermine his main argument against Wood's halfpence,[33] and answering Steele, he says, 'although I have often heard of a *solemn* Day, a *solemn* Feast, and a *solemn* Coxcomb, yet I can conceive no Idea to my self of a *solemn Barrier*' (VIII 53).

He frequently draws attention to Tindal's definitions. When the latter mentions 'their Executioner', Swift replies, 'He is fond of this Word in many Places, yet there is nothing in it, further than it is the Name for the Hangman' (II 91), and when Tindal uses the phrase 'constantly applying the same Ideas to them', Swift answers, 'This is, in old *English*, meaning the same Thing' (II 87), attacking his definition of 'definition'. He observes that Tindal 'hath a Talent of rattling out Phrases, which seem to have Sense, but have none at all: The usual Fate of those who are ignorant of the Force and Compass of Words, without which it is impossible for a Man to write either pertinently or intelligibly upon the most obvious Subjects' (II 78), with the result that his ignorance of words vitiates his reasoning: 'the Strength of his Arguments is equal to the Clearness of his Definitions. For, having most ignorantly divided Government into three Parts, whereof the first contains the other two; he attempteth to prove that the Clergy possess none of these by Divine Right. And he argueth thus . . .' (II 81).

A final example will show Swift's attack on Tindal's argument through an attack on definition (of government, as in the preceding example), including a rare instance of Swift's offering to rephrase an entire argument to improve its clarity.[34] Tindal says, 'It will be necessary to show what is contained in the Idea of Government', and Swift responds:

> Now, it is to be understood, that this refined Way of Speaking was introduced by Mr. *Locke*: After whom the Author limpeth as fast as he was able. All the former Philosophers in the World, from the Age of *Socrates* to ours, would have ignorantly put the Question, *Quid est Imperium*? But now it seemeth we must vary our Phrase; and since our modern Improvement of Human Understanding, instead of desiring a Philosopher to describe or define a Mousetrap, or tell me what it is; I must gravely ask, what is contained in the Idea of a Mouse-trap?[35] But then to observe

how deeply this new Way of putting Questions to a Man's Self, maketh him enter into the Nature of Things; his present Business is to shew us, what is contained in the Idea of Government. The Company knoweth nothing of the Matter, and would gladly be instructed; which he doth in the following Words.   (II 80)

With a subsequent apology for the length of the quotation, Swift now gives an example of what he considers the obscurity of his opponent's definition, which begins, 'It would be in vain for one intelligent Being to pretend to set Rules to the Actions of another . . .', and continues for several lines consisting of abstractions like 'Good', 'Evil', 'Convenience' and 'Inconvenience'.

If what is said is not clear, the answerer should not hesitate to say that he does not understand it (*Top.*, 160ª21–2) and Swift, not hesitating, replies sarcastically and offers to improve it: 'therefore let us melt this refined Jargon into the *Old Style*, for the Improvement of such, who are not enough conversant in the *New.*'[36] Exact account of definition is more scientific than dialectical and is properly the business of the *Posterior Analytics* (II 3–13) and not the *Topics*, where it is usually said that definition should simply express essence (101ᵇ21, 39; 139ª34). Essence, Swift believed, is usually best expressed through examples and comparisons whose illustrations are relevant and familiar (*Top.*, 157ª14–15), so that when he rephrases Tindal's explanation he offers a simple, commonplace example:

If the Author were one that used to talk like one of us, he would have spoke in this Manner: I think it necessary to give a full and perfect Definition of Government, such as will shew the Nature and all the Properties of it;[37] and, my Definition is thus. One Man will never cure another of stealing Horses, merely by minding him of the Pains he hath taken, the Cold he hath got, and the Shoe-Leather he hath lost in stealing that Horse; nay, to warn him, that the Horse may kick or fling him, or cost him more than he is worth in Hay and Oats, can be no more than Advice. For the Gallows is not the natural Effect of robbing on the High-Way, as Heat is of Fire: And therefore, if you will govern a Man, you must find out some other Way of Punishment, than what he will inflict upon himself.[38]   (II 80–1)

Following this explanation he gives another example, referring to the idea of a mousetrap he mentioned earlier, to show how a man, to keep a mouse from eating his cheese, must convince her with punishment, not with advice about the harmful effects of eating too much cheese. In both these examples he keeps to a thin line between clear explanation and *reductio ad absurdum* in the colloquial sense, or more precisely, diminution.

CONTEMPT FOR OPPONENT'S REASONING

Defending the Tory position on the war in 1712 Swift remarks, 'And here I cannot, without some Contempt, take notice of a sort of Reasoning offered by several People' (vi 90), which he gives and counters with three concise replies. Belittling an attempt to foist something like a dilemma on the nation, he observes of provisions of the Barrier Treaty obviously not in Britain's best interest, although Britain is bearing the brunt of the fighting: 'This I humbly conceive to be perfect Boys Play, *Cross* [heads] *I win*, and *Pile* [tails] *you lose*; or, *What's yours is mine*, and *What's mine is my own*' (vi 92). Of Steele's *Guardian* essays he says, 'Well, but he tells you, he *cannot offer against the* Examiner *and his other Adversary, Reason and Argument without appearing void of both.* What a singular Situation of the Mind is this! How glad should I be to hear a Man *offer Reasons and Argument, and yet at the same time appear void of both*!' He continues quoting from Steele and responding and concludes, 'he will make an admirable Reasoner in the House of Commons' (viii 12–13), to which Steele had been elected that year (1713). Near the conclusion of his attack on Steele's *Crisis*, he says, 'I have now finished the most disgustful Task that I ever undertook: I could with more Ease have written *three* dull Pamphlets, than remarked upon the Falshoods and Absurdities of *One*' (viii 66–7).

He also records his disapproval of poor reasoning in marginal notes to books he reads. In Burnet's *History of My Own Times* (1724–34) he finds sophistry, wrong and weak arguing and 'A lawyer's way of arguing, very weak'.[39] In the margins of other books he remarks, 'Very false Reasoning' (v 254), 'Are you serious?' (v 252) and 'O Jesus' (v 262).

EXPOSING FALLACIOUS REASONING

Swift obviously knew the wide variety of fallacies categorised in the

Sophistical Elenchi and repeated in most seventeenth-century logic manuals. He exposes the fallacy of composition (or combination) in his sermon 'On the Trinity', following his reference to those people of 'corrupted Reason' who 'conclude, that the Truth of the whole Gospel must sink along with that one Article' which they find questionable (IX 159).[40] This fallacy provides the basis both of the remark about the crumbling edifice of Christianity in the 'Argument against Abolishing Christianity', where an equivocal text on the Trinity undermines the entire religion,[41] and of the passage in 'A Letter concerning the Sacramental Test', where his opponents are shown trying to unite all Protestants against the Papists. In the face of this fallacy of composition Swift argues the propriety of maintaining divisions (II 120–1). He cites the fallacy *petitio principii*,[42] or begging the question, after discussing at some length Steele's theory of government: 'All this, our Author tells us, with extreme Propriety, *is what seems reasonable to common Sense*; that is, in other Words, it seems *reasonable* to *Reason*' (VIII 44).

Hotspur's remark about Glendower's grandiloquent description of his own birth[43] exposes the fallacy of consequent, which Aristotle in the *Poetics* says is useful in the art of fiction, as Homer has shown.[44] This fallacy has no place in dialectic, however, once it is discovered. 'Answer it. No such Consequence at all' (II 85), Swift replies to one of Tindal's assertions. In response to one of Tindal's proofs, he asks, 'Is it any Sort of Proof that I have no Right, because a Stronger Power will not let me exercise it? Or doth all, that this Author says through his Preface, or Book itself, offer any other Sort of Argument but this, or what he deduces the same Way?' (II 82). He has pointed out in Tindal's argument the fallacy of the convertible consequent: it is wrong to suppose that because B is, A necessarily is, following the supposition that when A is, B necessarily is. For example, it does not follow that if a man with a fever is hot, a man who is hot must have a fever; or that since after rain the ground is consequently wet, one should suppose that if the ground is wet it has been raining (*Soph. El.*, 167ᵇ1–20).

In marginalia to Burnet's *History of My Own Times* Swift charges: 'No consequence' (V 268), 'Abominable assertion, and false consequence' (V 289).[45] Answering a letter attacking the *Examiner*, he says, 'This Writer wonders how I *should know their Lordship's Hearts, because he hardly knows his own.* I do not well see the Consequence of this: Perhaps he never examines into his own Heart, perhaps it keeps no correspondence with his Tongue or his

Pen: I hope at least, it is a Stranger to those foul Terms he has strowed throughout his Letter; otherwise I fear *I know it too well*: For *out of the abundance of the Heart, the Mouth speaketh*' (III 195). Here is an example of Swift's shifting from logic to personal attack enlivened with wit and a trace of humour approaching satire, as he does also when he says, 'The Scripture tells us, that *Oppression makes a wise Man mad*; therefore, consequently speaking, the Reason why some Men are not *mad*, is because they are not *wise*: However, it were to be wished that *Oppression* would, in Time, teach a little *Wisdom* to *Fools*' (IX 18). In the former example he is exposing the fallacy of consequent, in the latter simply denying the consequent, a valid logical procedure. When he adds paradox, irony, nonsense, ridicule or humour, or a combination of some of these, in his shifts from dialectic to what one can call dialectical satire the transformation from the dialectical to the literary art is more pronounced.

'The Reformation', Swift says, 'owed nothing to the good Intentions of King *Henry*: He was only an Instrument of it, (as the Logicians speak) by Accident' (IV 73).[46] When Tindal says, 'They suspected the Love of Power natural to Churchmen', Swift, aware of the fallacious argument from accident, replies, 'Truly, so is the Love of Pudding, and most other Things desirable in this Life; and in that they are like the Laity, as in all other Things that are not good. And, therefore, they are held not in Esteem for what they are like in, but for their Virtues. The true Way to abuse them with Effect, is to tell us some Faults of their's, that other Men have not, or not so much of as they, &c. Might not any Man speak full as bad of Senates, Dyets, and Parliaments, as he can do about Councils; and as bad of Princes, as he doth of Bishops?' (II 86). Tindal's distinction of the clergy's love of power is, after the humorous diminution of the pudding analogy, shown to be a false distinction, a fallacy of accident:[47] love of power is natural to men, whether they happen to be princes or bishops; it is as natural to them as the love of pudding. After this solution comes the effective stratagem of showing the opponent how he should have argued.

CITING OPPONENT'S DIALECTICAL TRICKS

Some of the sophistical arguments perpetrated by Swift's opponents can be more naturally viewed as dialectical stratagems than as one of the six fallacies *in dictione* or one of the seven *extra dictione*. He speaks in general of those who gain 'by deceiving us with plausible arguments' (IX 237) and again in general he observes, 'It is in Disputes as in Armies; where the weaker Side sets up false Lights, and makes a great Noise, that the Enemy may believe them to be more numerous and strong than they really are' (I 243). More particularly, he reminds opponents who would extend an argument that their point 'doth not belong to the Question' (XII 288) and he observes of others that 'when we drive them thus far, they always retire to the main Body of the Argument. . . . Now, whether this be a sincere Way of arguing, I will appeal to any other Judgment but theirs' (II 123). When the *Medley* publishes a thinly disguised libel on the Speaker of the House of Commons, so worded that the reader cannot easily mistake the object of attack, Swift attacks in turn and comments, 'I shall be pleased to see him have Recourse to the old Evasion, and say, that I who make the Application, am chargeable with the Abuse: Let any Reader of either Party be Judge' (III 156). Burnet, he shows, argues from the assumption that the other side are scoundrels,[48] and turning the tables on him Swift shows how deceitful the trick is (IV 63–4, 83). 'But what disgusts me from having any thing to do with this Race of *Answer-jobbers*', he says, 'is, that they have no sort of Conscience in their Dealings'. He points out how by altering terms and phrases to suit himself – to make his argument telling – his opponent maliciously distorts the meaning of what he tries to refute.[49] 'This is what the *Whigs* call answering a Book' (VI 96–7). He exposes the same stratagem when he says, 'It is grown a mighty Conceit, among some Men, to melt down the Phrase of a *Church established by Law*, into that of the *Religion of the Magistrate*; of which Appelation it is easier to find the Reason [behind it] than the Sense: If, by the *Magistrate*, they mean the *Prince*, the Expression includes a Falshood; for when King *James* was *Prince*, the Established Church was the same as it is now: If, by the same Word they mean the Legislature, we desire no more' (II 115).[50]

Although Swift denounces opponents' altering terms to suit themselves in establishing views, he uses the manoeuvre himself, for example in his explanation of how 'many of the Clergy and other learned Men, deceived by a dubious Expression, mistook the *Object* to which *Passive Obedience* was due' (II 16). Similarly he employs the stratagem of claiming an unproved conclusion as proved, which Aristotle calls 'the most highly sophistical of all the unfair tricks of questioners'.[51] Swift had used the stratagem as the Examiner in 1713, as his Whig opponents recalled in 1727 (v xiv), and yet Swift as a competent answerer will not allow questioners to use the stratagem against him. He will not allow an opponent's assertion or affirmation to pass as 'a Thing granted' (III 198; IV 76) or 'as Matters fully determined on' (IV 69). 'These are the Facts he all along takes for granted, and argues accordingly' (IV 68), he says of Burnet. 'A pretty artful Episcopal Method is this', he says again of Bishop Burnet, 'of calling his Brethren as many injurious Names as he pleaseth. It is but quoting a Text of Scripture, where the Characters of evil Men are described, and the Thing is done' (IV 77).

ATTACKING METAPHORS

Dialectical disputation must not employ metaphors, Aristotle warns (*Post. An.*, 97^b37–40), because they are always obscure, making it possible for an answerer to argue sophistically against the user of a metaphorical expression as though he had used it in its literal sense.[52] Swift makes superficial comments on opponents' metaphors: for example, when Burnet says, 'in the management of that run of success', and Swift glances, 'A metaphor, but from gamesters' (v 275). Tindal observes, 'And the Body Politick, whether Ecclesiastical, or Civil, must be dealt with after the same Manner as the Body Natural', and Swift replies, 'What, because it is called a Body, and is a Simile, must it hold in all Circumstances' (II 94). He ridicules this metaphor in *Gulliver's Travels* (iii 6): 'Whereas all Writers and Reasoners have agreed, that there is a strict universal Resemblance between the natural and the political Body; can there be anything more evident, than that the Health of both must be preserved, and the Diseases cured by the same Prescriptions?' but he uses it at the opening of the 'Contests and Dissensions'.

In a passage in *The Rights of the Christian Church*, Tindal makes much of his metaphorical definition that clergymen are God's ambassadors and therefore they are sent from heaven and cannot be made on earth. Swift replies, 'But you know an Ambassador may leave a Secretary' (II 91), a reference to Tindal's suggestion that clergymen are at best 'only Commentators, Note-makers, or Sermon-makers on those Doctrines which the Embassadors of God [Christ and his Apostles] once deliver'd to the Saints' (p. 78). This holding of Tindal to the literal sense of his metaphor[53] occurs again when

Tindal makes an assertion which includes the qualifying parenthetical expression 'if Fame be not a Liar'. Swift answers, 'It is fair to produce Witnesses, is she a Lyar or not?' (II 90). Tindal personified Fame and Swift calls her into court. Tindal questioned her truthfulness and Swift holds him to that also.

Burnet uses a metaphor to describe his party, who 'make themselves a Wall for their Church and Country', which Swift quotes, replying, 'a *South* Wall, I suppose, for all the best Fruit of the *Church and Country* to be nailed on' (IV 81). Then he names his dialectical manoeuvre: 'Let us examine this Metaphor', which he does more appropriately in a martial defence sense than in the former sense of ripening political plums. He quotes Burnet again, 'They lie in the Dust, mourning before him', and answers, 'Hang me, if I believe that, unless it be figuratively spoken. But suppose it to be true, Why do *they lie in the Dust*? Because they love to *raise* it; for what do *they mourn*? Why, for Power, Wealth and Places. There let the Enemies of the Queen and Monarch, and the Church *lie* and *mourn*, and *lick* the *Dust* like *Serpents*, till they are truly sensible of their Ingratitude, Falshood, Disobedience, Slander, Blasphemy, Sedition, *and every evil Work*' (IV 82). The shift from taking the metaphor literally to attacking the opponent is forthright and largely devoid of logical parody, wit, humour, irony, paradox or nonsense, often found in Swiftian dialectic. The next chapter will show how ripostes like the one above can turn into satire with the infusion of humour bred of witty analogies and various kinds of toying with logic.

The use of metaphors in dialectic is unwise because, as Aristotle warns and Swift shows, the metaphorical element can serve an opponent as a syllogistic term ready for drawing a conclusion surprisingly different from what the user of the metaphor might have expected, and one to his disadvantage in argument, even to his embarrassment. The method is similar to the *reductio ad impossibile* to the extent that it uses the terms given by an opponent to turn back on him a conclusion logically sound but far from what he had expected.

EXPOSING WIT AND SOURCES

In order to discomfit his opponent Tindal, Swift points out instances when Tindal would pass lamely for a wit. When Tindal compares

churches with traps and churchmen with trap-setters, Swift replies
simply, 'Remark his Wit' (II 90),[54] and when Tindal applies a
Babylonian metaphor to the contemporary church, Swift responds,
'I will do him Justice, and take Notice, when he is witty' (II 90).
Tindal uses a simile, 'Kings and People, who (as the Indians do the
Devil) adored the Pope out of Fear', and Swift answers, 'I am in
doubt whether I shall allow that for Wit or no, &c. Look you in
these Cases, preface it thus; if one may use an old Saying' (II 90).[55]
Tindal uses the phrase, 'Play the Devil for God's Sake', and Swift
replies, 'If this meant for Wit; I would be glad to observe it, but in
such Cases I look whether there be common Sense' (II 99), and to
Tindal's phrase, 'The Pope, and other great Church Dons', Swift
replies, 'I suppose he meaneth Bishops: But I wish, he would
explain himself and not be so very witty in the midst of an
Argument; it is like two Mediums; not fair in disputing' (II 95).

Denying stratagems and devices to others which one uses oneself
might be called at least inconsistency, which might challenge the
view of Swift as a consistent moralist. These instances in themselves
are negligible, but together with other examples of Swiftian
inconsistency in argument they suggest that Swift was more a
dialectical pamphleteer than a moralist. His own sense of dialectical
superiority[56] and of the inconsistency natural to men[57] tends to
confirm this suggestion, especially if one believes with Aristotle in
parts of the *Topics* and with Schopenhauer that the dialectician is
out for victory rather than truth, the latter being determined for him
by whatever passes for the opinions currently received by the wise
or the majority or both. An example is Swift's assurance that he was
on the side of truth when defending the Tories because the queen
preferred them as ministers and the people had elected them to a
majority in the Commons. To be fair, however, one should
acknowledge that Swift responded to many attacks of various kinds
over many years and initiated some, and yet his principles remained
reasonably steady in spite of some contradictory positions he took in
the excitement of dialectical combat or in the delight of ironic,
playful satire.

A good dialectician does not miss a chance to display his own
knowledge and belittle his opponent's, both of which can be effected
by citing an opponent's sources. In a single paragraph Swift
disparages the legal authorities Tindal uses and Tindal's interpretation
of them, mentions Tindal's authorities' utter ignorance of early
historical sources 'further than a Quotation or an Index' and shows

that when they do have recourse to ancient history for support they rely on Tacitus, although 'they might have deduced it much more fairly from *Aristotle* and *Polybius*' (II 83). Exposing Tindal's attempt at wit by citing his source, Swift quotes a line from Tindal, 'Churches serve to worse Purposes than Bear-Gardens', and says only, 'This from *Hudibras*' (II 118). To a remark of Tindal's about the state of nature, he replies, 'False; he doth not seem to understand the State of Nature, although he hath borrowed it from Hobbes' (II 88).[58] He uses the same tactic against Steele: 'This Paragraph of Mr. *Steele*'s, which he sets down as an Observation of his own, is a miserable mangled Translation of six Verses out of that famous Poet' Virgil, and Swift translates part of the passage as a further insult (VIII 43–4). When Steele tries to excite fear of the Pretender, Swift observes: 'this is the Spittle of the Bishop of *Sarum*, which our Author licks up, and swallows, and then coughs out again, with an Addition of his own Phlegm' (VIII 36). The scorn in this attack is similar to many of Swift's remarks about his opponents' style, which with other kinds of personal attack in dialectic will be the subject of the concluding sections of this chapter.

CRITICISING STYLE

The fourth of the five aims of 'those who argue as competitors and rivals to the death' is to reduce the opponent to solecism: that is, to make him, in consequence of the argument, use an ungrammatical expression (*Soph. El.*, 165^{b}12–22). Aristotle suggests this aim as the questioner's, but Swift as answerer frequently takes pains to point out his opponent's faults in grammar and style, although he did not cause them. This stratagem would obviously have an effect upon an opponent guilty of poor style in pamphlet controversy. In the *Tale* Swift calls the style of Thomas Vaughan 'unintelligible Fustian' (p. 127) and that of Wotton 'laborious Eloquence' (p. 129), and in his 'Predictions' he remarks that Partridge, Gadbury and other astrologers 'do not so much understand Grammar and Syntax' and thus write unintelligible English (II 142). Tindal's book is 'motley, inconsistent', with a 'Flatness of Thought and Stile' (II 68), 'his Stile is naturally harsh and ungrateful to the Ear', his lines 'perfect Nonsense and Blunder' (II 78) and his definitions merit only sarcastic praise (II 80). Complimenting his own style, Swift speaks of 'the *Examiner*, a Paper writ with plain Sense, and in a tolerable Style'

(III 87), and when an opponent borrows a phrase and turns it back on him, Swift comments parenthetically, 'a Phrase I unwillingly lend him, because it cost me some Pains to invent' (III 201).

He particularly criticises Steele, who 'hath no Invention, nor is Master of a tolerable Style' (VIII 5–6) and whose faults lie in 'studying Cadence instead of Propriety, and filling up Nitches with Words before he has adjusted his Conceptions to them' (VIII 22). The Whigs, who sponsored Steele's *Crisis*, care not for wit, style and argument, but only for the scratching out of pamphlets (VIII 31);[59] yet they have in Steele a writer above the inferior class, 'provided he would a little regard the Propriety and Disposition of his Words, consult the Grammatical Part, and get some Information in the Subject he intends to handle' (VIII 32). The *Crisis*, Swift says, is characterised by follies, falsehoods, absurdities (VIII 34), plausible nonsense, barrenness and flatness (36), improprieties (44) and solecisms (46). Swift closely examines Steele's five maxims on liberty: 'In the Second, He *desires to be understood to mean*; that is, he desires to be meant to mean, or to be understood to understand' (46), and after giving an abbreviated form of the fifth maxim Swift says he will leave it to Steele to make it out (47).

He criticises Burnet's style almost as much as he does Steele's. He is forced only by necessity to apply the word 'Stile' to the expressions of Burnet and other Whig writers (IV 57). 'I would advise him, if it be not too late in his Life, to endeavour a little at mending his Style, which is mighty defective in the *Circumstances* of Grammar, Propriety, Politeness and Smoothness', so that his manner is 'very grating to an *English* Ear',[60] partly because 'endeavouring at Rhetorical *Flowers*, he gives only Bunches of Thistles [the Scottish national emblem] of which I could present the Reader with a plentiful Crop; but I refer him to every Page and Line of the Pamphlet itself' (IV 82–3). Although Swift had criticised Bentley's invective style in controversy in the *Tale* (pp. 251–2), he seems to prefer that 'plain *Billingsgate* Way of calling Names' (IV 69) to Burnet's circumlocutions, which are equally abusive. In the margin of Burnet's *History of My Own Times* he criticises the mean Scots expressions (v 183) and translates some of them (v 278, 280); he points out inconsistencies in tense (v 281) and annoying repetitions of verbs (269) and the word *that* (272);[61] he observes 'This wants grammar' (269), and concludes generally, 'I never read so ill a style' (266).

Criticism of an opponent's style in pamphlet warfare would seem to have an effect similar to that produced by a disputant's air of calm superiority in a disputation in which the opponents face each other. 'In Scholastic Disputes', Swift observes in the *Tale*, 'nothing serves to rouze the Spleen of him that *Opposes*, so much as a kind of Pedantick affected Calmness in the *Respondent*' (p. 140). Few effective retorts apply to a valid criticism of one's style.

PERSONAL ATTACK

Two kinds of personal attack are distinguishable in argument: *ad hominem* and *ad personam*. The *argumentum ad hominem* passes from the objective discussion of the subject (*argumentum ad rem*) to the statements or admissions one's opponent has made about the subject, and the *argumentum ad personam* is a total neglect of the subject for an attack upon the opponent's person with offensive and spiteful remarks.[62] The argument *ad hominem*, as Whately points out, actually establishes a conclusion: not the absolute and general one in question, but one relative and particular to the opponent; not that *x* is true, but that the opponent, in accordance with his line of reasoning, or his conduct or situation, must admit its truth.[63]

Both Wotton[64] and Oldmixon,[65] among others, criticised Swift, a clergyman, for writing a book like *A Tale of a Tub*. Swift himself was no stranger to the tactic of argument *ad hominem*,[66] which he knew conformed with one of his maxims: 'In all Contests the safest way is to put those we dispute with, as much in the Wrong as we can' (VIII 96). In a characteristically clear and concrete explanation he says that

> when Books are written with ill Intentions to advance dangerous Opinions, or destroy Foundations; it may be then of real Use to know from what Quarter they come, and go a good Way towards their Confutation. For Instance, if any Man should write a Book against the Lawfulness of punishing Felony with Death; and upon Enquiry the Author should be found in Newgate under Condemnation for robbing a House; his Arguments would not very unjustly lose much of their Force, from the Circumstances he lay under. So, when *Milton* writ his book of Divorces, it was presently rejected as an occasional Treatise; because every Body knew, he had a Shrew for his Wife. Neither can there be any Reason imagined, why he might not, after he was blind, have writ

another upon the Danger and Inconvenience of Eyes.[67] But, it is a Piece of Logic which will hardly pass on the World; that because one Man hath a sore Nose, therefore all the Town should put Plaisters upon theirs. (II 67–8)

In several places he directs this kind of argument to Tindal: 'the Author introduceth the Arguments he formerly used, when he turned Papist in King *James*'s Time; and, loth to lose them, he gives them a new Turn; and they are the strongest in his Book, at least have most Artifice' (II 106).[68] Tindal's design, he says, 'is either to run down Christianity, or set up Popery; and the latter is more charitable to think, and, from his past Life, highly probable' (II 106). He is similarly quick to use this kind of argument on Burnet. 'That early love of liberty he boasts of is absolutely false; for the first book that I believe he ever published is an entire treatise in favour of passive obedience and absolute power; so that his reflections on the clergy, for asserting, and then changing those principles, come very improperly from him' (V 183). As one of the affluent Whig episcopacy who disparaged the impecunious lower clergy,[69] Burnet especially irritated Swift. 'But nothing is so hard for those, who abound in Riches, as to conceive how others can be in Want. How can the neighbouring Vicar feel Cold or Hunger, while my Lord is seated by a good Fire in the warmest Room of his Palace, with a dozen Dishes before him?' (IV 65).

When one is looking for methods other than direct logical refutation in an attempt to gain victory over an opponent, Aristotle suggests that 'there is anger and contentiousness, for when agitated everybody is less able to take care of himself. Elementary rules for producing anger are to make a show of the wish to play foul, and to be altogether shameless' (*Soph. El.*, 174^{a}20–3). Seventeenth-century logic manuals sometimes pass on this advice, as does, for example, Thomas Granger's *Syntagma Logicum*, where in a chapter on answering merely apparent objections he suggests angering an opponent so that he goes for his sword, a procedure especially useful if the provoker is more strong than wise.[70] Dryden in the epilogue to *All for Love* (1674) observes, 'Poets, like disputants, when reasons fail/Have one sure refuge left, and that's to rail'. Speaking in the *Tale* of the effect of satire, Swift says that 'Anger and Fury, though they add Strength to the *Sinews* of the *Body*, yet are found to relax those of the *Mind*, and to render all its Efforts feeble and impotent' (p. 215). In his 'Vindication of Isaac Bickerstaff' he shows a mock aversion to this tactic, the *argumentum ad personam* – 'Scurrility and Passion, in a Controversy among *Scholars*, is just so much of nothing to the Purpose; and, at best, a tacit Confession of a weak Cause' (II 159) – but he sometimes uses it in his dialectic. He says he will not call his opponents 'the Vilest and most Ignorant among Mankind' but he does call them 'those Wretches' (II 113) and because his opponents call the Examiner names like an 'abandon'd Wretch' (III 249), 'a poor *Paper-Pedlar*, every *Thursday*, like the veriest *Rascals* in the Kingdom' and include him with the '*Scum of Mankind*' (III 256), he sometimes returns the attack, as he does to the Whig paper, the *Medley*, at which he directs these words: 'Factious Rancour, false Wit, abandoned Scurrility, impudent Falshood, and servile Pedantry' (III 154). Regarding Wood, he is determined 'to shew the insupportable Villany and Impudence of that incorrigible Wretch'.[71]

Because the polished insult employs the logic which is the basis of much of his witty, ironical and satirical dialectic, it is more natural to Swift than is straightforward abuse. It is no surprise that the objects of some of his best insults are Steele, Burnet and Tindal. A mild example occurs in 'The Importance of the *Guardian* Considered', a pamphlet in the form of a letter to the Bailiff of Stockbridge, a borough which had recently elected Steele as its representative in parliament. 'I would therefore place the *Importance* of this Gentleman before you in a clearer Light than he has given himself the Trouble to do; without running into his early History, because I owe him no Malice' (VIII 5). In 'The Publick Spirit of the Whigs' he comments on Steele's allegations concerning the French King and the Duke of Savoy. 'This is one of those Facts wherein I am most inclined to believe the Author, because it is what he must needs be utterly ignorant of, and therefore might possibly be true' (VIII 64). In like manner he says of a legal point in church history made by Burnet, 'I shall believe it to be so, although I happen to read it in his Lordship's History' (IV 66). In these last two examples, like the two which follow, it is the implication in the form of the buried premise of the enthymeme which carries the insult to Burnet. 'It is a famous Saying of his', Swift says, '*That he looks upon every Layman to be an honest Man, until he is by Experience convinced to the contrary: And every Clergyman as a Knave, until he finds him to be an honest Man.* . . . I am afraid they [lower clergy, as opposed to bishops] would think such a Conviction might be no very advantageous Bargain; to gain the Character of an honest Man with his Lordship, and lose it with the rest of the World' (IV 71). Another example of logical inversion, or argument from contraries, concludes with a frequent Swiftian device, the clinching of his argument with an apt, concrete analogy:

> By crying out *Halters, Gibbets, Faggots, Inquisition, Popery, Slavery*, and the *Pretender* . . . , he little considers what a World of Mischief he doth to his Cause. It is very convenient, for the present Designs of that Faction, to spread the Opinion of our immediate Danger from *Popery* and the *Pretender*. His Directors therefore ought, in my humble Opinion, to have employed his Lordship in publishing a Book, wherein he should have asserted, by the most solemn Asseverations, that all things were safe and well: For, the World hath contracted so strong a Habit of believing him backwards, that I am confident nine Parts in ten of those who have read or heard of his *Introduction*, have slept in greater Security ever since. It is like the melancholy Tone of a Watchman at Midnight, who thumps with his Pole, as if some Thief were breaking in; but you know by the Noise, that the Door is fast. (IV 81)

A frequent dialectical reply of Swift in his 'Remarks' on Tindal's book, sometimes with *ad personam* overtones, is the lie at one of its seven removes.[72] He quotes part of a line from Tindal, 'Demonstrates I could have no Design but the promoting of Truth, &c.', and replies simply, 'Yes, several Designs, as Money, Spleen, Atheism, &c.' (II 87). Or more explicitly he responds to another of Tindal's assertions, 'This is false', and shows it by drawing a distinction (II 89). Most of his answers of this kind resemble the more quarrelsome of Touchstone's categories, the reply churlish, the reproof valiant and the lie direct. 'This is abominably absurd; shew it'; 'This is false'; 'This Account false in Fact' (II 90, 92, 94). Some tend toward the lighter reproofs, the retort courteous and the quip modest: 'That is a Mistake' (II 91). A new category might be the insult artistic, which he gives in reply to another of Tindal's remarks: 'Some deny *Tindall* to be the Author, and produce Stories of his Dullness and Stupidity. But what is there in all this Book, that the dullest Man in England might not write, if he were angry and bold enough, and had no Regard to Truth?' (II 87). The doubly insulting inverted compliment concedes his stupidity and asserts in addition his mendacity.

The next chapter shows the transformation of the artistic insult into satire, the move from argument to art.

9

Dialectic and Satire

SATIRE

Satire, the limits of whose definition do not seem to have been fixed, is a broad enough term to include dialectical irony, wit and humour, and paradox, all of which are considered below. Readers of Swift, besides often agreeing that his satire has a logical basis,[1] often agree also that no satisfactory definition of satire exists[2] and leave an inviting door open to an explanation that logic in its aggressive and defensive forms is indeed the basis of satire, is indeed the *sine qua non* of satire which has so far escaped those who would find the DNA, as it were, of this elusive mode of literature.

The main argument of an older attempt, but one of the better ones, to define or at least to corral the word 'satire' can help show the need of a theory of the dialectical basis of satire. Rosenheim suggests that, unlike the purely imaginative writer, the satirist 'is crucially concerned with *opinion* – opinion to be exploited or altered, as the case may be, yet never to be forgotten in his pursuit of the satiric mission' (p. 176). The wit, ingenuity and imagination in satire are equally useful in literal argument, he says, and the indignation of satire finds a similar release in direct frontal assault (p. 168), no doubt because 'a considerable number of satiric works strive for goals which are substantially the same as those of polemic rhetoric,[3] and to such works the term "attack" seems readily applicable' (p. 12). While punitive satire pleases the audience by the satiric and often comic invention used in discomfiting a culpable victim, persuasive satire by means of its fiction induces 'the audience to discover premises, draw inferences, detect resemblances and ultimately formulate conclusion by affirmative acts of understanding' (pp. 109–10), as the audience see how the 'victim is exposed, is refuted, or otherwise "suffers" in the course of the satiric performance' (p. 51). But attack, according to Rosenheim, lies just outside the boundary of satire and does not become satire until 'a palpable but vital fiction' (p. 169) transforms it, in which case

181

'traditional polemic rhetoric discards literal argument in favor of manifest fiction' (p. 31) and we have satire. 'If the rhetorician', in other words, 'departs at any point from literal truth into a deliberate fiction which he intends the audience to recognize for what it is, if this fiction is a means for conveying or augmenting his literal argument, and if that argument involves an "attack" . . . , then the rhetoric assumes, however transiently and transparently, the character of satire!' (p. 18). Rosenheim's argument is coherent and shows how close one can approach the dialectical tradition of satire without actually drawing what should by now be an obvious conclusion.

A reader can take Rosenheim's argument and comments like Starkman's that 'chop logic . . . is one of the most useful weapons of the satirist'[4] and view them from the opposite direction: not that logic is a part of satire, but that satire is a part of logic or dialectic, agreeing with Chesterton, for example, that 'True satire is always, so to speak, a variation or fantasia upon the air of pure logic'.[5] When Swift speaks of 'a large Vein of Wrangling and Satyr, much of a Nature and Substance with the *Spider*'s Poison',[6] he is not equating disputation[7] and satire but, as the description of the dispute between the spider and the bee shows, suggesting that satire can be a quality of dialectical debate. Similarly Collins observes that 'the solemn and grave can bear a solemn and grave Attack: That gives them a sort of Credit in the World, and makes them appear considerable to themselves, as worthy of a serious Regard. But *Contempt* is what they, who commonly are the most contemptible and worthless of Men, cannot bear to withstand, as setting them in their true Light, and being the most effectual Method to drive Imposture, the sole Foundation of their Credit, out of the World.'[8] Satire, synonymous here with contempt, is, according to the view from the opposite direction, an adjunct of dialectical disputation. Some opponents are to be refuted gravely and logically, some by scoffing humorously at their logical fallacies or their principles, and some by a mixture of the two methods.

When Swift, for example, answers a remark of Tindal's by saying, 'His great Error all along is, that he doth not distinguish between a Power, and a Liberty of exercising that Power', he is solving his opponent's fallacious argument, but when he says immediately afterwards, 'I would appeal to any Man, whether the Clergy have not too little Power, since a Book like his, that unsettleth Foundations, and would destroy all, goes unpunished' (II 95), he is concluding an argument consisting of two parts, the first half directed objectively towards the point at issue, the second half personally towards the opponent, or *argumentum ad rem* enlivened by an element *ad personam*. Seventeenth-century dictionaries generally define satire as a witty or biting laying open of men's vices,[9] which Swift is attempting to do in the answer above, just as he does with regard to Partridge. In both instances, in the protogenetic satiric answer in the incomplete 'Remarks' to Tindal and in the polished Bickerstaff Papers, the satire has a dialectical foundation.

> I shall only prove, that Mr. *Partridge* is not alive. And my first Argument is thus. . . . Neither did I ever hear that Opinion disputed: So that Mr. *Partridge* lies under a *Dilemma*, either of disowning his Almanack, or allowing himself to be *no Man alive*. . . . Thirdly, I will plainly prove him to be dead. . . . there lies the Sophistry of his Argument. . . . I think I have clearly proved, by *invincible Demonstration* . . .[10]

In one respect the Bickerstaff Papers are Swift's supreme example of dialectic, because he not only defeats his opponent but effectively destroys him, the hope but seldom the realisation of some dialecticians. Swift had easily managed to get the laughers on his side (XII 34), a dialectical stratagem Sprat especially feared. Experimental science, he says, will serve the wits, whose humorous writings are evidence of that infection which is 'the present *Genius* of the *English Nation*'.[11] Swift himself speaks of the current 'detracting Age' (III 21) and says that 'it is the Talent of our Age and Nation, to turn Things of greatest Importance into Ridicule' (II 164).[12] Temple, Shaftesbury and Collins,[13] among others, also point out that this age in particular is a bantering, drolling age, which reinforces by chronology the suggestion that satire can naturally be regarded as an adjunct of dialectic. The dialectical tradition had affected thought and writing for centuries before the burgeoning seventeenth-century banter, wit, raillery and humour[14] were enlisted in support of dialecticians, particularly in religious and political disputes.

These considerations correspond with the element of argument, which lies just outside Rosenheim's satiric spectrum until fiction transforms argument into satire. The untruth of fiction often finds its way into Swift's satire through the entrée of the untruth of irony, 'a deliberate fiction which [the satirist] intends the audience to recognize for what it is'.[15] Rosenheim suggests that irony is 'an innocuous term' and prefers the phrase 'manifest fiction' instead.[16] But Swift prided himself on his use of irony, a word not to be discarded.

IRONY

In its seventeenth- and eighteenth-century contexts, irony does not seem to be any more of an innocuous term than it does near the end of the twentieth century, its employment then as now being for the purpose of mockery or contempt. Dudley Fenner's *Art of Rhetoric* (1681)[17] couples *Ironia* with *Scurrility* under jests, saying that the former pleases oneself and the latter pleases others (p. 133). Other rhetorics are more explicit in pointing out the aggressive quality of irony: that it denotes derision, for example, or a mock or sarcasm,[18] or scorn.[19] Shaftesbury remarks that 'if Men are forbid to speak their minds seriously on certain Subjects, they will do it ironically', which is the origin of raillery; he adds, ''Tis the persecuting Spirit has rais'd the *bantering* one'. Collins speaks of 'tart biting Ironies' and Amhurst of 'vile Irony',[20] phrases reflected in the definitions of 'irony' in the dictionaries of Blount, Phillips, Bailey and the *Glossographia Anglicana Nova* (1707), which, after saying that the word means speaking contrary to one's meaning, refer to the mocking or scoffing quality in argument and to deriding and despising. Johnson defines it simply as meaning contrary to the words used, but his example agrees with the others' qualifying definitions: 'Bolingbroke was a holy man'.[21]

At this point it is too soon to go to the disturbing and penetrating irony of a pamphlet like 'A Modest Proposal', but if *'satire consists of an attack by means of a manifest fiction upon discernible historic particulars'*,[22] a step-by-step analysis will show that irony also consists of attack, as the preceding paragraph indicates, and that irony also uses fiction, unless one must exclude speaking by contraries from the definition of fiction. If it must be excluded, there still remain Rosenheim's words, which so clearly describe irony while describing the fictitious element in satire that one does not need the concession that speaking by contraries is fiction: 'if the rhetorician departs at any point from literal truth into a deliberate fiction which he intends the audience to recognize for what it is, if this fiction is a means for conveying or augmenting his literal argument, and if that argument involves an "attack" . . . , then the rhetoric assumes, however transiently and transparently, the character of satire!'[23] These words are given again because they contain important elements which lead to a conclusion other than that Rosenheim intends, and one needs to keep the elements in mind. In effect he says that a rhetorician using a winking fiction in attack is a satirist and further that this act is the origin of satire. That 'dialectician' could, and probably should, be substituted for 'rhetorician' here is so obvious that it needs no proof. That dialectic is *a* if not *the* starting point for satire, therefore, is equally obvious. This conclusion is based on the almost fundamental rightness of Rosenheim's definition of satire, a rightness struggling for life close to the *terra firma* of the dialectical tradition, heretofore *terra incognita* to definers of satire.

Words 'to be understood by contrary' (viii 9) is a definition of irony in general, but Swift uses at least two broad categories of irony, one of which is 'That Irony which turns to Praise' of Voiture, whose 'Genius first found out the Rule/For an obliging Ridicule',[24] the kind Swift displays in his Dedication to Lord Somers in the *Tale*. The other category, presumably to which he was referring when he remarked that 'I was born to introduce,/Refin'd it first, and shew'd its Use',[25] is not openly scoffing or deriding, 'vile' or 'tart biting', but an enigmatic, deeply penetrating kind that disturbs our conceptual patterns, like that in the 'Digression on Madness', 'A Modest Proposal' and Gulliver's Fourth Voyage. These are unquestionably satiric in intent, but they are also ironic. As Swift is probably suggesting, however, they are refined, and therefore they cannot even with forcing and twisting be made to fit comfortably into a scheme of satire as raw dialectic, because that would leave too many questions unanswered concerning their satiric, ironic, philosophic and comic elements. A reader must, then, like Rosenheim, beware the lure of the concept of irony, but he or she should not do it the affront of subsuming it under satire.[26]

To speak in general terms, one can say that a correspondence exists between the fictional element in satire, the fiction or feigning in irony and the feigning aspect of arguing either side of a question in dialectic. And the dialogue between opponents in a disputation bears an obvious resemblance to the repartee of characters in drama. Such general correspondences suggest the usefulness of an inquiry into the way they come about, into the manner in which dialectic – since one of the suggestions here is that dialectic is an origin of satire – in the process of argument undergoes a metamorphosis into satire.[27]

WIT AND HUMOUR

Some things are too serious to be 'spoken in jest, or to be understood by contrary' (VIII 9): for example, the miserable condition of Ireland, which Swift briefly praises as flourishing until he is forced to confess, 'my Heart is too heavy to continue this Irony longer' (XII 10). However, as Collins points out in his *Discourse concerning Ridicule and Irony in Writing*, 'a Jest, or witty Saying, is more fitted to operate and make Impression [on readers] than long Deductions and Reasonings' (p. 17), and citing Burnet's *History of My Own Times*, he suggests that 'it may with more Propriety be said, that King *James* II. and *Popery* were *laughed* or *Lillibullero'd*, than they were *argu'd* out of the Kingdom' (p. 35). Swift agrees in *Intelligencer* no. 3 (XII 33) and 'An Epistle to a Lady'[28] that humorous satire is more effective at laughing men out of their follies and vices than harsh satire is at lashing them to reformation. Like the satirist, the dialectician who is a *committed* author[29] defends principles he strongly believes in and attacks those he believes foolish or vicious or both, as shown in part by the dialectician's preference for dilemmas which place his opponent in the undesirable position of having to choose between dishonesty and incompetence.[30] It is but small work for a writer of Swift's wit (invention) to add what Rosenheim calls the required fiction to argument to transform the attack into satire, a process Swift usually effects by means he is able to control: that is, by similes, which are reasonable in the sense that they are announced to the intellect as comparisons or analogies not to be confused with identification, which metaphors, being addressed more to the emotions, are likely to assume. Intensity of feeling – scorn, scoffing, derision and mocking – is injected into Swift's dialectical analogies, but the intellect is always in control, pointing out that this opponent is like this animal, and so forth, so that through the intellect the comic can operate, as opposed to playing to the emotions by means of a deriding epithet or a scornful metaphorical identification.

Accordingly in the 'Preface to the Bishop of Sarum's Introduction' he says that Presbyterianism is only one third as bad a system of

Christian religion as Popery, but the danger from the former is greater. 'There is no doubt, but Presbytery and a Commonwealth are less formidable Evils than Popery, Slavery, and the Pretender; for, if the Fanaticks were in Power, I should be more in Apprehension of being starved than burned: But there are probably in *England* forty Dissenters of all Kinds, including their *Brethren* the *Free-thinkers*, for one Papist; and allowing one Papist to be as terrible as three Dissenters, it will appear by Arithmetick, that we are thirteen Times and one Third more in Danger of being ruined by the latter than the former' (IV 78). Here complex relationships among religious sects are reduced to order through numbers so that they can be manipulated by the writer in a manner uncommon to the usual 'rational' approach to the subject; and this strategem is an important factor in the art of creating nonsense,[31] in which Swift may be considered almost as competent as Lear and Carroll. But is the near-nonsensical reduction to numbers in this passage fiction? It is certainly attack, and if it is 'a deliberate fiction' then by Rosenheim's definition it is satire. Its true character may stand out more sharply compared with a passage in the 'Letter concerning the Sacramental Test' which concludes an argument against Anglicans' uniting with dissenters against Roman Catholics. 'It is agreed, among Naturalists, that a *Lyon* is a larger, a stronger, and more dangerous Enemy than a *Cat*; yet if a Man were to have his Choice, either a *Lyon* at his foot, bound fast with three or four Chains, his Teeth drawn out, and his Claws pared to the Quick, or an angry *Cat* in full Liberty at his Throat; he would take no long Time to determine' (II 122). The point Swift is making is virtually the same as that in the former passage, that Roman Catholicism is inherently more dangerous than Presbyterianism, but in Britain in the reign of Anne the far greater danger lies in the latter. Can one say that this lion–cat analogy employs fiction and the argument from numbers does not, or vice versa? Or that they both employ fiction but one to a greater degree? The aim here is not to attack Rosenheim's definition, but to suggest that it is true and limited. His definition has an admirable precision if one pretends to know when fiction starts and stops in argument, but if one does not know that, satire returns to its undefined state.

It seems Rosenheim has linked satire and argument correctly but viewed them from the wrong direction. Satire's unmistakable relationship with argument is better seen from a perspective which views argument (dialectic) as seeking victory, truth being as evasive to most dialecticians as it was to Pilate, because general opinion, on which the truth in dialectic and in satire is based, is unstable, changing as it does from age to age, from generation to generation or more frequently, and from country and institution to country and institution; it often disagrees with the opinions of the wise, the philosophers, and it is ultimately not demonstrable, not provable in the most absolute sense we know. Satire like dialectic assumes a position from which to attack, just as irony assumes a view of the truth from which it speaks by contraries; and dialectic, the mother of rational attack, as opposed to emotionally-based invective, for example, is a wider term than satire or irony, including at various times, in fact, satire, irony, comedy, nonsense and paradox in its goal of refuting an opponent. All of these, in spite of a greater or lesser degree of emotion in their composition, are known as modes of discourse which speak more to the mind than to the heart.

Satire does in fact occupy a middle space between argument ('polemic rhetoric') and comedy, employing elements of both. But rather than view Swift's satire in relation to the concept of satire *per se*, it is more accurate to view satire, and Swift's particularly, as an adjunct of dialectic and thus to place his satire in its historical, biographical and philosophical contexts. One can then see the origins of Swiftian satire in its first bud as it grows out of dialectic, which in turn serves to clarify some of the enigmatic aspects of his satire when it appears to pass into an almost philosophic realm beyond satire.

In its inchoate or incipient form Swift's satire generally occurs as an outgrowth of dialectic in the form of an analogy to clinch an argument, an analogy characterised obviously by wit, in the sense of invention,[32] and often by humour, but 'What Humor is, not all the Tribe/Of Logick-mongers can describe'.[33] Tindal's *Rights of the Christian Church*, Swift says, like most products of freethinkers, shows 'the same weak Advances towards Wit and Raillery; the same Petulancy and Pertness of Spirit; . . . the same Affectation of forming general Rules upon false and scanty Premisses. And lastly, the same rapid Venom sprinkled over the Whole, which, like the dying impotent Bite of a trodden benumbed Snake, may be nauseous and offensive, but cannot be very dangerous' (ii 68). Attack and invention are here, certainly, but the presence of humour is debatable. Later he asks, What should the clergy do to silence men like Tindal, who seem to think that by attacking the faith they will be bribed with money or preferment to cease? If the clergy should bestow this Man Bread enough to stop his Mouth, it will but open those of a hundred more, who are every whit as well qualified to rail as he. And truly when I compare the former Enemies of Christianity, such as *Socinus, Hobbes,* and *Spinosa*; with such of their Successors, as *Toland, Asgil, Coward, Gildon,* this Author of the *Rights,* and some others; the Church appeareth to me like the sick old Lion in the Fable, who, after having his Person outraged by the Bull, the Elephant, the Horse, and the Bear, took nothing so much to Heart, as to find himself at last insulted by the Spurn of an Ass. (II 72)

With the force of the passage withheld until the last word, this analogy is especially effective, and it seems to rise above insult to comic satire.

In a dilemmatic remark about Steele he says, 'A Writer with a weak Head, and a corrupted Heart, is an over-match for any single Pen; like a hireling Jade, dull and vicious, hardly able to stir, yet offering at every Turn to kick' (VIII 43). In another place he refers to 'a poor Whore of my Acquaintaince . . . who being big with Whig, was so alarmed at the Rising of the Mob, that she had like to have miscarried upon it; for the Logical Jade presently concluded, (and the Inference was natural enough) that if they began with pulling down Meeting-houses, it might end in demolishing those Houses of Pleasure, where she constantly paid her Devotion; and, indeed, there seems a close Connexion between *Extempore* Prayer and *Extempore* Love' (VI 154).[34] Wood, he says, 'hath Liberty to *Offer* his Coyn, and We have *Law, Reason, Liberty* and *Necessity* to refuse it. A knavish Jocky may Ride an old Foundred Jade about the Market, but none are obliged to buy it.'[35] In this and the satiric analogy concluding the argument against Steele given above, Swift chooses a horse to help make his point, as he does in the concluding 'analogy' in *Gulliver's Travels*. In these places, in the dispute between the Ancients and the Moderns which breaks out into an analogous dispute between a bee and a spider, in other examples given above and in other places the wit is evident but not always so the humour, which is admittedly hard to define. In the analogies clinching his arguments and in the witty, ironic arguments themselves one is often both surprised and delighted, which by Swift's definition is an indication of the presence of humour.[36] A greater problem in Swift's satire, however, is that raised by the question when the satire grows not comic but philosophic.

PARADOX

Wit derives from distortion of the true meanings of words,[37] and one is surprised by the new conjunctions or divisions of ideas or images suggested by the invented remark, passage or account. Distortion of the true meanings of words leads to *falsehood*, and it has been objected from time to time that (literary) fiction is lying and should be condemned. Truth and falsehood, in turn, are the essence of philosophy, just as they are in a less rigorous sense the essence of dialectic. Like dialectic, that paradox which is a part of philosophy is concerned with chameleon truth, the direct confrontation of two counterposed truths being the essence of paradox. One of them must give way, general opinion must shift, Copernicus must eventually triumph over Ptolemy in the world's eyes, Newton over his predecessors.[38] The opposed 'truths' defended by the dialectician and his opponent become, when the opposition shifts from a dialectical to a philosophical arena within a single mind, the opposed 'truths', for example, of the Modest Proposer, whose scheme is true in so far as it is mathematically and economically sound and true in so far that by ironic inversion it is an attack on the falsest values imaginable, values which perhaps cause and certainly ignore the plight of the poor Irish, the great majority. Both are true, yet one is based on an obvious 'fallacy' of ignoring humanity. Nevertheless, by arguing from a kind of law as opposed to (human) nature, a scheme like the Modest Proposer's might be seriously maintained or even put into practice, as the history of just the present century suggests.

Paradox can also be said to derive from a valid argument whose conclusion contradicts one of its premises, so that in some cases our accepted inference processes lead to unacceptable conclusions.[39] This occurs, for example, if someone draws a circle and writes within it, 'Everything written in this circle is false'. Logicians and philosophers can often solve self-referential paradoxes like this one and that of the Liar: 'Epimenides the Cretan said truthfully that all Cretans are liars'.[40] Perhaps logic and philosophy can solve the major problem of *Gulliver's Travels*, which is thoroughly concerned with truth and falsehood, as Gulliver frequently reminds us in his assertions that he has been 'not so studious of Ornament as of Truth' (iv 12), is 'chiefly studious of Truth' (ii 1), has an 'inviolable . . . Attachment to Truth' (iv 11), so that he utterly detests all falsehood and disguise and determines to sacrifice everything to truth (iv 7). It should not disturb us that he lied to the Japanese

Emperor and the Dutch ship's crew, telling them he was Dutch (iii 9, 11), because he had not yet met the truthful Houyhnhnms. But when Gulliver's master, who as a Houyhnhnm cannot tell *the thing which was not*, consents to keep Gulliver's wearing of clothes a secret from his family and friends, we might wonder how the master could avoid deception approaching or equalling falsehood when every visiting Houyhnhnm, the reader is told, shows incredulity and astonishment concerning Gulliver's covering (clothes) (iv 12). This, however, is not as important as the larger question of Gulliver the soothsayer.

When in his conclusion Gulliver says that in writing his *Travels* it was always his practice '*strictly*' to '*adhere to Truth*' (iv 12), a statement supported in the subsequent letter to his Cousin Sympson and in the publisher's preface, a reader is put in the strange position of knowing that Gulliver is a fictitious character who visited fictitious countries and yet who solemnly vows truth in all his accounts, a situation different from a character in a novel who strikes one as real, because in the prefatory letter Gulliver (not a novelist different from his main character) is arguing a point with us, his readers. The best solution to this problem, it seems, is to see it as a dialectical paradox generated by self-reference: not a reference of a given statement to itself, like a sentence within a circle, but a reference of a speaker to one of his own current utterances. Gulliver–Epimenides, the magnificent liar (*Splendide Mendax*),[41] while defending his truthfulness cites the famous liar Sinon (iv 12), who also lied to gain the admittance of a horse, as 'wooden' as a Houyhnhnm, through defences; but those defences were physical, not mental. Like Socrates, Swift seems to have 'played fast and loose' in his arguing,[42] and not with a 'discernible, historically authentic particular'[43] but with the reader,[44] as he seems to have done also in the two central paragraphs in the 'Digression on Madness'. Also like Socrates, Swift in his best satire was more suited to raise doubts than to resolve them: an aim of paradox, to force a reader to inspect more closely the 'truths' by which he or she lives.

The 'truth' of the principles from which Swift attacks historic particulars in *Gulliver's Travels*; the 'truth' of the nature of man placed in this middle state, as suggested in the Fourth Voyage, all in a framework of outrageous fiction (outsized giants, flying island, talking horses), as told by an apparently untrustworthy, gullible narrator; the 'truth' of the 'Digression on Madness' arguing for an acceptance of surfaces and deception which, one sees from Swift's other writings, he both embraced and rejected – such counterposing of truths reflects the counterposing of truths in dialectic, those maintained by the questioner and answerer 'who argue as competitors and rivals to the death' (*Soph. El.*, 165ᵇ13). Instead of fiction, formal dialectic has fallacy, which generally characterises the arguments of the questioner. Yet, as Schopenhauer observes, in dialectic outside the schools we usually do not know which side is in the right.

Swift's 'higher dialectic' which raises philosophical questions produces an internal dialectic for readers, as though Swift had sawed off our occiputs and changed them round, so that the debate over his meaning continues. 'It is a Point of Wit to advance Paradoxes, and the bolder the better, but the Wit lies in maintaining them', which a poor paradoxist neglects, forming 'imaginary Conclusions from them, as if they were true and uncontested' (II 101).⁴⁵ Like paradox, nonsense, 'whose Property it is neither to affirm or deny' (II 78), maintains a counterposition of truths, of the logical⁴⁶ and the illogical. It distorts normal reality in order to reach a sometimes disturbing intuitive reality beyond the rational world, as in the ultimate inability of reason to cope with appearance and reality in the 'Digression on Madness' and in the unsettling view that 'reason' is ultimately incompatible with human society in Gulliver's Fourth Voyage,⁴⁷ or in order to uncover and demonstrate another piece of nonsense,⁴⁸ as in 'Mr Collins's Discourse of Free-Thinking' (IV 25– 48). In a sense Swift's distinctive style both in his witty dialectic against a historically authentic opponent and in his satiric masterpieces is the result of a metalanguage in which his wit (invention) distorts the true meaning of words in order to draw the reader's attention more sharply to what he is saying and to shock the reader out of complacency, using falsehood or distortion to illuminate truth, nonsense to find sense and paradox to raise doubts in order to force reinspection of old 'truths'. Jests too, like wit, are mock-fallacies,⁴⁹ and in Swift what is said in jest is often meant in truth.

One applies logic to *test* the validity of conclusions or arguments, dialectic to *find* logical arguments⁵⁰ and, by definition, satire. The distortion of logic, advanced by the questioner in attacking the answerer's position, requires logical solution, and that is a reader's responsibility. It is Swift the questioner who is primarily the ironic, comic, paradoxical and nonsensical satirist. The master of wit through distortion, surprising readers by his juxtaposition of ideas and images, raising doubts, using nonsense and irony to penetrate reason to reach an intuitive reality beyond, making us laugh at what he thinks is wrongly held in serious regard: this our provoker as well as Tindal's and Steele's opponent is Swift the dialectician.

Thus Swift helps us to see that satire, rather than using logic or dialectic, is in fact an adjunct of dialectic, is the child of disputation. To gain strength and live, satire passes over inert error and stupidity to attack self-generating knavery and folly: living forces which are related as answerer to questioner in a disputation, as a defender and justifier of evil is to one who probes, questions and exposes what is dangerous because it thrives and spreads. Satire is only half an argument: it is the *opponent* in dialectic facing the *respondent* before an audience. And sometimes in Swift the respondent is the gentle reader who does not know how to respond to an opponent of the celebrated reason by which we attempt to live. Leaving the targets of knavery and folly and focusing on rationality, Swift in the dialectical tradition rejoins dialectic to philosophy, satirising mankind's imperfect attempt at a life of reason.

Appendix 1
Dialectic and Demonstration

Aristotle's distinction between demonstration and dialectic (*An. Pr.*, 24^{a}22–^{b}16; *Top.*, 100^{a}25–^{b}23) is one between *different kinds of argument*. A distinction can also be drawn between Aristotelian Dialectic (capital 'D' distinguishes it from the sense of 'dialectic' in the preceding sentence) and logic, which would be a distinction between *different kinds of study of arguments*. In this sense Dialectic, as an *ars disputandi*, is the study of *how* to find valid arguments, which is distinguished from logic, the study of *whether* arguments are valid. If this is correct, we might speak of the Dialectic of demonstration (how to find demonstrations) or the logic of demonstrations (what makes a valid demonstration), or again the Dialectic of dialectical arguments (how to find them) or the logic of dialectical arguments (what makes a valid piece of dialectic).

In a narrower sense of logical validity (truth preservation: 'P, therefore Q', where the premises of an argument logically imply the conclusion) the logic of demonstration and of dialectical arguments is the same, providing the premises logically imply the conclusions: thus the syllogistic developed in the *Prior Analytics* applies to both demonstrative and dialectical arguments. In a broader sense of logical validity (requiring self-evidence or persuasive power: 'P, therefore R, therefore S, therefore T, . . . , therefore Q', *showing that* Q follows from P, so that we can *follow* the argument and *see* that it is valid) the logic – or validity – of a demonstration requires that its premises should be true, primary, self-evident, necessary, prior to and better known than the conclusion (*Post. An.*, 71^{b}20–2); otherwise the argument will not serve as a demonstration or proof of the conclusion. For dialectical arguments, on the other hand, there is no corresponding requirement imposed on the premises, and this seems to be why Aristotle's discussion of the logic (in the broader sense) of demonstration, in the *Posterior Analytics*, has no full-blown analogue for dialectical arguments. Conversely, the special requirements on demonstration mean that the Dialectic of demonstration is an impoverished subject compared with the Dialectic of dialectical arguments, for there is far less freedom of choice of premises for a demonstration than for a dialectical argument; hence the study of how best to devise demonstrations is circumscribed compared to the study of how to devise dialectical arguments. This would explain why the discussion of the Dialectic of dialectic in the *Topics* has no full-blown analogue for demonstrations. The two uses of the word 'dialectic', therefore, have a special connection, but this in no way diminishes the need to keep them separate.

The distinction between *how* to find valid arguments and *whether* arguments are valid would correspond to the roles of the questioner and answerer in a dialectical disputation; see the beginning of Chapter 7. The distinction helps to explain why Swift as questioner using his creative imagination disturbs us with his satire far more than he does as answerer refuting the arguments of others, witty and forceful though he might be in the refutations.

Appendix 2

University Logic Studies – an Epilogue

In spite of the temporary excitement caused by the dialectic of Ramus, which proved to be of little importance, logic had neither progressed nor regressed since the time of Aristotle, as Kant pointed out;[1] it simply underwent refinement. Angus De Morgan said in 1846 that the Aristotelian syllogism had remained in the state in which the medieval schoolmen had left it,[2] but in the nineteenth century the scope of logic was broadened. The formal logics of Hamilton[3] and Mansel[4] came under Kantian influence; Mill's logic was influenced by the sensationalist metaphysics of Hobbes, Locke and Hume;[5] Boole's logic was mathematical[6] and Whewell's inductive.[7] As usual the universities were slow to respond. An Oxford statute of 1803 said that Aristotle was 'the master of logic', and in spite of a modified examination system between 1807 and 1809 there was still dissatisfaction over the importance given to logic and denied to mathematics and other sciences.[8] Whately's *Elements of Logic* (1826),[9] written with an Oxford bias suggesting that logic be required not universally but for honours only, helped put an end to logic as a fundamental university course.

One of the last attempts at Cambridge to reinforce the old system of dialectical disputations was Wesley's *Guide to Syllogism* (1832),[10] but seven years later the ancient forms of disputation (determination, inception, etc.) were things of the past. In a brief period final examinations changed in character from medieval to modern. A BA examination question in 1869 was, 'Construct an argument in Ferison, & reduce to Fig. 1';[11] in 1883: 'Compare Aristotle's treatment of Fallacies with that of any modern writer'; in 1884: 'Explain Aristotle's view of the relation of Dialectic to Science; compare it with Plato's; and discuss the connection of either view with the Socratic method of investigation'.[12]

Logic in the twentieth century has tended to be mathematical. 'Modern logic is not purely an outgrowth of the traditional formal logic. Problems in the foundation of mathematics have been an independent source of motivation.'[13] To see the difference in language between traditional and modern logic, one can compare the statement of an ancient paradox, that of the Liar – Epimenides the Cretan said, 'All Cretans are liars'[14] – with the statement of Russell's Paradox (1901) as found in a modern logic:[15]

(1) $(\exists y) (x) [x\epsilon y \; \cdot \equiv - (x\epsilon x)]$

(2) $(x) [x\epsilon y \; \cdot \equiv - (x\epsilon x)]$ (1) y

(3) $y\epsilon y \; \cdot \equiv - (y\epsilon y)$ (2)

(4) $(\exists y) [y\epsilon y \; \cdot \equiv - (y\epsilon y)]$ (3)

As could be expected, there have been complaints against the domination of modern logic by mathematicians;[16] but the other extreme, verbal logic applied to any subject in the language of that subject, does not seem to have been satisfactory. Oxford and Cambridge stopped requiring formal disputation for degrees in the 1830s, and although Trinity College, Dublin, seemed still to require them in 1845,[17] such conservatism was fighting a losing battle.

Appendix 3

British Library MS Cotton Faustina D. II First Opponent's Disputation on the First Question

Questio: sufficit in rebus humanis scite locum esse in carcere.

In the affairs of human life [as opposed to eternal punishment and reward] it is enough to know that there is room for a man in prison.

Op. . . . . Eadem ratio quae suadet vt carceri sit obiectum aliquod suadet etiam ut patibulum sit obiectum ultimum.

Op. . . . . The same line of thought which leads us to accept prison as a deterrent, leads also to the conclusion that the gallows is the ultimate deterrent.

Ergo ratio quaestionis tuae hoc suadet.

Therefore this is the conclusion to be drawn from your argument.

B. Nego antecedens.

B. I deny the antecedent.

Op. Ratio cur carcer sit obiectum aliquod scientiae haec est quod deterreat à scelere et maleficio. Sed patibulum magis deterret à scelere et maleficio.

Op. The reason why prison is a deterrent is that knowledge of its existence might discourage criminals and malefactors. But the gallows discourages them to a greater degree.

Ergo patibulum est obiectum vltimum scientiae in rebus humanis.

Therefore knowledge of the gallows is the ultimate deterrent in human life.

B. Concedo omnia. Habet enim iste syllogismus quatuor terminos . . .

B. I accept everything! Your syllogism indeed has four terms . . . [See above, Ch. 3, 'The disputation'.]

Op. Multi deterrentur à maleficio ipsius patibuli recordatione qui

Op. Many are deterred from wrong-doing by recollection of

198

carcerum non metuunt.

Ergo scire locum esse in carcere non sufficit ad admonitionem ne grauius homines peccent.

B. Nego antecedens.
[*Op.*] Quo grauior est poena eo longius arcet à maleficio. Grauior est poena patibuli quam carceris.

Ergo patibulum quam carcer longius arcet à maleficio.

B. Major propositio non est semper vera.
Op. Neque est semper verum cruci suffigi delinquentis sed contigenter vt igitur uera est occasio verum etiam erit argumentum.

B. Proba maiorem propositionem.
Op. Primum ex ipsis naturae fontibus illam confirmo deinde ex proportione certa inter poenam et delictum. Addo praxin quae apud nos in vsu est Postremo Platonis authoritatem De legib(us).

B. Valde peritus es in istis patibuli misteriis sed gratissimum mihi feceris si hac omissa ratione ad aliam te conferas. Non enim nimium mihi placet hoc dicendi genus.

the gallows itself who do not fear prison.

Therefore to know of the existence of prison is not a sufficient deterrent to prevent men from doing the more serious kinds of wrong.

B. I deny the antecedent.
Op. The more serious the punishment, the more it deters a man from misdeed. The penalty of the gallows is more serious than that of prison.

Therefore the gallows deters a man from misdeed more than prison.

B. The major premise is not always true.
Op. Neither is it always true that offenders are hanged [crucified], but only contingently; the result of this is that since there is a real possibility of its happening, the argument is valid.

B. Prove the major premise.

Op. My first proof is drawn from the very nature of man; the second I prove from the definable relationship between punishment and crime. In addition to this, according to our usual practice, I cite the authority of Plato in the last book of the *Laws*.

B. You are very experienced in the mysteries of the gallows, but you will do me a great favour if you will leave this train of thought and turn to another. This kind of talk gives me very little pleasure.

Neminem istius scientiae paenitebit qui tuam primis ut aiunt labris degustauerit philosophiam. Adeo enim humana et benigna est vt suos auditores in carcere non deserat sed deducat ad patibulum. Tam enim expedit alicui ut tua opinione doctus habeatur scire locum esse in cruce quam locum in carcere. Vereor certe ne istarum rerum inscitia discipulis tuis periculum creet quam peritiam. Non placet fortasse argumentum quod illi respondere nequeas. Aut igitur obicem tolle aut fatere ignorantiam. . . . Sed obserua quaeso te dum ad furcas caudinis cursu ferris praecipite meam prorsus perdidisse quaestionem.

No one will regret having this kind of knowledge who has – as one might say – tasted your philosophy with the tip of his tongue. Your philosophy is so kind-hearted and humane that it does not abandon its followers in prison, but leads them to the gallows. A man's knowing of room for himself in prison is as good, in your opinion, as his knowing of a place for himself on the gallows. I am really very afraid that ignorance of such matters will lead your disciples into danger rather than into wisdom. Perhaps you do not like an argument to which you find no answer. Therefore either remove the impediment or admit your ignorance.[1] . . . But notice that in your headlong rush to the Caudine Forks you have completely forgotten my proposition.

Op. Hoc tuis potius praestigiis tribuendum quod cu(m) opprimere ratione tibi sub patibulo ubi neminem aliquando te quaesiturum existimabas compares subterfugium sed non patiar hoc mihi extorqueri praeiudicium. Ad legem ad consuetudinem ad Judicem ad Philosophos prouocaui. Tu ut nullo uerbo conficias negotium iocaris lepide respondes nihil. Ita fortasse videtur tibi quod ego te non disserentem sed volantem sequari. Ita enim versutus es atq(ue) varius ut vix ullum locum

Op. Surely this is the fault of your verbal juggling. When, in the shadow of the gallows where you thought no one would ever find you, you are overwhelmed with the force of argument, you think up some way of escape. But I will not allow this injustice to be forced upon me. I make my appeal to Law and Custom and Justice and Philosophy. In your efforts to avoid ending the matter with a single word, you make clever jokes but no real response. Perhaps, therefore, it seems to you that I am following satis stabile inuenio dum tuis insisto vestigiis vbi figam pedem. Quaestionem igitur tuam si placet consule: Est enim locus in carcere.

a man who is not arguing but flying through the air. You are so cunning and twisty that when I follow your footsteps I can find hardly anywhere to plant my feet firmly. If you please, therefore, consider the subject of discussion: 'There is indeed room in prison'.

B. Scenam ornat histrio scholam Philosophus. Spartam nactus es hanc orna. Aut disputa quod tuam decet personam aut tace quod modestiam.

B. The glory of the stage is the actor, of the lecture room the philosopher. You have reached Sparta,[2] so add to its glory. Either carry on the disputation as befits the part you are playing, or be quiet as befits an humble man.

Op. Mallem te meo argumento respondere quam moderari libertati. Dicam ingenue quod sentio tu si scholam ornas responde vt philosophus. Axioma contra te protuli ex ratione supplicii iudicari de delicto.

Op. I would rather that you would answer my argument than control my freedom. I will tell you frankly what I think. If you are a credit to the School, reply as a philosopher. I have proposed against you the principle that crime is estimated in proportion to the punishment.

Moderatoris authoritate secundus est euocatus.

On the authority of the Moderator, the next man was called out.[3]

(This is the conclusion of the first opponent's disputation against Boyes's first question.)

Notes

INTRODUCTION

1. See 'Scholasticism' in Chapter 3, especially the ideas of Hugh Kearney, on whom much in this paragraph is based.
2. C. B. Schmitt, 'Towards a Reassessment of Renaissance Aristotelianism', *History of Science*, 11 (1973) 176.
3. E. J. Ashworth, *Language and Logic in the Post-Medieval Period* (Boston: D. Reidel, 1974) p. ix. Her reference is to W. Risse, *Die Logik der Neuzeit. Band I. 1500–1640* (Stuttgart–Bad Connstatt, 1964). See also W. Risse, *Bibliographia Logica. I. 1472–1800* (Hildesheim, 1965).
4. In the past fifteen years or so a growing but as yet insufficient selection of essays and a few books have begun to focus on scholastic dialectic and the disputation in the Renaissance to the seventeenth century. These include N. W. Gilbert, 'The Early Italian Humanists and Disputation', *Renaissance Studies in Honor of Hans Baron*, ed. A. Molho and J. A. Tedeschi, Biblioteca Storica Sansoni, Nuova Serie XLIX (Florence, 1971) pp. 203–26; C. B. Schmitt, 'Towards a Reassessment of Renaissance Aristotelianism', cited above (note 2); E. J. Ashworth, *Language and Logic in the Post-Medieval Period*, cited above (note 3); L. Jardine, 'Humanism and Dialectic in Sixteenth-Century Cambridge, A Preliminary Investigation', in *Classical Influences on Renaissance Culture*, ed. R. R. Bolgar (Cambridge University Press, 1976) pp. 141–55; L. Jardine, 'Lorenzo Valla and the Intellectual Origins of Humanistic Dialectic', *Journal of the History of Philosophy*, 15 (1977) 143–64; and A. R. Perreiah, 'Humanistic Critiques of Scholastic Dialectic', *Sixteenth Century Journal*, 13 (1982) 3–22.
5. D. W. Jefferson, 'An Approach to Swift', *Pelican Guide to English Literature*, ed. B. Ford, IV *From Dryden to Johnson* (London: Penguin, 1957) pp. 236, 240. R. S. Crane seems to have been the first to suggest the significance of textbooks in analysing Swift's writings in his essay 'The Houyhnhnms, the Yahoos, and the History of Ideas', 1st pub. in *Reason and the Imagination: Essays in the History of Ideas, 1600–1800*, ed. J. R. Mazzeo (New York: Columbia University Press, 1962) reprinted in R. S. Crane, *The Idea of the Humanities and Other Essays, Critical and Historical* (University of Chicago Press, 1967) vol. II, pp. 261–82. For all the valuable and often recognised service of Crane in pointing to the logic Swift studied at Trinity College, few have stated as accurately as J. E. Gill 'the background which Crane presents seems to this writer to be inadequate', in 'Man and Yahoo: Dialectic and Symbolism in Gulliver's "Voyage to the Country of the Houyhnhnms"', in *The Dress of Words: Essays on Restoration and Eighteenth-Century Literature in Honor of Richmond P. Bond*, ed. R. B. White, University of Kansas Library Series no. 42 (1978) p. 89

n. 16. I. Ehrenpreis in his *Mr Swift and His Contemporaries*, vol. I of *Swift: The Man, His Works, and the Age* (London: Methuen, 1962) p. 200, mentions the disputation exercises for the BA degree and the logic textbooks at Trinity College, Dublin; 'The Rhetoric of Satire', ch. 3 of J. M. Bullitt, *Jonathan Swift and the Anatomy of Satire* (Cambridge, Mass.: Harvard University Press, 1953), contains useful insights into Swift's use of logic to gain powerful satiric effect, but the chapter, as its title suggests, has a rhetorical rather than a dialectical emphasis.

6. W. B. Carnochan, 'Swift's *Tale*: On Satire, Negation, and the Uses of Irony', *Eighteenth-Century Studies*, 5 (1971) 122–44.

7. Cf. related problems: 'Deserts of circularity' in Swift's satires, noted by R. C. Elliott in 'Swift's Satire: Rules of the Game', *ELH*, 41 (1974) 413, citing C. Rawson, and Rawson's later observation, 'The ironic subversions of the *Tale* are so universal that they become self-subversions; and the applied appeal to a simplifying authority is itself subverted by that fact': 'The Character of Swift's Satire: Reflections on Swift, Johnson, and Human Restlessness', in *The Character of Swift's Satire: A Revised Focus*, ed. C. Rawson (Newark, N.J.: University of Delaware Press, 1983) p. 65. Chapter 9 below attempts to deal with some of the problems raised by Carnochan, Elliott, Rawson and others.

8. P. H. Wells, 'The Poetry of Swift: Dialectical Rhetoric and the Humanist Tradition', unpublished PhD thesis, New York University, 1971; A. B. England, 'The Subversion of Logic in Some of Swift's Poems', *Studies in English Literature*, 15 (1975) 409–18; J. Kellerman, 'Comedy, Satire, Dialectics', unpublished PhD thesis, State University of New York at Buffalo, 1977 – a focus on Molière's *Misanthrope* in terms of comedy, satire and Hegelian dialectics; J. E. Gill, 'Man and Yahoo', in *Dress of Words*, cited above (note 5).

CHAPTER 1

1. L. Feder, 'John Dryden's Use of Classical Rhetoric', *PMLA* (*Publications of the Modern Language Assocation*), 69 (1954) 1263, 1278. Closer to the mark is J. D. Garrison, *Dryden and the Tradition of Panegyric* (University of California Press, 1975), which shows the connection between the tradition of panegyric and satire but on a smaller scale than that between the tradition of dialectic and satire. See Chapter 9 below.

2. University Library Cambridge MS Dd. 5. 47, an anon. seventeenth-century logic notebook, gives the open hand/closed fist analogy, fol. 26, as does Emmanuel College, Cambridge, MS 3. 1. 11, p. 57, Joshua Barnes' reduction (c. 1696) of Holdsworth's 'Directions for a Student in the Universitie' (c. 1648), Emmanuel College MS 1. 2. 27. The latter mentions the connection between logic and rhetoric (p. 20) without Zeno's analogy.

3. [Thomas Hobbes], *The Art of Rhetoric* (London, 1681) pp. 2, 5, 96–8.

The book is actually Dudley Fenner's translation of a rhetoric by Talaeus. See W. S. Howell, *Logic and Rhetoric in England, 1500–1700* (Princeton University Press, 1956) p. 279.

4. A. Schopenhauer, *The World as Will and Idea*, trans. R. B. Haldane and J. Kemp (London: Routledge & Kegan Paul, 1948) vol. I p. 285.

5. Aristotle, *Topics*, 160ᵇ21–2, shows that audiences were present at dialectical debates and that they could be critical of the style of argument. Quotations from Aristotle are from the Oxford translation, ed. J. A. Smith and W. D. Ross, 12 vols (1908–53).

6. See W. V. Quine, *Methods of Logic*, 2nd ed., rev. (London: Routledge & Kegan Paul, 1962) pp. 33, 39–40.

7. For example, *Prior Analytics*, 24ᵃ21–ᵇ16; *Posterior Analytics*, 81ᵇ17–23; *Top.*, 100ᵃ25–ᵇ23; *Soph. El.*, 172ᵃ15–21; *Metaphysics*, Γ 2.

8. See Appendix 1.

9. For Plato's view of 'the power of dialectic alone' revealing 'the absolute truth' see the *Republic*, VII 533a–534d; for Aristotle's view of the truth attained by philosophy (demonstration) compared with 'only' the general opinion of dialectic, see *Top.*, 105ᵇ30–2 and *Post. An.*, 81ᵇ17–23; for the Middle Ages' higher regard for dialectic than for demonstration see, for example, John of Salisbury, *Metalogicon* II 3, trans. D. D. McGarry (University of California Press, 1955) p. 79. Quotations from Plato are from the translation of B. Jowett, 4 vols, 4th ed. (Oxford: Clarendon Press, 1953). For a criticism of Plato and Aristotle, especially the latter's harm to students to whom his ideas are taught and a criticism of his dialectic, see J.-C. Margolin, 'Vivès, Lecteur et Critique de Platon et d'Aristote', in *Classical Influences on European Culture, A.D. 1500–1700*, ed. R. R. Bolgar (Cambridge University Press, 1976) pp. 248, 254.

10. Robert Sanderson, *Logica Artis Compendium*, 9th ed. (Oxford, 1680) p. 1; Narcissus Marsh, *Institutiones Logicae, In Usum Juventutis Academicae Dubliniensis* (Dublin, 1681) p. 1. At Harvard too the terms were used interchangeably: the first logical thesis for disputation at commencement, 1689, was '*Dialectica est Ars rationis*'; S. E. Morison, *Harvard College in the Seventeenth Century*, Pt I (Cambridge, Mass.: Harvard University Press, 1936) p. 186 n. 1. For the (lack of) difference between the terms 'logic' and 'dialectic' in the period, see E. J. Ashworth, *Language and Logic in the Post-Medieval Period* (Boston: D. Reidel, 1974) p. 22.

11. Univ. Lib. Cambr. MS Dd. 5. 47, fol. 26.

12. Ibid. MS Add. 4359, fol. 5ᵛ, a logic notebook dated 1652. Bodleian MS Cherry 46, a logic treatise, 1683, has a subsection whose title is the same question: '*An Logica sit Speculativa vel Practica?*' (Whether logic is speculative or practical).

13. Thomas Blount, *Glossographia: or, a Dictionary*... (London, 1656); J. B., *An English Expositour, Or Compleat Dictionary* (Cambridge, 1684); Edward Phillips, *The New World of Words or, Universal English Dictionary*, 6th ed. (London, 1706); Anon., *Glossographia Anglicana Nova: or a Dictionary*... (London, 1707); Nathaniel Bailey, *An Universal*

Etymological Dictionary, 6th ed. (London, 1733); Samuel Johnson, *A Dictionary of the English Language* (London, 1755).

14. Antoine Arnauld and Pierre Nicole, *Logic; or, the Art of Thinking*, 2nd ed. (London, 1693): see the preface, 'The Translators to the Reader' – this is the famous Port Royal Logic, *L'Art de Penser* (1662); [René Rapin], *The Whole Critical Works of Monsieur Rapin* (London, 1706) vol. II pp. 408–9.

15. *Top.*, 105ᵇ30–2; *Met.*, Γ 2.

16. *Top.*, II 5, 156ᵃ7–157ᵃ5, 163ᵇ34–7; *Soph. El.*, *passim*, esp. ch. 15.

17. The origin of the word 'dialectic' in the verb διαλέγεσθαι, to discuss, is reflected in the many places in which Aristotle describes the art as one which proceeds by question and answer; e.g. *Top.*, 100ᵃ20, 108ᵃ22–31, 111ᵇ32–112ᵃ15; *An. Pr.*, 24ᵇ1–2.

18. *An Pr.*, 24ᵃ26–7, 46ᵃ9–10; *Post. An.*, 71ᵃ5.

19. See the questions raised by R. Adamson, *A Short History of Logic*, ed. W. R. Sorley (Edinburgh: Blackwood, 1911) pp. 43–5.

20. G. E. L. Owen, 'Dialectic and Eristic in the Treatment of the Forms', *Aristotle on Dialectic: The Topics. Proceedings of the Third Symposium Aristotelicum*, ed. G. E. L. Owen (Oxford: Clarendon Press, 1968) pp. 103–25.

21. A. Schopenhauer, 'The Art of Controversy', *The Art of Controversy and Other Posthumous Papers*, trans. T. B. Saunders (London: Swan Sonnenschein, 1896) pp. 2–9. The essay is also printed in *The Essential Schopenhauer* (London: Unwin Books, 1962) pp. 165–96. Schopenhauer was not the first to see dialectic as a programme of study which should skirt philosophical issues and concentrate instead on cut-and-thrust argument. In an admirable treatise called *Dialecticae Disputationes*, Lorenzo Valla (1407–57) provides the formal foundation for such a programme of study. See L. Jardine, 'Humanism and Dialectic in Sixteenth-Century Cambridge, A Preliminary Investigation', in *Classical Influences on Renaissance Culture*, ed. R. R. Bolgar (Cambridge University Press, 1976) p. 145.

CHAPTER 2

1. *An Pr.*, 41ᵃ23–41, 45ᵇ9–11, 50ᵃ29–38, 60ᵇ18–36, 62ᵇ29–41; *Post. An.*, 87ᵃ1–22; *Top.*, 162ᵇ16–22; *Soph. El.*, 167ᵇ21–6, 170ᵃ2. For the danger involved in this kind of argument see *Top.*, 157ᵇ34–158ᵃ2.

2. W. V. Quine, *Methods of Logic*, 2nd ed., rev. (London: Routledge & Kegan Paul, 1962) p. 173.

3. Aristotle, *Metaphysics*, 987ᵇ33: 'the early thinkers [Pythagoreans, Heracliteans, etc.] had no tincture of dialectic'. Aristotle acknowledges Zeno as the inventor of dialectic (according to Diogenes Laertius, *Vitae Philosophorum* VIII 57, IX 25 and Sextus Empiricus, *Adversus Mathematicos* VII 7) but only by practice, not by a developed theory or explained technique. Zeno's discovery was presumably the use of the *reductio ad impossibile*.

4. B. Jowett, Introduction to the *Euthydemus*, in *The Dialogues of Plato*, 4th ed. (Oxford: Clarendon Press, 1953) vol. ɪ p. 200.
5. Aristotle's view of dialectic as opposed to Plato's is discussed in Frederick Solmsen, 'Dialectic without the Forms' pp. 55, 67–8 and in L. Elders, 'The *Topics* and the Platonic Theory of Principles of Being' pp. 127–8, both essays found in *Aristotle on Dialectic: The Topics, Proceedings of the Third Symposium Aristotelicum*, ed. G. E. L. Owen (Oxford: Clarendon Press, 1968). For a more complete account of Plato's view of dialectic and the controversy over its interpretation see R. Robinson, *Plato's Earlier Dialectic*, 2nd ed. (Oxford: Clarendon Press, 1953) pp. 146–79.
6. Besides the sources cited, the section 'Dialectic in Ancient Greece' draws on Kneale, Moraux, Lee, Guthrie, O. F. Owen, Ross (ed., Aristotle's *Analytics*), John of Salisbury and Hamblin, cited in the bibliography.
7. Quoted in L. Thorndike, *University Records and Life in the Middle Ages* (New York: Columbia University Press, 1944) pp. 3–4.
8. Besides the source cited in note 7 the section 'Scholasticism' draws on the *Cambridge Medieval History*, John of Salisbury, Hamblin, Gilson, Leff, Copleston, Russell, and Church, Goodman & Bochenski, cited in the bibliography.
9. S. E. Morison, *The Founding of Harvard College* (Cambridge, Mass.: Harvard University Press, 1935) p. 10. The brief survey in 'The seven liberal arts' draws on the *Cambridge Medieval History*, Bolgar's *Classical Heritage*, Leff and McPherson, cited in the bibliography.
10. Some translations directly from the Greek by Latin scholars were probably the result of the capture of Constantinople by the Fourth Crusade in 1204.
11. The section 'Aristotle and the Arabs' draws on Peters, Gilson, Eby and Arrowood, and the *Cambridge Medieval History*.
12. *Chartularium Universitatis Parisiensis*, ed. H. Denifle and A. Chatelain, vol. ɪ (Paris, 1889) pp. 78–9 (or ɪ no. 20). The section 'The founding of the universities' draws also on Gilson, Morison's *Founding*, Leff, McPherson, Paetow's *Arts Course* and the *Cambridge Medieval History*, cited in the bibliography.
13. Oxford was generally more scientifically oriented than Paris, Bologna was a renowed centre for law and Salerno, Padua and Montpellier for medicine.
14. *Documents Relating to the University and Colleges of Cambridge* (no ed.) (London, 1852) vol. ɪ p. 459. For the importance of dialectic in the *trivium* in the late medieval curricula, see J. A. Weisheipl, 'Curriculum of the Faculty of Arts at Oxford in the Early Fourteenth Century', *Medieval Studies*, 26 (1964) 143–85. Besides these two sources, the section 'Dialectical, literary and scientific studies' draws on Leff, Lawson, Bolgar's *Classical Heritage*, Paetow's *Arts Course* and *Guide*, Morison, Gibson and Copleston vol. ɪɪ, cited in the bibliography.
15. *Chart. Univ. Paris.* vol. ɪ p. 78 (or ɪ no. 20).
16. Ibid. vol. ɪ p. 229 (or ɪ no. 201).
17. L. M. De Rijk, '*Logica Cantabrigiensis*: A Fifteenth-Century Cambridge

Manual of Logic', *Revue Internationale de Philosophie*, 29 (1975) 297–315. See also De Rijk, '*Logica Oxoniensis*: An Attempt to Reconstruct a Fifteenth-Century Oxford Manual of Logic', *Medioevo: Rivista di storia della filosofia medievale*, 3 (1977) 121–64; his attempt is only to give manuscript evidence of the (supposed) Oxford logic textbook from sources more scattered than those at Cambridge. The section 'Medieval university textbooks' also draws on Leff, Thorndike, Anstey vol. I and Gibson, cited in the bibliography.

18. The 1252 Paris statutes give regulations for candidate bachelors of arts determining in Lent (*determinandis in Quadragesima*): *Chart. Univ. Paris.* vol. I p. 229, no. 201. The 1366 Paris statutes explain the requirements for scholars 'determining in arts': Thorndike p. 246 and *Chart. Univ. Paris.* vol. III pp. 143–6. According to the 1408 Oxford statutes the student had to swear, as a determining bachelor in the faculty of arts, that he had met certain requirements, including disputing, proving and acting as respondent in preliminary disuptations called 'responsions' (*et se ibidem disputando, arguendo, et respondendo doctrinaliter exercentes*): Anstey vol. I p. 242. The 1431 Oxford statutes are the regulations for the licence and inception: Leff p. 146.

19. The four classes of undergraduates, corresponding to their four years at the university, were Junior and Senior Freshmen and Junior and Senior Sophisters. The names were used by Trinity College, Dublin, from its foundation.

20. Besides the sources cited, the sections 'The BA and MA courses' draw on both of Heywood's books, Skånland, Fowler, 'Luther' (*Encyc. Brit.*, 1911), W. Taylor, A. Clark, Lawson, Leff, Amhurst, Leach, Wordsworth's *Scholae Academicae*, Green, Eby and Arrowood, Hackett, Hodges' *Congreve, The Man*, Anstey, Peacock, and Heywood and Wright, cited in the bibliography.

21. Focusing on Leonardo Bruni and Petrarch, N. W. Gilbert gives a balanced view of dialectical disputations (or 'British' logic) and humanistic learning in fourteenth- and fifteenth-century Italy, showing how highly some students and others regarded the usefulness of disputations, in 'The Early Italian Humanists and Disputation', *Renaissance Studies in Honor of Hans Baron*, ed. A. Molho and J. A. Tedeschi, Biblioteca Storica Sansoni, Nuova Serie XLIX (Florence, 1971) pp. 203–26. Besides Gilbert the section 'Medieval and Renaissance disputations' draws on 'Duns Scotus' (*Encyc. Brit.*, 1911), Cant, Eby and Arrowood, Thorndike, Heywood's *Collection of Statutes*, Fuller's *History*, Powicke's 'Problems' and Marsden, cited in the bibliography. On the place of canon law in the universities and its relation to the king's divorce, see H. Kearney, *Scholars and Gentlemen: Universities and Society in Pre-Industrial Britain, 1500–1700* (London: Faber, 1970) pp. 15–20. See also Richard Cumberland, *Memoirs of Richard Cumberland, Written by Himself* (London, 1806) pp. 80, 84, cited near the end of the section 'The disputation' in Chapter 3, where Cumberland opposes a north-country, black-bearded philosopher in disputation at Cambridge.

CHAPTER 3

1. The section 'Scholasticism' draws on Leff, Pringle-Pattison, Cranston, White, Costello and Kearney, to whom much of this and the next section is indebted. All are cited in the bibliography. L. Jardine, 'The Place of Dialectic Teaching in Sixteenth-Century Cambridge', *Studies in the Renaissance*, 21 (1974) 61–2, disagrees with Kearney that sixteenth-century and early seventeenth-century Cambridge was conservatively Aristotelian after a brief embracing of Ramism. She suggests rather that the dialectic taught at Cambridge in the second half of the sixteenth century was a response to the humanist view of learning, focusing on classical literature as well as logical debates. This 'humanist' dialectic served as a basic training for a broad programme of liberal studies preparing young men for all professions appropriate to the sons of the gentry and professional classes.

2. Keckermann, *Praecognitorum Logicorum Tractatus III* (Hanoviae, 1606) p. 109; cited in E. J. Ashworth, *Language and Logic in the Post-Medieval Period* (Boston: D. Reidel, 1974) p. ix. This is not Keckermann's popular *Systema Logicae* (1606).

3. Printed with English trans. in L. M. Quiller Couch (ed.), *Reminiscences of Oxford by Oxford Men 1559–1850* (Oxford: Clarendon Press, 1892) pp. 14–17.

4. National Library of Scotland MS 9381.

5. Bodleian MS Add. A. 65.

6. University Library Cambridge MS Add. H. 2640.

7. Ibid. MS Add. 3854.

8. Ibid. MS Add. 4368.

9. Ibid. MS Add. 4359, fols. 51–190, dated 1652.

10. St John's College, Cambridge, MS Aa. 3.

11. Robert Sanderson, *Logicae Artis Compendium* (Oxford, 1615); other eds in 1618, 1631, 1657, 1664, 1672, 1680, 11th ed. 1741. For a discussion of Sanderson's logic see W. S. Howell, *Eighteenth-Century British Logic and Rhetoric* (Princeton University Press, 1971) pp. 16–21.

12. Henry Aldrich, *Artis Logicae Compendium* (Oxford, 1691); several eds in the eighteenth century and 6 eds in a rev. form in the nineteenth century. See W. S. Howell pp. 42–60.

13. Bodleian MS Rawl. D. 1178.

14. A. de Jordy and H. F. Fletcher (eds), *A Guide for Younger Schollers*, by Thomas Barlow (c. 1655) (Urbana, Ill.: University of Illinois Press, 1961); Kearney, pp. 124–5; G. C. Moore Smith in *The Eagle*, 40 (1919) 98–115. MS copies are found in the libraries of Durham University, St John's College, Cambridge, Worcester College, Oxford, and the British Library.

15. Richard Holdsworth, D'Ewes' tutor at St John's and Master of Emmanuel 1637–43, was for long the reputed author of the 'Directions'. See Emmanuel College, Cambridge, MS 1. 2. 27; Costello p. 42; M. H. Curtis, *Oxford and Cambridge in Transition* (Oxford: Clarendon Press, 1959) pp. 109–13; H. F. Fletcher, *The Intellectual Development of John*

Milton, vol. II (Urbana, Ill.: University of Illinois Press, 1961) pp. 84–8: appendix 2 (vol. II pp. 624–55) prints the entire 'Holdsworth' MS. From evidence in Bodleian MS Rawl. D. 200, Kearney (p. 198) says the 'Directions' is the work of John Merryweather, BA (Cantab.); see also Kearney pp. 102–5.

16. Emmanuel College, Cambridge, MS 3. 1. 11.

17. Trinity College, Cambridge, MS O. 10A. 33, ed. G. M. Trevelyan in *The Cambridge Review*, 44 (1943) 328–30; see Costello pp. 9–10 and Curtis pp. 113–14.

18. For the influence of Ramus on logic in the sixteenth and seventeenth centuries see W. S. Howell, *Logic and Rhetoric in England, 1500–1700* (Princeton University Press, 1956) pp. 210, 280, 299–309; W. S. Howell, *Eighteenth-Century British Logic and Rhetoric* pp. 16–21, 23–8; and Kearney ch. 3, 'The Ramist Challenge', pp. 46–70.

19. The 'Advice' was printed piratically in 1729; a 2nd ed. came out in 1730 and another ed. in 1740; rpt. in Christopher Wordsworth, *Scholae Academicae. Some Account of the Studies at English Universities in the Eighteenth Century* (Cambridge University Press, 1877) app. 3 pp. 330–7.

20. William Duncan, *The Elements of Logick* (London, 1748); other London eds 1752, 1754, 1759, 1764, 1770, 1776, 1787; Edinburgh eds 1776, 1807. Also popular at the universities in the eighteenth century was the book of Isaac Watts, *Logick, or the Right Use of Reason in the Enquiry after Truth* (London, 1725); other London eds 1726, 1733, 1736, 1740, 1745, 1797, 1801, 1827; Berwick, 1793; Edinburgh, 1807; 5 eds in the USA by 1812. With Duncan's, Watts's was one of the very few eighteenth-century logics written in English.

21. Nicholas Amhurst, *Terrae-Filius: or, The Secret History of the University of Oxford* (London, 1726) vol. I p. 110; from speech no. 21, dated Wednesday, 28 March 1721. Amhurst (1697–1742) was educated at Merchant Taylors' School and St John's College, Oxford, 1716 until 1719, when he was expelled. Under the pseudonym of Caleb D'Anvers he was later to edit the important *Craftsman* journal, which expressed the views of Bolingbroke and other members of the Tory opposition to the Walpole administration.

22. Wordsworth, *Scholae Academicae*, p. 86.

23. University Library Cambridge MS Add. 4319, fol. 65^r.

24. Ch. 7 was probably written by Arbuthnot, possibly with help from Swift and Parnell; see C. Kerby-Miller (ed.), *Memoirs of the Extraordinary Life, Works, and Discoveries of Martinus Scriblerus* (New Haven, Conn.: Yale University Press, 1950) pp. 50–60.

25. *Gentleman's Magazine*, 50 (1780) 119–20.

26. It was practical or commercial mathematics, like political arithmetic, which, along with other sciences with utilitarian implications, was excluded from the university curricula: see Kearney p. 162, Clarke pp. 67–8.

27. Wordsworth, *Scholae Academicae*, app. 3 p. 336.

28. Richard Cumberland, *Memoirs of Richard Cumberland, Written by Himself* (London, 1806) p. 81. The eighteenth-century curriculum at

Cambridge was not only more mathematical but generally more scientific than at Oxford, as reflected, for example, in a notebook of Thomas Sympson, Trinity College, Cambridge, 8th wrangler in 1748, entitled 'A Course of Lectures in Experimental Philosophy, by W. S. Powell, Fellow of St John's Coll: Cambridge, 1746' (St John's College, Cambridge, MS O. 84). The notes contain 119 observations on mechanics (experiments with magnets, rules on the laws of motion, etc.) and 29 observations on hydrostatics and pneumatics (the properties of fluids, buoyancy, etc.). An eighteenth-century MS at Gonville and Caius College, MS 689/776, lists disputation questions almost all of which are mathematical or scientific: '*Si quando vis variantur ut distantia, area confecta ex lineis, quae repraesentant vires, sit triangulum*', '*Recte statuit Hami[l]tonus de ascensu vapor[iu]m*', and so forth; many begin, '*Recte statuit Newtonus . . .*'. Besides the sources cited, this section on 'University logic studies' draws on Locke's *Educational Writings*, Fuller's *Holy State and Profane State*, Fletcher vol. I, Clarke, Davies, 'Laud' (*Encyc. Brit.*, 1911), Morgan, Beaufort, Wordsworth's *Social Life*, Green, Fuller's *History*, D'Ewes, Morison's *Harvard College* and Wallis, cited in the bibliography.

29. And those insufficiently appraised. See A. B. Cobban, *The King's Hall within the University of Cambridge in the Later Middle Ages* (Cambridge University Press, 1969) p. 2. However, since K. M. Burton said 'Our knowledge of Cambridge education in the seventeenth century is still in rather an elementary stage' ('Cambridge Exercises in the Seventeenth Century', *The Eagle*, 54 [Jan. 1951] 248), several books like those of Costello, Kearney and Fletcher have made up some of the deficiency.

30. British Library MS Cotton Faustina D. II.

31. Written c. 1420. Parts of these stylised disputations are printed in app. C. pp. 643–7 of *Statuta Antiqua Universitatis Oxoniensis*, ed. S. Gibson (Oxford: Clarendon Press, 1931).

32. Fols. 262–309, c. 1450.

33. This was a traditional question for disputation in the Middle Ages. In the light of the conclusion of Amhurst's example, which concerns the deference of undergraduates to the authority of the vice-chancellor who is '*in distans*', the disputation question may be translated 'Whether an effect is caused from a distance'.

34. The vice-chancellor was present at this disputation.

35. Amhurst, *Terrae-Filius*, speech no. 21 (28 March 1721) vol. I p. 113.

36. The title of Swift's rhyme '*Probatur Aliter*', a 48-line series of riddles whose answers are triple puns, is a reference to the moderator's directions at disputations: 'Let (the proposition) be proved another way'. Cf. Wordsworth, *Scholae Academicae*, p. 371: 'The Moderator, who has been acting all the while as umpire, when the disputation has begun to slide into free debate, says to the Opponent, *Probes aliter*, whenever an argument has been disposed of'. See also C. Wesley, *A Guide to Syllogism, or, A Manual of Logic; Comprehending an Account of the Manner of Disputation Now Practiced in the Schools at Cambridge* (Cambridge, 1832) p. 112. An opponent could announce, '*Probo aliter*',

when he felt the respondent was impervious to attack along the line of argument he had been attempting. See Wordsworth, *Scholae Academicae*, p. 373; Gonville and Caius College, Cambridge, MS 689/776, n. pag.: '*Prob. Aliter*', in mathematical disputations; 'Observations on the University of Oxford', *Gentleman's Magazine*, 50 (1780) 278: '*Opp.* I prove it otherwise . . .'; Costello p. 20: '*Arguo ex alio capite*', or 'I prove from another principle', a variation of *Probo aliter*.

37. 'Observations on the University of Oxford', *Gentleman's Magazine*.
38. Costello pp. 19–24, 173 n. 47.
39. British Library MS Cotton Faustina D. II, fol. 8^r. A syllogism with more than three terms is invalid, one of the basic rules of logic. Part of this disputation is given in Appendix 3.
40. Actually 'P', but it is unlikely that the Father or Pater (advocate from the disputing undergraduate's college) would have interceded here.
41. The confusion in the text of the manuscript can be resolved by assigning responses as indicated in square brackets. Missing punctuation has been added throughout.
42. In accordance with the universities' function of upholding the status quo in society, the first thesis in the Boyes disputation, that knowledge of the existence of prisons is sufficient crime deterrent, might have been held in the affirmative in the moderator's concluding determination, and the second thesis, that the possession of private property does not violate the law of nature, would certainly have been held in the affirmative.
43. '*Introductio ad Logicam in qua Brevi Synopsi Argumentandi Formulae explicantur*', undated (apparently seventeenth-century) Edinburgh University Library MS Dc. 8. 17. Also containing sections '*de Legibus disputandi*' are Edinburgh University Library MS Dc. 8. 56, p. 13, the notes of Charles Futt taken from the logic lectures of James Duncan in 1720, and National Library of Scotland MS 9834, '*Exercitationes Logicae*', a volume of lecture notes taken by William Blair at Glasgow University from the lectures of his regent John Tran in 1686.
44. Edinburgh University Library MS Dc. 7. 91, p. 14, app. to ch. 1.
45. MS Dc. 8. 17, p. 18; MS Dc. 7. 91, pp. 13–14. A Collège de Sorbonne statute of 1344 required that the master impose silence if the disputants seemed 'to contend for vanity rather than truth': L. Thorndike, *University Records and Life in the Middle Ages* (New York: Columbia University Press, 1944) p. 198.
46. Wordsworth, *Scholae Academicae*, pp. 216–17.
47. G. Peacock, *Observations on the Statutes of the University of Cambridge* (Cambridge, 1841) pp. 8–10; app. B, pp. lxix–lxxii, lxxxi. These descriptions are drawn largely from sources like Queens' College Library Archives MS 89, pp. 42–51, Gonville and Caius College MS 744/249, fols. 32–41, 59–67, and University Library Cambridge MSS Mm. 5. 42 and Mm. 1. 35, pp. 234–7. For a concise general description of disputations see E. Porter, *Cambridgeshire Customs and Folklore* (London: Routledge & Kegan Paul, 1969) pp. 273–4. For a brief

description of how a disputation was carried out between master and student, see A. Perreiah, 'Humanistic Critiques of Scholastic Dialectic', *Sixteenth Century Journal*, 13 (1982) 18–20.

48. Wordsworth, *Scholae Academicae*, pp. 39–40, expands an argument of three conditional syllogisms from Wesley's *Guide*.

49. In *Parerga and Paralipomena* (1851).

50. Costello pp. 14–26.

51. *Aristotle on Dialectic: The Topics. Proceedings of the Third Symposium Aristotelicum*, ed. G. E. L. Owen (Oxford: Clarendon Press, 1968) pp. 277–311.

52. Whewell's *On the Principles of English University Education* (London, 1837) pp. 7–8 and *Of a Liberal Education in General; and with Particular Reference to the Leading Studies of the University of Cambridge* (London, 1845) pp. 150–1 comment on the disputation as a teaching device; H. D. P. Lee, *Zeno of Elea, A Text, with Translation and Notes* (Cambridge University Press, 1936) pp. 113–19, and C. L. Hamblin, *Fallacies* (London: Methuen, 1970) pp. 54–66, provide discussions of the dialectical background of disputations. L. Jardine, 'Lorenzo Valla and the Intellectual Origins of Humanist Dialectic', *Journal of the History of Philosophy*, 15 (1977) 143–64, provides a good discussion of the origins of the kinds of dialectical contest one finds in the seventeenth century, those based on probability rather than certainty.

53. N. Bernard, *The Life and Death of Dr. James Usher* (London, 1656) pp. 31–2.

54. The bishop of Ely, Lancelot Andrewes, was so pleased with the performances of four of the disputants (from his college, Pembroke) that he sent them 20 gold angels apiece. Of the many accounts of this particular Act, several modern ones are those of J. B. Mullinger, in *Cambridge Characteristics in the Seventeenth Century* (Cambridge University Press, 1867) pp. 50–3, who implies wrongly that it took place in 1611; Wordsworth, *Social Life at the English Universities in the Eighteenth Century*, pp. 258–9; and Costello pp. 24–6.

55. Chappel was later Provost of Trinity College, Dublin, 1634–40. See W. B. S. Taylor, *History of the University of Dublin* (London, 1845) pp. 235–6; D. C. Heron, *The Constitutional History of the University of Dublin* (Dublin, 1847) p. 51.

56. Bodleian MS Rawl. D. 1104, fol. 6^{r-v}.

57. Quoted in *The Educational Writings of John Locke*, ed. J. L. Axtell, pp. 42–3 (see bibliography).

58. Emmanuel College, Cambridge, MS 1. 2. 27, pp. 7–8.

59. He had a similar success in the seven remaining arguments, to the amazement and delight of an audience who had not expected the young undergraduate to defeat the older man. Cumberland, *Memoirs* (1806) pp. 74–6.

60. Wordsworth, *Scholae Academicae*, pp. 321, 25, 301, 29. This section on 'The disputation' also draws on Case, Sidney Sussex College, Cambridge, MS Notebooks 12, 13, 17 & 19, Morison's *Harvard College*, Craig and Shaftesbury vol. I p. 5, cited in the bibliography.

61. Thorndike, p. 372; G. P. Mayhew, 'Swift and the Tripos Tradition', *Philological Quarterly*, 45 (1966) 86–7.
62. B. Smith and D. Ehninger, 'The Terrafilial Disputations at Oxford', *Quarterly Journal of Speech*, 36 (1950) 333.
63. Wordsworth, *Scholae Academicae*, pp. 19–21.
64. J. Heywood and T. Wright (eds), *Cambridge University Transactions During the Puritan Controversies of the 16th and 17th Centuries* (London: Bohn, 1854) vol. II pp. 228 and 31; *Maii 8, 1626*.
65. C. W. Scott-Giles, *Sidney Sussex College: A Short History* (Cambridge University Press, 1951) p. 52.
66. [J. H. Marsden], *College Life in the Time of James the First, as Illustrated by an Unpublished Diary of Sir Symonds D'Ewes . . . of St. John's College, Cambridge* (London: Parker, 1851) pp. 84–9; the quotation is from 'Mr. Buck's Book' (1665), Queens' College, Cambridge, Library Archives MS 89, quoted in Peacock, *Observations on the Statutes*, app. B p. lxix.
67. G. Dyer (ed.), *The Privileges of the University of Cambridge; Together with Additional Observations on Its History, Antiquities, Literature, and Biography* (London, 1824) vol. I pp. 328–9.
68. Smith and Ehninger, p. 339.
69. Anthony à Wood, *Athenae Oxoniensis*, ed. P. Bliss, 3rd ed. (London, 1813) vol. I p. xci, under the entry for 9 July 1681.
70. D. Neal, *The History of the Puritans, or Protestant Non-Conformists, from the Reformation to the Death of Queen Elizabeth*, ed. J. Toulman, vol. IV (Bath, 1793) p. 442 n., quoted in Smith and Ehninger, p. 334 n. 7.
71. [Marsden] p. 89.
72. Anthony Wood, *The Life and Times of Anthony Wood, Antiquary, of Oxford, 1632–1695, Described by Himself, Collected from His Diaries and Other Papers*, ed. A. Clark (Oxford: Clarendon Press, 1894) pp. 105–6.
73. Costello pp. 27–30; K. M. Burton, 'Cambridge Exercises in the Seventeenth Century', *The Eagle*, 54 (Jan. 1951) 248–58.
74. William Wotton, *Observations upon The Tale of a Tub* (1705), printed in part in app. B of the Guthkelch-Smith ed. of the *Tale*: see 2nd ed. (Oxford, 1958) pp. 318, 326. The lewdness of Swift's language is obvious in sections 7, 8 and 11 of the *Tale* and in section 2 of *The Mechanical Operation of the Spirit*, not to mention places in his other works. Swift and the tripos at TCD will be discussed in the next chapter.
75. The Musick Speech at the Lesser Act in the spring was similar to the tripos or prevaricator speech.
76. Possibly Henry Thurman, Christ Church, BA 1652. If he made the speech at his degree ceremony, it would have been in July 1654 when he took the MA, and not in February 1652 when he took his BA: on fol. 42^r – see MS ref. in note 77 – there is a reference to 'this hotte weather'.
77. University Library Cambridge MS Dd. 6. 20. Costello pp. 27–9 looks at

another part of this manuscript. This speech of Thurman and another brief one of his following it contain several gibes at Cambridge (fols. 19ᵛ, 22ᵛ, 24ᵛ), as common a practice in Oxford speeches as was the converse at Cambridge. Another common subject for both wit and serious consideration was the relative antiquity of the two universities (MS Dd. 6. 30, fol. 39ʳ). St John's College, Cambridge, MS Aa. 3, p. 356, says Cambridge was founded about 630 AD and Oxford about 895.

78. Anon., seventeenth-century University Library Cambridge MS Dd. 6. 30; the address to the ladies is on fols. 41ʳ–45ʳ. Costello, pp. 27–9, looks at another part of this manuscript; see also Fletcher, *Intellectual Development of Milton*, vol. I p. 262.

79. MS Dd. 6. 30, fol. 42ᵛ. Cf. *A Tale of a Tub*, pp. 147, 157, 201.

80. *Chartularium Universitatis Parisiensis*, ed. H. Denifle and A. Chatelain, vol. I (Paris, 1889) pp. 27–9, trans. Thorndike, *University Records and Life in the Middle Ages*, p. 16.

81. The references from Colet to Rabelais are from Perreiah, pp. 4–12.

82. Thomas Sprat, *The History of the Royal-Society* (1667), ed. J. I. Cope and H. W. Jones (St Louis, Mo.: Washington University Studies, 1959) p. 338; see also pp. 15–16, 325–7, 332, 430. The spider/bee metaphor is Baconian. For an explanation of why Renaissance humanists objected to the *language* of scholastic dialectic, see Perreiah pp. 19–20.

83. Bodleian MS Eng. misc. f. 4, 'A Synopsis of Natual Philosophy according to the Method of the Ancients, but improved & augmented with the Notions of later Philosophers. By Charles Morton, M.A., 1680', p. 2.

84. Concerning laws like those of gravitation and of motion: 'Have we any reason, assuming that they have always held in the past, to suppose that they will hold in the future? . . . All arguments which, on the basis of experience, argue as to the future or the unexperienced parts of the past or present, assume the inductive principle; hence we can never use experience to prove the inductive principle without begging the question.' Bertrand Russell, 'On Induction', ch. 6 of *The Problems of Philosophy* (1912; London: Oxford University Press, 1959). For a defence of scientific conclusions as necessary or conclusive, see S. Toulmin, *The Uses of Argument* (Cambridge University Press, 1958) p. 168. Were they conclusive, however, there might be fewer or no (what our world calls) advances in the sciences.

85. p. 33. When Webster complained that the scholastic disputations were about 'Notions and paper Idols', Seth Ward of Wadham College, Oxford, replied in his *Vindicae Academicarum* (Oxford, 1654) p. 41, 'Was there ever, or can there be, a Disputation about anything else but Notions?' Quoted in J. B. Mullinger, *The University of Cambridge*, vol. III (Cambridge University Press, 1911) p. 465.

86. Cf. 'the stately son of demonstration, who proves with mathematical formality what no man has yet pretended to doubt', *Idler*, no. 36, Sat. 23 Dec. 1758.

87. *History of the Royal Society*, p. 18; *Some Thoughts concerning Education*, in *The Educational Writings of John Locke*, ed. Axtell,

pp. 296–7. Schopenhauer, *The Art of Controversy*, trans. T. B. Saunders (London: Swan Sonnenschein, 1896) pp. 5–6, seems to justify the apparent dishonesty of pursuing victory rather than truth in disputation.

88. Roger North, *The Autobiography of the Hon. Roger North*, ed. A. Jessopp (London: Nutt, 1887) p. 16.

89. Amhurst, *Terrae-Filius*, vol. I p. 106; see also, vol. II pp. 227–8, 230. Pope, *Dunciad* (1743 ed) ii 240–2; cf. ii 379–81, iv 189–200, 477 n. and 501 n. (H. Davis (ed.), London: Oxford University Press, 1966); 'Epistle to Dr. Arbuthnot', ll. 398–9; 'Epistle to Bathurst', ll. 15–16; *Essay on Man*, ii 81–6. Cowper, *The Task* (1785) ii 731–9; see also ll. 748–50, iv 723–6. Vicesimus Knox, *Essays Moral and Literary*, vol. I (London, 1782) pp. 332–3, rpt. in L. M. Quiller Couch (ed.), *Reminiscences of Oxford*, p. 162.

90. Blake, 'The Marriage of Heaven and Hell', *Complete Writings of Blake*, ed. G. Keynes (London: Oxford University Press, 1966) p. 157: 'in the mill was Aristotle's Analytics', etc.; 'Jerusalem', ch. 1 plate 10 ll. 7–17, 20–1 and ch. 1 plate 15 ll. 9–20; ibid., pp. 629 and 635–6. Keats, *Lamia*, pt II ll. 227–30, 234–7; letter to B. Bailey, 22 Nov. 1817: 'I have never yet been able to perceive how any thing can be known for truth by consequitive [*sic*] reasoning'.

91. Immanuel Kant, *Logic*, trans. J. Richardson (London, 1819) pp. 17–18.

92. A grace of the Cambridge Senate (1684) concerns 'huddling': University Library Cambridge MS Mm. 5. 42, fols. 83ᵛ–84ʳ, printed in Dyer (ed.), *The Privileges of the University of Cambridge*, vol. I pp. 265–6; see Wordsworth, *Scholae Academicae*, p. 214.

93. Wordsworth, *Scholae Academicae*, pp. 62, 218.

94. Ibid., p. 222 n. 3, p. 63.

95. Angus De Morgan, 'Mock Disputations', *Notes and Queries*, 2nd Series, 8 (3 Sept. 1859) 191; Wordsworth, *Scholae Academicae*, pp. 41–2, 61, 218.

96. In addition to works cited above, the section on 'The tripos or prevaricator speeches' draws in order on John Evelyn, *The Diary of John Evelyn*, under the entry for 10 July 1669; Henri d'Andeli, 'La Battaille des VII Ars', quoted in part in S. E. Morison, *The Founding of Harvard College* (Cambridge, Mass.: Harvard University Press, 1935) p. 10; Ralegh, *Works* (New York, Burt Franklin, n.d.) vol. II p. xlv; Crites in Dryden's *Essay of Dramatic Poesy*, 16th par.; *Hudibras*, i 65–80; *Essay Concerning Human Understanding*, III 10 pp. 7–8, 12; IV 17 pp. 4, 6; *Leviathan*, ch. 46, *passim*; Bacon, *The Advancement of Learning*, vol. II p. 13; Benjamin Hoadly, 'Dedication to the Pope', *An Account of the State of the Roman-Catholick Religion Throughout the World* (London, 1715) p. xliv (the Dedication is often attributed to Richard Steele); Simonds D'Ewes, *Autobiography*, vol. I p. 140; 'D'Ewes, Sir Simonds', *DNB* (*Dictionary of National Biography*), vol. V p. 901; and the *Cambridge Medieval History*.

CHAPTER 4

1. According to Archbishop Loftus, Henry Usher, one of the three fellows of the college at its founding, 'laid the foundation of his Learning in Paris & at Cambridge': Bodleian, Smith MS 21, p. 8. This manuscript contains 'The Charter of ye Foundacon of the Collidge by Dublin', pp. 9–11. On Emmanuel's connection with Harvard, see A. Heimert, '"Let Us Now Praise Famous Men"', *Cambridge Review*, 106 (November 1985) 177–82.
2. From the sixteenth to the twentieth centuries undergraduates at TCD have been divided into four classes, Junior and Senior Freshmen and Junior and Senior Sophisters, a nomenclature borrowed from Cambridge.
3. C. E. Maxwell, *A History of Trinity College, Dublin, 1591–1892* (Dublin: The University Press, 1946) p. 51; H. L. Murphy, *A History of Trinity College, Dublin, from Its Foundation to 1702* (Dublin: Hodges, Figgis, 1951) p. 200.
4. Robert Bolton, *A Translation of the Charter and Statutes of Trinity-College, Dublin* (Dublin, 1749) pp. 35, 83–4, 78.
5. See R. S. Crane, 'The Houyhnhnms, the Yahoos, and the History of Ideas', 1st pub. in *Reason and the Imagination: Essays in the History of Ideas, 1600–1800*, ed. J. R. Mazzeo (New York: Columbia University Press, 1962), rpt. in R. S. Crane, *The Idea of the Humanities and Other Essays, Critical and Historical* (University of Chicago Press, 1967) vol. II pp. 261–82, esp. pp. 281–2; I. Ehrenpreis, *Mr Swift and His Contemporaries*, vol. I of *Swift: The Man, His Works, and the Age* (London: Methuen, 1962) pp. 49–50.
6. E. J. Furlong, 'The Study of Logic in Trinity College, Dublin', *Hermathena*, 60 (1942) 40; Maxwell, p. 138 n. 23; W. M. Dixon, *Trinity College, Dublin* (London: Robinson, 1902) p. 171.
7. Bolton, p. 72. The distinction between 'Syllogistically' and the 'Flourishes of Rhetoric' is a free translation of the original Latin which refers to Zeno's metaphor of the closed fist v. the open hand: '*volumus, ut Logice, id est, Pugnis tractentur, non Palma rhetorica*'; *Chartae et Statuta Collegii Sacrosanctae et Individuae Trinitatis, Reginae Elizabethae, juxta Dublin* ([Dublin], 1768) p. 59.
8. Drawing on the *Dublin University Calendar* for 1847, D. C. Heron, *The Constitutional History of the University of Dublin* (Dublin, 1847) p. 118, describes the *pro forma* disputations for the BA degree, which consisted of three papers, each containing four sets of questions to be systematically defended and opposed by the disputants. W. B. S. Taylor, *History of the University of Dublin* (London, 1845) p. 145, describes the same ceremony. Neither the 1847 *Calendar* nor the two histories say that the syllogisms were written out beforehand, but whether they were advanced extempore (from memory) or read, the procedure described is as wooden and ritualistic as that in Wesley's *Guide to Syllogism* (1832), which shows the Cambridge procedure in the nineteenth century. (See C. Wordsworth, *Scholae Academicae* [Cambridge, 1877] pp. 37–8, for another description of the degenerated

Cambridge disputations at BA final examinations, 1772–1827.) The TCD reforms of 1833 abolished disputations as part of the preliminary exercises for degrees (see DU Calendars for 1833 and 1834) although, as a provost of the college explained, the empty form of written-out syllogisms survived to 1860; J. P. Mahaffy, 'Students' Fees and Tutorial Duties', *Hermathena*, 18 (1919) 198. The most recent and readable biography of Swift, that by D. Nokes, repeats observations made by R. S. Crane, and the more misleading ones by Ehrenpreis regarding Swift's practice of dialectical disputation in college: *Jonathan Swift, A Hypocrite Reversed: A Critical Biography* (Oxford University Press, 1985) pp. 11–12.

9. More than the 1685 tripos (British Library Add. MS 38671, fols. 19–28), that of 1688 (TCD MS I. 5. 1, pp. 142–77) has been the object of debate over whether Swift wrote all or part or none of it. G. P. Mayhew, 'Swift and the Tripos Tradition', *Philological Quarterly*, 45 (1966) 85–6, agrees with Walter Scott, F. E. Ball and H. Williams that Swift may have contributed to the tripos of 1688, and he agrees with Ball that Swift may have contributed to that of 1685. Ehrenpreis (p. 67) believes the evidence of Swiftian authorship of the 1688 tripos is insignificant. John Barrett's *Essay on the Earlier Part of the Life of Swift* (London, 1808) overstates the case for Swift's writing the 1688 tripos and Walter Scott seems to have been the first to limit the conjecture to its present state of uncertainty, on pp. xxii–xxiii of app. 2 to vol. I of *The Works of Jonathan Swift* (Edinburgh, 1814). He prints the tripos in vol. I, app. 2, pp. xxiv–xliv; Barrett discusses Swift's part in the tripos on pp. 18–22 and prints it on pp. 46–77. J. Forster, *The Life of Jonathan Swift* (London: J. Murray, 1875) p. 33, says, 'I have vainly attempted, in two careful readings, to discover in it anything that should recall Swift, however distantly. It is simply an outrage on his memory to call it his.'

10. For example, Forster says that in the passage 'the truth substantially is related, no doubt; but with colouring from the ironical tone which he so often gave to his mention of the Irish college in the days when it was written': pp. 28–9. Ehrenpreis calls Swift's claim of dullness a clear exaggeration: p. 62; Nokes says it was possibly an exaggeration: p. 10. Cf. p. ix of the intro. to *The Prose Writings of Jonathan Swift*, ed. H. Davis, vol. I (Oxford: Blackwell, 1939). The passage is found in vol. v p. 192.

11. John Potenger, *Private Memoirs of John Potenger*, ed. C. W. Bingham (London, 1841) p. 29; quoted by L. M. Quiller Couch (ed.), *Reminiscences of Oxford by Oxford Men, 1559–1850* (Oxford: Clarendon Press, 1892) p. 53. Cf. Ehrenpreis, pp. 62–3.

12. The original statutes for Corpus Christi College, 1517, supplemented in 1528, called for undergraduates 'to be lectured in logic and assiduously practised in arguments and the solution of sophisms': T. Fowler, *The History of Corpus Christi College* (Oxford: Clarendon Press, 1893) p. 41.

13. Thomas Sheridan, *The Life of Swift* (London, 1784) pp. 4, 5–6.

14. Forster pp. 31–2.
15. *Swift*, in English Men of Letters Series (London: Macmillan, 1882) ch. 1.
16. Forster, pp. 28–9. On the untrustworthiness of Swift's autobiographical recollections see Nokes's biography, pp. 4–5, 356, 387–8. In addition to the sources cited Ch. 4 draws on Morison's *Founding*, Urwick, Kearney, Bernard, Stanford, Hodges' *Congreve, the Man* and *Congreve: Letters and Documents* and Gosse, cited in the bibliography.

CHAPTER 5

1. D. Donoghue, *Jonathan Swift: A Critical Introduction* (Cambridge University Press, 1969) p. 172; I. Ehrenpreis, *Dr Swift* (London: Methuen, 1967), vol. II of *Swift: The Man, His Works, and the Age*, pp. 50–3. E. W. Rosenheim suggests that the competent consideration of universal propositions in whatever light is the effort of the philosophic mind, and therefore the 'Voyage to the Houyhnhnms', which attempts to answer universal questions about the human condition, lies in the province not of satire but of philosophy: *Swift and the Satirist's Art* (University of Chicago Press, 1963) pp. 30, 99, 101. On Swift's lack of intelligence see F. R. Leavis, 'The Irony of Swift', *Scrutiny*, 2 (1934) 378. On his lack of commitment to helping the poor Irish see Nokes's discussion of the Irish pamphlets in *Jonathan Swift: A Hypocrite Reversed* (Oxford University Press, 1985).
2. Ehrenpreis (p. 51), from whom I borrow this statement, uses 'polemicist', Rosenheim several times refers to Swift's 'polemic' or 'polemical rhetoric', e.g. pp. 169, 173, 175. In these instances 'polemic' is indistinguishable from what has traditionally been understood as 'dialectic'.
3. 'Intelligence', according to Leavis, seems to imply commitment.
4. Recorded in Magdalene College Library, Cambridge, MS F. 4. 21, p. 202, an anon, mid-seventeenth-century commonplace book.
5. K. Williams, *Jonathan Swift and the Age of Compromise* (Lawrence, Kansas: University of Kansas Press, 1958) p. 137.
6. See also L. A. Landa, 'Introduction to the Sermons', in the Davis ed. of Swift's prose writings, IX 118, 122.
7. In *Examiner* no. 25 Swift groups together atheists, deists and Socinians (III 71) as he does in the 'Argument against Abolishing Christianity' (II 36). See Landa, in Davis IX 102 and IV xvii–xix.
8. *Examiner* no. 35 is devoted to a description of Whig and Tory as Swift saw them in 1711; no. 36 traces the Whig Party from its Puritan origins in the Civil War; no. 43 gives the history of the political meanings of Whig and Tory.
9. In two of the most indignant passages in the essay he mentions landlords devouring tenants and England eating up Ireland.
10. On 14 August 1775 Swift wrote to Ford, 'I have finished my Travels . . .; they are admirable Things, and will wonderfully mend the World':

Letters of Jonathan Swift to Charles Ford, ed. D. Nichol Smith (Oxford: Clarendon Press, 1935) p. 101.

11. For example: XIII 22; XII 75; *Drapier's Letters*, p. 3.

12. For example, his concern with various forms of tyranny in the *Contests and Dissentions*; in 'The Publick Spirit of the Whigs' (VIII 37); in the 'Voyage to Brobdingnag' (ch. 7), where he says of the giants: 'in the Course of many Ages they have been troubled with the same Disease, to which the whole Race of Mankind is Subject; the Nobility often contending for Power, the people for Liberty, and the King for absolute Dominion'; and in 'Memoirs, Relating to that Change in the Queen's Ministry' (VIII 120), where he speaks of his 'having been long conversant with the Greek and Roman authors, and therefore a lover of liberty'.

13. Aristotle, *Topics*, 100^{a}30–^{b}23.

14. 'To Lord Chancellor Midleton', *Drapier's Letters*, p. 137.

15. III 33; XII 202; IX 236; and VI 129, where he offers friendly advice on which opinions a Whig in 1712 may and may not hold.

16. 'For purposes of philosophy we must treat of these things according to their truth, but for dialectic only with an eye to general opinion': Aristotle, *Top.*, 105^{b}30–2. 'The virtue of the subject is certainly not wisdom, but only true opinion': *Politics*, 1277^{b}27–8.

17. *Euthydemus*, 303c–d. Cf. *Top.*: 'reasoning . . . is "dialectical", if it reasons from opinions that are generally accepted. . . . those opinions are "generally accepted" which are accepted by every one or by the majority or by the philosophers – i.e. by all, or by the majority, or by the most notable and illustrious of them' (100^{a}30–1, ^{b}21–3); cf. also 104^{a}3–15: 'no one in his senses would make a proposition of what no one holds' (104^{a}5–6).

18. Emmanuel College, Cambridge, MS 3. 1. 11, p. 33. Barnes was fellow of Emmanuel College from 1678 and Professor of Greek at Cambridge from 1695.

19. *Drapier's Letters*, p. 154.

20. *Contests and Dissentions*, p. 114.

21. 'A Letter from Dr Swift to Mr Pope' (IX 31), where he declares his objection to 'a Popish Successor to the Crown', except where established by law or desired by 'the sentiments of the Vulgar', because 'discontent among the meaner people', especially over the right of inheritance, can lead to grave civil turmoil.

22. Ehrenpreis, *Dr Swift*, pp. 50–1, mentions some of the epistemological problems of Swift's shifting positions and claiming that the majority is with him.

23. 'all Church of *England* Men agree', *Tale*, p. 8; 'the universal Opinion of almost every *Clergyman* in the Kingdom' (XII 200); 'If I might venture to guess the Opinion of the Clergy upon this Matter, I believe they could wish . . .' (IV 64).

24. 'many learned Men agree' (IX 142); 'the greatest Part of the men of Wit and Learning' (IV 16); 'it hath been in all Ages defended by many learned Men' (II 142).

25. 'I agree with the Opinion of many wise Persons' (IX 203); 'I hear, it is

the Opinion of many wise Men' (xɪɪ 198); 'in the Opinion of wise Men' (ɪx 144).

26. Most of 'the Legislators of all Ages . . . seem to agree in this' (*Contests and Dissentions*, p. 83); 'the chief Professors have universally agreed' (*The Mechanical Operation of the Spirit*, p. 283); 'the Opinion of the best Writers upon Government' (ɪɪ 24); 'I have been confirmed in my Sentiments by the Opinion of some very judicious Persons, with whom I consulted. They all agreed . . .' (ɪv 5).

27. A dialectical thesis 'is a supposition of some eminent philosopher that conflicts with the general opinion' (*Top.*, 104ᵇ19–20).

28. *Contests and Dissentions*, p. 121; ɪɪɪ 158–9. As often, Swift maintains elsewhere an apparently contrary thesis: cf. ɪx 160 and 'It is the mistake of wise and good men that they expect more Reason and Virtue from human nature, than taking it in the bulk, it is in any sort capable of' (v 79).

29. *Drapier's Letters*, p. 36.

30. *Gulliver's Travels*, iv 10.

31. The 'author' of the *Tale* says that among the subjects dealt with in his treatise is 'an Universal Rule of Reason, or Every Man his own Carver', a reference to the two famous, central paragraphs in the 'Digression on Madness'.

32. See Ch. 1 above.

33. Gulliver's master explains to him 'That, in the last general Assembly, when the Affair of the *Yahoos* was entered upon, the Representatives had taken Offence at his keeping a *Yahoo* (meaning myself) in his Family more like a *Houyhnhnm* than a Brute Animal'. The Houyhnhnm Master says in this explanation that the Yahoos have a 'natural Pravity' (iv 10).

34. Because of lack of empirical evidence the Houyhnhnms could not have established the minor premise of this inductive inference.

35. The major premise of this deduction is the conclusion of the preceding induction. 'We often induce in order to deduce, ascending from particular to universal and descending from universal to particular in one act as it were': 'Logic', *Encyclopaedia Britannica*, 11th ed., 1911.

36. At a celebrated public disputation at Cambridge in 1614 performed in the presence of James I, Matthew Wren, uncle of Sir Christopher Wren, was respondent and John Preston of Emmanuel College was first opponent, disputing the question, 'Whether dogs can make syllogismes'. For an account of the disputation, see W. T. Costello, *The Scholastic Curriculum at Early Seventeenth-Century Cambridge* (Cambridge, Mass.: Harvard University Press, 1958) pp. 24–6.

37. R. S. Crane in his essay, 'The Houyhnhnms, the Yahoos, and the History of Ideas', *The Idea of the Humanities and Other Essays* (University of Chicago Press, 1967) ɪɪ pp. 261–82, discusses seventeenth-century logical definitions of man and animal as rational and irrational, but not the question of the ability of animals to reason.

38. Narcissus March, *Institutiones Logicae, In Usum Juventutis Academicae Dubliniensis* (Dublin, 1681) p. 202.

39. II 19 (99^{b}15–100^{b}17). Cf. Aristotle's *Metaphysics*, A 1, where he explains the difference between wisdom and sense perception.
40. Ehrenpreis, *Dr Swift*, p. 87.
41. Lines 103–10; cf. *Dunciad*, iv 471–8:
    'We nobly take the high Priori Road,
    And reason downward, till we doubt of God:
    Make Nature still incroach upon his plan:
    And shove him off as far as e'er we can:
    Thrust some Mechanic Cause into his place;
    Or bind in Matter, or diffuse in Space.
    Or, at one bound o'er-leaping all his laws,
    Make God man's Image, Man the final Cause.'
42. In deduction, although 'the premises contain the conclusion, neither premise alone contains it, and a man who knows both but does not combine them does not draw the conclusion; it is the synthesis of the two premises which at once contains the conclusion and advances our knowledge; and as a syllogism consists, not indeed in the discovery, but essentially in the synthesis of two premises, it is an inference and an advance on each premise and on both taken separately': 'Logic', *Encyclopaedia Britannica*, 11th ed., 1911.
43. Near the end of the Fourth Voyage the Houyhnhnm Assembly still believes that Gulliver swam to their island, but his master has by then accepted his account of sea travel (iv 10).
44. II 19, an obscure chapter which has drawn much commentary. For an excellent discussion of the problems raised in it see R. Adamson, *A Short History of Logic*, ed. W. R. Sorley (Edinburgh: Blackwood, 1911), upon which I draw in this paragraph.
45. Charles Wesley, *A Guide to Syllogism, or, A Manual of Logic; Comprehending an Account of the Manner of Disputation Now Practiced in the Schools at Cambridge* (Cambridge, 1832) p. 58 n. The italics are his.
46. This quality has been called in question. See e.g. F. C. S. Schiller, 'Aristotle's Refutation of "Aristotelian" Logic', *Mind*, 23 (1914) esp. 3, 8, 14 & 16.
47. Bertrand Russell, *The Problems of Philosophy* (1912; London: Oxford University Press, 1959) p. 1.
48. Ibid., ch. 1, 'Appearance and Reality'; ch. 2, 'The Existence of Matter'. On 'the general fraudulence of the senses' see G. Ryle, *Dilemmas* (Cambridge University Press, 1954) ch. 7, 'Perception'. Gulliver says, after testing the trustworthiness of his senses by trying to pinch himself out of a dream, 'I absolutely concluded, that all these Appearances could be nothing else but Necromancy and Magick' (iv 2), thus displaying distrust of sense perception, subsequent conviction of his senses and finally a (mistaken) reliance on deductive inference. Cf. in Ch. 6 the quotation from the letter to the Earl of Peterborough, in the section 'Prove, reason, deduce . . .'.
49. Jeremy Taylor, educated at Gonville and Caius College, Cambridge, and later fellow of All Souls College, Oxford, reflects the logical

training of all seventeenth-century undergraduates in his reference to 'a most necessary and most probable truth' in the prayers following ch. iv sec. 6 of *The Rule and Exercises of Holy Living* (1650).

50. 'When a Man's Fancy gets *astride* on his Reason, when Imagination is at Cuffs with the Senses, and common Understanding, as well as common Sense, is kickt out of Doors . . .': *Tale*, p. 171. Cf. 'it is to be understood, that in the Language of the Spirit, *Cant* and *Droning* supply the Place of *Sense* and *Reason*, in the Language of Men': *The Mechanical Operation of the Spirit*, p. 278; and 'the *Senses* in men are so many Avenues to the Fort of *Reason*': ibid., p. 269.

51. On Swift's knowledge of history see H. Davis, intro. to Swift's prose writings, v xxxvii–viii; Ehrenpreis, *Dr Swift*, pp. 59–65; and J. R. Moore, 'Swift as Historian', *Studies in Philology*, 49 (1952) 583–604. Swift points out, for example, Burnet's historical errors in his 'Preface to the Bishop of Sarum's Introduction' and Collins's historical errors in 'Mr. Collins's Discourse of Free-Thinking', as does the learned Bentley in *Remarks upon a Late Discourse of Free-Thinking* (London, 1713).

52. For example, Gulliver, having seen his first Brobdingnagians and fearing for his life, recalls Lilliput, 'where I was able to draw an Imperial Fleet in my Hand, and perform those other Actions which will be recorded for ever in the Chronicles of that Empire' (ii 2).

53. A joking reference in *The Battle of the Books*, p. 224, masks one of his true beliefs: 'I, being possessed of all Qualifications requisite in an *Historian*, and retained by neither Party'. On Swift's ambition to Historiographer Royal, see *Prose Writings*, v x. Among other places, he displays his knowledge of history in the following writings: 'Sentiments of a Church-of-England Man' (II 23): Greek and Roman politics; 'A Fragment of the History of England from William Rufus' (v 36): Greek, Roman and German politics; *Examiners* nos 16 and 27 (III 22–3, 83–6) criticising Marlborough's avarice, show a detailed knowledge of Roman history; *Examiner* no. 20 (III 40–2): history of governments' relations with their armies, in Greece, Rome, Macedon, Carthage, England, Venice and Holland; 'An Enquiry into the Behaviour of the Queen's Last Ministry' (VIII 171–2): great events in history result from petty causes; ibid. (pp. 174, 180): political lessons from Greek and Roman history; 'A Letter to a Whig-Lord' (VI 134): Cato and Brutus v. Caesar and Pompey, related to current quarrels; 'Some Arguments against Enlarging the Power of Bishops' (IX 48): Roman economics; *Gulliver's Travels* (iii 8): judgments on ancient and modern history. The practice of academic disputations may have contributed to Swift's habit of drawing on historical examples. See the concluding response in the Boyes disputation in Ch. 3.

54. See his reliance on history in refuting Steele in 'The Publick Spirit of the Whigs' (VIII 37) and Tindal in 'Remarks upon a Book, Intitled, The Rights of the Christian Church Asserted' (II 83).

55. Cf. 'Three *Cambridge Sophs* and three pert *Templars* came': *Dunciad* (1728 version) ii 335; (1743 version) iii 337–8; iv 189–200; and contemporary footnotes to iii 37, 199.

56. II 33–4. He denounces the 'Practice of . . . reviling the Universities, as

Maintainers of Arbitrary Power' (III 6); the late Whig ministry wanted 'to remove the Care of educating Youth out of the hands of the Clergy, who are apt to infuse into their Pupils too great a Regard for the Church and the Monarchy' (III 37); the Whig *Observator* and *Review* for many years have called 'the Universities . . . Seminaries of the most pernicious Principles in Church and State' (III 189); see also II 103, III 71 and VI 125.

57. The influence of the disputation upon literature in the seventeenth and eighteenth centuries has been noted in passing in several places, among them, 'Not a few writers of this period delight to import into the productions of the closet, the smartness, bluster, and quibblings of a regular disputation': J. B. Mullinger, *Cambridge Characteristics in the Seventeenth Century* (Cambridge University Press, 1867) p. 71; Costello pp. 146–7; V. H. H. Green, *British Institutions: The Universities* (Harmondsworth: Penguin, 1969) p. 194; '"Cambridge Disputations" Illustrative of Shakespeare', *Notes and Queries*, 1st Ser., VI 217, 4 Sept. 1852; H. F. Fletcher, *The Intellectual Development of John Milton*, vol. I (University of Illinois Press, 1956) p. 267, subsection: 'The Permanent Effects of Disputing on Milton'; G. P. Mayhew, 'Swift and the Tripos Tradition', *Philological Quarterly*, 45 (1966) 90: influence of the tripos tradition on Nahum Tate, Southerne, Farquhar, Congreve and Swift; M. L. Clarke, *Classical Education in Britain, 1500–1900* (Cambridge University Press, 1959) p. vii: influence of classical education on literature.

58. He criticises the moral philosophy of Plato, Aristotle, Thales, Solon, Diogenes, Zeno and Epicurus (IX 246–7).

59. 'Which has the Faculty of teaching its Readers to find out a Meaning in every Thing but it self': *Tale*, p. 85.

60. 'Character of Aristotle' (V 345). Cf. another criticiser of scholasticism, Nicholas Amhurst, who after denouncing the contemporary reliance of Oxford on Aristotle says, 'This old *Pagan* was undoubtedly a very learned man in his time, and has left several notable treatises behind him; nay, I will suppose, in his behalf, that we have had nothing like them published ever since, except . . . the inspired books of the *New Testament*'. *Terrae-Filius* (London, 1726) vol. I p. 110.

61. 'Ode to Sir William Temple' (1692) ll. 24, 34. Cf. 'the incohaerent Jargon of the Schools': 'Ode to the Athenian Society' (1692) l. 205, and Hobbes who, speaking of the incomprehensibility of the schoolmen's jargon, translates the title of ch. 6 bk 1 of Suarez, *Of the Concourse, Motion, and Help of God* – 'The first cause does not necessarily inflow any thing into the second, by force of the Essentiall subordination of the second causes, by Which it may help it to worke' – and asks, 'When men write whole volumes of such stuffe, are they not Mad, or intend to make others so?' *Leviathan*, i 8.

62. 'A Panegyric on the Reverend Dean Swift' (1730) ll. 29–30.

63. *Gulliver's Travels*, ii 3.

64. For other examples of parody of scholastic terminology, see the *Tale*, pp. 151 n. 2, 152 nn. 1, 2, 170 n. 2, 222 n.3.

65. Aristotle, *Posterior Analytics* (99^a1–6). Cf. also 93^b21–8.

66. II 16. Cf. the disputation question 'started by one of the Schoolmen' (II 268).
67. 'Ode to Dr. William Sancroft' (1692) ll. 10, 12–13.
68. *The Battle of the Books*, p. 241.
69. *Characteristicks of Men, Manners, Opinions, Times*, 4th ed. (London, 1727) vol. I p. 67.
70. 'On the Death of Mrs. Johnson' [Stella] (v 235).
71. 'Diogenes said Socrates was a madman; the disciples of Zeno and Epicurus, nay of Plato and Aristotle, were engaged in fierce disputes about the most insignificant trifles' (IX 250).
72. *Battle of the Books*, p. 251.
73. Ibid., pp. 251–2.
74. Ibid., p. 252. Bentley's 'railing' mentioned on pp. 251 and 252 is of course a verb denoting the use of abusive language, as opposed to the noun 'raillery', which is good-humoured ridicule or rallying. As one would expect, Swift is concerned over the rudeness of railing: 'For Conversation well endu'd;/She calls it witty to be rude;/And, placing Raillery in Railing,/Will tell aloud your greatest Failing': 'The Furniture of a Woman's Mind', (1727) ll. 17–20; 'They rail, and scold, and storm': 'The Journal of a Modern Lady' (1729) l. 270; 'thy Raillery is Railing': 'To Betty the Grizette' (1730) l. 28; see also 'The Life and Character of Dean Swift' (1731) ll. 166–7; IX 262; IX 221; IX 174, 176, 178; and 'If what you call *Insult, Buffoonery, Banter, Ridicule*, and *Irony, Mockery* and *bitter Railing* be Crimes in Disputation, you will find none more deeply involv'd in it than our most famous Writers, in their controversial Treatises about *serious* Matters': Anthony Collins, *A Discourse concerning Ridicule and Irony in Writing* (London, 1729) p. 5.

CHAPTER 6

1. W. B. C. Watkins, *Perilous Balance: The Tragic Genius of Swift, Johnson and Sterne* (1939; rpt. Cambridge, Mass.: Walker–de Berry, 1960) p. 21.
2. E. W. Rosenheim, *Swift and the Satirist's Art* (University of Chicago Press, 1963) pp. 43, 50, 122, 147, 152.
3. I. Ehrenpreis, *Dr Swift* (London: Methuen, 1967) pp. 125–7.
4. 'The Sentiments of a Church-of-England Man' just mentioned, e.g., is not strongly dialectical; yet, as the first paragraph shows, Swift is concerned with difference of opinion of opposing political parties. Later in the essay the language is more dialectical: 'It is reckoned ill Manners, as well as unreasonable, for Men to quarrel upon Difference in Opinion; . . . But this I do not conceive to be an universal infallible Maxim, except in those Cases where the Question is pretty equally disputed among the Learned and the Wise: . . . a Man of tolerable Reason . . . may apprehend he is got into a wrong Opinion . . .'.
5. J. M. Bullitt, *Jonathan Swift and the Anatomy of Satire* (Cambridge,

Mass.: Harvard University Press, 1953) p. 73; ch. 3 has useful insights, but the chapter is more an analysis of rhetoric than of dialectic.

6. Rosenheim pp. 12, 31. Ehrenpreis, *Mr Swift and His Contemporaries* (London: Methuen, 1962) p. 62, seems to be using 'formal rhetoric' for 'dialectic'.

7. Ehrenpreis, *Mr Swift and His Contemporaries*, p. 200.

8. D. W. Jefferson, 'An Approach to Swift', *Pelican Guide to English Literature,* ed. B. Ford, vol. IV (London: Penguin, 1957) p. 236. The last sentence in the quotation in the text is debatable, because the new philosophers and scientists of the seventeenth and eighteenth centuries seem to have had but little effect on the universities, the mainstays and largely the promulgators of dialectic (see Chs 3 and 4 above). Johnson's review of Jenyn's *Free Inquiry into the Nature and Origin of Evil* and the letters of Junius (e.g. that to the Printer of the *Public Advertiser*, 19 July 1769) might be considered evidence that dialectic had not greatly diminished in the 'Age of Reason'.

9. 'Professors in most Arts and Sciences are generally the worst qualified to explain their Meanings to those who are not of their Tribe' (IX 66).

10. 'The art of examining does not consist in knowledge of any definite subject. For this reason, too, it deals with everything: for every "theory" of anything employs also certain common principles. Hence everybody, including even amateurs, makes use in a way of dialectic and the practice of examining: for all undertake to some extent a rough trial of those who profess to know things. What serves them here is the general principles: for they know these of themselves just as well as the scientist. . . . All, then, are engaged in refutation; for they take a hand as amateurs in the same task with which dialectic is concerned professionally; and he is a dialectician who examines by the help of a theory of reasoning' (*Soph. El.*, 172ª28–37).

11. Dialectic is useful 'in relation to the ultimate bases of the principles used in the several sciences. For it is impossible to discuss them at all from the principles proper to the particular science in hand, seeing that the principles are the *prius* of everything else: it is through the opinions generally held on the particular points that these have to be discussed, and this task belongs properly, or most appropriately, to dialectic: for dialectic is a process or criticism wherein lies the path to the principles of all inquiries' (*Top.*, 101ª37–ᵇ4).

12. *Tale*, p. 192.

13. *Gulliver's Travels*, iii 6.

14. See *Top.*, 156ª7–157ª15, and *Soph. El.*, Ch. 15.

15. 'The Publick Spirit of the Whigs' (VIII 50).

16. 'If what is claimed by the questioner be relevant but too generally rejected, the answerer, while admitting that if it be granted the conclusion sought follows, should yet protest that the proposition is too absurd to be admitted' (*Top.*, 160ª6–8).

17. 'To the Lord Chancellor Midleton', *Drapier's Letters*, p. 124.

18. 'Do not be insistent, even though you really require the point: for insistence always arouses the more opposition' (*Top.*, 156ᵇ24–5).

19. *Battle of the Books*, p. 227.

20. Disputation questions or theses in the sixteenth, seventeenth and eighteenth centuries often began with 'whether' (*An* or *Utrum*). At Vespers (the first part of the Inception disputation – see above, 'The BA course' in Ch. 2) at Oxford in 1584 one question disputed was whether humours or evil spirits are the cause of madness (*Utrum humores an demones sint furoris causae?*). In the Act (*Comitia*) on the Monday following Saturday Vespers one of the disputation questions reflects the scholastic concern with the status quo: Whether factions should be supported in a republic (*Utrum factiones in republica sint nutriendae?*); and another interesting one was: Whether Aristotle ought to be blamed for not mentioning a good wife among the blessings of the fortunate (*An reprehendendus sit Aristoteles quia inter bona felicis bonam uxorem non commemoravit?*), Oxford Act, 1606, 3rd Question: A. Clark (ed.), *Register of the University of Oxford*, vol. ii pt 1 (Oxford: Clarendon Press, 1887) pp. 171, 175. Cf. the disputation example from Amhurst in Ch. 3 above: *An datur actio in distans?* The notebook of Thomas Smith of Oxford (c. 1680) lists questions for debate: *An Philosophia moralis sit disciplina practica? An Ethica sit Prudentia?* Bodleian MS Smith 128, fol. 391^r. Gulliver refers to the old debate, the only one ever to occur in Houyhnhnmland: 'The Question to be debated was, Whether the *Yahoos* should be exterminated from the Face of the Earth. One of the *Members* for the Affirmative offered several Arguments of great Strength and Weight' (iv 9). See the scholastic disputation question cited by Swift (ii 16).

21. *Top.*, 158^{a}14–21; *De Interp.*, 20^{b}22–30; *An Pr.*, 24^{a}22–5; *Post. An.*, 77^{a}34–5; 'Now so far as the selection of his ground is concerned the problem is one alike for the philosopher and the dialectician; but how to go on to arrange his points and frame his questions concerns the dialectician only' (*Top.*, 155^{b}7–10); *Soph. El.*, 172^{a}15–21; 174^{a}39–^{b}7. Cf. Johnson's attempt to place his opponent in an unacceptable either/or predicament in the 'Review of a Free Enquiry into the Nature and Origin of Evil', *Works of Johnson* (London, 1787) vol. x p. 222: 'I am told, that this pamphlet is not the effort of hunger: what can it be then but the product of vanity?' Cf. also the clever dialectical turn of the question whether or not to heal a withered hand on the sabbath: 'And he said unto them, Is it lawful to do good on the sabbath days, or to do evil? to save life, or to kill? But they held their peace' Mark 3:4.

22. See above, 'The disputation' in Ch. 3.

23. *Gulliver's Travels*, i 5; 'all the usual Topicks of *European* Moralists' (ii 7); iii 25; viii 89.

24. Of Henry VIII and the Reformation: 'He was only an Instrument of it, (as the Logicians speak) by Accident' (iv 73); 'whether a Logician might possibly put a Case that would serve for an Exception' (ix 66); 'several *Well-willers* to Infidelity might be discouraged by a shew of Logick' (iv 27); 'you are taught thus much in the very Elements of Philosophy, for one of the first Rules in Logick is, *Finis est primus in intentione*' (ix 334); 'The Place of the Damn'd' (1731) l. 3: 'if Hell may by *Logical* Rules be defin'd'; 'Upon the horrid Plot discovered by Harlequin the Bishop of Rochester's French Dog' (1722) l. 41: '*Whig*. I

prov'd my Proposition full'; ll. 71–2: '*Tory*. I own it was a dang'rous Project;/And you have prov'd it by *Dog-Logick*'.

25. The figure of a syllogism is determined by the position of the middle term in the two premises. See virtually any logic manual, eighteenth-century or earlier. Cf. *Hudibras*, i 77–80:

'He'd run in debt by disputation
And pay with ratiocination.
All this by syllogism, true
In mood and figure, he would do.'

For a concise description of the various moods and figures of syllogisms, 'Barbara, Celarent', etc., see L. Jardine, 'The Place of Dialectic Teaching in Sixteenth-Century Cambridge', *Studies in the Renaissance*, 21 (1974) p. 38 n. 19.

26. Cf. 'an uncontroulable Argument' (III 45), i.e. one that cannot be refuted.

27. 'By an argument's being stated in regular logical form, is meant, its being so arranged, that the conclusiveness of it is manifest from the mere force of the expression, *i.e.* without considering the meaning of the terms.' Charles Wesley, *A Guide to Syllogism* (Cambridge, 1832) p. 2. 'Whenever one or more statements may be taken as conclusive evidence for a further statement merely on account of their form – that is to say, merely on account of the way the words are put together – the inference from one to the other is said to be logical.' J. C. Cooley, *A Primer of Formal Logic* (New York, 1942) p. 3.

28. *Top.*, 105^{a}11–19. 'You should display your training in inductive reasoning against a young man, in deductive against an expert' (164^{a}12–13).

29. *Drapier's Letters*, p. 59.

30. Peter, 'the Scholastick Brother' (p. 89), 'proved by a very good Argument, that *K* was a modern illegitimate Letter, unknown to the Learned Ages', and so justified the wearing of shoulder knots (p. 84). The Author playfully announces, 'Having thus amply proved the Antiquity of *Criticism* . . .' (p. 102).

31. The title of the pamphlet sometimes called 'A Letter to a Whig-Lord' is 'Some Reasons to Prove, That no Person is obliged by his Principles, as a Whig, To Oppose Her Majesty or Her Present Ministry. In a Letter to a Whig-Lord' (VI 121).

32. Reasoning or proof 'is a "demonstration", when the premises from which the reasoning starts are true and primary, or are such that our knowledge of them has originally come through premises which are primary and true: reasoning, on the other hand, is "dialectical", if it reasons from opinions that are generally accepted' (*Top.*, 100^{a}27–31). Aristotle discusses the relation of opinion to knowledge in the *Post. An.*, I 33 (88^{b}30–89^{b}29).

33. 'That mode of investigation step by step, which crowns the process of the student by the demonstration and discovery of positive and mathematical truth, must of necessity so exercise and train him in the habits of following up his subject, be it what it may, and working out his proofs, as cannot fail to find their uses, whether he, who has them,

dictates from the pulpit, argues at the bar or declaims in the senate; nay, there is no lot, no station, . . . in which the man, once exercised in these studies, though he shall afterwards neglect them, will not to his comfort experience some mental powers and resources, in which their influence shall be felt.' Richard Cumberland, *Memoirs of Richard Cumberland, Written by Himself* (London, 1806) p. 81.

34. *Mechanical Operation of the Spirit*, p. 275.

35. For example, deductions of 'Oratorical Machines', fanaticism, the mechanical operation of the spirit: *Tale*, pp. 60, 105, 276, 283. In two of his few logical uses of 'deduce' and its derivatives he says in Gulliver's 'Letter to His Cousin Sympson' that reformations in Britain from abuses and corruptions 'were plainly deducible from the Precepts delivered in my Book' and in his 'Remarks' to Tindal that the latter's ideas on the state of nature are 'a very wrong Deduction of paternal Government' (II 88).

36. The Author of the *Tale* says, 'Reflecting upon all this . . . , I easily concluded' (p. 97) and 'from all which, I have justly formed this Conclusion to my self' (p. 174). In the *Battle of the Books*, anyone 'may form just Conclusions upon the Merits of either Cause' (p. 219). See also the *Contests and Dissentions*, p. 111, and the sermon 'On Mutual Subjection', where he logically concludes twice (IX 141, 147).

37. *Contests and Dissentions*, p. 89.

38. Letter to the Earl of Peterborough, 18 May 1714: *Correspondence of Swift*, ed. H. Williams, vol. II (Oxford: Clarendon Press, 1963) p. 22.

39. 'A syllogism is discourse in which, certain things being stated, something other than what is stated follows of necessity from their being so': *An. Pr.*, 24ᵇ18–20. '*Syllogismus est oratio, in qua quibusdam positus, aliud quiddam ab iis, quae posita sunt, necessario accidit, eo quod haec sunt*': Narcissus Marsh, *Institutiones Logicae* (Dublin, 1681) p. 127. Burgersdicius's definition is virtually the same: '*nesessario sequitur*', etc. *Institutio Logicarum* (Cambridge, 1680) p. 332. Cf. 'Syllogism . . . a most perfect kinde of Argument, which gathers a necessary conclusion out of two premises'. Thomas Blount, *Glossographia; or, a Dictionary Interpreting . . . Hard Words* (London, 1656).

40. From II 2, the first of 3 chapters on the drawing of true conclusions from false premises in the three syllogistic figures. Cf. *Top.*, 162ᵃ8–11.

41. See above, Ch. 3; App. 3; and W. T. Costello, *The Scholastic Curriculum at Early Seventeenth-Century Cambridge* (Cambridge, Mass.: Harvard University Press, 1958) pp. 21–4.

42. The 'If . . . , and . . . , then' form of syllogism is more properly Aristotelian than is the categoric form used for centuries in modern logic books. See Jan Lukasiewicz, *Aristotle's Syllogistic*, 2nd ed. (Oxford: Clarendon Press, 1957) pp. 1–3. In my examples I use singular terms and premises, but Aristotle does not introduce them into his system.

43. The Aristotelian 'If . . . , and . . . , then' form of categorical syllogisms cannot be used with hypothetical syllogisms without producing an awkward construction, like 'If if-A-is-B-then-E-is-F; and if-C-is-D-then-G-is-H . . .'. I have therefore used the traditional form.

44. *Drapier's Letters*, pp. 129–30.
45. See above, 'The disputation', in Ch. 3.

CHAPTER 7

1. 'An argument is clear in one, and that the most ordinary sense, if it be so brought to a conclusion as to make no further questions necessary: in another sense, and this is the type most usually advanced, when the propositions secured are such as compel the conclusion, and the argument is concluded through premises that are themselves conclusions' (*Top.*, 162^{a}35–^{b}2).
2. For commentary on the questioner–answerer concept of dialectic in Aristotle or in university disputations, see Charles Wesley, *A Guide to Syllogism, . . . Comprehending an Account of the Manner of Disputation Now Practiced in the Schools at Cambridge* (Cambridge, 1832) pp. 97–101; W. D. Ross, *Aristotle* (London: Methuen, 1923) p. 56; W. T. Costello, *The Scholastic Curriculum at Early Seventeenth-Century Cambridge* (Cambridge, Mass.: Harvard University Press, 1958) pp. 20–4; P. Moraux, 'La joute dialectique d'après le huitième livre des *Topiques', Aristotle on Dialectic: The Topics, Proceedings of the Third Symposium Aristotelicum*, ed. G. E. L. Owen (Oxford: Clarendon Press, 1968) esp. pp. 279–86; Gilbert Ryle, 'Dialectic in the Academy', ibid., p. 74.
3. In the 8th book of the *Topics* there is a distinction between dialectical discussion and philosophical inquiry (e.g. 155^{b}7–16) which does not appear in books 2 to 7. For a discussion of these different concepts of dialectic see Moraux, pp. 307–10.
4. See G. E. L. Owen, 'Dialectic and Eristic in the Treatment of the Forms', *Aristotle on Dialectic*, pp. 103–4. Also indicative of the combative rather than the philosophical end in Aristotelian dialectic is the constant attention paid to refutation (e.g. *An. Pr.*, II 20), especially in the *Topics*, where the aim is usually to 'demolish' the opponent's conclusion: 109^{a}24; 110^{b}9; 111^{a}23; 112^{a}1–3, 23; 153^{a}7; 155^{a}7, 36 *et passim*; cf. *Soph. El.*, 176^{b}36.
5. *Memoirs of Martinus Scriblerus*, ed. C. Kerby-Miller (New Haven, Conn.: Yale University Press, 1950) p. 118.
6. Schopenhauer, *The Art of Controversy and Other Posthumous Papers*, trans. T. B. Saunders (London: Swan Sonnenschein, 1896) pp. 4–5, 10.
7. For comment on the inconsistent nature of the system of dialectic in the *Topics*, see Moraux, pp. 286, 303.
8. For example, 'It is well to expand the argument and insert things that it does not require at all, as do those who draw false geometrical figures: for in the multitude of details the whereabouts of the fallacy is obscured. For this reason also a questioner sometimes evades observation as he adds in a corner what, if he formulated it by itself, would not be granted' (157^{a}1–5).
9. *Sophistical Elenchi*, 171^{b}6–34; *Topics*, 100^{b}23–101^{a}4, 108^{a}30–7.

10. In this and the two succeeding references to the *Examiner*, Swift assumes the role of questioner attacking the Whigs. Usually in the *Examiner* essays he is the defender of the Tories against the attacking Whigs, as the next chapter shows in the section 'The answerer'.

11. Apology to the *Tale*, pp. 11, 12, 10.

12. That portion of Wotton's *Observations*, 3rd ed. (London, 1705), which 'deals directly with the *Tale*' is printed as app. B of the Guthkelch-Smith ed. of the *Tale*, pp. 315–28.

13. 'It is a good rule also, occasionally to bring an objection against onself: for answerers are put off their guard against those who appear to be arguing impartially' (*Top.*, 156ᵇ18–20).

14. Cf. Schopenhauer: 'we make it a rule to attack a counter-argument, even though to all appearances it is true and forcible, in the belief that its truth is only superficial, and that in the course of the dispute another argument will occur to us by which we may upset it, or succeed in confirming the truth of our statement. . . . generally a disputant fights not for truth, but for his proposition', *Art of Controversy*, p. 6.

15. Cf. Swift's insulting of Burnet, IV 66, 71.

16. Junius to the Printer of the *Public Advertiser*, 22 April 1771.

17. See the similar concession offered with more bitter irony in IV 114.

18. Besides attacks in the newspapers there were *An Answer to the Conduct of the Allies*, *Remarks on the Tories New Idol* and *Remarks on a False, Scandalous and Seditious Libel*, etc. See Davis ed., VI ix, x.

19. Davis ed., VI xi.

20. For other examples of Swift's inconsistency in controversy, see XII xlv and xlvii, where his inconsistency is detected by a dialectical opponent. More detailed examples of an opponent's superiority to Swift in argument are given in Ch. 8.

21. *An Pr.*, 66ᵇ9–12; *Soph. El.*, 165ᵃ3, 168ᵃ37.

22. The major term in a syllogism is the predicate of the conclusion; the minor term is the subject of the conclusion.

23. If the major premise is true: but Wotton's major premise is not attacked in this part of the reply. Swift's statement is directed not to the question of borrowing, but to the inherent wit in the names.

24. In dialectic, arguments that are properly reasoned are solved by demolishing them, but merely apparent arguments are solved by drawing distinctions (*Soph. El.*, 176ᵇ35–6), which Swift does, sophistically implying that Wotton's argument was only apparent.

25. In spite of the pulled punch of 'I think', Swift's reply is made with effective accuracy. Buckingham's pamphlet was first printed, apparently, in 1705. See the *Tale*, p. 14 n. 1.

26. *Ignoratio elenchi* is one of the seven fallacious refutations not dependent on diction. See *Soph. El.*, 166ᵇ24, and Ch. 6.

27. *Top.*, 111ᵇ32–3. In another respect Swift is doing here what Aristotle advised in *Soph. El.*, 173ᵃ22–3, that is, leading his opponent into views opposite to the majority and the philosophers.

28. See *Drapier's Letters*, p. 15 n. to l. 25.

29. Ibid., p. xlii.

30. *Soph. El.*, 172ᵇ19; *Top.*, 111ᵇ32–3.

31. Schopenhauer, *Art of Controversy*, p. 33, Stratagem 26. See Costello p. 21.

32. *Drapier's Letters*, p. 21.

33. Cf. Cowper, *The Task*, iii 100–4:
    'Hypocrisy, detest her as we may, . . .
    May claim this merit still – that she admits
    The worth of what she mimics with such care,
    And thus gives virtue indirect applause.'

34. 'Whenever one forsees any question coming, one should put in one's objection and have one's say beforehand: for by doing so one is likely to embarrass the [opponent] most effectually' (*Soph. El.*, 176^{b}26–8).

35. An arguer should 'bring a negative instance against [his proposition]: for the negative instance will be a ground of attack upon the assertion' (*Top.*, 110^{a}10–12). Cf. 160^{b}13–16, 163^{a}37–^{b}8.

36. Swift changes the contingent 'might' of the objection to a ready belief in the necessity of the objection.

37. Many of these kinds of argument are listed in C. L. Hamblin, *Fallacies* (London: Methuen, 1970) p. 41, and some are discussed, pp. 42–4.

38. *Drapier's Letters*, pp. 10–11.

39. Ibid., p. 13. This regard for legal authority is unusual in Swift. In the 3rd, 4th, 5th and 6th *Drapier's Letters* lawyers, and particularly legal precedents, come under Swift's criticism: ibid., pp. 52, 72, 108, 141.

40. *Top.*, 104^{b}19–24; *Rhetoric*, 1398^{b}18.

41. See, e.g., App. 3 for the opponent's inability to meet the dilemma with reasoned argument.

42. *Drapier's Letters*, p. 104. F. M. Cornford noticed the applicability of the argument *ab utili* to the academic world in his brief *Microcosmographia Academica, Being a Guide for the Young Academic Politician* (Cambridge, 1908; rpt. London: Bowes & Bowes, 1983) pp. 2–3.

43. 'A Letter to a Member of Parliament in Ireland, upon the Chusing a New Speaker There' (II 129–35).

44. Blake, a vigorous opponent of scholastic logic, took issue with 'systematic reasoning' in general and especially with the system of 'contraries' in Aristotle's *Organon*. In 'Jerusalem', ch. 1 pl. 17 ll. 33–9, Los gives a paradoxical view of contraries. Cf. ch. 1 pl. 10 ll. 7–16, 20–1, 'The Marriage of Heaven and Hell', pls 17–20, 'A Memorable Fancy', and pls 21–2. At the end of a description of the angel's eternal lot, which is as disgusting as parts of Milton's hell or *Gulliver's Travels*, Blake says: 'as the stench terribly annoy'd us both, we went into the mill, & I in my hand brought the skeleton of a body, which in the mill was Aristotle's Analytics'. When the angel objects to what he has been shown, Blake replies, 'it is but lost time to converse with you whose works are only Analytics'. And to the reader he adds, 'I have always found that Angels have the vanity to speak of themselves as the only wise; this they do with a confident insolence sprouting from systematic reasoning.'

45. *Top.*, 163^{a}37–^{b}12. Socrates recommends this kind of training in the *Parmenides*, 135e–136c.

46. In 'A Vindication of Lord Carteret' (1730).

47. *Top.*, 112^{b}27–113^{a}19, shows how to select which of two contraries is useful in demolishing or establishing a thesis. The fourth Drapier's Letter, 'To the Whole People of Ireland', shows the difficulty of establishing the Drapier's thesis and demolishing Wood's when the audience knows only one side of the argument. The English hear only Wood's side and believe him in the right; the Drapier quotes extracts from English pamphlets defending Wood to show their falsehoods in fact and reasoning: *Drapier's Letters*, pp. 80–3.

48. Quoted in *Drapier's Letters*, p. lxv. For a similar stratagem used by Swift against Godolphin over remission of First Fruits in Ireland, see D. Nokes, *Jonathan Swift: A Hypocrite Reversed* (Oxford University Press, 1985) pp. 89–91.

49. For example, pp. 10–13.

50. Presumably 'natural' and not legal justice.

51. *Soph. El.*, 174^{a}39–^{b}7; 172^{a}15–21; *Top.*, 112^{a}24–31; *De Interp.*, 20^{b}22–30; *An. Pr.*, 24^{a}25; *Post. An.*, 73^{b}18–24. 'To postulate that the division exhausts the genus is not illegitimate if the opposites exclude a middle; since if it is the differentia of that genus, anything contained in the genus must lie on one of the two sides' (97^{a}19–22). On the law of excluded middle, see also *Metaphysics*, Γ 7.

52. Schopenhauer gives this manoeuvre as his Stratagem 13: 'To make your opponent accept a proposition, you must give him the counter-proposition as well, leaving him his choice of the two; and you must render the contrast as glaring as you can, so that to avoid being paradoxical he will accept the proposition, which is thus made to look quite probable. . . . It is as though you were to put grey next black, and call it white; or next white, and call it black' (p. 26).

53. As did some academic disputations – see Christopher Wordsworth, *Scholae Academicae* (Cambridge University Press, 1877) p. 22.

54. Denis Donoghue notices the either/or aspect in Swift's writing and attributes it to his imagination, contrasting it with the both/and cast of Sterne's imagination: *Jonathan Swift: A Critical Introduction* (Cambridge University Press, 1969) p. 116.

55. Kathleen Williams believes that Swift offers two unacceptable extremes in order to propose a middle way. This is what she means by compromise in *Jonathan Swift and the Age of Compromise* (Lawrence, Kansas: University of Kansas Press, 1958) pp. 142, 146.

56. Ibid., pp. 141–2; M. Price, *Swift's Rhetorical Art* (New Haven, Conn.: Yale University Press, 1953) pp. 94, 110; cf. H. D. Kelling, 'Reason in Madness: *A Tale of a Tub*', *PMLA*, 69 (1954), 216–18. Swift's use of the formal dilemma – see the next section – suggests that often he is not implying a middle path between the two unacceptable extremes he offers but is adroitly framing an argument which will discomfit an opponent. In the 'Digression on Madness' the opponent seems to be the reader.

57. Swift points out the similarity or complicity of the Roman Catholics and Calvinists (or dissenters) in several places: *Tale* (p. 204); 'Sentiments of a Church-of-England Man' (II 9); 'Letter concerning the Sacramental Test' (II 124–5); 'The Life and Character of Dean Swift' (1731) ll. 148–

53; 'Queries Relating to the Sacramental Test' (xII 255, 256–7, 258); 'The Presbyterians Plea of Merit' (xII 269).

58. See the ref. to the Caudine Forks in the disputation in App. 3.

59. By Chrysippus and the Stoic logicians. W. & M. Kneale, *The Development of Logic* (Oxford: Clarendon Press, 1962) p. 178. Dilemma (δις, twice, two; λημμα, an assumption) was understood in the sixteenth, seventeenth and eighteenth centuries usually as an argument rather than as a practical predicament (see above, n. 41): Thomas Wilson, *The Rule of Reason* (1551; rpt. London, 1553) fol. 34ᵛ; Robert Sanderson, *Logicae Artis Compendium*, 9th ed. (Oxford, 1680) pp. 135–6; Burgersdicius, *Institutionum Logicarum* (Cambridge, 1680) p. 342; Narcissus March, *Institutiones Logicae* (Dublin, 1681) pp. 195–6. It would naturally be defined as an argument in these and other logics of the time, but it was also defined as such in the dictionaries: Thomas Blount, *Glossographia: or, a Dictionary* . . . (London, 1656); J. B., *An English Expositour, Or Compleat Dictionary* (Cambridge, 1684); Edward Phillips, *The New World of Words or, Universal English Dictionary*, 6th ed. (London, 1706); Anon., *Glossographia Anglicana Nova: or a Dictionary* . . . (London, 1707); Nathaniel Bailey, *An Universal Etymological Dictionary*, 6th ed. (London, 1733); and Johnson's 1755 dictionary. The word 'dilemma' (διλημμα) in its modern formal-logical sense was not used until the second century AD, when Hermogenes (*De Inventione*, IV 6) used the word διλημματον as Cicero had used *complexio* (*De Inventione*, I 57), to mean two questions equally awkward to answer: Kneale p. 178.

60. 'Dilemma', Johnson, *Dictionary*.

61. 'Dilemma', defined in Burgersdicius, *Monitio Logica: or an Abstract and Translation of Burgersdicius His Logick. By a Gentleman* (London, 1697) p. 56.

62. Wilson fol. 34ᵛ; Sanderson p. 135; Burgersdicius, *Institutionum Logicarum*, p. 342; *Monitio Logica*, pp. 56–7; Henry Aldrich, *Artis Logicae Compendium* (Oxford, 1691) p. 29; University Library Cambridge MS Add. 3072, fol. 39ᵛ. The dilemma example is from Aulus Gellius, *Noctes Atticae* (c. AD 150) v 11.

63. Richard Whately, *Elements of Logic*, 6th ed. (London, 1836) p. 115.

64. Whately p. 118 and Wesley, *A Guide to Syllogism*, p. 47 give only three forms, denying the existence of a simple destructive dilemma. Others accept the simple destructive as a valid form of a dilemma: G. H. Joyce, *Principles of Logic*, 2nd ed. (London: Longmans, Green, 1916) p. 210; S. H. Mellone, *Elements of Modern Logic*, 2nd ed. (London: University Tutorial Press, 1945) p. 168; M. R. Cohen and E. Nagel, *An Introduction to Logic* (Harbinger Books; New York: Harcourt Brace Jovanovich, 1962) p. 106; S. F. Barker, *The Elements of Logic* (New York: McGraw-Hill, 1965) p. 98.

65. Referred to in Marsh p. 197; given as an example in Thomas Blundeville, *The Art of Logike*, 3rd ed. (London, 1619) p. 178; Burgersdicius's *Institutionum Logicarum*, p. 201 and his *Monitio Logica*, p. 57; Joyce pp. 213–14; I. M. Copi, *Introduction to Logic*, 2nd ed. (New York: Macmillan, 1961) pp. 231–2.

66. Sanderson p. 135. '*Dilemma est Syllogismus Disjunctivus . . .*': Marsh pp. 195–6.
67. Cf. Marsh p. 196:
    > If misfortune (or pain, sorrow) should be feared, it is either because it is long or because it is great;
    > but long misfortune is light, and great misfortune is brief;
    > therefore misfortune should not be feared.
68. The Aristotelian 'If . . . , and . . . , then . . .' form of syllogism cannot be used with dilemmas without producing an awkward construction:
    > If if-A-is-B-then-E-is-F, and if if-C-is-D-then-E-is-F,
    > and either A is B or C is D,
    > then E is F.
    I have therefore used the traditional categoric form in the minor premise and conclusion when reducing dilemmas to syllogistic form.
69. Another constructive dilemma is found in the section 'Against Anger' (IV 8), concerning one's reaction to a friend.
70. He shows his friends Harding the printer (*Drapier's Letters*, p. 115) and Gay ('To Mr. Gay on his being Steward to the Duke of Queensberry' (1731) ll. 129–30) to be caught in practical dilemmas.
71. 'The message to Pilate from his wife furnishes an instance of a single word ("*just*") suggesting a Major-premiss, while the Conclusion is stated in the form of an *exhortation*: "Have thou nothing to do with that *just* man". And the succeeding sentence must have been designed to convey a hint of Arguments for the Proof of each of the Premises on which that Conclusion rested': Whately, *Elements of Logic*, 9th ed. (London: Longmans, 1864) p. 78. The ref. is to Matt. 27: 19.
72. The dilemmatic conclusion offering the choice between dishonesty and lack of intelligence seems to be a favourite with writers of logics, at least since the eighteenth century. Wesley offers the choice between not honest and not competent, pp. 49–50; Whately between not wise and not good, 6th ed., p. 218; and Joyce between unintelligent and dishonest, p. 211. The form of all of these, being negative and disjunctive in the conclusion, is complex destructive.
73. Thomas Sprat, *The History of the Royal Society*, ed. J. I. Cope and H. W. Jones (St Louis, Mo.: Washington University Studies, 1959) p. 354.
74. The ironic elements in this passage are mentioned in I. Ehrenpreis, 'Swift and Satire', *College English*, 13 (1952) 309.

CHAPTER 8

1. For Swift's contribution to the Tory cause in the *Examiner* papers and in 'The Conduct of the Allies', 'The Importance of the *Guardian* Considered', 'The Publick Spirit of the Whigs' and other writings, and for the background of the *Medley* and other Whig journals, see J. A. Downie, *Robert Harley and the Press: Propaganda and Public Opinion in the Age of Swift and Defoe* (Cambridge University Press, 1979) esp. pp. 122, 174.

2. Cf. 'The Respondent, in a Disputation, being always supposed to maintain a true proposition, the argument of the Opponent, whose province it is to support the contradictory, must be presumed to be founded on some fallacy': Charles Wesley, *Guide to Syllogism* (Cambridge, 1832) p. 97.

3. *Top.*, 161ª30–2. Cf. *Soph. El.*, 176ª22–3. Apparent solutions 'must sometimes be advanced rather than true solutions in contentious reasonings and in the encounter with ambiguity'. Cf. also Schopenhauer, *The Art of Controversy and Other Posthumous Papers*, Stratagem 21.

4. 'Some Remarks upon a Pamphlet, Entitl'd, A Letter to the Seven Lords of the Committee, Appointed to Examine Gregg. By the Author of the Examiner' (1711) III 203.

5. 'The Publick Spirit of the Whigs' (1714) VIII 59.

6. 'The Importance of the *Guardian* Considered' (1713) VIII 4. See Ch. 7, 'Turning of opponent's argument'. For a brief account of the ill will between Swift and Steele, see D. Nokes, *Jonathan Swift: A Hypocrite Reversed* (Oxford University Press, 1985) pp. 181–4. J. A. Downie, *Jonathan Swift: Political Writer* (London: Routledge & Kegan Paul, 1984) pp. 184–6, gives the background of Swift's attacks on Steele in the winter of 1713–14.

7. 'Some Observations upon a Paper, Call'd, The Report of the Committee of the Most Honourable the Privy Council in England, Relating to Wood's Half-Pence', *Drapier's Letters*, p. 62.

8. Matthew Tindal, *The Rights of the Christian Church*, 2nd ed. (London, 1706) p. 89.

9. To counter a universal or generic assertion, examine its species one by one, and if any inconsistency is shown, the problem is demolished (*Top.*, 109ᵇ13–15, 23–4).

10. The *reductio ad impossibile* is discussed in many places in Aristotle: e.g. *An. Pr.*, 41ª23–41, 50ª29–38, 60ᵇ18–36, 62ᵇ29–41; *Post An.*, 87ª1–11, 14–22; *Top.*, 163ª30–7; *Soph. El.*, 167ᵇ21–6, 34–6, 170ª2. See the section below, '*Reductio ad impossibile*'.

11. The conclusion of Swift's answer is self-referential, adding nothing of substance: 'This is some Allusion, but the Thing is plain, as it seemeth to me, and wanteth no Subterfuge, &c.' It seems to imply an acknowledgement that his physician allusion was not as to the point as it might have been.

12. Wide knowledge is obviously of use to a dialectician (*Soph. El.*, 170ª20–33).

13. *An. Pr.*, 66ᵇ9–12. In other places Aristotle says a refutation involves the *contradiction* of an opponent's conclusion: e.g. *Soph. El.*, 165ª3. Propositions opposed as contraries cannot both be true, but may both be false. Those opposed as contradictories cannot both be true, nor can they both be false; one must be true and the other false. See *De Interp.*, 17ᵇ17–23.

14. Vol. I was pub. in 1679, vol. II in 1681 and vol. III in 1714. The 'Introduction' to the 3rd vol. was pub. in 1713, as was Swift's 'Preface' to the 'Introduction'.

15. *Soph. El.*, 165ª3, 168ª37, 170ᵇ1.

16. Swift is quoting from Burnet's 'Introduction', pp. 27–8.
17. Cf. *Top.*, 112ª16–23. In the constructive form, *modus ponens*, the antecedent is affirmed and therefore so is the consequent, as in the opponent's first proof in Amhurst's sample disputation, Ch. 3 above, in the section 'The disputation'. See also the opening of Ch. 2 above.
18. The contradictory of his own conclusion is Tindal's conclusion.
19. For the distinction between the two kinds of argument, see Kneale, pp. 7–9. For Aristotle's only reference, apparently, to the *reductio ad absurdum* in the *Top.* or *Soph. El.*, see *Top.*, 162ᵇ19.
20. See below, Ch. 9 n. 36.
21. Turning the tables in argument suggests the conversion of an argument, explained in *Top.*, 163ª30–6. This explanation, one of three ways of converting an argument shown in the *Topics*, is the same as the *reductio ad impossibile* explained in the *Analytics*.
22. *Letters of Junius*, ed. J. Wade (London: Bohn, 1850) I 4.
23. Aristotle recommends arguing from contraries, *Top.*, 119ª37–ᵇ1.
24. See the section on the formal dilemma in Ch. 7. The academic disputation in App. 3 contains a dilemmatic manoeuvre described as the Caudine Forks.
25. *De Interp.*, 20ᵇ22–30, *An. Pr.*, 24ª24–5; *Top.*, 158ª14–20; *Soph. El.*, 174ª39–ᵇ7; Schopenhauer, Stratagem 13.
26. Cf. 'Reason is certainly in the Right', used ironically in the *Tale* (p. 173) as here.
27. 'A Preface to the Bishop of Sarum's Introduction to the Third Volume of the History of the Reformation of the Church of England' (1713).
28. Cf. *Letters of Junius*, I 176: 'in this, as in almost every other dispute, it usually happens that much time is lost in referring to a multitude of cases and precedents which prove nothing to the purpose, or in maintaining propositions which are either not disputed, or, whether they be admitted or denied, are entirely indifferent as to the matter in debate, until, at last, the mind, perplexed and confounded with endless subtleties of controversy, loses sight of the main question, and never arrives at truth'.
29. *Drapier's Letters*, p. 22.
30. 'The Defence of Poesie', *The Prose Works of Sir Philip Sidney*, ed. A. Feuillerat (1912; rpt. Cambridge University Press, 1962) III 3. The argument concerns the superiority of the horse to all other beasts and, Sidney implies, to man. For Swift's knowledge of the 'Defence', see IX 327, 328, 332, 335, 340.
31. Burgersdicius, *Institutionum Logicarum Libri Duo* (1626; rpt. Cambridge, 1680) p. 352. See Narcissus Marsh, '*Fallacia Compositionis*', *Institutiones Logicae* (Dublin, 1681) p. 251; Henry Aldrich, *Artis Logicae Compendium* (Oxford, 1691) p. 39; John Sanderson, *Institutio Dialecticarum Libri Quatuor* (Oxford, 1602) p. 322.
32. [Thomas Good], *A Brief English Tract of Logick* (Oxford, 1677); Burgersdicius, *Monitio Logica: or an Abstract and Translation of Burgersdicius His Logick* (London, 1697).
33. *Drapier's Letters*, pp. 50–1.
34. He sometimes emphasises clarity in his own arguments: 'I will set in as

clear Light as I can, what I conceive to be . . .' (II 74); 'It will be therefore necessary to set this Matter in a clear Light' (II 76).

35. Referring again to Tindal's phrase 'Idea of Government' he remarks, 'A canting, pedantic Way, learned from *Locke*' (II 85); cf. another glance at Lockean terminology: 'This Word *People* is so delicious in him, that I cannot tell what is included in the Idea of the *People*. Doth he mean the Rabble or the Legislature . . . ?' (II 99).

36. 'You should say that we ought to use our terms to mean the same things as most people mean by them' (*Top.*, 110^{a}16–17).

37. 'Let us . . . call that part which indicates the essence a "definition", while of the remainder let us adopt the terminology which is generally current about these things, and speak of it as a "property" ' (*Top.*, 101^{b}20–3). The preceding four references to the *Topics* show only that Swift might have had Aristotle in mind in his attack on Tindal's argument to establish a definition. This last reference, however, suggests that he did have in mind Aristotle, or a Peripatetic logician, and consequently the preceding four references seem the more justified.

38. Cf. the question and the debate in App. 3.

39. v 286, 269, 277, 279, 285, 291.

40. The fallacy of composition occurs when what is true of a part is therefore asserted to be true of the whole: see n. 31 above. C. L. Hamblin, *Fallacies* (London: Methuen, 1970) pp. 18–22.

41. II 38. The sorites Swift mentions in this passage is analysed by J. M. Bullitt, *Jonathan Swift and the Anatomy of Satire* (Cambridge, Mass.: Harvard University Press, 1953) pp. 93–5.

42. *Soph. El.*, 167^{a}37–9; 181^{a}15–21; Marsh pp. 255–6; Burgersdicius, *Inst. Log.*, p. 271. Hamblin pp. 32–5.

43. *Henry IV Part I*, III i.

44. *Poetics*, ch. 24 (1460^{a}19–25).

45. The fallacy of consequent, like the fallacy of accident mentioned in the next paragraph of the text, is explained in both Marsh and Burgersdicius. Their logics follow the *Soph. El.* in dividing fallacies into those dependent on diction (ambiguity, amphiboly, etc.) and those not dependent on diction (accident, *ignoratio elenchi, petitio principii*, consequent, false cause, etc.), as do some seventeenth-century logic notebooks, such as Queens' College Library, Cambridge, MS Horne 39, which consists of a '*Tractatus de Fallaciis in Dictione*' and one '*extra Dictione*'.

46. 'An Accident is that which *in any One* and *the same thing may be, and not be*. Or thus: An Accident is that which is either present or absent, without the Ruine of the Subject'. Burgersdicius, *Monitio Logica*, p. 42. Cf. *Top.*, 102^{b}6–7, 21–2, 26.

47. 'Fallacies . . . that depend on Accident occur whenever any attribute is claimed to belong in a like manner to a thing and to its accident' (*Soph. El.*, 166^{b}29–30). Cf. 179^{a}25–32; 168^{a}33–4, 38–40: 'Fallacies that depend on Accident are clear cases of *ignoratio elenchi*. . . . If, then, there is no proof as regards an accident of anything, there is no refutation. For supposing, when *A* and *B* are, *C* must necessarily be, and *C* is white, there is no necessity for it to be white on account of the syllogism.' 'In

Gulliver's moral universe, the first error is to treat the accident of a thing as if it were its essence': the Lilliputians plan to impeach Gulliver for urinating on the queen's palace, because they treat the urine as the essence and putting out the fire as the accident. D. Donoghue, *Jonathan Swift: A Critical Introduction* (Cambridge University Press, 1969) p. 72.

48. Sir William Draper was later to accuse Junius of a similar stratagem, and Junius refutes the accusation by saying that if he asked *a most virtuous man* whether he ever committed theft or murder it would not disturb his peace of mind: *Letters of Junius*, i 129–30.

49. When the Rev. John Horne distorts Junius's meaning by taking only half of a composite idea and using it in print to make a point, Junius replies, 'In what school this gentleman learned his ethics I know not. His *logic* seems to have been studied under Mr. Dyson', etc.: ibid., i 393.

50. Aristotle advises altering a term to suit oneself in order to establish or overthrow a view ($111^a 8$–13), as does Schopenhauer, Stratagem 2.

51. *Soph. El.*, $174^b 8$–10. Cf. Schopenhauer, Stratagems 14 and 20.

52. *Top.*, $139^b 32$–6; cf. $112^a 32$–5; $158^b 8$–15.

53. For other examples and comment on this practice of Swift's, see M. Quinlan, 'Swift's Use of Literalization as a Rhetorical Device', *PMLA*, 82 (1967) 516–21.

54. The reply is somewhat inconsistent with Swift's earlier suggestion that Tindal should use commonplace examples in his explanations, showing him, in fact, the way to do so in his restatement of Tindal's abstract explanation of the nature of governing, using the horse-stealing analogy (ii 80–1).

55. If he will not allow it for wit he condemns his own wit a decade earlier in the *Mechanical Operation of the Spirit*, where he used the same device, the Indians' worshipping of the Devil, to belittle religious fanatics (p. 274).

56. See the section 'Dialectical superiority' earlier in this chapter.

57. In 'Thoughts on Various Subjects' (i 244).

58. 'Authorities which your opponent fails to understand are those of which he generally thinks the most': Schopenhauer, Stratagem 30, p. 36.

59. He was still making this charge more than a decade later: 'It seems to me that all the writers are on one side, and all the railers on the other' (v 96).

60. Burnet was born in Edinburgh and was educated at Marischal College, Aberdeen.

61. He sarcastically praises Wharton's overuse of the word *such* (vi 153).

62. Schopenhauer p. 13; Stratagem 38, p. 46.

63. Cited in Hamblin p. 174.

64. *Observations on The Tale of a Tub*, in the *Tale* vol., pp. 322, 327.

65. See intro. to Swift, *Prose Writings*, Davis ed., iv xiv.

66. I. Ehrenpreis, *Dr Swift* (London: Methuen, 1967) pp. 269–70, comments on Swift's use of the argument *ad hominem*.

67. Cf. Jack's praise of blindness: *Tale*, p. 193.

68. Cf. a similar comment, ii 105.

69. A 'perennial topic of dissension' (iv xxiii).

70. Thomas Granger, *Syntagma Logicum, or The Divine Logike* (London, 1620) pp. 384–5.
71. *Drapier's Letters*, p. 83.
72. *As You Like It*, v iv.

CHAPTER 9

1. See above, the section 'Dialectic' in Ch. 6.
2. For example, J. M. Bullitt, *Jonathan Swift and the Anatomy of Satire* (Cambridge, Mass.: Harvard University Press, 1953) p. 68; E. W. Rosenheim, *Swift and the Satirist's Art* (University of Chicago Press, 1963) p. 6; I. Ehrenpreis, *Dr Swift* (London: Methuen, 1967) p. 297; and issue after issue of the *Satire Newsletter*.
3. A compound term which seems to be a periphrastic avoidance of the word 'dialectic'.
4. M. K. Starkman, *Swift's Satire on Learning in A Tale of a Tub* (Princeton University Press, 1950) p. 60.
5. Quoted in Bullitt p. 68.
6. *Battle of the Books*, p. 234.
7. A wrangler was traditionally one who disputed publicly on a thesis, and at Cambridge undergraduates placed in the first class of the mathematical tripos were honoured with the title Wranglers.
8. [Anthony Collins], *A Discourse concerning Ridicule and Irony in Writing* (London, 1729) p. 7.
9. Thomas Blount, *Glossographia: or, a Dictionary* . . . (London, 1656); J. B., *An English Expositour, Or Compleat Dictionary* (Cambridge, 1684); Edward Phillips, *The New World of Words or, Universal English Dictionary*, 6th ed. (London, 1706); cf. a speech delivered at the Oxford commencement on 12 July 1658 by Robert South: '*An magis ad Virtutem amant Satyrici quam Panegyrici?*' (Whether satirists love virtue more than do panegyricists?), which was held in the affirmative: Bodleian MS Rawl. D. 1111, fol. 29^v.
10. 'A Vindication of Isaac Bickerstaff', II 162, 164.
11. Thomas Sprat, *The History of the Royal Society* (1667) ed. J. I. Cope and H. W. Jones (St Louis, Mo.: Washington University Studies, 1959) p. 413.
12. Cf. *Tale*, p. 48 n. 1.
13. See Temple's letter of August 1667 to Lord Lisle, quoted in Ehrenpreis, *Mr Swift and His Contemporaries* (London: Methuen, 1962) p. 111; Shaftesbury, *Characteristicks of Men, Manners, Opinions, Times*, 4th ed. (London, 1727) vol. I p. 171; [Collins], *Discourse concerning Ridicule*, pp. 23–4, 61–2.
14. See H. MacDonald, 'Banter in English Controversial Prose after the Restoration', *Essays and Studies*, 32 (1947) 21–39.
15. Rosenheim p. 18.
16. Ibid. p. 21.
17. Published under Hobbes's name: see W. S. Howell, *Logic and Rhetoric in England, 1500–1700* (Princeton University Press, 1956) p. 279.

18. Benjamin Keach, Τροπολογια: *A Key to Open Scripture Metaphors* (1682; another ed., London, 1779) p. 30.
19. [Bernard Lamy], *De L'Art de Parler* (Paris, 1679) p. 321.
20. Shaftesbury vol. I pp. 71–2; [Collins], *Ridicule and Irony*, p. 8; Amhurst vol. II p. 201; all cited in the bibliography.
21. For various contexts of the word in the seventeenth and eighteenth centuries see N. Knox, *The Word Irony and Its Context, 1500–1755* (Durham, N.C.: Duke University Press, 1961).
22. Rosenheim p. 31; cf. p. 25.
23. Ibid. p. 18.
24. 'To Mr Delaney' (1718) ll. 34–6.
25. 'Verses on the Death of Dr Swift' (1731) ll. 57–8.
26. As Rosenheim does, pp. 21, 39.
27. Gabriel Harvey, public lecturer in rhetoric at Cambridge from 1574 to 1576, says in his *Ciceronianus* and *Rhetor* (London, 1577) that dialectic is the basis for all critical analysis and for composing what we call literature. See L. Jardine, 'Humanism and Dialectic in Sixteenth-Century Cambridge, A Preliminary Investigation', in *Classical Influences on Renaissance Culture*, ed. R. R. Bolgar (Cambridge University Press, 1976) pp. 145–6. See also R. W. Uphaus, who notes a similar metamorphosis, from panegyric to satire, in 'From Panegyric to Satire: Swift's Early Odes and *A Tale of a Tub*', *Texas Studies in Literature and Language*, 13 (1971) 55–70.
28. (1733) ll. 205–8, 235–6.
29. See the beginning of Ch. 5.
30. See above, the section 'The dilemma' in Ch. 7; cf. the two central paragraphs in the 'Digression on Madness'.
31. See E. Sewell, *The Field of Nonsense* (London: Chatto & Windus, 1952).
32. 'by Wit is onely meant/Applying what we first invent': 'To Mr Delaney' (1710) ll. 17–18.
33. Ibid., ll. 19–20. In this and several of the following observations by Swift, one can see the explicit language of logic or dialectic in dealing with humour, wit, satire and dialectic.
34. Cf. *The Mechanical Operation of the Spirit*, pp. 287–9, where a long paragraph given to the same comparison concludes in a similar apt, humorous analogy.
35. *Drapier's Letters*, p. 59.
36. After summoning a brief physician analogy to refute one of Tindal's assertions, Swift reminds himself in a note, 'Jest on it' (II 98), and then gives a brief soldier analogy. Stock analogies are part of his jesting technique, one he recommends to other writers and talkers ironically (IV 103; IX 336) and for which he ridicules Steele (VIII 41). Two of Swift's favourite stock answers (analogies) are those concerning physicians (II 96, 104; IV 39–40; XII 79; *Drapier's Letters*, p. 21) and soldiers (II 97, 98–9; *Drapier's Letters*, p. 104).
37. *Soph. El.*, 182^{b}13–20; Cicero, *De Oratore*, II 256; Quintilian, *Institutio Oratoria*, VI 6–7, 89.

38. The fact that 'truths' can have counter-truths and arguments counter-arguments generates dialectic.
39. C. L. Hamblin, *Fallacies* (London: Methuen, 1970) pp. 230–1.
40. Or: 'Epimenides said truthfully, "I am lying"; therefore he was lying when he said, "I am lying".'
41. See the frontispiece in vol. III of Faulkner's ed. (1735) rpt. in the Davis ed., vol. XI.
42. *Gorgias*, 482e–83a.
43. Rosenheim, pp. 25, 31.
44. For comments on this technique, see H. W. Sams, 'Swift's Satire of the Second Person', *ELH*, 26 (1959) 36–44.
45. For the sixteenth- and seventeenth-century background of the paradox, see R. L. Colie, *Paradoxia Epidemica: The Renaissance Tradition of the Paradox* (Princeton University Press, 1966).
46. Literary nonsense, or the absurd, is generally considered to have a logical foundation. See Sewell, *The Field of Nonsense*; A. E. Dyson, 'Method in Madness: A Note on Edward Lear', *English*, 10 (1955) 221; M. Esslin, *The Theatre of the Absurd* (New York: Anchor-Doubleday, 1961) pp. 309–10; E. Husserl, *Ideas: General Introduction to Pure Phenomenology*, trans. W. R. Boyce Gibson (London: Allen & Unwin, 1931) pp. 159 n. 1, 168, 169.
47. A suggestion underscored by Gulliver's attitude in the letter to his Cousin Sympson.
48. Sigmund Freud, *Jokes and Their Relation to the Unconscious*, trans. and ed. J. Strachey (London: Routledge & Kegan Paul, 1960) pp. 57, 69.
49. Richard Whately, *Elements of Logic*, 9th ed. (London, 1864) p. 149.
50. See App. 1.

APPENDIX 2

1. Kant, *Kritik der Reinen Vernunft*, 2nd ed. (1787) preface, p. 17; E. Carruccio, *Mathematics and Logic in History and in Contemporary Thought*, trans. I. Quigly (London: Faber, 1964) p. 75; Kant, *Logic*, trans. J. Richardson (London, 1819) p. 23.
2. Angus De Morgan, 'On the Structure of the Syllogism', *Trans. Camb. Phil. Soc.*, 8 (1846) 379; rpt. in A. De Morgan, *On the Syllogism and Other Logical Writings*, ed. P. Heath (London: Routledge & Kegan Paul, 1966) p. 1.
3. W. Hamilton, *Lectures on Metaphysics and Logic*, ed. H. L. Mansel and J. Veitch, 4 vols (Edinburgh: Blackwood, 1859–60): vols 3–4 contain *Lectures on Logic*.
4. H. L. Mansel, *Prolegomena Logica, an Inquiry into the Psychological Character of Logical Processes* (Oxford: Graham, 1851) and *The Limits of Demonstrative Science, considered in a Letter to the Rev. William Whewell* (Oxford: Graham, 1853) 46 pp.

242 *Notes*

5. J. S. Mill, *A System of Logic*, 2 vols (London, 1843); F. Ueberweg, *System of Logic and History of Logical Doctrines*, trans. T. M. Lindsay (London: Longmans, Green, 1871) pp. 572–3.
6. G. Boole, *The Mathematical Analysis of Logic* (Cambridge, 1847). De Morgan, also a mathematician, also contributed to the renaissance of logic in modern times.
7. W. Whewell, *History of the Inductive Sciences*, 3 vols (London, 1837), *The Philosophy of the Inductive Sciences, Founded upon Their History*, 2 vols (London, 1840) and *Of Induction, with Especial Reference to Mr J. Stuart Mill's System of Logic* (Cambridge, 1849).
8. W. R. Ward, *Victorian Oxford* (London: Cass, 1965) pp. 14, 56, 57.
9. Richard Whately (Oriel), *Elements of Logic*; see 6th ed., rev. (London, 1836) pref., pp. xxv–vii. Whately's logic was popular in both Britain and the United States and went to 9 eds by 1848.
10. Charles Wesley (Christ's), *A Guide to Syllogism, or A Manual of Logic, Comprehending an Account of the Manner of Disputation Now Practiced in the Schools at Cambridge; with Specimens of the Different Acts* (Cambridge, 1832).
11. University Library Cambridge MS Add. 7323, p. 15, a notebook of J. N. Keynes on examination questions in logic at Cambridge, 1865–85 (partly MS, partly print clipped from Tripos exam. papers). Most of the questions in this notebook are based on the logics of Whately and Mill.
12. University Library Cambridge MS Add. 7322, p. 173, another of Keynes's notebooks on logic questions at Cambridge, 1865–85. The questions are concerned with the logic of Aristotle, Bacon, Locke, Kant, De Morgan, Whewell, Hamilton, Mansel and Boole.
13. W. V. Quine, *Elementary Logic*, rev. ed. (Cambridge, Mass.: Harvard University Press, 1966) p. vii, from the preface to the 1941 ed. Cf. Bertrand Russell, *The Principles of Mathematics*, intro. to the 2nd ed. (London: Allen & Unwin, 1937) p. v, where he says the book's 'fundamental thesis . . . that mathematics and logic are identical, is one which I have never seen any reason to modify'.
14. Aristotle may be referring to this paradox in the *Soph. El.*, 180^{b}2–7; Paul, apparently without realising that it is a puzzle, refers to it in Titus 1:12–13.
15. W. V. Quine, *Methods of Logic*, 2nd ed., rev. (London: Routledge & Kegan Paul, 1962) p. 249.
16. See, e.g., S. Toulmin, *The Uses of Argument* (Cambridge University Press, 1958) p. 147.
17. See W. B. S. Taylor, *History of the University of Dublin* (London, 1845) p. 145.

APPENDIX 3

1. See 'The dilemma', Ch. 7.
2. In Laconia, whose inhabitants were noted for their few words.
3. Fols 8^r–10^r.

Select Bibliography

MANUSCRIPT MATERIAL

London

British Library
Cotton Faustina D. II   1594–1600

Lambeth Palace Library
221   c. 1450

Cambridge

University Library

Dd. 5. 47	17th C.
Dd. 6. 30	mid-17th C.
Mm. 1. 35	c. 1678–1740
Mm. 5. 42	17th C.
Add. 3072	early 17th C.
Add. 3854	late 17th C.
Add. 4319	1755
Add. 4359	1652
Add. 4368	1703
Add. 7322–3	1865–85
Add. H. 2640	1681

Emmanuel College Library

1. 2. 27	1651/2
3. 1. 11	c. 1696

Gonville and Caius College Library

689/776	18th C.
744/249	17th C.

Magdalene College Library

F. 4. 21	mid-17th C.

Queens' College Library

Archives MS 89	1665
Horne 39	17th C.
Unclassified MS	1651

St John's College Library

A. a. 3	1684–6
K. 38	c. 1652
O. 84	1746
S. 34	17th C.

Sidney Sussex College Library
Samuel Ward MS
Notebooks 12, 13,   early 17th C.
17, 19

Trinity College Library

O. 10A. 33	1650–60

Oxford

Bodleian Library

Cherry 46	1683
Eng. misc. f. 4	1680
Lat. misc. e. 38	1670–90
Rawl. D. 200	1651/2
Rawl. D. 1104	1647
Rawl. D. 1110	1662
Rawl. D. 1111	1658
Rawl. D. 1178	1700
Rawl. D. 1442	1681
Smith 21	1648–53
Smith 128	1679/80
Add. A. 65	1677

Edinburgh

Edinburgh University Library

Dc. 7. 90	1668
Dc. 7. 91	1724
Dc. 8. 17	17th C.
Dc. 8. 56	1720
La. III. 154	1680–1

National Library of Scotland   **Dublin**
2741   1697
9380   1648–9   *Trinity College Library*
9381   1628   I. 5. 1   1688
9383   1681–2   2642   17th C.
9834   1686   Add. 38671   1685
Adv. 22. 7. 2   1691

PRINTED MATERIAL

Adamson, R., *A Short History of Logic*, ed. W. R. Sorley (Edinburgh: Blackwood, 1911).

Aitken, G. A., *The Life and Works of John Arbuthnot* (Oxford: Clarendon Press, 1892).

Aldrich, H., *Artis Logicae Compendium* (Oxford, 1691).

Amhurst, N., *Terrae-Filius: or, The Secret History of the University of Oxford; in Several Essays* (London, 1726).

Anon., ' "Cambridge Disputations" Illustrative of Shakespeare', *Notes and Queries*, 1st Ser., VI (4 Sept. 1852) 217.

—— *The College-Examination: A Poem* (Dublin, 1731).

—— *The Difficulties and Discouragements which Attend the Study for a Fellowship in the College of Dublin* (Dublin, 1735).

—— *Glossographia Anglicana Nova: or, a Dictionary, Interpreting Such Hard Words of Whatever Language, as are at present used in the English Tongue* (London, 1707).

—— 'Observations on the University of Oxford', *Gentleman's Magazine*, 50 (1780) 119–20, 277–8.

Anstey, H., *Munimenta Academica, or Documents Illustrative of Academical Life and Studies at Oxford*, 2 vols (London: Longmans, 1868).

Aristotle, *The Organon, or Logical Treatises, with the Introduction of Porphyry*, trans. O. F. Owen, 2 vols (London: Bohn, 1853).

—— *Prior and Posterior Analytics*, ed. W. D. Ross (Oxford: Clarendon Press, 1949).

—— *The Works of Aristotle*, trans. into English under the editorship of W. D. Ross, 12 vols (Oxford: Clarendon Press, 1908–52).

Arnauld, A., and P. Nicole, *Logic: or, the Art of Thinking*, trans. from the French (2nd ed., London, 1693).

[Arnauld, A., and P. Nicole], *La Logique, ou l'Art de Penser* (4th ed., Paris, 1674).

Ashworth, E. B., *Language and Logic in the Post-Medieval Period* (Boston: D. Reidel, 1974).

B. J., Dr. of Physick, *An English Expositour, or Compleat Dictionary Teaching the Interpretation of the Hardest Words, and Most Useful Terms of Art Used in our Language* (Cambridge, 1684).

Bacon, F., *The Advancement of Learning*, ed. G. W. Kitchin (London: Everyman's Library, 1915).

Bailey, K. C., *A History of Trinity College, Dublin: 1892–1945* (Dublin: The University Press, 1947).

Bailey, N., *An Universal Etymological English Dictionary* (6th ed., London, 1733).

Baldwin, T. W., *William Shakspere's Small Latine & Lesse Greeke*, 2 vols (Urbana, Ill.: University of Illinois Press, 1944).

Barker, S. F., *The Elements of Logic* (New York: McGraw-Hill, 1965).

Barlow, T., *A Library for Younger Schollers*, ed. A. De Jordy and H. F. Fletcher, Illinois Studies in Language and Literature (Urbana, Ill.: University of Illinois Press, 1961).

Barrett, J., *An Essay on the Earlier Part of the Life of Swift* (London, 1808).

Beaufort, Margaret, *Early Statutes of Christ's College, Cambridge*, trans. H. Rackham (Cambridge University Press, 1927).

B. E. N., 'Swift: Dryden: Herrick', *Notes and Queries*, 21 Aug. 1875.

Bentley, R., *Remarks upon a Late Discourse of Free-Thinking* (London, 1713).

Bernard, N., *The Life and Death of Dr. James Usher* (London, 1656).

Blake, W., *The Complete Writings of William Blake*, ed. G. Keynes (London: Oxford University Press, 1966).

Blount, T., *Glossographia; or, a Dictionary Interpreting All Such Hard Words . . . Now Used in Our Refined English Tongue* (London, 1656).

Blundeville, T., *The Arte of Logike* (3rd ed., London, 1619).

Bolgar, R. R., *The Classical Heritage and Its Beneficiaries* (Cambridge University Press, 1958).

—— (ed.), *Classical Influences on European Culture, A.D. 1500–1700; Proceedings of an International Conference Held at King's College, Cambridge, April 1974* (Cambridge University Press, 1976).

Boole, G., *The Mathematical Analysis of Logic* (Cambridge, 1847).

Bolton, R., *A Translation of the Charter and Statutes of Trinity College, Dublin* (Dublin, 1749).

Bullitt, J. M., *Jonathan Swift and the Anatomy of Satire* (Cambridge, Mass.: Harvard University Press, 1953).

Burgersdicius, F., *Institutionum Logicarum Libri Duo* (Leyden, 1626; rpt. Cambridge, 1680).

—— *Monitio Logica: or an Abstract and Translation of Burgersdicius His Logick. By a Gentleman* (London, 1697).

Burnet, G., *An Introduction to the Third Volume of the History of the Reformation of the Church of England* (London, 1714).

Burton, K. M., 'Cambridge Exercises in the Seventeenth Century', *The Eagle*, 54, no. 238 (Jan. 1951) 248–58.

Cant, R. G., *The University of St. Andrews, A Short History* (Edinburgh: Oliver & Boyd, 1946).

Carney, J. D., and R. K. Scheer, *Fundamentals of Logic* (New York: Macmillan, 1964).

Carnochan, W. B., 'Swift's *Tale*: On Satire, Negation, and the Uses of Irony', *Eighteenth-Century Studies*, 5 (1971) 122–44.

Carruccio, E., *Mathematics and Logic in History and in Contemporary Thought*, trans. I. Quigly (London: Faber, 1964).

Case, J., *Summa Veterum Interpretum in Universam Dialecticam Aristotelis* (Oxford, 1598).

Chartae et Statuta Collegii Sacrosanctae et Individuae Trinitatis, Reginae Elizabethae, juxta Dublin ([Dublin], 1768).

Chartularium Universitatis Parisiensis, ed. H. Denifle and A. Chatelain, vol. I (Paris, 1889).

Chaucer, G., *The Works of Geoffrey Chaucer*, ed. F. N. Robinson (2nd ed., Boston: Houghton Mifflin, 1957).

Church, A., N. Goodman and I. M. Bochenski, *The Problem of Universals* (University of Notre Dame Press, 1956).

Cicero, *Brutus*, trans. G. L. Hendrickson, Loeb Classical Library (London: Heinemann, 1939).

—— *De Finibus*, trans. H. Rackham, Loeb Classical Library (London: Heinemann, 1914).

—— *De Oratore*, trans. H. Rackham, 2 vols, Loeb Classical Library (London: Heinemann, 1942).

—— *Orator*, trans. H. M. Hubbell, Loeb Classical Library (London: Heinemann, 1939).

—— *De Partitione Oratoria*, in *De Oratore* vol. II, trans. H. Rackham, Loeb Classical Library (London: Heinemann, 1942).

—— *Tusculan Disputations*, trans. J. E. King, Loeb Classical Library (1927; rev. ed. London: Heinemann, 1945).

Clark, A. (ed.), *Register of the University of Oxford*, vol. II (1571–1622) pt I (Oxford: Clarendon Press, 1887).

Clark, G. N., *The Later Stuarts, 1660–1714* (2nd ed., Oxford: Clarendon Press, 1955).

Clarke, M. L., *Classical Education in Britain, 1500–1900* (Cambridge University Press, 1959).

Cobban, A. B., *The King's Hall within the University of Cambridge in the Later Middle Ages* (Cambridge University Press, 1969).

Cohen, M. R., and E. Nagel, *An Introduction to Logic* (New York: Harbinger–Harcourt Brace Jovanovich, 1962).

Colie, R. L., *Paradoxia Epidemica: The Renaissance Tradition of the Paradox* (Princeton University Press, 1966).

[Collins, A.], *A Discourse of Free-Thinking, Occasion'd by the Rise and Growth of a Sect Call'd Free-Thinkers* (London, 1713).

—— *A Discourse Concerning Ridicule and Irony in Writing, in a Letter to the Reverend Dr. Nathanael Marshall* (London, 1729).

—— *An Essay Concerning the Use of Reason in Propositions, The Evidence Whereof Depends upon Human Testimony* (London, 1707).

Cooley, J. C., *A Primer of Formal Logic* (2nd ed., New York: Macmillan, 1942).

Copi, I. M., *Introduction to Logic* (2nd ed., New York: Macmillan, 1961).

Copleston, F., *A History of Philosophy* (8 vols, London: Burns, Oates & Washbourne, 1947–66; 9th vol., London: Search Press, 1975).

Corbett, E. P. J., *Rhetorical Analyses of Literary Works* (New York: Oxford University Press, 1969).

Cornford, F. M., *Microcosmographia Academica, Being a Guide for the*

Young Academic Politician (Cambridge, 1908; rpt. London: Bowes & Bowes, 1983).

Costello, W. T., *The Scholastic Curriculum at Early Seventeenth-Century Cambridge* (Cambridge, Mass.: Harvard University Press, 1958).

Cowan, J. L., 'The Uses of Argument – An Apology for Logic', *Mind*, 73 (1964) 27–45.

Craig, H., 'Shakespeare and Formal Logic', *Studies in English Philology: A Miscellany in Honor of Frederick Klaeber,* ed. K. Malone and M. B. Ruud (Minneapolis: University of Minnesota Press, 1929) pp. 380–96.

Crane, R. S., 'The Houyhnhnms, the Yahoos, and the History of Ideas', *The Idea of the Humanities and Other Essays, Critical and Historical* (University of Chicago Press, 1967) II pp. 261–82.

Cranston, M., *John Locke, A Biography* (London: Longmans, Green, 1957).

Cumberland, R., *Memoirs of Richard Cumberland, Written by Himself* (London, 1806).

Curtis, M. H., *Oxford and Cambridge in Transition, 1558–1642. An Essay on Changing Relations Between English Universities and English Society* (Oxford: Clarendon Press, 1959).

Davies, G., *The Early Stuarts, 1603–1660* (2nd ed., Oxford: Clarendon Press, 1959).

Deanesly, M., 'Medieval Schools to c. 1300', *Cambridge Medieval History*, 5 (Cambridge University Press, 1926) pp. 765–79.

De Morgan, A., 'Mock Disputations', *Notes and Queries*, 2nd Ser., 8 (3 Sept. 1859) 191.

—— *On the Syllogism and Other Logical Writings*, ed. P. Heath (London: Routledge & Kegan Paul, 1966).

De Rijk, L. M., '*Logica Cantabrigiensis*: A Fifteenth Century Cambridge Manual of Logic', *Revue Internationale de Philosophie*, 29 (1975) 297–315.

—— '*Logica Oxoniensis*: An Attempt to Reconstruct a Fifteenth-Century Oxford Manual of Logic', *Medioevo: Rivista di storia della filosofia medievale*, 3 (1977) 121–64.

D'Ewes, S., *The Autobiography and Correspondence of Sir Simonds D'Ewes, Bart., During the Reigns of James I and Charles I*, ed. J. O. Halliwell, 2 vols (London, 1845).

Dixon, W. M., *Trinity College, Dublin* (London: Robinson, 1902).

Documents Relating to the University and Colleges of Cambridge (no ed.) vol. I (London, 1852).

Donoghue, D., *Jonathan Swift: A Critical Introduction* (Cambridge University Press, 1969).

Downie, J. A., *Jonathan Swift: Political Writer* (London: Routledge & Kegan Paul, 1984).

—— *Robert Harley and the Press: Propaganda and Public Opinion in the Age of Swift and Defoe* (Cambridge University Press, 1979).

Du Trieu, P., *Manuductio ad Logicam* (Douai, 1615).

Duncan, W., *The Elements of Logick* (London, 1748).

Duport, J., *Rules to Be Observed by Young Pupils & Schollers in the*

University, ed. G. M. Trevelyan under the Title 'Undergraduate Life under the Protectorate', *Cambridge Review*, 64 (22 May 1943) 328–30.

Dyer, G. (ed.), *The Privileges of the University of Cambridge; Together with Additional Observations on Its History, Antiquities, Literature, and Biography*, 2 vols (London, 1824).

Dyson, A. E., 'Method in Madness: A Note on Edward Lear', *English*, 10 (1955) 221–4.

Eby, F., and C. F. Arrowood, *The History and Philosophy of Education, Ancient and Medieval* (New York: Prentice-Hall, 1951).

Edwards, P., 'Bertrand Russell's Doubts about Induction', *Logic and Language*, 1st Ser., ed. A. G. N. Flew (Oxford: Blackwell, 1951).

Ehrenpreis, I., *Swift: The Man, His Works, and the Age* (London, Methuen) vol. I, *Mr Swift and His Contemporaries* (1962); vol. II, *Dr Swift* (1967); vol. III, *Dean Swift* (1983).

—— 'Swift and Satire', *College English*, 13 (1952) 309–12.

Elders, L., 'The *Topics* and the Platonic Theory of Principles of Being', *Aristotle on Dialectic: The Topics. Proceedings of the Third Symposium Aristotelicum*, ed. G. E. L. Owen (Oxford: Clarendon Press, 1968) pp. 126–37.

Elliott, R. C., 'Swift's Satire: The Rules of the Game', *ELH*, 41 (1974) 413–28.

Encyclopaedia Britannica, 11th ed. (1911), articles 'Duns Scotus', 'Laud', 'Luther'.

England, A. B., 'The Subversion of Logic in Some of Swift's Poems', *SEL (Studies in English Literature)*, 15 (1975) 409–18.

Esslin, M., *The Theatre of the Absurd* (Garden City, N.Y.: Anchor-Doubleday, 1961).

Evelyn, J., *The Diary of John Evelyn*, ed. A. Dobson, 3 vols (London: Macmillan, 1906).

Feder, L., 'John Dryden's Use of Classical Rhetoric', *PMLA (Publications of the Modern Language Association)*, 69 (1954) 1258–78.

Fitch, F. B., *Symbolic Logic: An Introduction* (New York: Ronald Press, 1952).

Fletcher, H. F., *The Intellectual Development of John Milton*, 2 vols (Urbana, Ill.: University of Illinois Press, 1956–61).

Forster, J., *The Life of Jonathan Swift* (London: J. Murray, 1875).

Fowler, T., *The History of Corpus Christi College* (Oxford: Clarendon Press, 1893).

Freud, S., *Jokes and Their Relation to the Unconscious*, trans. and ed. J. Strachey (London: Routledge & Kegan Paul, 1960).

Fuller, T., *The History of the University of Cambridge*, ed. J. Nichols (London, 1840).

—— *The Holy State and The Profane State* (1642; London, 1840).

Furlong, E. J., 'The Study of Logic in Trinity College, Dublin', *Hermathena*, 60 (1942) 38–53.

Garrison, J. D., *Dryden and the Tradition of Panegyric* (Berkeley: University of California Press, 1975).

Gilbert, N. W., 'The Early Italian Humanists and Disputation', *Renaissance Studies in Honor of Hans Baron*, ed. A. Molho and J. A. Tedeschi,

Biblioteca Storica Sansoni, Nuova serie XLIX (Florence: G. C. Sansoni, 1971) 203–26.

Gill, J. E., 'Man and Yahoo: Dialectic and Symbolism in Gulliver's "Voyage to the Country of the Houyhnhnms" ', in *The Dress of Words: Essays on Restoration and Eighteenth-Century Literature in Honor of Richmond P. Bond*, ed. R. B. White, University of Kansas Library Series no. 42 (Lawrence, Kansas: University of Kansas Libraries, 1978) pp. 67–90.

Gilson, E., *History of Christian Philosophy in the Middle Ages* (London: Sheed & Ward, 1955).

Good, H. G., and J. D. Teller, *A History of Western Education* (3rd ed., London: Collier-Macmillan, 1970).

[Good, T.], *A Brief English Tract of Logick* (Oxford, 1677).

Gosse, E., *Life of William Congreve* (1888; 2nd ed., rev., London: Heinemann, 1924).

Green, V. H. H., *British Institutions: The Universities* (Harmondsworth: Penguin, 1969).

Granger, T., *Syntagma Logicum, or The Divine Logike* (London, 1620).

Guthrie, W. K. C., *A History of Greek Philosophy*, vol. III (Cambridge University Press, 1969).

Hackett, M. B., *The Original Statutes of Cambridge University: The Text and Its History* (Cambridge University Press, 1970).

Hamblin, C. L., *Fallacies* (London: Methuen, 1970).

Hamilton, W., *Lectures on Metaphysics and Logic*, ed. H. L. Mansel and J. Veitch, 4 vols (Edinburgh: Blackwood, 1859–60).

Heereboord, A., *Logica, seu Synopseos Logicae Burgersdicianae Explicatio, Tum per Notas tum per Exempla* (Cambridge, 1680).

Heron, D. C., *The Constitutional History of the University of Dublin* (Dublin, 1847).

Heywood, J., and T. Wright (eds), *Cambridge University Transactions During the Puritan Controversies of the 16th and 17th Centuries*, 2 vols (London: Bohn, 1854).

Heywood, J. (ed.), *Collection of Statutes for the University and the Colleges of Cambridge: Including Various Early Documents* (London, 1840).

—— (ed.), *Early Cambridge University and College Statutes in the English Language* (London: Bohn, 1855).

Hoadley, B., *An Account of the State of the Roman-Catholick Religion throughout the World* (London, 1715).

[Hobbes, T.], *The Art of Rhetoric, with a Discourse of the Laws of England* (London, 1681). Actually a trans. by D. Fenner of a rhetoric by Talaeus.

Hodges, J. C., *William Congreve, the Man: A Biography from New Sources* (New York: Modern Language Association, 1941).

—— (ed.), *William Congreve: Letters and Documents* (London: Macmillan, 1964).

Howell, A. C., '*Res et Verba*: Words and Things', *ELH*, 13 (1946) 131–42.

Howell, W. S., *Eighteenth-Century British Logic and Rhetoric* (Princeton University Press, 1971).

—— *Logic and Rhetoric in England, 1500–1700* (Princeton University Press, 1956).

Husserl, E., *Ideas: General Introduction to Pure Phenomenology*, trans. W. R. Boyce Gibson (London: Allen & Unwin, 1931).

Jardine, L., 'Humanism and Dialectic in Sixteenth-Century Cambridge, A Preliminary Investigation', in *Classical Influences on European Culture, A.D. 1500–1700; Proceedings of an International Conference Held at King's College, Cambridge, April 1974*, ed. R. R. Bolgar (Cambridge University Press, 1976) pp. 141–55.

—— 'Lorenzo Valla and the Intellectual Origins of Humanist Dialectic', *Journal of the History of Philosophy*, 15 (1977) 143–64.

—— 'The Place of Dialectic Teaching in Sixteenth-Century Cambridge', *Studies in the Renaissance*, 21 (1974) 31–62.

[Jebb, R. C.], 'Rhetoric', *Encyclopaedia Britannica*, 1952.

Jefferson, D. W., 'An Approach to Swift', *Pelican Guide to English Literature*, ed. B. Ford, IV: *From Dryden to Johnson* (London: Penguin, 1957) pp. 230–49.

John of Salisbury, *The Metalogicon*, trans. D. D. McGarry (Berkeley: University of California Press, 1955).

Johnson, S., *A Dictionary of the English Language* (London, 1755).

—— *The Works of Samuel Johnson*, 11 vols (London, 1787).

Joyce, G. H., *Principles of Logic* (2nd ed., London: Longmans, Green, 1916).

Junius, *The Letters of Junius*, ed. J. Wade, 2 vols (London: Bohn, 1850).

Kant, I., *Logic*, trans. J. Richardson (London, 1819).

—— *Kritik der Reinen Vernunft* (2nd ed., Riga, 1787).

Keach, B., Τϱοπολογια: *A Key to Open Scripture Metaphors* (1682; another ed. London, 1779).

Kearney, H., *Scholars and Gentlemen: Universities and Society in Pre-Industrial Britain, 1500–1700* (London: Faber, 1970).

Kellerman, J., 'Comedy, Satire, Dialectics', unpubl. PhD Thesis (State University of New York at Buffalo, 1977).

Kelling, H. D., 'Reason in Madness: *A Tale of a Tub*', *PMLA*, 69 (1954) 198–222.

Kerby-Miller, C. (ed.), *Memoirs of the Extraordinary Life, Works, and Discoveries of Martinus Scriblerus*, by John Arbuthnot *et al.* (New Haven, Conn.: Yale University Press, 1950).

Kierkegaard, S., *The Concept of Irony, with Constant Reference to Socrates*, trans. L. M. Capel (New York: Harper & Row, 1965).

Kneale, W., and M. Kneale, *The Development of Logic* (Oxford: Clarendon Press, 1962).

Knox, N., *The Word Irony and Its Context, 1500–1755* (Durham, N.C.: Duke University Press, 1961).

[Lamy, B.], *De L'Art de Parler* (Paris, 1679).

Landa, L. A., and J. E. Tobin, *Jonathan Swift: A List of Critical Studies Published from 1895 to 1945* (New York: Cosmopolitan Science & Art Service Co., 1945).

Lawson, J., *Medieval Education and the Reformation* (London: Routledge & Kegan Paul, 1967).

Leach, A. F., *Educational Charters and Documents, 598–1909* (Cambridge University Press, 1911).

Leavis, F. R., 'The Irony of Swift', *Scrutiny*, 2 (1934) 364–78.

Lee, H. D. P., *Zeno of Elea, A Text, with Translation and Notes* (Cambridge University Press, 1936).

Leff, G., *Paris and Oxford Universities in the Thirteenth and Fourteenth Centuries, An Institutional and Intellectual History* (New York: Wiley, 1968).

Lemmon, E. J., *Beginning Logic* (London: Nelson, 1965).

Lever, R., *The Art of Reason, Rightly Termed Witcraft, Teaching a Perfect Way to Argue and Dispute* (London, 1653).

Locke, J., *The Educational Writings of John Locke*, ed. J. L. Axtell (Cambridge University Press, 1968).

—— *An Essay Concerning Human Understanding*, ed. J. W. Yolton, 2 vols (London: Everyman–Dent, 1961).

'Logic', *Encyclopaedia Britannica*, 11th ed. (1911).

Lukasiewicz, J., *Aristotle's Syllogistic, From the Standpoint of Modern Formal Logic* (2nd ed., Oxford: Clarendon Press, 1957).

MacDonald, H., 'Banter in English Controversial Prose after the Restoration', *Essays and Studies by Members of the English Association*, 32 (1947) 21–39.

McPherson, R. G., *Theory of Higher Education in Nineteenth-Century England*, University of Georgia Monographs no. 4 (Athens, Georgia: University of Georgia Press, 1959).

Mahaffy, J. P., *An Epoch in Irish History: Trinity College, Dublin. Its History and Fortunes (1591–1660)* (London: T. Fisher Unwin, 1903).

—— 'On the History of Sizarship in Trinity College', *Hermathena*, 13 (1905) 315–18.

—— (ed.), *The Particular Book of Trinity College, Dublin* (London: T. Fisher Unwin, 1904).

—— 'Students' Fees and Tutorial Duties', *Hermathena*, 18 (1919) 184–203.

Mansel, H. L., *The Limits of Demonstrative Science, considered in a Letter to the Rev. William Whewell* (Oxford: W. Graham, 1853).

—— *Prolegomena Logica, an Inquiry into the Psychological Character of the Logical Processes* (Oxford: W. Graham, 1851).

Margolin, J.-C., 'Vivès, Lecteur et Critique de Platon et d'Aristote', in *Classical Influences on European Culture*, ed. R. R. Bolgar (Cambridge University Press, 1976) pp. 245–58.

[Marsden, J. H.], *College Life in the Time of James the First, as Illustrated by an Unpublished Diary of Sir Symonds D'Ewes . . . For Some Time a Fellow-Commoner of St. John's College, Cambridge* (London: Parker, 1851).

Marsh, N., *Institutio Logicae* (Dublin, 1679).

—— *Institutiones Logicae, In Usum Juventutis Academicae Dubliniensis* (Dublin, 1681).

Maxwell, C. E., *A History of Trinity College, Dublin, 1591–1892* (Dublin: The University Press, 1946).

Mayhew, G. P., 'Swift and the Tripos Tradition', *Philological Quarterly*, 45 (1966) 85–101.

Mazzeo, J. R. (ed.), *Reason and the Imagination: Essays in the History of Ideas, 1600–1800* (New York: Columbia University Press, 1962).

Mellone, S. H., *Elements of Modern Logic* (2nd ed., London: University Tutorial Press, 1945).

Mill, J. S., *A System of Logic*, 2 vols (London, 1843).

Milton, J., *Of Education, To Master Samuel Hartlib* (London, 1644).

—— *The Works of John Milton*, gen. ed. F. A. Patterson, 18 vols (New York: Columbia University Press, 1931–40).

Moore, J. R., 'Swift as Historian', *Studies in Philology*, 49 (1952) 583–604.

Moore Smith, G. C., 'Hints for Forming a Library, by a Seventeenth-Century Scholar', *The Eagle*, 40 (1919) 98–101.

Moraux, P., 'La joute dialectique d'après le huitième livre des *Topiques*', *Aristotle on Dialectic*, ed. G. E. L. Owen (Oxford: Clarendon Press, 1968) pp. 227–311.

Morgan, A. (ed.), *University of Edinburgh: Charters, Statutes, and Acts of the Town Council and Senatus, 1583–1858* (Edinburgh: Oliver & Boyd, 1937).

Morison, S. E., *The Founding of Harvard College* (Cambridge, Mass.: Harvard University Press, 1935).

—— *Harvard College in the Seventeenth Century*, Part I (Cambridge, Mass.: Harvard University Press, 1936).

Mullinger, J. B., *Cambridge Characteristics in the Seventeenth Century or, The Studies of the University* (Cambridge University Press, 1867).

—— *The University of Cambridge*, vol. III: *From the Election of Buckingham to the Chancellorship in 1626, to the Decline of the Platonist Movement* (Cambridge University Press, 1911).

Murphy, H. L., *A History of Trinity College, Dublin, from Its Foundation to 1702* (Dublin: Hodges, Figgis, 1951).

Murray, R., *Artis Logicae Compendium* (London, 1773).

Newton, J., *An Introduction to the Art of Logick* (London, 1671).

Nokes, D., *Jonathan Swift, A Hypocrite Reversed: A Critical Biography* (Oxford University Press, 1985).

North, R., *The Autobiography of the Hon. Roger North*, ed. A. Jessopp (London: Nutt, 1887).

Nugent, E. M. (ed.), *The Thought and Culture of the English Renaissance: An Anthology of Tudor Prose, 1481–1555* (Cambridge University Press, 1956).

Oulton, J. E. L., 'The Study of Divinity at Trinity College, Dublin, since the Foundation', *Hermathena*, 58 (1941) 3–29.

Owen, G. E. L., 'Dialectic and Eristic in the Treatment of the Forms', *Aristotle on Dialectic*, ed. G. E. L. Owen (Oxford: Clarendon Press, 1968) pp. 103–25.

Owen, O. F. (trans.), Aristotle, *The Organon, or Logical Treatises, with the Introduction of Porphyry*, 2 vols (London: Bohn, 1953).

Paetow, L. J., *The Arts Course at the Medieval Universities, with Special Reference to Grammar and Rhetoric* (Champaign, Ill.: University of Illinois Press, 1910).

—— *A Guide to the Study of Medieval History* (1917; rev. ed., New York: F. S. Crofts, 1931).

Parker, F. H., and H. B. Veatch, *Logic as a Human Instrument* (New York: Harper, 1959).

Parker, W. R., *Milton: A Biography*, 2 vols (Oxford: Clarendon Press, 1968).

Peacock, G., *Observations on the Statutes of the University of Cambridge* (Cambridge: Deighton, 1841).

Peters, F. E., *Aristotle and the Arabs: The Aristotelian Tradition in Islam* (New York University Press, 1968).

Perelman, C., 'Rhétorique, Dialectique et Philosophie', in *Rhetoric Revalued*, ed. B. Vickers, Medieval & Renaissance Texts & Studies, Monog. 19:1 (Binghamton, N.Y.: Center for Medieval & Early Renaissance Studies, 1982) pp. 277–81.

Perreiah, A., 'Humanist Critiques of Scholastic Dialectic', *Sixteenth Century Journal*, 13 (1982) 3–22.

Phillips, E., *The New World of Words or, Universal English Dictionary* (6th ed., London, 1706).

Plato, *The Dialogues of Plato*, trans. B. Jowett, 4 vols (4th ed., Oxford: Clarendon Press, 1953).

Pope, A., *Poetical Works*, ed. H. Davis, Oxford Standard Authors (London: Oxford University Press, 1966).

Porter, E., *Cambridgeshire Customs and Folklore* (London: Routledge & Kegan Paul, 1969).

Potenger, J., *Private Memoirs of John Potenger*, ed. C. W. Bingham (London, 1841).

Powicke, F. M., 'Some Problems in the History of the Medieval University', *Transactions of the Royal Historical Society*, 17 (1934) 1–18.

—— 'Universities and Scholarship', *The Character of England*, ed. E. Barker (Oxford: Clarendon Press, 1947) pp. 236–51.

Price, M., *Swift's Rhetorical Art* (New Haven, Conn.: Yale University Press, 1953).

Pringle-Pattison, A. S., 'Scholasticism', *Encyclopaedia Britannica*, 11th ed. (1910).

Quiller Couch, L. M. (ed.), *Reminiscences of Oxford by Oxford Men, 1559–1850* (Oxford: Clarendon Press, 1892).

Quine, W. V. O., *Elementary Logic* (rev. ed., Cambridge, Mass.: Harvard University Press, 1966).

—— *Methods of Logic* (2nd ed., rev., London: Routledge & Kegan Paul, 1962).

Quinlan, M., 'Swift's Use of Literalization as a Rhetorical Device', *PMLA*, 82 (1967) 516–21.

Quintilian, *De Institutione Oratoria*, trans. H. E. Butler, Loeb Classical Library (London: Heinemann, 1921).

Ralegh, W., *The Works of Sir Walter Ralegh*, 8 vols (1829; New York: Burt Franklin, n.d.).

Ramus, P., *Dialectique* (Paris, 1555; trans. of his *Dialecticae Institutiones*, Paris, 1543).

[Rapin, R.], *The Whole Critical Works of Monsieur Rapin*, 2 vols (London, 1706).

Rashdall, H., 'The Medieval Universities', *Cambridge Medieval History*, 6 (Cambridge University Press, 1929) 559–601.

—— *The Universities of Europe in the Middle Ages*, rev. and ed. F. M.

Powicke and A. B. Emden, 3 vols (Oxford: Clarendon Press, 1936).

Rawson, C., 'The Character of Swift's Satire: Reflections on Swift, Johnson, and Human Restlessness', in *The Character of Swift's Satire: A Revised Focus*, ed. C. Rawson (Newark: University of Delaware Press, 1983).

Reade, W. H. V., 'Philosophy in the Middle Ages', *Cambridge Medieval History*, 5 (Cambridge University Press, 1929) 780–829.

Risse, W., *Bibliographia Logica I. 1472–1800* (Hildesheim, 1965).

—— *Die Logik der Neuzeit. Band I. 1500–1640* (Stuttgart–Bad Connstatt, 1964).

Robinson, R., *Plato's Earlier Dialectic* (Oxford: Clarendon Press, 1953).

Rodino, R. H., *Swift Studies: 1965–1980: An Annotated Bibliography* (New York: Garland, 1984).

Rosenheim, E. W., *Swift and the Satirist's Art* (University of Chicago Press, 1963).

Ross, W. D., *Aristotle* (London: Methuen, 1923).

Russell, B., *The Principles of Mathematics* (2nd ed., London: Allen & Unwin, 1937).

—— *The Problems of Philosophy* (1912; London: Oxford University Press, 1959).

Ryle, G., 'Dialectic in the Academy', *Aristotle on Dialectic*, ed. G. E. L. Owen (Oxford: Clarendon Press, 1968) pp. 69–79.

—— *Dilemmas* (Cambridge University Press, 1954).

Sams, H. W., 'Swift's Satire of the Second Person', *ELH*, 26 (1959) 36–44.

Sanderson, J., *Institutionum Dialecticarum Libri Quatuor* (3rd ed., Oxford, 1602).

Sanderson, R., *Logicae Artis Compendium* (9th ed., Oxford, 1680).

Schiller, F. C. S., 'Aristotle's Refutation of "Aristotelian" Logic', *Mind*, 23 (1914) 1–18.

Schmitt, C. B., 'Towards a Reassessment of Renaissance Aristotelianism', *History of Science*, 11 (1973) 159–93.

Schopenhauer, A., *The Art of Controversy and Other Posthumous Papers*, trans. T. B. Saunders (London: Swan Sonnenschein, 1896).

—— *The Essential Schopenhauer* (London: Unwin Books, 1962).

—— *The World as Will and Idea*, trans. R. B. Haldane and J. Kemp, 2 vols (1883; rpt. London: Routledge & Kegan Paul, 1948).

Scott, W. (ed.), *The Works of Jonathan Swift*, 19 vols (Edinburgh, 1814).

Scott-Giles, C. W., *Sidney Sussex College: A Short History* (Cambridge University Press, 1951).

Scouten, A. H., and H. Teerink, *A Bibliography of the Writings of Jonathan Swift* (2nd ed., Philadelphia: University of Pennsylvania Press, 1963).

Sewell, E., *The Field of Nonsense* (London: Chatto & Windus, 1952).

Shaftesbury, Anthony, Third Earl, *Characteristicks of Men, Manners, Opinions, Times* (4th ed., 3 vols, London, 1727).

Sheridan, T., *The Life of Swift* (London, 1784).

Sidney, P., *The Prose Works of Sir Philip Sidney*, ed. A. Feuillerat, 4 vols (1912; rpt. Cambridge University Press, 1962).

Skånland, V., *The Earliest Statutes of the University of Cambridge* (Oslo: Universitetsforlaget, 1965).

Smiglecius, M., *Logica, Selectis Disputationibus . . . in qua Quicquid in*

Aristotelico Organo vel Cognita Necessarium (Oxford, 1658).

Smith, B., and D. Ehninger, 'The Terrafilial Disputations at Oxford', *Quarterly Journal of Speech*, 36 (1950) 333–9.

Solmsen, F., 'Dialectic without the Forms', *Aristotle on Dialectic*, ed. G. E. L. Owen (Oxford: Clarendon Press, 1968) pp. 49–68.

Spence, J., *Observations, Anecdotes, and Characters of Books and Men*, ed. J. M. Osborn, 2 vols (Oxford: Clarendon Press, 1966).

Sprat, T., *The History of the Royal-Society of London, For the Improving of Knowledge* (1667), ed. J. I. Cope and H. W. Jones (St Louis: Washington University Studies, 1959).

Stanford, W. B., 'Classical Studies in Trinity College, Dublin, since the Foundation', *Hermathena*, 57 (1941) 3–24.

Starkman, M. K., *Swift's Satire on Learning in A Tale of a Tub* (Princeton University Press, 1950).

Stathis, J. J., *A Bibliography of Swift Studies: 1945–1965* (Nashville, Tenn.: Vanderbilt University Press, 1967).

Statuta Antiqua Universitatis Oxoniensis, ed. S. Gibson (Oxford: Clarendon Press, 1931).

Stephen, L., *Swift*, English Men of Letters Series (London: Macmillan, 1882).

Stubbs, J. W., *The History of the University of Dublin from Its Foundation to the End of the 18th Century* (Dublin: Hodges, Figgis, 1889).

Suarez, F., *Metaphysicarum Disputationum, in Quibus at Universa Naturalis Theologia Ordinate Traditure & Quaestiones ad Omnes Duodecim Aristotelis Libros Pertinentes, Accurate Disputantur* (1597; Cologne, 1614).

Swift, J., *The Correspondence of Jonathan Swift*, ed. H. Williams, 5 vols (Oxford: Clarendon Press, 1963–5).

—— *A Discourse of the Contests and Dissentions Between the Nobles and Commons in Athens and Rome*, ed. F. H. Ellis (Oxford: Clarendon Press, 1967).

—— *The Drapier's Letters to the People of Ireland against Receiving Wood's Halfpence*, ed. H. Davis (Oxford: Clarendon Press, 1935).

—— *Letters of Jonathan Swift to Charles Ford*, ed. D. Nichol Smith (Oxford: Clarendon Press, 1935).

—— *Poetical Works*, ed. H. Davis, Oxford Standard Authors (London: Oxford University Press, 1967).

—— *The Prose Writings of Jonathan Swift*, ed. H. Davis, 14 vols (Oxford: Blackwell, 1939–68).

—— *A Tale of a Tub*, etc., ed. D. Nichol Smith and A. C. Guthkelch (2nd ed., Oxford: Clarendon Press, 1958).

Sylvester, D. W. (ed.), *Educational Documents, 800–1816* (London: Methuen, 1970).

Taylor, A. E., *Plato, The Man and His Work* (3rd ed., London: Methuen, 1929).

Taylor, J., *The Rule and Exercises of Holy Living* (London, 1650).

Taylor, W. B. S., *History of the University of Dublin* (London, 1845).

Thomas, E. C., *History of the Schoolmen* (London: Williams & Norgate, 1941).

Thorndike, L., *University Records and Life in the Middle Ages* (New York: Columbia University Press, 1944).

Tindal, M., *The Rights of the Christian Church Asserted, Against the Romish, and All Other Priests Who Claim an Independent Power Over It* (2nd ed., London, 1706).

Toulmin, S. E., *The Uses of Argument* (Cambridge University Press, 1958).

Ueberweg, F., *System of Logic and History of Logical Doctrines*, 3rd ed., trans. T. M. Lindsay (London: Longmans, Green, 1871).

Uphaus, R. W., 'From Panegyric to Satire: Swift's Early Odes and *A Tale of a Tub*', *Texas Studies in Literature and Language*, 13 (1971) 55–70.

Urwick, W., *The Early History of Trinity College, Dublin, 1591–1660, as Told in Contemporary Records, on Occasion of Its Tercentenary* (Dublin: Hodges, Figgis, 1892).

Vickers, B., 'Swift and the Baconian Idol', *The World of Jonathan Swift: Essays for the Tercentenary*, ed. B. Vickers (Oxford: Blackwell, 1968) pp. 87–128.

Vieth, D. M., *Swift's Poetry, 1900–1980: An Annotated Bibliography of Studies* (New York: Garland, 1982).

[Walker, O.], *Of Education, Especially of Young Gentlemen* (Oxford, 1687).

—— *Some Instructions Concerning the Art of Oratory, Collected for the Use of a Friend, a Young Student* (Oxford, 1682).

Wallis, J., *Institutio Logicae, ad Communes Usus Accommodata* (Oxford, 1687).

Walsh, J. J., 'Scholasticism in the Colonial Colleges', *New England Quarterly*, 5 (1932) 483–532.

Ward, S., *Vindicae Academicarum* (Oxford, 1654).

Ward, W. R., *Victorian Oxford* (London: Cass, 1965).

Watkins, W. B. C., *Perilous Balance: The Tragic Genius of Swift, Johnson and Sterne* (1939; rpt. Cambridge, Mass.: Walker–de Berry, 1960).

Watts, I., *Logick, or the Right Use of Reason in the Enquiry after Truth* (London, 1725).

Webster, J., *Academiarum Examen* (London, 1654).

Weisheipl, J. A., 'Curriculum of the Faculty of Arts at Oxford in the Early Fourteenth Century', *Mediaeval Studies*, 26 (1964) 143–85.

Wells, P. H., 'The Poetry of Swift: Dialectical Rhetoric and the Humanist Tradition', unpubl. PhD Thesis (New York University, 1971).

Wesley, C., *A Guide to Syllogism, or, A Manual of Logic; Comprehending an Account of the Manner of Disputation Now Practiced in the Schools at Cambridge; with Specimens of the Different Acts* (Cambridge, 1832).

Whately, R., *Elements of Logic* (6th ed., London, 1836; 9th ed., London: Longmans, 1864).

Whewell, W., *History of the Inductive Sciences*, 3 vols (London, 1837).

—— *Of Induction, with Especial Reference to Mr. J. Stuart Mill's System of Logic* (Cambridge, 1849).

—— *Of a Liberal Education in General; and with Particular Reference to the Leading Studies of the University of Cambridge* (London, 1845).

—— *The Philosophy of the Inductive Sciences, Founded upon their History*, 2 vols (London, 1840).

Whewell, W., *On the Principles of English University Education* (London, 1837).

Whitaker, V. K., *Shakespeare's Use of Learning: An Inquiry into the Growth of His Mind and Art* (San Marino, Calif.: Huntington Library, 1953).

White, R. J., *Dr. Bentley, A Study in Academic Scarlet* (London: Eyre & Spottiswoode, 1965).

Willcock, G. D., 'Shakespeare and Rhetoric', *Essays and Studies by Members of the English Association*, 29 (1943) 50–61.

Williams, K., *Jonathan Swift and the Age of Compromise* (Lawrence, Kansas: University of Kansas Press, 1958).

Wilson, T., *The Rule of Reason* (1551; rpt. London, 1553).

Wood, A., *Athenae Oxoniensis*, ed. P. Bliss, 4 vols (3rd ed., London, 1813–20).

—— *The Life and Times of Anthony Wood, Antiquary, of Oxford, 1632–1695, Described by Himself, Collected from his Diaries and Other Papers*, ed. A. Clark (Oxford: Clarendon Press, 1894).

Wordsworth, C., *Scholae Academicae. Some Account of the Studies at the English Universities in the Eighteenth Century* (Cambridge University Press, 1877).

—— *Social Life at the English Universities in the Eighteenth Century* (Cambridge: Deighton, Bell, 1874).

Index

Page numbers followed by n *refer to the notes*

Abelard, Peter, 14, 23, 24, 28, 33, 45
Addison, Joseph, 2
Albert the Great, St, 26
Alcuin of York, 22, 25
Aldrich, Henry, 41, 94
Alexander of Aphrodisias, 13
Amhurst, Nicholas, 46, 59, 60, 61, 69,
    184, 209n
analogical inference, 87, 91
Anglican Church, 6
    pamphlets, 92
    in Swift, 76–8, 80, 122, 123–4: as
        answerer, 147–9
    and Trinity College, Dublin, 64
Anne, Queen, 77, 78, 94, 173
Anselm, St, 22
answerer, Swift as, 144–80, 195
    and criticism of style, 174–6
    and definitions, 164–7
    and dialectical superiority, 149–52, 173
    and the dilemma, 159–60
    and distinctions, 163–4
    and metaphors, 171–2
    opponents, 147–9: dialectical tricks,
        169–71; manipulating arguments,
        161–3; personal attacks on, 176–
        80; reasoning of, 167–9; wit and
        sources in, 172–4
    and refutation, 152–9
    role of answerer, 144–7
    and unacceptable extremes, 160–1
Aquinas, St Thomas, 23–4, 25, 26, 37,
    93, 96
Arabs, and Aristotle, 26
argument, in Swift, 105–7
    argumenta ad, 125–7
    from contraries, 128–32
    attacking definitions, 164–7
    demonstration and dialectic, 194–5
    drawing distinctions, 163–4
    manipulating opponent's arguments,
        161–3
    and opinion, 83
    refutation of, 119–21, 152–9
    and satire, 187–8
    turning of opponent's, 122–4
    unacceptable extremes of, 160–1

'Argument against Abolishing
    Christianity' (Swift), 109, 168
argumenta ad, 125–7
Aristotelianism
    and Swift, 95–6
    at Trinity College, Dublin, 64, 66
Aristotle, 15, 19–21
    and the answerer, 144
    and the Arabs, 26
    and argument, 83, 125, 128, 131
    Categories, 21, 22, 30
    criticism of, 57, 58
    demonstration and dialectic, 194
    dialectic and rhetoric, 11
    and the dialectical theologians, 23–4
    and the dilemma, 134–5
    and disputation, 49, 50–1
    and extension of opponent's thesis,
        121, 122
    Of Generation and Corruption, 41
    On Interpretation, 21, 22, 30
    Logic, 32
    and logic studies, 41, 42, 43, 196
    and the medieval universities, 27, 28,
        29, 30
    and metaphors, 171, 172
    Metaphysics, 14, 64
    Nicomachean Ethics, 64
    Organon, 21, 22, 23, 26, 27, 30, 40,
        64, 89
    and personal attacks on opponents,
        177
    Physics, 64
    Politics, 26
    and the questioner, 125–6, 144, 170–1
    questioner–answerer method of
        dialectic, 16–18
    and reason, 88, 89, 106
    and the *reductio ad impossibile*, 154
    Rhetoric, 34
    and scholasticism, 39, 97
    and the Scottish universities, 40–1
    and Suarez, 25
    and Swift, 6, 95–6
    see also Posterior Analytics; *Prior
        Analytics*; *Sophistical Elenchi*;
        Topics

259

Asgill, John, 95
Atterbury, Francis, 95
Averroës, 26
Avicenna, 26

Bacon, Francis, 4, 15, 23, 35, 41, 57, 58, 95
Bacon, Roger, 29, 57–8
Bailey, B., 60
Bailey, N., 15, 184
Barlow, Thomas, 42
Barnes, Joshua, 42, 82
Barrow, Isaac, 42
Battle of the Books (Swift), 54, 80, 92, 93, 95–6, 99, 121, 132, 145
Bellarmine, St Robert, 93, 96
Bentley, Richard, 37, 43, 92, 95, 96, 99, 100, 175
Bickerstaff Papers, 177–8, 183
Blake, William, 4, 60, 231n
Blois, Peter of, 25, 57
Blount, Thomas
    Glossographia, 14, 184
Blundeville, Thomas
    Arte of Logike, 14
Boethius, Anicius Manlius Severinus, 21, 22, 23, 25, 29, 30, 34
Bolde, Alexander, 56
Bolingbroke, Henry St John, 1st Viscount, 107
Boole, G., 196
Boyle, Charles, 92, 94
Boyle, Hon. Robert, 55
British Library MS
    Cotton Faustina D. II, 46, 48–51, 68, 198–201
Brown, John, 40
Burgersdicius, F., 38, 42, 43, 65, 66, 71, 88, 164
Burke, E., 66
Burnet, Gilbert, 6, 34, 72, 89, 100, 103, 104, 118
    History of My Own Times, 167, 168, 175, 186
    and Swift as answerer, 151, 152–3, 162, 170, 171, 172, 175: personal attacks on, 177, 178–9
Burton, K. M., 56
Butler, Joseph, 58
Byzantium, 26

Callicles, 131
Cambridge University
    disputations at, 31, 33, 34, 35, 36, 44, 45, 52, 53: comic (tripos), 54–5, 56, 69
    eighteenth-century curriculum, 210n
    founding of, 26, 214n
    logic studies, 40, 41, 42, 196
    in medieval times, 29, 30
    and scholasticism, 37, 43, 208n
    and Swift, 94
    and Trinity College, Dublin, 63–4
Capella, Martianus, 25
Carnochan, W. B., 5–6
Carteret, John, 1st Earl Granville, 122
Case, John, 45, 46
Catholic education
    and scholastic disputation, 16
    see also Roman Catholics
Chappel, Dr William, 53
Charlemagne, 22, 25
Charles II, King of England, 119
Chaucer, Geoffrey, 29, 59
Church of England *see* Anglican Church
Cicero, 11, 105, 144
    Topics, 22
    Tusculan Disputations, 45, 116
civil war, English, 39
Coghill, Dr, 129–30
Colet, John, 58
Collins, A., 77, 78, 95, 182, 183, 184, 186, 192
Cologne, Albert of, 23–4
comic disputations, 54–7, 61–2
    at Trinity College, Dublin, 69
complex constructive dilemmas, 139, 141
complex destructive dilemmas, 137–8, 234n
conclusions, in Swift, 108
'Conduct of the Allies, The' (Swift), 119, 137, 138, 150
consequence, in Swift, 108–9
Contests and Dissentions (Swift), 78, 83–4, 102, 171
contraries, argument from, 128–32
controversy, and Swift, 98–100
Copernicus, Nicholas, 41
Cordova, Fernando of, 35
Costello, W. T., 48, 52, 56
Courçon, Robert de, 27
Cowell, John, 41
Cowper, William, 60
Crane, R. S., 5, 202n
Cranmer, Thomas, 36
Crichton, James ('the Admirable'), 35–6
Cumberland, Richard, 36, 43, 53, 61, 69, 107, 108

D'Ewes, Simonds, 36, 42, 61
De Morgan, Angus, 196
deduction, 106
   in Swift, 90, 108
deductive inference, 87–8, 90
definitions, attacks on, and Swift as
   answerer, 164–7
Defoe, Daniel, 2
demonstration and dialectic, 194–5
Descartes, René, 41, 96
dialectic, definition of, 11
dictionaries
   and definitions of logic, 15
   and definitions of satire, 183
'Digression on Madness' (Swift), 185,
   191, 192
dilemma, and Swift
   as answerer, 159–60
   as questioner, 134–43, 234n
disjunctive propositions, and the
   dilemma, 135–6
disputations, 3–4, 31–6, 197
   for BA courses, 31–4, 67, 68, 101
   comic, 54–7, 61–2
   contemporary accounts of, 53–4
   criticism of, 57–62
   language of, 103–5
   for MA courses, 34–5, 68
   rules of, 51–2
   and satire, 182: of scholasticism,
      97–8
   in the seventeenth century, 44–54
   and Swift, 51, 67, 68–9, 70–2
   at Trinity College, Dublin, 66–72, 101,
      197
dissenters, and Swift, 78, 187; *see also*
   religion
Dissoi Logoi, 19
Docker, Henry, 41
Donne, John, 102
Drapier's Letters (Swift), 78, 79, 102–3,
   112–13
   and Swift: as answerer, 147, 163; as
      questioner, 122, 123, 125, 126,
      132
Dryden, John, 1, 2, 58, 95, 102
   All for Love, 177
   dialectic and rhetoric in, 11
   'Hind and the Panther', 96
   and satire, 34
Duncan, William, 43
Duns Scotus, Johannes, 24, 25, 35, 37,
   93, 96, 99
Duport, J., 42, 52

Edinburgh University
   seventeenth-century curriculum, 40
Ehrenpreis, Irvin, 5, 69, 101, 102
either/or question, and Swift as
   questioner, 132–3
Epicureans, 21
Erasmus, 58
eristic and dialectic, 15–18
Euathlus, 135, 141, 142
Euclid, 19
Evelyn, John, 55
examinations, university, 3, 15, 196
Examiner, 78
   and Swift as answerer, 145–6, 149,
      151, 168–9, 174–5
Exeter, Bishop of, 53, 55

fallacious arguments, Swift's
   manipulation of, 161–3
fallacious reasoning, Swift's exposure of,
   167–9
Fell, Dr John, 37
Fenner, Dudley
   Art of Rhetoric, 184
Forster, J., 71
freethinkers, in Swift, 76–7, 78, 82, 96,
   108, 187
Fuller, Thomas, 40, 45

Gadbury, 174
Galen, 41
Gellius, 135
Glossographia Anglicana Nova (1707),
   184
Goldsmith, Oliver, 66
Good, Thomas
   Brief English Tract of Logick, 14
Gorgias, 19
Granger, Thomas
   Syntagma Logicum, 177
Greece, Ancient
   and dialectic, 19–21
   and logic, 13
Grosseteste, Robert, 29
Guardian (Whig paper), 167
Gulliver's Travels (Swift), 78–9, 85, 86–
   91, 92, 94, 95
   and argument from contraries, 130
   and dilemma, 140–1, 142
   irony in, 185
   and the language of dialectic, 104, 105
   and metaphors, 171
   and paradox, 190–1, 192
   and satire, 189

Gulliver's Travels – continued
  and Swift as answerer, 145, 149
  'Voyage to the Houyhnhnms', 62, 75,
    77, 80, 86–90, 100, 140, 191, 192,
    218n, 220n, 221n

Hamblin, C. L.
  Fallacies, 13
Hamilton, W., 196
Hare, Francis, 119
Harley, Robert, 1st Earl of Oxford, 94,
  119
Harley ministry, 83, 93
  and Swift as answerer, 146, 160
Hartlib, Samuel, 42
Harvard University, 63
  disputations at, 45–6
Harvey, William, 41
Hegelian dialectic, 5, 6
Henry II, King of England, 36
Henry VIII, King of England, 36, 169
history, in Swift, 92
*History of the Four Last Years of the
  Queen* (Swift), 92
History of My Own Times (Burnet), 167,
  168, 175, 186
*History of the Reformation of the Church
  of England* (Burnet), 152–3
Hoadly, Bishop, 59
Hobbes, Thomas, 12, 35, 40, 58, 196
Hody, John Humphrey, 41
Holdsworth, Richard, 42, 53
Homer, 95, 168
Hugh of St Victor, 23
Hume, David, 196
humour, in Swift, 186–9; *see also* satire

'Importance of the *Guardian* considered'
  (Swift), 178
induction, 106
  in Swift, 90–1
inductive inference, 87
irony, in Swift, 6, 184–6
  as answerer, 145

James I, King, 53, 68
James II, King, 63
James of Venice, 22
Jefferson, D. W., 5, 102
Johnson, Dr Samuel, 15, 184
Jones, John, 69
Jowett, Benjamin, 20
Junius, 118, 160

Kant, Immanuel, 60–1, 196
Keats, John, 4, 60
Keckermann, B., 39–40, 42, 65, 71
Kilkenny Grammar School, 63
Knox, Vicesimus, 60, 69

ladies, prevaricators' addresses to, 56–7
language
  of dialectic, 101–3
  of disputation, 103–5
  of the syllogism, 109–13
Leibniz, Gottfried Wilhelm von, 25
'Letter to a Member of Parliament in
  Ireland' (Swift), 121–2
'Letter to a Whig Lord' (Swift), 102
liberty, in Swift, 78–9
literature, disputation in, 44
Locke, John, 37, 58, 125
  and disputations, 4, 35, 51, 59
  *Essay concerning Human
    Understanding*, 38, 43
  and logic, 40, 41, 196
Loftus, Adam, 63
logic
  criticism of, 57–62
  definition of, 11, 164
  of demonstration, 194
  and dialectic, 11, 12–15
  and dilemma, 135
  language of, 101–13
  lectures, on, 51
  in the post-medieval period, 3
  and rhetoric, 11–12
  and satire, 181, 182
  at Trinity College, Dublin, 64–6
  in university studies, 196–7:
    seventeenth century, 39–43
Lombard, Peter, 23
Luther, Martin, 31, 36

majority opinion, 21, 132, 134
  in Swift, 83–5: as answerer, 162
Mandeville, Bernard, 127
mankind, benefit of, in Swift, 78–9
Mansel, H. L., 196
Marlowe, Christopher, 2
Marprelate, Martin, 92
Marsden, J. H., 55
Marsh, Narcissus, 58–9, 64, 65, 88, 141
mathematics
  and dialectic, 20
  and logic, 196–7
  and proof, 107
  and scholasticism, 43

Mechanical Operation of the Spirit (Swift), 77, 97, 145
medical degrees, seventeenth-century curriculum for, 38
medieval disputations, 35–6
medieval scholasticism, 22–5
medieval universities, 25–30
Medley (Whig Paper), 146, 170, 178
Memoirs of Martinus Scriblerus, 22, 25, 43, 59, 115
metaphors, Swift's attacks on, 171–2
Meurer, Wolfgang, 36
Mill, J. S., 196
Miller, Serjeant, 61
Milton, John, 4, 12, 35, 36, 37, 40, 58, 59, 95
Mitchell, Jonathan, 45
mock disputations *see* comic disputations
mock logic, in Swift, 61–2
'Modest Proposal, A' (Swift), 184, 185, 190
monarchy, and Swift as answerer, 157–9
Moore, Thomas, 60
moralist, Swift as, 173
Moraux, Paul, 52
More, St Thomas, 2, 58
Murray, Richard, 65

New Scientists, 15–16, 57
nineteenth century
  decline of dialectic in, 15
  and disputations, 52: mock, 61
North, Lord, 159–60

Observator (Whig paper), 146, 161, 223n
Observations on the Tale of a Tub (Wotton), 77, 117
Ockham, William of, 25, 37
'Ode to the Athenian Society' (Swift), 89
Oldmixon, John, 119, 176
'On the Poor Man's Contentment' (Swift), 133
'On the Trinity' (Swift), 133, 168
opinion in Swift
  importance of, 80–1
  and satire, 181
  singularity of, 81–3
  unacceptable extremes of, 133–4
  of the wise and the majority, 83–5, 132, 134, 162
opponents of Swift *see* answerer, Swift as; questioner, Swift as
Oxford University
  and disputations, 31–2, 33, 34, 35, 36,

46, 52, 197: comic (*terrae-filius*), 54, 56–7, 69
  founding of, 26, 214n
  logic studies, 40, 41–2, 43
  medieval curriculum, 29
  and scholasticism, 37–8
  and Swift, 94

Padua, University of, 26
pamphlet warfare
  criticism of opponent's style, 175–6
  and extremes of opinion, 160–1
  and Swift, 91–4
paradox
  in Aristotle, 134
  in Swift, 190–3
Paris, medieval University of, 29–30, 34
  and disputations, 31, 32, 35
Parmenides, 19
Partridge, John, 95, 174, 183
Peacock, G., 52
Peripatetics, 21
Philipart, F. J., 43
Phillips, Edward, 15, 184
Plato, 11, 14, 16, 18, 19, 24, 96, 115
  Euthydemus, 20, 44
  Swift's criticism of, 95
poets, and criticism of dialectic, 60
Poitiers, Peter of, 23
politics *see* Tories; Whigs
Pope, Alexander, 2, 20, 35, 38, 59–60, 95
Porphyry, 25
  Isagoge, 22, 30, 40, 64
Porrée, Gilbert de la, 23
Posterior Analytics (Aristotle), 21
  and definition, 166
  dialectic and logic in, 13, 14, 194
  and disputation, 48
  and experimental science, 58
  and medieval scholasticism, 22, 30
  and metaphors, 171
  and reason, 88, 89, 90
  and the *reductio ad impossibile*, 154
Potenger, John, 70
prevaricator speeches, 54–7, 69
Prior Analytics (Aristotle), 19, 21, 194
  and consequence, 109
  dialectic and logic in, 13, 14
  and medieval scholasticism, 22, 30
  and the questioner, 115, 116
  and the *reductio ad impossibile*, 154

'Project for the Advancement of Religion and the Reformation of Manners' (Swift), 75, 108–9, 110, 123
proof, in Swift, 107
'Proposal for Correcting the English Tongue' (Swift), 119
Protagoras, 19, 135, 141–2
Protestant universities, 16
Ptolemy, 41
Pulteney, William, 128
Puritan pamphlets, 92

questioner, Swift as, 114–43, 195
    and argument from contraries, 128–32
    and the dilemma, 134–43
    and either/or questions, 132–3
    extension of opponent's thesis, 121–2
    offering two unacceptable extremes, 133–4
    and the opposition, 118–19
    and refutation, 119–21
    role of questioner, 114–18
    turning of opponent's argument, 122–7

Rabelais, François, 58
Raleigh, Walter, 58
Ramism, 37, 40
    at Trinity College, Dublin, 66
Ramus, P., 64, 196
    Dialectique, 14
reason, in Swift, 85–91, 107–8
reductio ad impossibile, 154–9, 162, 172
refutation, and Swift
    as answerer, 152–9
    as questioner, 119–21
religion, in Swift, 76–8, 85–6, 92
    as answerer, 147–9, 151–2, 154–8, 160, 171–2
    'Argument against Abolishing Christianity' 109, 168
    and consequence, 108–9
    and dilemma, 139
    and extremes of opinion, 134
    'On the Trinity', 133, 168
    'Project for the Advancement of Religion and the Reformation of Manners', 75, 108–9, 110, 123
    and the Sacramental Test abolition, 121–2, 127, 131, 168, 187
    'Sentiments of a Church-of-England Man', 101, 157–9, 224n
    'Sermon on the Excellence of Christianity', 95

wit and humour, 186–7, 188–9
Renaissance disputations, 3, 35–6
Reneu, William, 42
Review (Whig paper), 161, 223n
rhetoric, and dialectic, 11–12
Rights of the Christian Church (Tindal), 147–9, 171–2, 188
Risse, W., 3
Roberts, Dr, (Trinity College, Dublin), 53
Robertson, John, 40
Roman Catholics, 162, 187
Roscelin, Johannes Roscellinus, 22
Rosenheim, E. W., 181–2, 183, 184, 185, 186, 187, 218n
Russell, Bertrand, 90–1

Salisbury, John of, 23, 25, 28, 57
Sanderson, John, 51
Sanderson, Robert, 41, 46
satire
    and argument, 183, 187–8
    and dialectic, 1, 34, 181–3, 188, 192–3
    of pamphleteers, 93
    in Plato, 20
    in Swift, 6–7, 181–4, 186–9, 192–3: as answerer, 145, 152
    and the universities, 94
Scaliger, J. J., 99–100
scholasticism
    criticisms of, 57–62
    medieval, 22–5
    and science, 38, 39, 57–9
    since the sixteenth century, 37–9, 43
    Swift's satire on, 96–8
Schopenhauer, A., 12, 16–17, 52, 115, 121, 125, 126, 173, 192
science, and scholasticism, 38, 39, 57–9
Scottish universities
    lectures on logic, 51
    in the seventeenth century, 38, 40–1
Scriblerus, Cornelius, 115
Scriblerus memoirs, 22, 25, 43, 59, 115
sense perception, and reason, 88–90
'Sentiments of a Church-of-England Man' (Swift), 101, 157–9, 224n
seventeenth century
    logic and dialectic in, 14–15
    and mock disputations, 61
    role of universities, 2
    and scholasticism, 37–9: criticism of, 58–9
    and university logic studies, 39–43

Shaftesbury, Anthony Ashley Cooper, 3rd Earl of, 51, 98, 183, 184
Shakespeare, William, 51
  and disputations, 44
Sheridan, Thomas, 71
Sidney, Philip, 2
Smiglecius, M., 65, 71
Smith, John, 41
Smith, Samuel, 41
Socrates, 16, 18, 19, 44, 81, 115, 131
  and satire, 191
Sophistical Elenchi (Aristotle), 16, 20, 21
  dialectic and logic in, 13
  and disputation, 44–5, 52
  and medieval scholasticism, 22, 30
  and Swift: as answerer, 145, 148, 163, 164, 168, 177; as questioner, 114, 115, 116, 125–6, 135, 139, 140
sophistry, and dialectic, 15–18
Southwell, Edward, 129–30
Spenser, Edmund, 2
Sprat, T., 4, 15, 23, 35, 37, 58, 59, 138–9, 183
St Andrews University
  and disputations, 36
  founding, 27
  and logic studies, 38, 40–1, 51
St Paul's School, 40
Starkman, M. K., 182
state, the, in Swift, 76–8, 80
Steele, Sir Richard, 1, 2, 6, 72, 100, 103, 189, 193
  Crisis, 103, 160, 167, 175
  and Swift as answerer, 146–7, 153–4, 160, 165, 167, 168, 174, 175, 178
Stephen, Leslie, 71
Stoics, 21
style, criticism of, and Swift as answerer, 174
Suarez, Francisco, 25, 37, 96
syllogisms, 69
  and disputation, 46, 69
  language of, in Swift, 109–13
  and the questioner, 114–15
  and turning of opponent's argument, 124

Tale of a Tub, A (Swift), 61–2, 66, 80, 85, 93, 96–7, 106, 107
  irony in, 185
  and Swift as answerer, 145, 152, 174, 176, 177
  and Swift as questioner, 117–18, 119, 120, 133–4

Taylor, Jeremy, 136–7, 139
Temple, Sir William, 64, 95, 183
terrae-filius speeches, 54, 55, 56–7, 69
textbooks, in medieval universities, 29–30
Tindal, Matthew, 6, 72, 82, 85, 95, 96, 100, 103, 108, 193
  Rights of the Christian Church, 147–9, 171–2, 188
  and satire, 182–3
  and Swift as answerer, 147–9, 154–7, 162, 163, 165–7, 169, 172–4: personal attacks, 177, 178, 179–80
Toland, John, 95, 108
Toledo, Raymond, Archbishop of, 26
Tom, Eric
  Negation and Logic, 5
Topics (Aristotle), 20, 194
  dialectic and logic in, 13, 14
  and disputation, 45, 52
  and medieval scholasticism, 22, 23, 30
  and opinions, 21, 83
  questioner–answerer method of dialectic, 16, 17–18
  and Swift: as answerer, 148, 166, 173; as questioner, 114, 115
Topics (Cicero), 22
Tories
  and Swift, 83, 93, 110, 167, 173
  and the universities, 94, 95
  see also Harley ministry
Toulmin, Stephen
  Uses of Argument, 13
Trieu, Philippe du, 65
Trinity College, Dublin, 29, 30, 58, 63–72
  BA candidates, 101, 216n
  disputations, 32, 66–72, 101, 197, 216–17n: comic (tripos), 54, 69–70, 217n; public commencement, 67–8, 69
  founding and early development, 63–4
  logic studies, 43, 64–6
  Swift at, 5, 34, 63, 66, 69
  tripos speeches, 54–7, 69
  at Trinity College, Dublin, 69–70, 217n
Tusculan Disputations (Cicero), 45, 116

universities, 15–16
  logic studies, 39–43, 196–7
  medieval, 25–30, 27
  and scholasticism, 37–9
  in the seventeenth century, 2, 39–43

universities – *continued*
  and Swift, 94–8
  and the Whigs, 94, 95
  see also Cambridge; disputations;
    Oxford; Paris; Trinity College,
    Dublin
Usher, Bishop James, 53

Valla, Lorenzo, 58
Vaughan, Thomas, 174
Venice, Paul of
  Logica Parva, 58
Vilant, Colin, 51
'Vindication of Isaac Bickerstaff' (Swift),
  177–8
Vives, Juan Luis, 58

Walker, Obadiah, 12
Wallis, John, 43, 55
Walpole ministry, 94, 95
  and Swift, 94
Walsh, James, J., 16
Ward, Samuel, 45
Ward, Seth, (later Bishop of Exeter), 55
Waterland, Daniel, 42, 43
Webster, John, 59

Wesley, Charles
  Guide to Syllogism, 4, 52, 90, 196
Whately, R., 135, 137, 176, 196
Whewell, W., 196
Whigs
  and Swift, 78, 80, 81, 83–4, 93–4: as
    answerer, 151, 160, 175, 178
  'The Public Spirit of the Whigs', 178
  and the universities, 94, 95
Williams, Kathleen, 76
Wilson, Thomas
  Rule of Reason, 11, 14
wit, in Swift, 186–9
  exposure of, in opponents, 172–4
Wood, Anthony, 61
Wood, William, 112–13, 122, 123, 129,
  162–3
Wordsworth, Christopher, 52, 54, 61
Wordsworth, William, 4, 60
Wotton, William, 77, 92, 95, 117, 118,
  119, 120, 121, 174, 176

Xenophon, 18, 115

Yeats, W. B., 79

Zeno of Elea, 16, 19, 20, 154